LEGAL RESPONSES
TO WIFE ASSAULT

Legal Responses to Wife Assault
is under the general editorship of
Jon R. Conte, Ph.D.

LEGAL RESPONSES TO WIFE ASSAULT

CURRENT TRENDS AND EVALUATION

EDITED BY **N. ZOE HILTON**

SAGE Publications
International Educational and Professional Publisher
Newbury Park   London   New Delhi

For information address:

SAGE Publications, Inc.
2455 Teller Road
Newbury Park, California 91320

SAGE Publications Ltd.
6 Bonhill Street
London EC2A 4PU
United Kingdom

SAGE Publications India Pvt. Ltd.
M-32 Market
Greater Kailash I
New Delhi 110 048 India

Printed in the United States of America

Library of Congress Cataloging-in-Publication Data

Main entry under title:

Legal responses to wife assault : current trends and evaluation /
    [edited by] N. Zoe Hilton.
        p. cm.
    Includes bibliographical references and index.
    ISBN 0-8039-4552-3 (cl.) — ISBN 0-8039-4553-1 (pbk.)
        1. Wife abuse—United States. 2. Abused wives—Legal status,
    laws, etc.—United States. I. Hilton, N. Zoe.
    KF9322.A75L44 1993   93-3609
    362.82'92—dc20   CIP

93 94 95 96 97 10 9 8 7 6 5 4 3 2 1

Sage Production Editor: Judith L. Hunter

Contents

	Preface	vii
PART I:	OVERVIEW	
1.	Introduction *N. Zoe Hilton*	3
2.	Husbands Who Assault: Multiple Profiles Requiring Multiple Responses *Daniel G. Saunders*	9
PART II:	POLICE	
3.	Police Intervention and Public Opinion *N. Zoe Hilton*	37
4.	The Impact of Police Laying Charges *Peter G. Jaffe, Elaine Hastings, Deborah Reitzel,* and *Gary W. Austin*	62
5.	Irreconcilable Differences: Battered Women, Police, and the Law *Kathleen J. Ferraro* and *Lucille Pope*	96
PART III:	COURTS	
6.	The Criminal Prosecution of Wife Assaulters: Process, Problems, and Effects *David A. Ford* and *Mary Jean Regoli*	127

7.   Family Courts, Marital Conflict Mediation,
and Wife Assault   165
Desmond Ellis

8.   Court-Mandated Treatment of Men Who
Assault Their Partner: Issues, Controversies,
and Outcomes   188
L. Kevin Hamberger and *James E. Hastings*

PART IV: VICTIMS

9.   Battered Women as Defendants   233
Lenore E. A. Walker

10.   Self-Defense Jury Instructions in Trials of
Battered Women Who Kill Their Partner   258
Alan J. Tomkins, Mary K. Kenning,
Jessica P. Greenwald, and *Gregory R. Johnson*

PART V: SUMMARY

11.   Legal Responses to Wife Assault: Future
Prospects for Intervention and Evaluation   289
Ronald Roesch, Stephen D. Hart, and
Laurene J. Wilson

Author Index   307

Subject Index   317

About the Contributors   325

Preface

In the 1980s and 1990s, legal responses to wife assault have been increasing. Police officers have been encouraged, sometimes required, to take a more interventionist approach when called to scenes of wife assault. No-drop prosecution policies and victim-witness support programs have been implemented to respond to some of the difficulties faced by battered women who must testify against their partner. Both incarceration and court-mandated treatment programs for wife assaulters have also increased over the past 10 to 15 years. These changes have largely occurred as a response to controversy about the legal system's adequacy in dealing with wife assault. The controversy, however, continues. On the one hand, many people believe that the legal system still is not doing enough to fight wife assault. On the other hand, the appropriateness of increasing the powers of the criminal justice system in order to meet the needs of battered women has been questioned.

Often, the questions raised about legal responses to wife assault are based more on ideals than on the demonstrated effectiveness or failure of the recent innovations. This is hardly surprising, as relevant research has lagged behind program development, and work that has been done to evaluate legal responses to wife assault tends to be published in disparate academic journals or inaccessible government reports. Yet, well-conducted research that is accessible to policymakers and others active in the field is essential to guide our efforts and to channel funding into the most appropriate and effective interventions.

In this book, we aim to promote appropriate and effective legal responses to wife assault by not only exploring the debates surrounding current trends, but also drawing together recent evaluation research in this field. Each chapter begins with a review of the main developments and literature in a specific area, be it police response, mediation, prosecution, treatment for wife assaulters, or legal defenses for battered women who kill their partner. The authors have extensive familiarity with their respective areas as researchers, practitioners, or both. The chapters also highlight the authors' own work, mostly in the form of research that illustrates the points made in the literature review, gives a clear example of the kind of evaluation work that is being done, and describes some of the most recent work in the field in more detail than can be covered in a simple literature review.

Researchers and scholars using this book will find of value the extensive reviews of existing studies, such as in the chapter by Hamberger and Hastings, who point out shortcomings in wife assault treatment research that may be equally applicable to research regarding wife assault in general. The contributors also point to aspects of wife assault requiring more attention in the future; for example, both Jaffe and his colleagues and Roesch and his co-authors make a plea for more preventive efforts, which may be guided by theory-based research.

Knowledge of the existing literature and debates, and an awareness of current evaluation research can also be invaluable to clinicians, battered women's advocates, policymakers, and others whose practice brings them into contact with wife assaulters or their victims. As Roesch and his colleagues show, good research can help improve the circumstances of battered women. Improvement may be brought about when weaknesses of existing services are pointed out, as is done, for example, by Ferraro and Pope in their analysis of problems in communication and service provision between police and battered women, and by Saunders, whose research emphasizes the need for interventions that are adapted to the characteristics of the wife as-saulter. Research and literature summaries can also provide useful information for those whose work necessitates lobbying for govern-ment funds. An understanding of the effects of proarrest policies and special instructions to the jury, the kinds of interventions people see as appropriate in wife assault, the outcomes of different approaches to prosecution, and the acceptability of expert witness testimony are offered by the chapters that follow.

In addition to the authors of these chapters, many people have contributed to this book during the course of its development. I wish to thank the Mental Health Centre, Penetanguishene, for providing me with the opportunity to work on this project. Pat Reid and Sandy Tessier provided invaluable library and research assistance, always giving cheerful service. I am very grateful to Sonja Dey, who typed numerous drafts and reformatted tables faster than I could think of new changes to make. Grant Harris's wisdom and humor saw me through all the trials of editing. And as always, I thank Brad Fisher, a loving and gentle husband. This book is dedicated to our baby, in the hope that a peaceful world awaits him.

PART
I

OVERVIEW

1

Introduction

N. ZOE HILTON

Current Trends

When the women's movement first brought wife assault to the forefront of public attention in the 1970s, the police and other agents of the criminal justice system soon came under attack for failing to provide victims of wife assault with adequate protection (e.g., MacLeod, 1987; Schechter, 1982). It was claimed that legal remedies were less accessible to victims of wife assault than to victims of other forms of violence, and that, moreover, the lack of legal response, and the law itself, reflected society's tolerance and even acceptance of wife assault. The 1980s and 1990s, in contrast, have seen a growth in legal responses to wife assault. The use of incarceration for wife assaulters has increased since the 1970s (Endicott, 1987). In addition, there have been moves to create interagency cooperation, the best known examples being in Duluth, Minnesota (Pence, 1989), and London, Ontario (Jaffe & Burris, 1984). Here, the police, the courts, and services for wife assaulters and their victims provide not merely legal intervention but an integrated community response to wife assault. On a smaller scale, the criminal justice system is making use of the treatment programs that are increasingly being offered by mental health and social services, through probation orders or through diversion programs (see Caesar & Hamberger, 1989). And as our

3

awareness of the dynamics of wife assault and its consequences increases, courts are also beginning to consider the notion of the battered woman syndrome when dealing with battered women who have killed their partner (e.g., Ewing, 1990).

A trend towards increasing legal responses to wife assault, then, is evident in North America, largely in reaction to earlier calls for greater responsiveness by the legal system. Yet, none of these changes has occurred without controversy. For example, some states have enacted mandatory arrest policies for wife assault cases, in part to overcome the reluctance of prosecutors and judges to proceed with victim-initiated complaints (E. S. Buzawa & C. G. Buzawa, 1990). Some authors caution, though, that arrest might not be what all victims want (e.g., MacLeod, 1987; Schechter, 1982); mandatory arrest may be perceived by women as further disempowerment if they have been under the control of their violent partner prior to police intervention. Another example is the "no-drop" policy introduced by some jurisdictions, whereby a victim of wife assault does not have the option of withdrawing charges once the prosecution process is under way. The no-drop prosecution policy has been criticized when it has resulted in contempt of court procedures being invoked to punish battered women who refuse to testify against their partner (e.g., McGillivray, 1987).

Evaluation

Despite the important and politically sensitive debates surrounding responses to wife assault, few legislative or policy changes have been accompanied by large-scale, well-funded evaluation efforts by the governments responsible for their introduction. One exception has been the Sherman and Berk (1984) study of the effectiveness of arrest, followed by the series of replication attempts sponsored by the U.S. National Institute of Justice (Dunford, Huizinga, & Elliott, 1990; Hirschel, Hutchison, & Dean, 1992). Careful evaluation research can help resolve some of the debates over the value of legal and policy reforms, not only in terms of cost effectiveness but also as a measure of their actual as opposed to intended effects. There has been some concern, for example, that funding for treatment programs for wife assaulters places these programs in competition with existing, non-treatment services for battered women, including shelters (MacLeod, 1987). Also, at the same time that criminal courts are adopting a stronger response to wife assault, mediation services associated with family courts across Canada and the United States are gaining acceptance and authority in dealing with marital disputes, often including wife assaulters and their victims in their negotiations. It has been argued that increased attention to wife assault by the criminal justice system has placed a greater burden on the courts, which has led to an increased reliance on mediation, with negative consequences for battered women (Hilton, 1992).

When evaluating legal innovations, it is important not to lose the voice of the victims. In the field of clinical theories of wife assault, Ptacek (1988) has identified an increase in the use of gender-neutral language such as "spouse assault," which hides the greater risks of violence and nonphysical abuse suffered by women. Evaluations of legal responses that focus on whether a wife assaulter is physically violent to the same partner following intervention also risk obscuring the full picture of victimization. Battered women are not unlike other victims of violence in their recent attempts to play a larger role in decisions about offenders (e.g., Rosenfeldt, 1990). The victims of wife assault, however, face additional difficulties that merit particular attention from the criminal justice system. For example, a battered woman might be continuing her relationship with the offender and might see treatment rather than punishment as offering her a better chance of a violence-free future. On the other hand, a woman who is trying to end a violent relationship might fear having to face the offender in court and risk him knowing of her whereabouts. In this book, an attempt has been made to include research that is sensitive to the needs and wishes of the victims of wife assault.

The term "battered woman" has been used in this volume, not only because it specifies the female as the victim of wife assault, which is the subject of this book, but also because it reflects the repetitive nature of the violence suffered by most of these women (e.g., Straus, 1990). The words "battery" and "batterer," however, have been reserved by this editor for the legal offense of battery. While aware of different opinions including those of some chapter authors, I have changed "battering" and "wife beater" to the terms "assault" and "wife assaulter," with the intention of including all forms of aggressive physical contact, from the most serious, life-threatening attacks to comparatively minor slaps and shoves. Not all incidents of wife assault constitute severe violence; however, the fear and other psychological effects of each assault are compounded with the repeated, comparatively minor threats, restrictions, sexual assaults, and other degradations suffered by many battered women (e.g., Finkelhor & Yllö, 1985; Follingstad, Rutledge, Berg, Hause, & Polek, 1990; Russell, 1982). The word "abuse" has been used in this book to refer to nonphysical behaviors, such as taunting, isolation, humiliation, and other forms of aggression and control inflicted by wife assaulters on their victims (e.g., Follingstad et al., 1990).

It is hoped that people working in services for battered women will be among those who will find this book valuable. The book draws together new research about legal responses to wife assault in a form more easily accessible than the academic journals in which this information is usually found. Clinicians who work with wife assaulters will find a thorough review of treatment programs for wife assault and the debates surrounding treatment formats and philosophies, as well as chapters on aspects of the criminal justice system that may well affect their clients. Lawyers, judges, police and probation officers, and policymakers may profit not only from the debates and evidence about arrest, prosecution, mediation, and treatment and their effectiveness, but also from the insights offered about battered women as consumers of these services. Students and researchers will also find here critical reviews and new works in this growing area of evaluation research.

The book is divided into five sections. Part I includes a look at the need for different responses to wife assault depending on the profile of the wife assaulter (Saunders), a qualification that the reader should bear in mind when considering the remaining chapters. Part II concerns the police response to wife assault: first, the extent to which members of the public indicate they would like the police to intervene in cases of wife assault (Hilton); second, how effective such intervention is in reducing future violence (Jaffe, E. Hastings, Reitzel, and Austin); and third, how well suited the police response is to the needs and wishes of battered women (Ferraro and Pope). In Part III, the various functions of the courts are addressed. The effectiveness and problems of prosecution (Ford and Regoli) and mediation (Ellis) are explored, followed by a discussion of court-mandated treatment for wife assaulters and the success of treatment for wife assault in general (Hamberger and J. E. Hastings). Part IV considers the legal response to violence by battered women against their partner. The role of expert testimony about the battered woman syndrome and the dynamics of violent relationships (Walker) and the effects of jury instructions about psychological self-defense (Tomkins, Kenning, Greenwald, and Johnson) are discussed in this section. Part V presents a summary of the preceding chapters, along with an assessment of their contribution to current trends in intervention and evaluation of legal responses to wife assault (Roesch, Hart, and Wilson).

References

Buzawa, E. S., & Buzawa, C. G. (1990). *Domestic violence: The criminal justice response*. Newbury Park, CA: Sage.

Caesar, P. L., & Hamberger, L. K. (Eds.). (1989). *Treating men who batter: Theory, practice, and programs*. New York: Springer.

Dunford, F. W., Huizinga, D., & Elliott, D. S. (1990). The role of arrest in domestic assault: The Omaha police experiment. *Criminology, 28*, 183-206.

Endicott, T. A. (1987). The criminality of wife assault. *University of Toronto Faculty of Law Review, 45*, 355-391.

Ewing, C. P. (1990). Psychological self-defense: A proposed justification for battered women who kill. *Law and Human Behavior, 14*, 579-594.

Finkelhor, D. & Yllö, K. (1985). *License to rape: Sexual abuse of wives*. New York: Free Press.

Follingstad, D. R., Rutledge, L. L., Berg, B. J., Hause, E. S., & Polek, D. (1990). The role of emotional abuse in physically abusive relationships. *Journal of Family Violence, 5*, 107-120.

Hilton, N. Z. (1992). Mediating wife assault: Battered women and the "new family." *Canadian Journal of Family Law, 9*, 29-53.

Hirschel, J. D., Hutchison, I. W., & Dean, C. W. (1992). The failure of arrest to deter spouse abuse. *Journal of Research in Crime and Delinquency, 20*, 7-33.

Jaffe, P., & Burris, C. A. (1984). *An integrated response to wife assault: A community model*. Ministry of the Solicitor General, Canada.

MacLeod, L. (1987). *Battered but not beaten: Preventing wife battering in Canada*. Ottawa: Canadian Advisory Council on the Status of Women.

McGillivray, A. (1987). Battered women: Definition, models, and prosecutional policy. *Canadian Journal of Family Law, 6*, 15-45.

Pence, E. (1989). Batterer programs: Shifting from community collusion to community confrontation. In P. L. Caesar & L. K. Hamberger (Eds.), *Treating men who batter: Theory, practice, and programs* (pp. 24-50). New York: Springer.

Ptacek, J. (1988). The clinical literature on men who batter: A review and critique. In
    G. T. Hotaling, D. Finkelhor, J. T. Kirkpatrick, & M. A. Straus (Eds.), *Family abuse
    and its consequences* (pp. 149-162). Newbury Park, CA: Sage.
Rosenfeldt, G. (Ed.) (1990). Current affairs. *Victims of Violence Report* (July, August,
    September), 3-7.
Russell, D.E.H. (1982). *Rape in marriage*. New York: Macmillan.
Schechter, S. (1982). *Women and male violence*. London: Pluto.
Sherman, L. W., & Berk, R. A. (1984). The specific deterrent effects of arrest for domestic
    assault. *American Sociological Review, 49,* 261-272.
Straus, M. A. (1990). Injury and frequency of assault and the "representative sample
    fallacy" in measuring wife beating and child abuse. In M. A. Straus & R. J. Gelles
    (Eds.), *Physical violence in American families: Risk factors and adaptations to
    violence in 8,145 families* (pp. 75-91). New Brunswick: Transaction Books.

2

Husbands Who Assault

Multiple Profiles Requiring Multiple Responses

DANIEL G. SAUNDERS

- A police department receives a call from a woman who says that she is afraid of her estranged husband, who is outside her apartment door pleading to see her. She is referred to an agency that can help her file for a restraining order. She is reluctant to do this, partly because it could affect his reputation. He is a 44-year-old, highly respected physician. She reports that he broke her wrist a few months earlier, but she is now thinking of reuniting if he agrees to couples' counseling. Police records show a single arrest for a minor traffic accident while he was under the influence of alcohol.

- A police dispatcher receives a call from a hospital emergency room. A woman wants her boyfriend arrested for severely bruising her about the face and neck. He previously assaulted her to the point of causing a miscarriage. He is the same man the police arrested the night before for a drunken brawl with three men in a bar. He is a seasonal construction worker in his mid-30s. He has a long history of alcohol-related crimes, including an assault on a police officer when he was in his early 20s. After serving time for that assault, he served 2 years in prison for drug dealing. As a youth he lived in foster homes and juvenile treatment centers.

University of Michigan School of Social Work, 1065 Frieze Building, Ann Arbor, Michigan, 48109-1285.

- A suicide hot line worker calls the police for aid. She would like the police to check on a 23-year-old man who has called them several times threatening suicide. He now says he has a gun and wants to "execute" himself. He is separated from his wife and young son and realizes how much he has hurt her through his aggression. He has slapped her and ridiculed her severely. In the last episode of violence she was holding their son. He has no criminal justice history. As a child he was affected by his mother's severe mental illness and violence by his older brother.

These cases illustrate the great diversity among husbands who assault*: diversity in violence severity, alcohol use, social class, childhood experiences, and other factors. Some men are aggressive only at home, whereas others are aggressive in many settings and have a long criminal record. The violence may range from a few slaps and shoves to life-threatening beatings and use of weapons (Straus, Gelles, & Steinmetz, 1980). The backgrounds and hence the psychological traits of these men are also diverse. Although the patriarchal norms and structure of our society lay a strong foundation for men's violence against intimate partners (Yllö, 1984), the expression of their aggressive domination takes many complex forms. One example of the complexity arises from a paradox created in our patriarchal society: some aggressive men feel extremely powerless despite holding relatively powerful positions (Finkelhor, 1983).

With rare exceptions, diversity among husbands who assault has been ignored in criminal justice and treatment interventions. In this chapter, I will review the current literature on multiple profiles of men who assault their wife, with special attention to the need for considering multiple interventions. The review will first cover risk factors for all types of husbands who assault before proceeding to the more specific topic of subtypes.

Risk Markers for Assaultive Behavior

Recent empirical reviews comparing husbands who assault with other men reveal some consistent risk markers for wife assault

---

*The term *husbands who assault* is used to mean men who have used violence against a married or cohabitating partner or ex-partner.

(Hotaling & Sugarman, 1986; Tolman & Bennett, 1990). These are not necessarily causal factors but have merely been found to distinguish husbands who assault from nonassaulters. I will summarize these reviews here and integrate findings from additional studies. The reader should realize, however, that the failure of certain traits to distinguish between groups may be because men who assault their wife may not be too different from other men. In many ways, they are "like other men, only more so." The lack of distinguishing traits in general can also be attributed to the subtypes, to be described later. Thus, only a few factors are found consistently across the population of husbands who assault. Childhood violence, low income, and alcohol use are the strongest (see Table 2.1).

Childhood Violence

The notion that violence is transmitted across generations is well entrenched. As predicted by social learning theory and other theories, a consistent risk marker for domestic violence is a history of witnessing parental violence or being physically assaulted oneself (Hotaling & Sugarman, 1986). Even "ordinary punishment" must be a topic of concern, because it is associated in males with violence toward wife and children in adulthood (Straus, 1983). Witnessing violence appears to be a somewhat stronger predictor. If both witnessing and being the target of violence occurs, there is an additive effect, with rates five times higher than those with nonviolent childhoods (Straus et al., 1980).

Class and Subculture

Those in a position to help in cases of wife assault, including the police and prosecutors, sometimes minimize the problem by saying, "It's only in that part of town that we have a real problem." "That part of town" usually is home to the poorest residents or to a particular racial or ethnic group. Although wife assault occurs in all economic and ethnic groups, there is a kernel of truth to the notion that it is more prevalent in some sociocultural groups. For example, in a U.S. survey, the rate of wife assault in the lowest income families was over five times the rate of the highest income families (11% vs. 2%, Straus

Table 2.1 Risk Factors for Wife Assault

Risk Factors	Comments
PROMINENT RISK	
Childhood experience with violence	More risk if both saw abuse and was abused
Low income and education of man	More risk if woman has higher status
Alcohol use by man	Chronic alcoholism may be key factor
PROBABLE RISK	
Communication skills deficits	Especially if combined with need for power
Rigid sex-role attitudes	If based on woman's perceptions of man
Personality disorders	Heterogenous pattern of disorders
Abuse of children	Half of violent husbands severely abuse a child
Anger	Especially for marital situations
POSSIBLE RISK	
Stress	"Stressor" may be the result of violence
Depression	Low self-esteem may be better risk marker

SOURCE: Adapted from D. G. Saunders (in press).

et al., 1980). Blue-collar workers, the unemployed, and especially the partially employed also had higher rates. African Americans and Hispanic Americans also have higher rates of wife assault (Straus et al., 1980; Straus & Smith, 1990). The popular explanation—that these subcultures have proviolence norms—is not supported by the evidence. Rather, the stresses of unemployment, underemployment, and inner-city living appear to be the best explanatory variables (Straus & Smith, 1990). Hand in hand with the lower income of men who assault their wife is their lower educational level (Hotaling & Straus, 1989).

Of special note is the volatile mix that occurs when the man's religious background differs from his partner's (Hotaling & Sugarman, 1986). A somewhat less prominent risk marker occurs when the wife's education or occupational status is higher than her husband's. His patriarchal beliefs about who should be head of the household are likely to be challenged when this occurs.

Age

Consistent with other violent crime, men who assault their wife tend to be younger than nonviolent men. For example, in the U.S. survey by Straus et al. (1980), those under 30 had a rate of wife assault three times higher than those over 30 (9% vs. 3%). The reason for this difference is unclear. The decrease in violence with age does not appear to be attributable to the decreases in verbal abuse, alcohol use, and marital conflict that occur with aging (Suitor, Pillemer, & Straus, 1990). As with other crimes, biological changes or learning through experience may explain the reduction (Hirschi & Gottfredson, 1983).

Alcohol

Alcoholism theories operate as simplistically as "subculture of violence" theories for many law enforcement personnel; that is, "dry out" the man and he will not be violent anymore. Such notions about the alcohol-violence connection are challenged in the scientific literature. High rates of alcohol use or alcoholism are present in samples of husbands who assault (Tolman & Bennett, 1990), but the alcohol-violence relationship may be attributable to a factor influencing both violence and alcoholism. Personality, cultural norms, and mind-set are known to affect behavioral reactions to alcohol (Collins, 1983). In a macho culture, for example, men are expected to both "fight hard" and "drink hard." Also, the connection might be related more to chronic than to acute use of alcohol (Tolman & Bennett, 1990). Chronic use may produce family arguments about drinking, paranoia from cognitive deficits, or severe withdrawal symptoms, including irritability.

Behavioral Deficits

A popular notion about wife assault is that it is the "last ditch" effort to communicate by a man who is unskilled in verbal battle. There seems to be some truth to the notion that men who assault their wife have communication skills deficits. For example, in one study, it was found that husbands who assault were not as skilled as other men at making requests and initiating activities, although they could say "no" to requests (Maiuro, Cahn, & Vitaliano, 1986). In another study, researchers found that violent men were less competent in responding to perceived rejection, challenges from the wife, and situations involving jealousy (Holtzworth-Munroe & Anglin, 1991). These researchers did not find violent and nonviolent men to differ in their competency to respond to wives' requests or teasing. Difficulty in being assertive seems most strongly related to violence among men with the greatest need for power (Dutton & Strachan, 1987). These men may become especially frustrated and angry, with few assertive skills for expressing their feelings. Observational studies reveal that husbands who assault also have some behavioral excesses, including more negative voice quality and more signs of irritation and frustration than nonviolent men (Margolin, John, & Gleberman, 1988).

Personality Disorders

Although there is no strong evidence that more than a small fraction of offenders have severe mental disorders, they have more signs of psychopathology than once thought. Using broad definitions of psychopathology, such as personality disorders and alcoholism, most husbands who assault in treatment show clinical elevations on standardized instruments such as the Minnesota Multiphasic Personality Inventory (MMPI) and the Millon Clinical Multiaxial Inventory (MCMI) (Coates, Leong, & Lindsey, 1987; Hamberger & Hastings, 1986). MMPI profiles characterize the average abuser as alienated, isolated, insecure, and distrustful of others, and they appear to be overly concerned about their masculine image (Bernard & Bernard, 1984). No consistent pattern has been found on the MCMI. Patterns cluster around asocial/borderline, narcissistic/antisocial, and dependent/compulsive profiles (Hamberger & Hastings, 1986). Elevated scales on the MCMI seem to be related to alcoholism (Hamberger, Hastings, & Lohr, 1991).

Violence Toward Children

Violent husbands are seven times more likely to be violent toward their children than are nonviolent husbands (50% vs. 7%; Straus, 1983). Increasing attention is being paid to the children in these homes by battered women's advocates, family counselors, and child protection workers (Jaffe, Wolfe, & Wilson, 1990). The children are likely to suffer severe short-term and long-term effects from being physically assaulted, with additional effects from witnessing violence against their mothers.

Anger

Contrary to what might be expected, anger and hostility are not consistently related to violence. Some men may act not out of anger but out of a sense of a "duty to discipline" their wife, just like a parent who disciplines a child. Some men may keep their "cool" when seeking revenge. The inconsistent relation between anger and violence may result from individual differences among husbands who assault, discussed below in the section on subtypes.

The type of anger measure used may also contribute to the inconsistency. The Buss-Durkee Hostility Inventory, but not the Novaco Anger Index, shows elevated anger scores for assaultive husbands (Tolman & Bennett, 1990). When the Novaco Index is modified to include maritally specific items, however, it is related to women's reports of their partner's aggression (Saunders & Hanusa, 1986). Thus, when women transgress certain marital expectations, the men may erupt with anger. The men also reveal anger when their fears of abandonment are aroused, perhaps fears that stem from childhood traumas. In response to videotaped scenes of abandonment, they reported more anger than other violent and nonviolent samples of men (Dutton, 1988).

Stress

Stress from work may be as important a factor as stress from family life (Barling & Rosenbaum, 1986). The men may displace their anger, stress, and frustration from work onto those least likely to retaliate: their family members. Studies on this risk factor, however, are inconsistent and difficult to interpret. Some studies include items on the stress scales such as "divorce," "separation," and "problems with boss." It is unclear if these are the cause or the result of aggression.

Depression and Low Self-Esteem

The connection between depression and violence is also unclear. There is some indication that publicly identified husbands who assault (i.e., those who are arrested) are more depressed than those from community samples (i.e., those who complete anonymous questionnaires) (Hamberger & Hastings, 1988). Arrestees may be depressed over their arrest or their separation from their partner. Alternatively, community samples may be less willing to admit to problems. Any causal connection is impossible to establish with existing studies, which fail to assess depression over time or disentangle the effects of arrest, separation, co-occurring problems, and other factors.

Self-esteem as a trait may be less likely to be affected by situational or "state" factors. In the review by Hotaling and Sugarman (1986), the majority of studies showed that men who assault their wife had lower self-esteem than nonviolent men. Even this factor, however, may be affected by events just prior to the assessment of self-esteem (see discussion by Neidig, Collins, & Friedman, 1986). There is also evidence that husbands who assault do not differ on this trait from nonviolent husbands in distressed marriages (Telch & Lindquist, 1984).

Other Factors

Some factors may be related to violence by their simple co-occurrence. For example, sexual assault is a consistent correlate of wife assault (Hotaling & Sugarman, 1986). It is most commonly associated with severe violence (Gondolf, 1988) and has the most traumatic emotional effects on its victim (Shields & Hanneke, 1983).

Arguments and conflict are often found in violent relationships (O'Leary & Vivian, 1990; Straus et al., 1980). As with stress and other factors, however, it is unclear if these are causes or effects of violence. Verbal aggression is clearly a precursor of physical violence in young marriages (Murphy & O'Leary, 1989).

Violent crime outside of the home also appears as a risk marker. Early case studies suggested that most husbands who assault restricted their violence to the home (e.g., Faulk, 1974, 12%; Walker, 1979, 20%). More recent studies, on the other hand, reveal that the majority are violent outside the home and have a history of arrest (Hotaling & Straus, 1989).

Nonrisk Factors

Mention should also be made of a few traits that are commonly thought to characterize husbands who assault. Traditional sex-role beliefs have not generally been found to distinguish husbands who assault, at least on the basis of their self-reported attitudes and violence (Hotaling & Sugarman, 1986). Only when women are asked about their partner's attitudes does the predicted link between traditional attitudes and violence emerge (Smith, 1990; Walker, 1984). As we will see shortly, some types of violent husbands have stronger sexist attitudes than others.

Although cross-cultural studies clearly show that on a macrosocial level, patriarchal norms and male dominance are risk factors for wife assault (Levinson, 1989; Yllö, 1983), actual decision-making power or a psychological need for power have not been shown to be consistent factors on an individual level (Hotaling & Sugarman, 1986). The most rigorous study, however, does show that an abundance of decision-making power in the hands of one spouse, either husband or wife, is a risk marker (Straus et al., 1980). This is especially true, at least for "minor" violence, when conflict in the relationship is high (Coleman & Straus, 1986). Furthermore, subtypes of husbands who assault may have this trait. For example, the man's decision-making power is a risk factor among blue-collar workers with the fewest resources (Allen & Straus, 1980). Other types of power, such as the ability to restrict the woman's freedom, are implicated as risk markers for wife assault (Frieze & Browne, 1989). More research is clearly needed on the causal role of various types of power.

Summary

The most prominent risk markers for wife assault are childhood experiences with violence, low SES, and alcohol use. Several factors appear to be less prominent, but are likely to exert an influence: anger, communication skill deficits, personality disorders, and violence toward children. The roles of stress, depression, and patriarchal norms are less clear. Women's perceptions of the man's norms and cross-cultural evidence indicate patriarchal attitudes are significant risk markers. Sexual assault and marital conflict are consistent correlates of physical aggression. Finally, an imbalance of power is found as a risk marker in the most rigorous study and may be especially potent in some subtypes. Table 2.1 summarizes the most consistently found risk markers for wife assault and classifies them as "prominent," "probable," or "possible."

Types of Husbands Who Assault

Early empirical work indicated that men who assault their wife could be divided into two groups: those aggressive only at home and those aggressive both in and outside the home. The generally aggressive type was found to be more severely violent and more likely to abuse alcohol (Brisson, 1981; Fagan, Stewart, & Hansen, 1983; Shields, McCall, & Hanneke, 1988). Not surprisingly, these men seem to hold stronger proviolence attitudes and to have criminal life-styles (Shields et al., 1988). They appear to be the most likely to be violent toward their children and to sexually assault their partner (Gondolf, 1988). Most studies reveal that these men are more likely to have experienced severe violence in childhood (Caesar, 1986; Fagan et al., 1983; Hofeller, 1980). The general aggressor, then, may differ little from other violent criminals. Fagan (1988) points out the need to integrate criminological theories with theories of domestic violence, at least for this generally aggressive subtype.

Personality traits have also been assigned to these two types. The generally aggressive type has been labeled "dominant" and the family-only type labeled "dependent" (Hofeller, 1980). The dependent type, for example, is more affectionate in the marriage and may attempt suicide if divorce is imminent (Hofeller, 1980). The dependent type shows more remorse after being aggressive (Caesar, 1986; Gondolf, 1988; Hofeller, 1980). The generally aggressive type seems to have the trait of "undercontrolled" hostility, with the family-only type being "overcontrolled" (Hershorn & Rosenbaum, 1991).

Some researchers find more than two types of husbands who assault, with some other types appearing to be subtypes of the generally aggressive and family-only types. Caesar (1986), using the MMPI and a background questionnaire, found evidence for a dependent type who had tried to intervene in his parents' fights. He had chronic resentment but did not seem able to express it. Hamberger and Hastings (1986), using the MCMI, found a great deal of heterogeneity in their treatment sample. The largest "pure" type was dependent/compulsive and it comprised only 16% of the sample. They provide evidence that the most antisocial and aggressive men may not be the most angry.

The above studies usually relied either on reports of behavior or single psychological tests to determine different types. My recent study of wife assaulter types combined many of the background, behavioral, and attitude variables from the above studies into a single one (Saunders, 1992). Such an approach is likely to yield more accurate representations of different types of men who assault their wife.

Method

Participants were 165 men being assessed for treatment of wife assault. Their average age was about 30 and the majority did not have education beyond high school (59.5%). About three fourths were white, with African Americans being the next largest racial group (18.1%). About 70% of the men were referred from the courts or a deferred prosecution program.

The two major sources of data were a structured interview conducted by an intake counselor and standardized self-report measures. Generalized violence was measured in the intake interview based on the man's report that he was violent outside the home as well as inside. Arrest records were used to corroborate his reports. The men's victimization in childhood at the hands of parents or siblings was also assessed in this interview.

The men were then asked by the intake counselor about their history of psychologically and physically aggressive acts against their partner. A modified form of the Conflict Tactics Scale (Straus, 1979) was used. Several items of physical aggression were added (e.g., "physically forced sex on her"). Several were also added on psychological abuse (e.g., "interrupted her eating or sleeping," "said she could not leave or see certain people"). The four items classified as life-threatening in a factor analysis were given double the weight of other items.

The final measure taken from the intake interview was an estimation of the percentage of time that alcohol use by the man was associated with violence against his partner. This measure correlated significantly with the Michigan Alcohol Screening Test.

The following self-report measures were used: the Attitudes Toward Women Scale (Spence & Helmreich, 1978) of sexist attitudes; a short version of the Blood and Wolfe (Blood & Wolfe, 1960) scale of marital decision-making power; the Marital Conflict Index that was used in the first national study of family violence (Straus et al., 1980); a modified version of the Novaco Anger Index (Novaco, 1975) that included specific, hypothetical marital situations; romantic jealousy as measured with a scale developed by White (1977); and the Beck Depression Inventory.

A unique feature of the study was the adjustment of measures for response bias, as the study relied on self-reports likely to be contaminated by social desirability response bias. A 10-item version of the Marlowe-Crowne Social Desirability Scale was used as a measure of impression management, or the tendency to "fake good" (Greenwald & Satow, 1970).

The primary analysis was a cluster analysis of six variables (Euclidean distances with a complete linkage procedure). The derivation of clusters was followed by ANOVA comparisons for the variables used in clustering, as well as the remaining "external" variables to test the validity of the clustering. In order to uncover the overall association between the clusters and the clustering and external variables, a discriminant function analysis was also conducted. In a subsequent intake sample, the emotional traits of the different types found were correlated with personality scales of the Millon Clinical Multiaxial Inventory.

Table 2.2 Three Types of Husbands Who Assault Derived From Cluster Analysis

	Family Only (n = 86)	Generally Aggressive (n = 48)	Emotionally Volatile (n = 31)
General violence	$.30_a$	1.75_b	$.89_c$
Violence severity	10.39_a	21.18_b	11.67_a
Anger at partner	2.36_a	2.51_a	3.21_b
Depression	7.10_a	8.15_a	23.33_b
Liberal sex-role beliefs	27.32_a	24.51_b	31.73_c
Alcohol use	33.75_a	76.53_b	42.11_a
Jealousy	16.70_a	18.91_a	20.87_b
Marital satisfaction	9.56_a	$5.27b$	$6.06_{a,b}$
Psychological abuse	5.31_a	7.02_b	6.87_b
Marital conflict	2.39_a	2.69_b	2.88_b
Prior counseling	$36\%_a$	$44\%_{a,b}$	$59\%_b$
Severe abuse as child	$34\%_a$	$51\%_a$	$40\%_a$
Arrests for violence	$45\%_a$	$70\%_b$	$30\%_a$
MCMI correlates	Conformist	Antisocial	Passive-Aggressive Avoidant Borderline

NOTE: Means and percents are adjusted for social desirability response bias. Groups with different subscripts are significantly different from each other (Duncan's multiple range test or bivariate Chi-square analysis).
SOURCE: Adapted from D. G. Saunders (1992).

Results and Discussion

The results, shown in Table 2.2, revealed that family-only and general aggressors could be distinguished, as in other studies. A third type, distinguished by high levels of anger, depression, and jealousy, was also found. The results were similar to those of other studies in showing that the generalized aggressor was most likely to have a history of severe childhood abuse, to use alcohol when violent, and to be the type to severely assault his partner most often. The generalized aggressor had the least liberal sex-role attitudes. Although reporting the most severe violence, this type reported only moderate levels of anger and jealousy.

In contrast to the general aggressor, the family-only type was less likely to have severe childhood victimization and had more liberal sex-role beliefs and lower levels of anger. Of the three types, he reported less conflict and more satisfaction in his marriage. This type appeared to suppress his emotions (Marlowe-Crowne Scale) and to have a conformist personality (MCMI). Alcohol was associated with violence about a third of the time.

A third type of wife assaulter was also uncovered. This type was characterized by extreme jealousy, anger, and depression, including suicidal feelings. He was most likely to have sought help in the past for psychological problems and was most likely to be open about his problems, as revealed by the Marlowe-Crowne Scale (not shown on the table). He was least likely to use alcohol in connection with violence. He reported being less likely to use severe physical violence but admitted engaging in frequent psychological abuse. Of the three types, he reported his marriage to be the least satisfying. MCMI scales that correlated most strongly with the high levels of emotions associated with this type were passive-aggressive, avoidant, and borderline.

Returning to the case illustrations at the beginning of the chapter, even the small amount of information they provide suggests what types the men fit. Obviously much more information would have to be gathered in the assessment process. The physician was a family-only assaulter. He did not have a criminal record for violent offenses. His severe violence—breaking his wife's wrist—does not fit the pattern of family-only assaulters; however, the infrequency of this type of violence does fit the pattern. The pleading behavior he shows with his wife is typical of this type, usually following statements of remorse. The pleading may change to threats but is less likely to do so than for the other two types.

The man arrested for the barroom fight was a general aggressor. He clearly had a long history of aggressive and other antisocial behavior that was not only directed at female partners. His long history of alcohol-related crimes is typical of this type. Further assessment may reveal severe childhood traumas and a history of experimentation with several types of drugs.

The young, suicidal man fits the "emotionally volatile" type. His violence is rarely severe, yet he is the most self-blaming of the three types. His self-blame can quickly change to blaming others for his actions. He seems belatedly aware that even a slap can horribly degrade his partner and potentially injure her and their child. He is reaching out for help with repeated calls to a suicide hot line. His separation from his family may trigger the reexperiencing of a chaotic and painful childhood.

Because all three of these men are influenced by our society's norms about male-female roles and violence, their violence has a common etiology. Yet, their unique backgrounds and personalities also mean there are probably causes that are unique to each. Different approaches are likely to be needed to help each of these men end his violence. The childhood experiences of the three types may lead to very different ways of handling emotions and using alcohol. I speculate that the severe violence suffered by generalized aggressors resulted in post-traumatic stress symptoms such as "psychic numbing," with its blockage of feelings (van der Kolk, 1988). These men may use alcohol to deaden painful memories. They often try to justify their violence as "protection" against perceived or real threats. They probably lack empathy because they are cut off from their own pain. In addition, some men comment that they have little sympathy for their partner's suffering because it is much less severe than what they experienced in childhood. Family-only men, on the other hand, may overcontrol their feelings and use alcohol occasionally to help release feelings of anger or hurt. The emotionally volatile men probably suffered psychological, and perhaps sexual, abuse in childhood. This could explain their borderline personality traits and frequent psychological abuse of their partner.

Severe and Frequent Assaults

Decisions about legal and treatment interventions may hinge on predictions of who is most likely frequently or severely to assault his partner. For example, closer probationary monitoring or more immediate treatment may be called for in some cases. In extreme cases, practitioners are expected to make judgments about the dangerousness of offenders in order to warn victims or to notify legal authorities. The studies described above show that the most severely violent men are even more likely than other husbands who assault to have experienced violence in childhood and to abuse alcohol. Consistently, they are violent outside the home as well as inside. They appear to have a criminal life-style and to show little remorse for their violence. Most of these factors can be determined with interviews and background checks; thus, sophisticated psychological tests may not be required.

Less is known about the correlates of frequent violence, a dimension that is not necessarily related to violence severity (e.g., Bowker, 1983). In one study, women who were the most frequently assaulted experienced the most threats and a high rate of marital rape (Snyder & Fruchtman, 1981). In another study, frequent assault, just like severe assault, was associated with less education in the men, and with their having experienced and witnessed violence in childhood (Bowker, 1983). In Bowker's study, alcohol or drug involvement before marriage was more highly associated with frequency of assault in marriage than was premarital violence. It was also a stronger correlate than the wife's suspicion before marriage that her partner had a temper. An alcoholic aggressor may be the most adept at hiding his propensity toward violence until after marriage.

Do Different Types Respond Differently to Intervention?

Husbands who assault are likely to respond differently to different social policies and treatments depending on their type. The question about differential responding, however, cannot be answered directly at this time. Thus far, types of husbands who assault have not been assigned experimentally to different interventions. Cross-sectional analyses of interventions, however, do provide us with some clues about differential effects. Some risk factors are beginning to appear for those least likely to be affected by legal sanctions and treatment.

Criminal Justice Interventions

Many reports on the effect of arrest, restraining orders, and prosecution either do not assess or do not highlight the type of assaulter with whom intervention is most successful. Many of these findings and their implications will be presented in later chapters in this book (see Jaffe, Hastings, Reitzel, & Austin, this volume; Ford & Regoli, this volume). A couple of examples will be mentioned here. For ethical reasons, the influential Minneapolis Police Experiment and its replications did not include felony assault cases (Sherman & Berk, 1984). Thus, any effect of arrest may hold only for relatively nonsevere cases, and the replication experiments thus far completed do not show an arrest effect even for these cases (e.g., Dunford, Huizinga, & Elliott, 1990; Hirschel, Hutchison, & Dean, 1992). Indeed, Fagan (1989) presents nonexperimental evidence to suggest that arrest and prosecution may not be effective with those with a history of severe violence. In a study of the effects of restraining orders, the orders showed no effect on violence recidivism, even for family-only, nonsevere assaulters (Grau, Fagan, & Wexler, 1984). Nonsevere assaulters did show lower rates of harassment and verbal threats following a restraining order. The generalized aggressor, with experience in the criminal justice system, may know how weak its sanctions are and consequently may not be deterred. The family-only type, with a tendency to conform to social norms, may be more influenced by legal sanctions.

Risk Factors for Treatment Attrition

The above review of wife assaulter types noted that the emotionally volatile type seems the most willing to seek help voluntarily and is the most open to revealing his problems. He may still be very ambivalent about being in treatment, however, and he may be difficult to work with. Before a psychological assessment can be conducted to determine the type of assaulter, some easily gathered demographic information can be used to predict treatment compliance. For example, treatment follow-through is higher among those who are older, better educated, and employed (DeMaris, 1989; Grusznski & Carrillo, 1988).

Legal requirements to attend treatment do not seem to improve the motivation of these men. In fact, motivation may be lessened for some. These are the men most likely to be referred voluntarily or through a "first offenders" program, and they are the least likely to have the criminal record of the general aggressors (Saunders & Parker, 1989; cf. Hamberger & Hastings, this volume). Some studies also indicate that Caucasian clients are more likely to complete assessment and treatment (Saunders & Parker, 1989). Because minority, poor, and less educated men are at risk for attrition, agencies should assess their minority staffing patterns and the reading level of material used in psychoeducational programs. Methods for enhancing treatment motivation can also be tried, such as marathon orientation sessions or "sponsorship" programs in which volunteers are matched with new clients (e.g., Almeida & Bograd, 1991; Tolman & Bhosley, 1990).

Risk Factors for Recidivism
After Treatment

The recurrence of violence 6 months or more after treatment averages about 35% across a number of studies (Saunders & Azar, 1989; cf. Hamberger & Hastings, this volume). For men not completing treatment, the average across these studies is 52%. Few studies have reported on the characteristics of those who were violent after treatment. Hamberger and Hastings (1990) relied on the reports of men or their partner during the year after treatment. Those men who were violent after treatment were younger, reported alcohol as a problem, and scored higher on narcissism on the MCMI than other men. These men are likely to be antisocial, general aggressors.

DeMaris and Jackson (1987) relied on questionnaire responses mailed to the men after treatment. Those reporting recidivism were more likely to have alcohol problems and to have witnessed parental violence. Tolman (1988) found that longer histories of pretreatment violence predicted failure. Again, these are the characteristics of the general aggressor type. A weakness in the above studies is the failure to measure decreases in the magnitude of violence for those violent after treatment; any occurrence of violence was the criterion for failure. Given the history of pretreatment violence, it is quite possible that treatment lowered the frequency and severity of violence by these men.

Implications for
Policy and Intervention

Notable among the risk factors for assault is the violence experienced by the men in childhood. Both "ordinary" and severe punishment of boys, plus their exposure to marital violence, greatly increase the odds that they will become the next generation of husbands who assault their wife and child (Straus, 1983). Their violence is also likely to go beyond the closed doors of the family. Thus, prevention programs for boys at risk for violence are likely to reduce violent crime both in and outside the home. Legal and treatment interventions do not provide long-term solutions to the problem of domestic violence. Beyond work with high-risk groups, primary prevention must decrease male dominance in the family and society and the general pervasiveness of violence in our society (Straus & Smith, 1990).

Implications also exist regarding the risk factor of alcoholism. The causal connection between alcohol use and domestic violence is not entirely clear, but chemical effects alone cannot account for the connection. Because many men who assault their wife have alcohol problems, alcoholism and domestic violence agencies need to work closely together to arrive at a common understanding (e.g., Wright, 1985). Some domestic violence agencies are now choosing to treat their own clients for alcohol and other drug problems.

For many years, the goal of most researchers, policymakers, and practitioners has been to derive a uniform profile of the wife assaulter and to apply interventions to this unitary, "average" assaulter. Few exceptions could be found to this unitary approach. Brisson (1981), for example, speculated that the family-only type would benefit the most from insight-oriented approaches. One treatment program divides its clients into two different groups, one for voluntary clients and one for involuntary clients (DeMaris & Jackson, 1987). Through research and clinical experience, we have learned that there are some major differences among violent husbands. Although the typology presented in this chapter needs further validation, it is consistent with much prior research. I will use it as a framework to make a series of propositions to guide researchers and practitioners.

Generalized Aggressor

This man will require the longest and most diverse interventions, perhaps lasting up to 2 years. His problems are the most chronic and are typified by the man in the second case illustration, whose violence caused a miscarriage and who has a long history of violent crime outside the home. He may have the most invested in holding on to his aggression and alcohol abuse as a way to keep his childhood wounds covered. He is least able to empathize with his victims and thus shows little remorse. He probably needs the closest legal supervision because of the above factors and because he is at highest risk for severe violence and recidivism after treatment. Emphasis in his intervention should be on a wide variety of areas, not necessarily in this order:

- Close legal supervision
- Alcoholism assessment and counseling
- Cognitive restructuring to improve impulse control
- Gradually increasing awareness of childhood traumas
- Healing childhood traumas
- Reducing rigid sex-role beliefs
- Learning the assertive expression of feelings

Family-Only Type

This man may need the least amount of treatment. His violence is the least serious and he reports the most affection and satisfaction in his marriage. He may need to learn to see anger as a normal emotion. He will then need help learning to express anger and other emotions nonabusively. Couples' counseling may be a useful approach with these men if separate assessment sessions reveal that each partner is willing to work on the relationship and that it has been free of violence for a substantial period of time. Emphasis in intervention for this type should be on:

- Learning assertive and emotional rights, including the right to have a range of emotions
- Assertiveness training and other communication skills training
- Relaxation training as an alternative to alcohol use
- Alcoholism assessment and counseling

Emotionally Volatile

This type of assaulter will probably need long-term help, depending in part on the severity of his childhood psychological abuse. Legal sanctions may do little to deter him. Steinfeld (1986), for example, predicts that this type cannot weigh the possibility of arrest or other sanctions because his perceptions are too clouded by anger. Legal sanctions may still provide the initial impetus for self-control. More important, this type probably needs readily available support to help him through crises, followed by an intensive program for emotional control. Emphasis in his intervention should probably be on:

- Crisis intervention
- Learning to accept "weak" feelings without channeling them into anger
- Regulation of emotions through systematic desensitization and cognitive restructuring
- Increasing awareness of harm caused by rigid sex-role beliefs and psychological abuse

The emphasis in most programs has been on cognitive and behavioral interventions, with varying degrees of emphasis on sex-role resocialization and turning the men away from other-control toward self-control (e.g., Saunders, 1982; Sonkin, Martin, & Walker, 1985; Stordeur & Stille, 1989). The cognitive and behavioral interventions have included rational-emotive therapy, cognitive restructuring, stress inoculation, relaxation training, and assertiveness training. In the future, more emphasis may be needed on resolving childhood traumas, especially with the general and emotionally volatile aggressors.

Summary and Conclusions

Much progress has been made in recent years in the identification of risk markers for domestic violence. These risk markers can be used to guide policymaking, treatment, and research on causal factors. Recent research presents us with a more complex picture of men who assault their wife than we once had. Our public policies and treatment programs are likely to be more effective if we tailor them to particular types of husbands who assault. In this chapter, I reviewed available evidence on risk factors and types of assaulter. The propositions on what should be emphasized for each type of assaulter were offered to guide practitioners in the improvement of interventions. The knowledge in this area is new, and I hope researchers will be encouraged to test the propositions.

References

Allen, C. M., & Straus, M. A. (1980). Resources, power, and husband-wife violence. In M. A. Straus & G. T. Hotaling (Eds.), *The social causes of husband-wife violence* (pp. 188-210). Minneapolis: University of Minnesota.

Almeida, R. V., & Bograd, M. (1991). Sponsorship: Men holding men accountable for domestic violence. In M. Bograd (Ed.), *Feminist approaches for men in family therapy* (pp. 243-260). New York: Harrington Park.

Barling, J., & Rosenbaum, A. (1986). Work stressors and wife abuse. *Journal of Applied Psychology, 71,* 346-348.

Bernard, J. L., & Bernard, M. L. (1984). The abusive male seeking treatment: Jekyll and Hyde. *Family Relations, 33,* 543-547.

Blood, R. E., & Wolfe, D. M. (1960). *Husbands and wives.* Glencoe, IL: Free Press.

Bowker, L. H. (1983). *Beating wife-beating.* Lexington, MA: Lexington.

Brisson, N. (1981). Battering husbands: A survey of abusive men. *Victimology, 6,* 338-344.

Caesar, P. L. (1986, August). Men who batter: A heterogeneous group. In L. K. Hamberger (Chair), *The male batterer: Characteristics of a heterogeneous population.* Symposium presented at the annual meeting of the American Psychological Association, Washington, DC.

Coates, C. J., Leong, D. J., & Lindsey, M. (1987, July). *Personality differences among batterers voluntarily seeking treatment and those ordered to treatment by the court.* Paper presented at the Third National Family Violence Research Conference, University of New Hampshire, Durham.

Coleman, D. H., & Straus, M. A. (1986). Marital power, conflict, and violence in a nationally representative sample of American couples. *Violence and Victims, 1,* 41-157.

Collins, J. J. (1983). Alcohol abuse and expressive interpersonal violence: A proposed explanatory model. In E. Gottheil, K. A. Druley, T. E. Skoloda, & H. M. Waxman (Eds.), *Alcohol, drug abuse, and aggression* (pp. 5-26). Springfield, IL: Charles Thomas.

DeMaris, A. (1989). Attrition in batterers' counseling: The role of social and demographic factors. *Social Service Review, 63,* 142-154.

DeMaris, A., & Jackson, J. K. (1987). Batterers' reports of recidivism after counseling. *Social Casework, 68,* 458-465.

Dunford, F. W., Huizinga, D., & Elliott, D. S. (1990). The role of arrest in domestic assault: The Omaha Police Experiment. *Criminology, 28,* 183-206.

Dutton, D. G. (1988). Profiling of wife assaulters: Preliminary evidence for a trimodal analysis. *Violence and Victims, 3,* 5-29.

Dutton, D. G., & Strachan, C. E. (1987). Motivational needs for power and spouse-specific assertiveness in assaultive and nonassaultive men. *Violence and Victims, 2,* 145-156.

Fagan, J. A. (1988). Contributions of family violence research to criminal justice policy on wife assault: Paradigms of science and social control. *Violence and Victims, 3,* 159-186.

Fagan, J. A. (1989). Cessation of family violence: Deterrence and dissuasion. In L. Ohlin & M. Tonry (Eds.), *Family violence* (pp. 49-68). Chicago: University of Chicago Press.

Fagan, J. A., Stewart, D. K., & Hansen, K. V. (1983). Violent men or violent husbands? Background factors and situational correlates. In D. Finkelhor, R. J. Gelles, G. T. Hotaling, & M. A. Straus (Eds.), *The dark side of families: Current family violence research* (pp. 49-67). Beverly Hills, CA: Sage.

Faulk, M. (1974). Men who assault their wives. *Medicine, Science, and the Law, 14,* 180-183.

Finkelhor, D. (1983). Common features of family abuse. In D. Finkelhor, R. J. Gelles, G. T. Hotaling, & M. A. Straus (Eds.), *The dark side of families: Current family violence research* (pp. 17-28). Beverly Hills, CA: Sage.

Frieze, I. H., & Browne, A. (1989). Violence in marriage. In L. Ohlin & M. Tonry (Eds.), *Family violence* (pp. 163-218). Chicago: University of Chicago Press.

Gondolf, E. W. (1988). Who are those guys? Toward a behavioral typology of batterers. *Violence and Victims, 3,* 187-204.

Grau, J., Fagan, J., & Wexler, S. (1984). Restraining orders for battered women: Issues of access and efficacy. *Women and Politics, 4,* 13-28.

Greenwald, H.J., & Satow, Y. (1970). A short social desirability scale. *Psychological Reports, 27,* 131-135.

Grusznski, R. J., & Carrillo, T. P. (1988). Who completes batterer's treatment groups? An empirical investigation. *Journal of Family Violence, 3,* 141-150.

Hamberger, L. K., & Hastings, J. E. (1986). Personality correlates of men who abuse their partners: A cross-validation study. *Journal of Family Violence, 1,* 323-341.

Hamberger, L. K., & Hastings, J. E. (1990). Recidivism following spouse abuse abatement counseling: Treatment program implications. *Violence and Victims, 5,* 157-170.

Hamberger, L. K., Hastings, J. E., & Lohr, J. M. (1991). Personality correlates of men who batter and nonviolent men: Some continuities and discontinuities. *Journal of Family Violence, 6,* 131-148.

Hershorn, M., & Rosenbaum, A. (1991). Over- vs. undercontrolled hostility: Application of the construct to the classification of maritally violent men. *Violence and Victims, 6,* 151-158.

Hirschel, J. D., Hutchinson, I. W., & Dean, C. W. (1992). The failure of arrest to deter spouse abuse. *Journal of Research in Crime and Delinquency, 29,* 7-33.

Hirschi, T., & Gottfredson, M. (1983). Age and the explanation of crime. *American Journal of Sociology, 89,* 552-584.

Hofeller, K. H. (1980). Social, psychological and situational factors in wife abuse. *Dissertation Abstracts International, 41(1-B),* 408.

Holtzworth-Munroe, A., & Anglin, K. (1991). The competency of responses given by maritally violent versus nonviolent men to problematic marital situations. *Violence and Victims, 6,* 257-269.

Hotaling, G. T., & Straus, M. A. (1989). Intrafamily violence, and crime and violence outside the family. In L. Ohlin & M. Tonry (Eds.), *Family Violence* (pp. 315-375). Chicago: University of Chicago Press.

Hotaling, G. T., & Sugarman, D. B. (1986). An analysis of risk markers in husband to wife violence: The current state of knowledge. *Violence and Victims, 1,* 101-124.

Jaffe, P. G., Wolfe, D. A., & Wilson, S. K. (1990). *Children of battered women.* Newbury Park, CA: Sage.

Levinson, D. (1989). *Family violence in cross-cultural perspective.* Newbury Park, CA: Sage.

Maiuro, R. D., Cahn, T. S., & Vitaliano, P. P. (1986). *Violence and Victims, 1,* 279-290.

Margolin, G., John, R. S., & Gleberman, L. (1988). Affective responses to conflictual discussions in violent and nonviolent couples. *Journal of Consulting and Clinical Psychology, 56,* 24-33.

Murphy, C., & O'Leary, K. D. (1989). Psychological aggression predicts physical aggression in early marriage. *Journal of Consulting and Clinical Psychology, 57,* 579-582.

Neidig, P. H., Collins, B. S., & Friedman, D. H. (1986). Attitudinal characteristics of males who have engaged in spouse abuse. *Journal of Family Violence, 1,* 223-233.

Novaco, R. W. (1975). *Anger control.* Lexington, MA: Lexington.

O'Leary, K. D., & Vivian, D. (1990). Physical aggression in marriage. In F. D. Fincham & T. N. Bradbury (Eds.), *The psychology of marriage: Basic issues and applications* (pp. 323-348). New York: Guilford.

Saunders, D. G. (1982). Counseling the violent husband. In P. A. Keller & L. G. Ritt (Eds.), *Innovations in clinical practice: A sourcebook* (Vol. 1, pp. 16-29). Sarasota, FL: Professional Resource Exchange.

Saunders, D. G. (1992). A typology of men who batter: Three types derived from cluster analysis. *American Journal of Orthopsychiatry, 62,* 264-275.

Saunders, D. G. (in press). Prediction of wife assault. In J. C. Campbell (Ed.), *Assessing the risk of dangerousness.* Newbury Park, CA: Sage.

Saunders, D. G., & Azar, S. (1989). Family violence treatment programs: Descriptions and evaluation. In L. Ohlin & M. Tonry (Eds.), *Family violence* (pp. 481-546). Chicago: University of Chicago Press.

Saunders, D. G., & Hanusa, D. R. (1986). Cognitive-behavior treatment of men who batter: The short-term effect of group therapy. *Journal of Family Violence, 1,* 357-372.

Saunders, D. G., & Parker, J. C. (1989). Legal sanctions and treatment follow-through among men who batter: A multivariate analysis. *Social Work Research and Abstracts, 23,* 21-29.

Sherman, L. W., & Berk, R. A. (1984). The specific deterrent effects of arrest for domestic assault. *American Psychological Review, 49,* 261-272.

Shields, N. M., & Hanneke, C. R. (1983). Battered women's reactions to marital rape. In D. Finkelhor, R. J. Gelles, G. T. Hotaling, & M. A. Straus (Eds.), *The dark side of families: Current family violence research* (pp. 132-148). Beverly Hills, CA: Sage.

Shields, N. M., McCall, G. J., & Hanneke, C. R. (1988). Patterns of family and nonfamily violence: Violent husbands and violent men. *Violence and Victims, 3,* 83-97.

Smith, M. D. (1990). Patriarchal ideology and wife beating: A test of a feminist hypothesis. *Violence and Victims, 5,* 257-274.

Snyder, D. K., & Fruchtman, L. A. (1981). Differential patterns of wife abuse: A data-based typology. *Journal of Consulting and Clinical Psychology, 49,* 878-885.

Sonkin, D. J., Martin, D., & Walker, L. E. A. (1985). *The male batterer: A treatment approach.* New York: Springer.

Spence, J. T., & Helmreich, R. L. (1978). *Masculinity and femininity: Their psychological dimensions, correlates, and antecedents.* Austin, TX: University of Texas Press.

Steinfeld, G. J. (1986). Spouse abuse: Clinical implications of research on the control of aggression. *Journal of Family Violence, 1,* 197-208.

Stordeur, R. A., & Stille, R. (1989). *Ending men's violence against their partners.* Newbury Park, CA: Sage.

Straus, M. A. (1979). Measuring family conflict and violence: The conflict tactics scale. *Journal of Marriage and the Family, 41,* 75-88.

Straus, M. A. (1983). Ordinary violence, child abuse, and wife beating: What do they have in common? In D. Finkelhor, R. J. Gelles, G. T. Hotaling, & M. A. Straus (Eds.) *The dark side of families: Current family violence research* (pp. 213-234). Newbury Park, CA: Sage.

Straus, M. A., Gelles, R. J., & Steinmetz, S. K. (1980). *Behind closed doors: Violence in the American family.* New York: Doubleday/Anchor.

Straus, M. A., & Smith, C. (1990). Family patterns and primary prevention of family violence. In M. A. Straus & R. J. Gelles (Eds.), *Physical violence in American families* (pp. 245-260). New Brunswick, NJ: Transaction.

Suitor, J. J., Pillemer, K., & Straus, M. A. (1990). Marital violence in a life cycle perspective. In M. A. Straus & R. J. Gelles (Eds.), *Physical violence in American families* (pp.305-315). New Brunswick, NJ: Transaction.

Telch, C. F., & Lindquist, C. U. (1984). Violent versus nonviolent couples: A comparison of patterns. *Psychotherapy, 21,* 242-248.

Tolman, R. M. (1988, November). *The impact of criminal justice system involvement on the outcome of intervention with men who batter.* Paper presented at the 40th annual meeting of the American Society of Criminology, Chicago.

Tolman, R. M., & Bennett, L. W. (1990). A review of research on men who batter. *Journal of Interpersonal Violence, 5,* 87-118.

Tolman, R. M., & Bhosley, G. (1990). A comparison of two types of pregroup preparation for men who batter. In *Advances in Group Work Research* (pp. 33-43). New York: Haworth.

van der Kolk, B. A. (1988). Trauma in men: Effects on family life. In M. B. Straus (Ed.), *Abuse and victimization across the life span* (pp. 170-187). Baltimore, MD: Johns Hopkins University Press.

Walker, L.E.A. (1979). *The battered woman.* New York: Harper.

Walker, L.E.A. (1984). *The battered woman syndrome.* New York: Springer.

White, G. L. (1977). The social psychology of romantic jealousy. *Dissertation Abstracts International, 37,* 5449-B.

Wright, J. (1985). Domestic violence and substance abuse: A cooperative approach toward working with dually affected families. In E. M. Freeman (Ed.), *Social work practice with clients who have alcohol problems* (pp. 26-39). Springfield, IL: Charles C. Thomas.

Yllö, K. (1983). Sexual inequality and violence against wives in American states. *Journal of Comparative Family Studies, 14,* 67-86.

Yllö, K. (1984). Patriarchy and violence against wives: The impact of structural and normative factors. *Journal of International and Comparative Social Welfare, 1,* 16-29.

PART

II

POLICE

3

Police Intervention and Public Opinion

N. ZOE HILTON

The police have a central, and often criticized, role in initiating legal responses to wife assault. Arrest has been both discouraged and demanded by various groups over the past quarter of a century, and policing policy has varied over time and across jurisdictions throughout North America. Although arrest and further criminal justice intervention for wife assault has not been explicitly ruled out by policy, police officers are endowed with discretion in deciding whether arrest and charges are warranted. An apparent reluctance on the part of police to intervene in wife assault has been attributed to officers' attitudes, which are said to be shared by society. But is this true? What is public opinion on police intervention in wife assault, and to what extent should that opinion influence policing policy? In this chapter, I will first look at what is known about public and police attitudes toward wife assault and then describe a study in which researchers explored some of the factors distinguishing assaults that are seen by the public as more or less deserving of a legal response. Finally, some implications for policing practice will be considered.

Mental Health Centre, Penetanguishene, Ontario, L0K 1P0. Parts of this chapter first appeared in the *Journal of Family Violence, 4*(2), 1989. I would like to thank A. N. Doob, G. T. Harris, and D. G. Saunders for helpful suggestions, the Ontario Science Centre for permission to conduct the study, and Leslie Samuels for research assistance.

As a 24-hour emergency and public service, and the "gateway" of criminal justice (Faragher, 1985), the police very often can be the first professionals to intervene in a case of wife assault. They are one of the few services available when an assault occurs: 85% of domestic violence calls to the police are made outside normal business hours (Pierce, Spaar, & Briggs, 1988, cited by E. S. Buzawa & C. G. Buzawa, 1990). Many incidents of wife assault, meanwhile, go unreported to the police (e.g., R. E. Dobash & R. Dobash, 1979, p. 164; Dutton, 1988, p. 144), so that by the time the police are called to intervene they are often faced with a habitual wife assaulter (Burris & Jaffe, 1983). Thus, the police bear considerable responsibility for the transition of wife assault from a "private" matter to one subject to legal responses. As it has been argued that wife assault is unlikely to cease (Fagan, 1989) and likely to escalate (Burris & Jaffe, 1983) without intervention, the way police deal with wife assault could have a substantial effect on the continuation of the violence.

In the past, wife assault has been regarded as a private domestic matter rather than "real" crime (e.g., E. S. Buzawa & C. G. Buzawa, 1990; R. E. Dobash & R. Dobash, 1979, p. 210; Faragher, 1985; Jaffe, Wolfe, Telford, & Austin, 1986). For some years, the police have been under attack for failing to arrest wife assaulters and initiate a criminal justice response. Such criticisms began when wife assault first became a salient public issue (e.g., Pizzey, 1974) and have continued more recently (e.g., Edwards, 1989; Ferraro & Pope, this volume), reaching a sensational level with lawsuits in which police are charged with inadequate protection of wife assault victims (cf. E. S. Buzawa & C. G. Buzawa, 1990, for a description of the highly publicized Thurman case; see also Jaffe, Hastings, Reitzel, & Austin, this volume). In the last decade, however, policing philosophy has increasingly recognized the role of policing as a social service (e.g., Clairmont, 1991; Nordholt & Straver, 1983). Intervention into wife assault might be viewed more favorably by the police under this philosophy than it has been in the past (see Jaffe et al., this volume, for recent history of arrest practices).

It has been claimed that, in practice, the police are more concerned about doing what the public expects of them than about controlling crime (Tremblay & Rochon, 1991). A concern for public expectations is not necessarily incompatible with the general philosophy of contemporary policing, according to which police forces should liaise with the community to identify and ameliorate problems of crime and public disorder (Leighton, 1991). Although the "community" typically refers to a neighborhood unit (e.g., Greene & Taylor, 1988; Mastrofski, 1988), the consensus of a wider public is also of value to the police at a more general planning level (e.g., Mastrofski, 1988; Tremblay & Rochon, 1991). An awareness of what problems the public identifies as crimes is not difficult to obtain. Information of this type is already available in studies of public perceptions of the seriousness of legally defined crimes (e.g., Cullen, Link, & Polanzi, 1982; Wolfgang, Figlio, Tracy, & Singer, 1985). Less systematic evidence is available on whether police officers share public perceptions or attitudes toward law enforcement against specific crimes, and little is known about the factors that affect the public's preference for a criminal justice or alternative response to specific crimes. In the next sections of this chapter, I will consider the issues of perceived seriousness, police attitudes, and public perceptions of the appropriateness of a legal response with respect to wife assault.

Perceived Seriousness of Wife Assault

It has often been argued that, far from being considered a serious criminal offense, wife assault has a history of normative support (e.g., R. E. Dobash & R. Dobash, 1979; Greenblat, 1985; Straus, 1976). In 1970, Stark and McEvoy reported that 25% of men and 16% of women believed it was acceptable for a man to slap his wife on "appropriate" occasions. The figures for a woman slapping her husband were 26% and 19%. A decade later, it was found that 28% of men and 23% of women saw "a couple slapping each other" as normal (Straus, Gelles, & Steinmetz, 1980); lower frequencies but larger sex differences in the same direction were reported for those who saw such violence as "good" or "necessary." Among women surveyed by Gentemann (1984), only 3% agreed that it was acceptable if "once in a while" a man slaps his wife. When Greenblat (1985) asked college students to rate the moral wrongfulness of wife assault and 19 other events, including armed robbery and poison gas warfare, wife slapping was rated more wrong than husband slapping, and wife beating was rated worst of all events. High ratings of the seriousness of wife murder and, to a lesser extent, wife assault are also found in public surveys (Cullen et al., 1982; Wolfgang et al., 1985).

In reviewing this literature, Frieze and Browne (1989) conclude that since the Stark and McEvoy (1970) study, "Public attitudes have changed. There is no longer casual acceptance of violence against women" (p. 166). The above studies, however, are not necessarily comparable; they used different questions, different methods, and different samples. The complete picture, moreover, is somewhat more complex than simply which behaviors survey respondents condemn as morally wrong in the abstract. The continuing tendency toward victim blaming that Frieze and Browne (1989) note, for example, could affect people's perceptions of the seriousness of an assault and the appropriateness of legal intervention. In support of this argument, Gentemann (1984) found that 19% of the women surveyed saw wife slapping as acceptable when the wife was described as flirting, having an affair, being drunk, or nagging the husband. Among college women and men, 24% would approve of wife slapping, and 10% of wife beating if the wife was having an affair; these figures rose to 33% and 16% if the wife was found in bed with another man (Greenblat, 1985). Individual variables (e.g., respondent sex, sex-role attitudes) have also been found to affect the perceived wrongfulness of wife assault (Greenblat, 1985) and the belief that arrests should not be made (Saunders & Size, 1986). Thus, although no "norm" exists for public approval of wife assault, a true understanding of public opinion requires some account of possible mediating variables, such as the perceiver's sex or the behavior ascribed to the victim, that might influence the extent to which people see intervention as appropriate for wife assault.

Police Attitudes

Saunders and Size (1986) compared 116 police officers, 39 counselor-advocates from battered women's shelters, and 52 wife assault victims in the extent to which they viewed wife assault as criminal and arrest as the best response. All groups tended to rate "marital violence" (responses about husband assault and wife assault were statistically similar and so were combined) as bad in general. They also tended to see the violence as not normal, with the advocates being more extreme in this response. All groups agreed that marital violence was unjusti-fied, but police officers were significantly more likely than either victims or advocates to endorse the view that violence was justifiable in the specific case of infidelity by the victim. In addition, police were significantly less likely than other groups to believe "The best way to deal with marital violence is to arrest the offending party." Only 4% of the police agreed (mildly or strongly) with this statement, compared with 38% of advocates and 63% of victims.

Perceived responsibility for an assault, as mentioned above, could influence how appropriate arrest is seen as being. Saunders and Size (1986) found that police attributed a greater degree of responsibility to the victim than did victims and advocates. The researchers' measure of responsibility combined responses to questions about women "bring[ing] this violence on themselves," being able to avoid violence by being quiet, and experiencing pleasure or pain when hit. Using a different measure, Lavoie, Jacob, Hardy, and Martin (1989) also found that police officers attributed some responsibility for wife assault to the wife. In their study, 235 police officers were presented with vignettes describing domestic disturbance calls in which socio-demographic factors, characteristics of the abuse, and victim and offender behavior were varied. This approach allows for some explo-ration of the variables mediating the officers' attitudes toward wife assault. Ratings of the wife's responsibility were most affected by the type of abuse against the wife and alleged verbal antagonism by the wife. That is, when the wife complained of verbal threats rather than physical violence, and the husband alleged that she "was looking for a fight," she was judged as more responsible than in other cases. This suggests that as in the studies with nonpolice respondents reported above, information about the wife's behavior might affect perceptions of the husband's behavior. It must be noted, though, that this study dealt with nonphysical acts as well as physical assault, and it is not clear whether respondents were asked to assign responsibility for the husband's actions or for "the situation," which in some scenarios could essentially have been a mutual verbal conflict.

The type and extent of violence described in the Lavoie et al. (1989) scenarios also influenced officers' responses to a question more directly related to the likelihood of intervention. (The police in this study were not asked specifically whether they would make an arrest.)

When asked about whom they would side with in the dispute, the police officers indicated the greatest likelihood of siding with the victim when physical violence had occurred and had been frequent in the past. The victim's attitude toward making a complaint, however, although elsewhere cited as an important factor in the police decision to arrest or charge wife assaulters (e.g., E. S. Buzawa & C. G. Buzawa, 1990; Elliott, 1989; Jaffe et al., this volume), was not significantly related to the dependent measures used. This apparent inconsistency could be the result of the experimental control found in Lavoie et al. (1989), or it could point again to the limited interpretations that can be made of the questions used in this study.

Saunders (1980) and Stith (1990) more directly explored factors in the decision to arrest, with an emphasis on variables relating to the police themselves. In a study of 116 (including 6 female) police officers, Saunders (1980) found that reports of minimal intervention (e.g., warnings) by police in response both to scenarios and to actual encounters with wife assault were associated with the officers' traditional sex-role attitudes and approval of marital violence. This finding implies that such attitudes toward women and violence can indeed reduce the likelihood of a legal response to wife assault.

Stith (1990) surveyed 72 married male police officers about their likelihood of responding to scenarios of wife assault by arresting the alleged offender, talking with the couple, and warning or arresting the victim and discouraging arrest of the offender ("antivictim response"). The four variables in Stith's statistical model were sex-role attitudes, marital stress, approval of marital violence, and perpetration of marital violence. The model was statistically significant in predicting an antivictim response, and approached significance in predicting arrest. In a path analysis of responses to the scenarios, officers' perpetration of wife assault was related to their attitudes toward marital violence, which in turn had a significant contribution to the model's overall ability to explain the likelihood of an antivictim response. The strongest relation to arrest was with perpetration of marital violence; that is, officers who admitted to assaulting their own wife were less likely to arrest another alleged wife assaulter. Unfortunately, Stith does not indicate the overall likelihood the police gave of arresting the alleged offender; a very high or very low rate could limit the explanatory power of the officer variables in the study. The four-variable model accounted for 19% of the variance in antivictim responses and only 11% of the variance in arrest responses.

Summary

At this point, it is possible to summarize our knowledge about police attitudes toward arresting wife assaulters. This knowledge is very limited, but it seems that few police officers believe that arrest is the best option in cases of domestic violence. A partial explanation of this reluctance to arrest might be that the offender is not seen as wholly responsible for the offense. Officers are less likely than victims and advocates—who might well be more extreme in their opinions than the general public—to see the offender as responsible, and they perhaps even see him as justified when the victim has been unfaithful. Verbal antagonism by the victim is also seen to make her more responsible for the abuse. In general, police officers' attitudes (and behavior) regarding wife assault affect whether they see arrest of the wife assaulter as appropriate or inappropriate.

Police attitudes toward wife assault have received attention from social scientists that is not matched by a comparable literature on attitudes toward intervention in other forms of violence. It must be noted, though, that analyses of police files have found that the situational variables influencing police response to nonfamily violence are similar to those found in file analyses of wife assaults, that is, sociodemographic characteristics of the disputants, use of alcohol by the disputants, the setting of the dispute, and a request for police intervention by a third party (see review by Elliott, 1989). A study in which police attitudes and police response to wife assault and nonfamily violence are compared would be a valuable addition to the literature at this point.

Police Intervention

So far, I have reviewed police attitudes to wife assault and arrest and attempted to compare them with similar attitudes in the general public and specific interest groups. For example, it has been noted that the police appear more likely than victims and advocates to see wife assault as justified, particularly when the wife is unfaithful. In the previous section, we saw that college and public samples reveal a similar, relatively lenient attitude toward wife assault in cases of the wife's actual or suspected infidelity. This literature, however, is fairly limited.

Even more sparse is nonfile research on what the police actually do in real domestic disputes. This topic received much interest in the early 1980s when researchers observed that police were reluctant to initiate a legal response to wife assault (e.g., Chatterton, 1983; Oppenlander, 1982). There were calls for stronger law enforcement, including mandatory arrest policies (e.g., J. C. Humphreys & W. O. Humphreys, 1985; MacLeod, 1987; cf. Elliott, 1989). Sometimes the removal of police discretion was justified on the grounds that the police do not see arrest as necessary for wife assault (J. C. Humphreys & W. O. Humphreys, 1985), a claim that would be supported by studies reviewed in this chapter. One reason suggested for police reluctance to make arrests in wife assault cases is that there might be insufficient evidence that an assault has occurred (e.g., Dow, 1976); Faragher (1985) notes that the police tend to arrive after the dispute is over. Fear of injury to police officers has also been cited as a reason for their reluctance to intervene (e.g., Bard, 1971; Byles, 1980), and the danger of domestic disputes has been emphasized in police training programs (E. S. Buzawa & C. G. Buzawa, 1990). Ellis (1987), however, has persuasively argued that such fear is disproportionate to the risk actually faced. Traditionally, though, police training for domestic disputes was more concerned with minimizing the risk of physical harm to the intervening police officer (e.g., Levens & Dutton, 1980) and mediating between the disputants and avoiding an arrest (e.g., Bard, 1971) than with evaluating the benefits for the victims of violence. The mediation response to wife assault promoted by Bard in New York, for example, received much praise at the time despite its failure to reduce the repetition of wife assault (Elliott, 1989; Sherman & Berk, 1984).

Mediation was said to be disliked by many police officers who were reluctant to adopt a nontraditional, social work approach (E. S. Buzawa & C. G. Buzawa, 1990; Hirschel, Hutchison, & Dean, 1992). This approach was followed by studies suggesting that a proarrest policy can increase arrest rates and reduce repeated violence (Jaffe et al.,

1986; Sherman & Berk, 1984). More recent failures to find a difference between arrest, charges laid without arrest, and advice/separation in their effects on the reduction of wife assault (e.g., Hirschel et al., 1992; see also Jaffe et al., this volume, for the relative importance of charges and arrest) sustain the controversy over the value of arrest, at least for the less serious assaults (misdemeanors) that these studies consider.

In the past decade, police forces have increasingly adopted a pro-arrest policy for wife assault (see review by E. S. Buzawa & C. G. Buzawa, 1990). Attempts to study the effects of arrest by using arrest or some alternative intervention on a predetermined schedule have met with a tendency for police officers to use arrest more frequently than required by the schedule (e.g., Hirschel et al., 1992; Sherman & Berk, 1984). Yet, some resistance on the part of officers responding to domestic disputes has still been noted (e.g., Ferraro, 1989; E. S. Buzawa & C. G. Buzawa, 1990). Ferraro and Pope (this volume) and Jaffe et al. (this volume) discuss some of the organizational and attitudinal factors that might inhibit a legal response to wife assault. In the remainder of this chapter, I deal with another possible influence; that is, the extent of public support for such a response as the best solution to wife assault.

Public Attitudes Toward
Legal Responses to Wife Assault

Much of the known history of wife assault is, in fact, a history of social attitudes toward the phenomenon and appropriate intervention. From early Judeo-Christian times, religious teachings have been used to condone wife assault (R. E. Dobash & R. Dobash, 1979; Hilton, 1989). One of the first societies to take a stand against family violence, though, was the Puritan government of Massachusetts Bay (Pleck, 1987). Men who beat their wife (in the absence of provocation) could be brought before the church court. Pleck (1987) argues, however, that the goal of family violence legislators in the 17th-century colony was more to preserve the family and to demonstrate Christian virtue than to reflect public protest against wife assault. Feminist groups that emerged in the latter 19th century, on the other hand, directed much of their attention toward the alcoholic wife assaulter and at first had the support of the temperance movement (Pleck, 1987). The Victorian feminists struggled to rally public opinion around domestic law reform, which they saw as taking the form of liberal divorce laws rather than criminal justice intervention. They lost popular support within the temperance movement because of their radical stance on divorce. More conservative women reformers emerged and proposed legal protection for wives that they argued would support the survival of the family. Public attitudes sympathetic toward assaulted women were sufficiently strong to support the establishment of a protective agency for women and children in Chicago in 1886 (Gordon, 1988).

It was not until the latter part of the present century that the belief that wife assault is a criminal offense gained popularity beyond a fringe feminist movement (Hilton, 1989; Pleck, 1987). Yet, these authors argue that it was the women's movement's attention to the battered wife, in the aftermath of the recognition of the battered child, that challenged social indifference toward, if not acceptance of, wife assault. At first, the battered women's movement consisted of small, localized, and marginalized groups of women, responding to assaulted women in crisis and protesting against mainstream public attitudes. Later, the movement grew, established networks, and formed coalitions with more conservative women's groups. Successful public protest and lobbying led to government funding of investigations and to development of professional interest in confronting wife assault. The recognition of wife assault as a social problem in Canada (Hilton, 1989) and the United States (Pleck, 1987) has been well documented, and contemporary government-sponsored public education campaigns reflect the "official" public attitude that wife assault is wrong and that legal intervention is appropriate. What has yet to be established is to what extent the general public supports the criminalization of wife assault.

So far in this chapter, I have reviewed literature showing that the public generally disapproves of wife assault, although police officers do not see legal intervention as a priority. Police nonintervention has been criticized, and police officers' reluctance to intervene in wife assault has been attributed at least partially to their attitudes toward wife assault. Attitude surveys, however, may yield different results depending on the sample, methods, and questions used. It is still not clear what factors mediate attitudes toward wife assault, and whether similar factors affect attitudes toward wife assault and other forms of violence, particularly attitudes concerning the need for police intervention.

Of particular interest to policymakers in this regard would be an indication of whether the public believes that charging and making on-site arrests is the best police response to wife assault and how this belief compares with similar opinions concerning other forms of assault. The study reported below was designed to explore the public's attitudes toward police intervention in cases of wife assault and comparable assaults on women by male strangers. In this study, 240 adults were each given a questionnaire containing one scenario describing an assault. Seriousness of the act, and relative responsibility of the man and woman involved, which could be related to preferences for laying charges, were explored in this study. Two other aspects that could plausibly increase the need for legal intervention—the man's criminal record and his potential for future violence—were also studied.

Method

Design

Each of 240 participants read one of four scenarios in a two (wife vs. stranger assault) by two (first offender vs. recidivist) by two (female vs. male participant) between-subjects design (n = 30 per cell). The location of the assault (public bar, house, or apartment stairwell) was balanced across scenarios in order to control any effects that a public or private setting might have on how realistic the assault description was seen as being. Because there were no hypotheses concerning this variable, the analyses reported below use data collapsed across location.

Dependent Measures

There were four main dependent measures. The first two, responses to "How serious do you think the violence described in this scene is" and "How likely is it that the man will be violent to anyone in the near future?" were rated on a labeled, 5-point scale from "Not at all" to "Extremely." Ratings of who is "most to blame for the violence" were made on a 5-point scale labeled from "The woman is entirely to blame" to "The man is entirely to blame." Posing the question about responsibility in terms of who was most to blame allows for direct comparability of the relative blame attributed to the man and woman. It also uses a simple concept and, perhaps, an approach to assigning culpability that is more familiar to most people than assessing the degree of responsibility held by one actor independent of other actors in a situation. Use of the word "blame" avoids any potential confusion between "responsible" actions and "irresponsible" behavior. A fourth question about "the best thing for the police to do now" was followed by 10 options intended to cover most possibilities participants might recommend: leave the scene without doing anything; leave the scene but check later on that everything is all right; tell the man not to hit the woman again; tell the woman to lay charges privately; try to resolve the dispute, act as peacemakers; refer the woman to a medical service; refer the woman to a social service; remove the man from the scene without laying charges; charge the man without removing him from the scene; charge the man and remove him from the scene. Participants indicated the one "most important" police action. A recoding of the options into broader categories was anticipated.

In addition to the four main dependent variables, participants were asked whether laws in effect in Ontario deemed it a crime "for the man to hit the woman" and what the police must do "if this happens": charge the man, decide whether to charge him, or not charge him. These items were included in order to assess any influence of participants' understanding of the law on their responses to the four main questions.

Participants

Participants were recruited from adult visitors to a popular science museum in Toronto, Ontario, in 1988. Similar surveys regarding various beliefs about sentencing and aspects of the criminal justice system (e.g., Doob & Roberts, 1983; Gebotys, Roberts, & Das Gupta, 1988), although not specifically addressing wife assault, have found no notable overall dissimilarities between samples drawn from this museum and more representative samples of Canadians.

Participants included 120 women and 120 men, with a mean age of 34.4 years (SD = 12.5). Seventy-nine percent were Canadian citizens, the remainder being either permanent residents or visitors, predominantly from the United States. Most participants were currently in skilled or semiskilled occupations (35.9%) followed by professional and managerial jobs (26.7%). Unskilled workers comprised 12.5% of participants.

Procedure and Materials

Participants were recruited through a notice board and verbal invitations. Written and verbal instructions were given to each participant, who completed the questionnaire and then received a written debriefing. The following is an example scenario:

> The police are called to a disturbance by someone in the neighborhood who reported what sounded like a fight going on in a public bar. When they arrive, the dispute is already over. A woman tells the police that she has been hit by her husband. She wants to know what the police are going to do about it. She has a bruise on her arm and her left eye is cut. The man is still in the bar. He has not been known to the police before. He tells the police that the fight was about something trivial and that they can sort it out on their own now.

The scenario was written with the intention of portraying that a criminal offense had taken place and that the police had the option of laying charges; that is, there was evidence of injury, and the man did not dispute that he had hit the woman.

Results

Seriousness and Likelihood of Recidivism

There was some similarity between the ratings of seriousness and likelihood of recidivism; the Pearson correlation coefficient was .50. Mean ratings revealed a tendency for the violence to be seen as fairly

Table 3.1 Mean Ratings of Seriousness of the Violence

	Relationship		
Record	*Wife*	*Stranger*	*Total*
First-time			3.5
Females	3.7	3.5	
Males	3.4	3.3	
Recidivist			3.7
Females	3.9	3.8	
Males	3.7	3.5	

to very serious (see Table 3.1) and recidivism to be very likely (see Table 3.2). Assaults by the man who was known to the police were rated as more serious (M = 3.74 vs. 3.45; $F(1,233)$ = 6.44, $p < .05$) and more likely to be repeated (M = 4.18 vs. 3.63, $F(1,233)$ = 20.20, $p < .001$) than assaults by the first-time offender. Also, female participants rated the assaults as more serious (M = 3.72 vs. 3.48; $F(1,233)$ = 4.61, $p < .05$) and more likely to be repeated (M = 4.12 vs. 3.70; $F(1,233)$ = 12.45, $p < .01$) than male participants. There was no effect of victim-offender relationship.

Relative Blame

In all conditions, the mean ratings of relative blame indicated that participants placed more responsibility on the man (i.e., the offender) than the woman (i.e., the victim) (see Table 3.3). There was a significant interaction between the offender's police record and his relationship to the victim ($F(1,226)$ = 10.21, $p < .01$). The offender was held to blame most in the recidivist-stranger assault condition (M = 4.16) and least in the first-offense-stranger assault condition (M = 3.61). In the wife assault conditions, ratings were unaffected by whether the man was a first-time offender or recidivist (M = 3.95 vs. 3.90). Overall, female participants placed more blame on the man than male participants did (M = 4.03 vs. 3.78; $F(1,226)$ = 6.48, $p < .01$).

Table 3.2 Mean Ratings of Likelihood of Recidivism

Record	Relationship		Total
	Wife	Stranger	
First-time			3.6
Females	4.0	3.8	
Males	3.5	3.4	
Recidivist			4.1
Females	4.4	4.3	
Males	4.1	3.9	

Recommended Police Action

Laying Charges

The 10 police action options were recoded in a dichotomous variable indicating whether laying charges was recommended. Most participants (54%) did recommend charging the man. In all but two cases, charging was recommended in conjunction with removing the man from the scene. This variable was subject to significant main effects of the victim-offender relationship ($F(1,226) = 9.90$, $p < .01$) and the offender's record ($F(1,226) = 6.89$, $p < .05$). From Table 3.4, it can be seen that charging was recommended more often for stranger assault than wife assault. A record-by-relationship interaction approached significance ($F(1,226) = 3.28$, $p < .07$). As with relative blame, police record had its effect mostly in cases of stranger assaults. Participants recommended charges more for stranger assaulters who were known to the police than for first-time offenders.

Referral and Mediation

Other recommended police actions were also of interest, particularly referring the victim to a legal, medical, or social service and mediating (i.e., telling the man not to hit the woman again or trying to resolve the dispute). Referral was recommended by 21% of partici-

Table 3.3 Mean Ratings of Relative Blame

Record	Relationship		
	Wife	*Stranger*	*Total*
First-time			3.8
Females	4.0	3.7	
Males	3.9	3.5	
Recidivist			4.0
Females	4.0	4.3	
Males	3.8	4.0	

NOTE: Higher numbers indicate more blame of the man.

pants, more often for victims of wife assault and particularly in the case of recidivist wife assault. Mediation was recommended by only 6%, mostly for first-time offenders and least for recidivist wife assaulters (see Table 3.4).

Knowledge of Law

Most participants (81%) correctly believed that it was an offense for the man to hit the woman. There were no significant differences between conditions in recognition of the law. Responses to the question of what the police must do were more varied. There was no effect of victim-offender relationship on whether participants believed charging to be mandatory (in this jurisdiction, it was not). There was, though, a record-by-sex interaction ($F(1,233) = 6.28, p < .05$) whereby female participants indicated that charging was mandatory more for first offenders than recidivists and males vice versa. Inconsistent responses and comments made by the participants suggested that some might not have treated these questions as matters of fact; however, there was a highly significant association between whether charging was believed to be mandatory and whether charging was recommended ($r_t = .36 \ p < .001$). Participants who believed that the police have discretion were twice as likely to prefer an alternative action than to recommend charging, and they preferred charging less

Table 3.4 Percentages of Total Participants Recommending Police Action as a Function of Victim-Offender Relationship and Offender's Police Record

	Relationship		
Record	Wife	Stranger	Total
Charge Man			54
First-time	43	49	
Recidivist	48	76	
Refer Victim			21
First-time	23	15	
Recidivist	38	10	
Mediate			6
First-time	7	4	
Recidivist	0.5	1	

for wife assault than stranger assault ($F(1,93) = 8.70, p < .01$) (see Table 3.5). Those who believed that the police must charge were three times more likely to recommend charging than not. Even among these participants, however, 25% did not indicate that charging the man was the most important thing to do; in their choice of police option, they were influenced by an interaction of the offender's record and relationship to the victim ($F(1,103) = 4.49, p < .05$), in which recidivist strangers were the most likely to be charged and recidivist wife assaulters, the least.

Regression Analysis

A post hoc regression of the independent and dependent variables (other than knowledge of law) on the recommendation to charge was performed. The best-fitting model had an R^2 of .21 ($p < .001$) and included three variables: ratings of blame, victim-offender relationship, and ratings of seriousness. This model correctly predicted 66% of the recommendations, providing a relative improvement over chance (Loeber, 1990) of 32% ($p < .001$).

Table 3.5 Percentage of Participants in Each Condition Recommending
Charges

Record	Relationship		
	Wife	Stranger	Total
Charge Mandatory			75
First-time	73	68	
Recidivist	67	92	
Charge Optional			37
First-time	17	35	
Recidivist	26	64	

NOTE: Cell sizes 24-30.

Discussion

The seriousness of the assault, the likelihood of recidivism, and the man's relative responsibility for the violence were all rated significantly higher by females than males. This less "positive" rating of aggression by females is consistent with other research (e.g., Campbell & Muncer, 1987; Smith, 1984), although Harris (1991) reveals that this effect can vary with other factors such as sex of the offender and victim.

Seriousness and likelihood of recidivism ratings were higher when the offender was known to the police for violence than when he was not known to the police. As far as seriousness is concerned, no single explanation presents itself. No definition of "serious" was given to the participants. Perhaps people believe that an assault by someone with a record for violence could be more threatening or could cause more harm than someone without a history of offending. Also, repeated incidents might imply more violent intent; for example, one might imagine "losing control" on a single occasion and not intending as much harm as if the decision to use violence were (deliberately) made on more than one occasion. Related to the matter of intent is the presumption that an offender known to the police must know that his behavior is considered to be wrong; therefore, the repeat offender's violence is considered a more serious problem because he is violent despite knowing that it is wrong. Violence by a recidivist might also seem more serious because it poses a greater risk of further offending. This interpretation is supported by the correlation of seriousness and recidivism ratings. That the risk of recidivism was seen as greater for offenders already known to the police suggests that participants believe past behavior to be a good predictor of future behavior.

It is important to note that participants did not see wife assault as less serious or less likely to recur than stranger assault. There were differences between stranger and wife assault, however, in attributed blame and recommended police action.

Ratings of blame (attributed, on average, more to the man than the woman) were affected by victim-offender relationship as well as by the offender's record: the recidivist stranger assaulter was seen as more to blame for his violence than the stranger assaulter with no police record. It is possible that participants thought it unusual for a man with a clean record to assault an unknown woman, and they could have considered victim provocation a plausible explanation. It might seem less reasonable for the victim to share the blame in the case of recidivist stranger assault. This rationale, however, does not apply to wife assault, for which relative blame is unaffected by the offender's record. This finding could reflect a different causal interpretation of wife assault, according to which both first-time and repeated incidents of violence can be understood without much emphasis on the victim's role. Perhaps, though, the wife assaulter's police record is not seen as useful information, because it may be easier for a husband than for a stranger to commit assault several times without becoming known to the police; as stated in the introduction to this chapter, there is evidence to support the high incidence of unreported wife assault.

Criminal charges were recommended most for the recidivist stranger assaulter. This was also the offender who was seen as most to blame for his behavior, and a post hoc analysis revealed blame ratings to be the strongest single predictor of whether charges were recommended. The regression analysis shows, though, that the recommendation to charge is complexly determined and cannot be fully accounted for by simple measures whose effects are not themselves easily explained.

Participants were offered alternative police responses, and their preferences for these options are informative. After police-laid charges, the most popular option was to refer the victim to an alternative service, especially a social service. Such noncharging options were recommended particularly in cases of wife assault. Perhaps participants believe that criminal justice intervention is not appropriate for wife assault or that wife assault is less deserving of a criminal charge; however, the absence of an effect of relationship on seriousness and recidivism ratings argues against this view. Alternatively, other responses might be seen as especially suitable or more effective against wife assault. This approach is consistent with the view of wife assault as a "social" problem or a "family matter" rather than a problem for the criminal justice system. Moreover, social services such as shelters and counseling programs are known to exist for wife assault, but might not seem a feasible option for stranger assault. It could be that participants see liaison with existing social services as an important role for the police. Certainly, victim advocates (e.g., Gaudreault, 1991) have argued that it is imperative for the police to refer the victim to support groups and other community services at their first contact. Referral might be seen as particularly important for the victim who is unaware of available services, who fears retaliation, or whose decision-making ability could be undermined by the trauma of victimization.

Another possible explanation for the popularity of victim referral in wife assault cases is that the wife herself is seen as having a problem, especially if she is a repeatedly assaulted wife. It can be argued that referring the victim to a helping agency is advisable in cases where a victim can suffer unique problems as a result of being hurt by a loved one and can remain at risk from her husband even after his arrest (cf. Ford & Regoli, this volume). Perhaps, also, participants expect the assaulted wife to leave her husband and envision her being escorted to a shelter by the police. The questionnaire options are not sufficiently detailed to clarify this point. Another limitation of the options is that all service referrals concern the victim. Participants could have selected victim referral as the only way to recommend that the couple, or even the husband alone, seek treatment. The questionnaire focused on immediate police responses; it did not indicate, and many participants might be unaware, that criminal justice intervention can be used to encourage the offender to seek treatment.

It is worth noting that although noncharging responses were recommended more for wife assault than stranger assault, a mediation approach was rarely nominated as the best thing for the police to do. This seems to be a clear message from the public that mediation by police is no longer the preferred intervention for stranger or wife assault.

Some Questions for Police Intervention

Current policing philosophy promotes police-public interaction and community consultation, but it has been argued that police are underinformed about public opinion regarding crime and police work (Tremblay & Rochon, 1991). In this chapter, I have brought together research on these opinions as related to wife assault. Before any attempt to apply this information is made, though, three main questions should be considered: (a) What information do these studies really tell us and what do we still need to know? (b) Are the opinions of some members of the community more pertinent than others and are these people able to voice their opinion? (c) What role should meeting public expectation play in the police response to wife assault and what other factors should guide policy?

First, although the experimental investigations described in this chapter make a unique and important contribution to our knowledge, each one is necessarily limited, and even together they cannot give a complete account of public opinion regarding wife assault. As indicated by the research on attributions of blame, for example, people's attitudes are influenced by many variables, which must be arbitrarily selected and artificially recreated for a given study. Although large-scale, actuarial research is more reliable than anecdotal experience, not all situations and not all subgroups of the public could be expected to yield the general opinions reported in this chapter. Police could find they need more information about such situations and subgroups, and collaboration with researchers toward obtaining policy-specific public opinion data should be welcomed.

Second, certain members of the public might be better informed about the problems facing victims of violence before, during, and after police intervention, and the police might wish to place greater emphasis on their informed opinions. Victims themselves could be included in this group. This is not to say that police officers need to base their decision to charge wife assaulters on whether the victim at the scene indicates that she would be a willing witness. Assaulted women might be less assertive and more ambivalent than the victim in the study described above. On the other hand, research has demonstrated that although assaulted women might be afraid to denounce their partner before the police or in court, when consulted in less threatening contexts they express a wish for protection for themselves and for treatment for their abuser, and they look to the police to help them in this respect (Saunders & Size, 1986; though see Ferraro & Pope, this volume).

Whether legal intervention by police can help the victim in this way requires investigation. This brings us to the third question of what role public opinion should play. The fact that victims and the general public look to the police to initiate legal intervention or to act as a social referral agent should be considered in the context of how effective the police can be in such roles. Although much of the discussion that has taken place on this matter has approached it as an organizational question, it should also be addressed as an empirical question, the approach taken by other chapters in this book.

Summary and Conclusions

Although the police and the public do not generally condone wife assault, their perceptions of the phenomenon can affect their support of the use of arrest and laying charges in wife assault cases. The study reported in this chapter revealed that members of the public see criminal charges for assault against women as most useful for cases of repeat offenses by strangers. Charges were also recommended, though, in wife assault cases approximately 45% of the time. Referring the victim to alternative (social, medical, or legal) services was recommended predominantly for cases of wife assault, especially recidivist wife assault. The relative emphasis participants placed on nonlegal responses for wife assault does not indicate that wife assault was seen as less serious than stranger assault. A similar conclusion can be drawn from the study by Saunders and Size (1986), in which agreement that arrest is the best response to wife assault had only a small correlation with the belief that wife assault is not really "crime." Both the preference for arrest and the related variable, perception of blame, are complexly determined. Together with previous research (Lavoie et al., 1989), the present study indicates that people place blame largely on the offender but are influenced by relationship, offender, victim, and other variables.

It is apparent that the public sees wife assault as a serious offense requiring some intervention. The extent and nature of intervention deemed necessary depend on a number of individual and situational variables, including the degree to which the victim is blamed. Attention to public opinion is important in the development of acceptable policing policies; however, equally important is a consideration of the effectiveness of the intervention and its acceptability to the victims of wife assault.

References

Bard, M. (1971). The role of law enforcement in the helping system. *Community Mental Health Journal, 7,* 151-160.

Burris, C. A., & Jaffe, P. (1983). Wife abuse as a crime: The impact of police laying charges. *Canadian Journal of Criminology, 25,* 309-318.

Buzawa, E. S., & Buzawa, C. G. (1990). *Domestic violence: The criminal justice response.* Newbury Park, CA: Sage.

Byles, J. A. (1980). Family violence in Hamilton. *Canada's Mental Health, 28,* 4-6.

Campbell, A. , & Muncer, S. (1987). Models of anger and aggression in the social talk of women and men. *Journal for the Theory of Social Behaviour, 17,* 489-511.

Chatterton, M. R. (1983). Police work and assault charges. In M. Punch (Ed.), *Control in the Police Organization* (pp. 194-221). Cambridge, MA: MIT Press.

Clairmont, D. (1991). Community-based policing: Implementation and impact. *Canadian Journal of Criminology, 3,* 469-484.

Cullen, F. T., Link, B. G., & Polanzi, C. W. (1982). The seriousness of crime revisited. *Criminology, 20,* 83-102.

Dobash, R. E., & Dobash, R. (1979). *Violence against wives: A case against the patriarchy.* New York: Macmillan.

Doob, A. N., & Roberts, J. V. (1983). *Sentencing: An analysis of the public's view of sentencing.* Ottawa, Canada: Department of Justice.

Dow, M. (1976). In M. Borland (Ed.), *Violence in the family* (pp. 129-135). Manchester, England: Manchester University Press.

Dutton, D. G. (1988). *The domestic assault of women: Psychological and criminal justice perspectives.* Boston: Allyn & Bacon.

Edwards, S. S. M. (1989). *Policing domestic violence: Women, the law and the state.* London: Sage.

Elliott, D. S. (1989). Criminal justice procedures in family violence crimes. In L. Ohlin & M. Tonry (Eds.), *Family violence* (pp. 427-480). Chicago: University of Chicago Press.

Ellis, D. (1987). Policing wife abuse: The contribution made by domestic disturbances to deaths and injuries among police officers. *Journal of Family Violence, 3,* 319-333.

Fagan, J. (1989). Cessation of family violence: Deterrence and dissuasion. In L. Ohlin & M. Tonry (Eds.), *Family violence* (pp. 377-426). Chicago: University of Chicago Press.

Faragher, T. (1985). Police response to violence against women in the home. In J. Pahl (Ed.), *Private violence and public safety* (pp. 110-124). London: Routledge & Kegan Paul.

Ferraro, K. J. (1989). Policing woman battering. *Social Problems, 1,* 61-74.

Frieze, I. H., & Browne, A. (1989). Violence in marriage. In L. Ohlin & M. Tonry (Eds.) *Family violence* (pp. 163-218). Chicago: University of Chicago Press.

Gaudreault, A. (1991). La police et les victimes d'actes criminels: un partenariat encore fragile. *Canadian Journal of Criminology, 33,* 459-468.

Gebotys, R. J., Roberts, D. V., & DasGupta, B. (1988). News media use and public perceptions of crime seriousness. *Canadian Journal of Criminology, 30,* 3-16.

Gentemann, K. M. (1984). Wife beating: Attitudes of a nonclinical population. *Victimology, 9,* 109-119.

Gordon, L. (1988). *Heroes of their own lives: The politics and history of family violence.* New York: Penguin.

Greenblat, C. S. (1985). Don't hit your wife. . . unless. . . : Preliminary findings on normative support for the use of physical force by husbands. *Victimology, 10,* 221-241.

Greene, J. R., & Taylor, R. B. (1988). Community-based policing and foot patrol: Issues of theory and evaluation. In J. R. Greene & S. D. Mastrofski (Eds.), *Community policing: Rhetoric or reality* (pp. 195-223). New York: Praeger.

Harris, M. B. (1991). Effects of sex of aggressor, sex of target, and relationship on evaluations of physical aggression. *Journal of Interpersonal Violence, 6,* 174-186.

Hilton, N. Z. (1989). One in ten: The struggle and disempowerment of the battered women's movement. *Canadian Journal of Family Law, 7,* 313-335.

Hirschel, J. D., Hutchison, I. W., & Dean, C. W. (1992). The failure of arrest to deter spouse abuse. *Journal of Research in Crime and Delinquency, 29,* 7-33.

Humphreys, J. C., & Humphreys, W. O. (1985). Mandatory arrest: A means of primary and secondary prevention. *Victimology, 10,* 267-280.

Jaffe, P., Wolfe, D. A., Telford, A., & Austin, G. (1986). The impact of police charges in incidents of wife abuse. *Journal of Family Violence, 1,* 37-49.

Lavoie, F., Jacob, M., Hardy, J., & Martin, G. (1989). Police attitudes in assigning responsibility for wife abuse. *Journal of Family Violence, 4,* 369-388.

Leighton, B. N. (1991). Visions of community policing: Rhetoric and reality in Canada. *Canadian Journal of Criminology, 33,* 485-522.

Levens, B. R., & Dutton, D. G. (1980). *The social service role of police: Domestic crisis intervention.* Ottawa: Minister of Supply and Services Canada.

Loeber, R. (1990). Development and risk factors of juvenile antisocial behavior and delinquency. *Clinical Psychology Review, 10,* 1-41.

MacLeod, L. (1987). *Battered but not beaten: Preventing wife battering in Canada.* Ottawa: Canadian Advisory Council on the Status of Women.

Mastrofski, S. D. (1988). Community policing as reform: A cautionary tale. In J. R. Greene & S. D. Mastrofski (Eds.), *Community policing: Rhetoric or reality* (pp. 47-67). New York: Praeger.

Nordholt, E., & Straver, R. (1983). The changing police. In M. Punch (Ed.), *Control in the police organization* (pp. 36-46). Cambridge, MA: MIT Press.

Oppenlander, N. (1982). Coping or copping out. *Criminology, 20,* 449-465.

Pizzey, E. (1974). *Scream quietly or the neighbours will hear.* Harmondsworth, UK: Penguin.

Pleck, E. (1987). *Domestic tyranny: The making of social policy against family violence from colonial times to the present.* New York: Oxford University Press.

Saunders, D. G. (1980). *The police response to battered women: Predictors of officers' use of arrest, counseling or minimal action.* Unpublished doctoral dissertation, University of Wisconsin-Madison.

Saunders, D. G., & Size, P. B. (1986). Attitudes about woman abuse among police officers, victims, and victim advocates. *Journal of Interpersonal Violence, 1,* 25-42.

Sherman, L. W., & Berk, R. A. (1984). The specific deterrent effects of arrest for domestic assault. *American Sociological Review, 49,* 261-272.

Smith, T. W. (Ed.). (1984). The polls: Gender and attitudes toward violence. *Public Opinion Quarterly, 48,* 384-396.

Stark, R., & McEvoy, J. (1970, November). Middle-class violence. *Psychology Today,* pp. 52-54, 110-112.

Stith, S. M. (1990). Police response to domestic violence: The influence of individual and familial factors. *Violence and Victims, 5,* 37-49.

Straus, M. A. (1976). Sexual inequality, cultural norms, and wife-beating. *Victimology, 1,* 54-70.

Straus, M. A., Gelles, R. J., & Steinmetz, S. K. (1980). *Behind closed doors: Violence in the American family.* New York: Anchor.

Tremblay, P., & Rochon, C. (1991). D'une police efficace à une police informée: Lignes directrices d'un programme global de traitement de l'information. *Canadian Journal of Criminology, 33,* 407-420.

Wolfgang, M. E., Figlio, R. M., Tracy, P. E., & Singer, S. I. (1985). *The national survey of crime severity.* Washington, DC: U.S. Department of Justice.

4

The Impact of Police Laying Charges

PETER G. JAFFE

ELAINE HASTINGS

DEBORAH REITZEL

GARY W. AUSTIN

Background: The Police Arrest Debate

Recent History of Arrest Practices

Up until the last decade, battered women, more often than not, could not depend on police officers to lay assault charges when called to the scene of a "domestic dispute." Despite the fact that in most jurisdictions assault against a spouse is not separated legally from other types of assault, police have been reluctant to press charges in cases of conjugal violence. There are several sociocultural reasons to explain this stance. For centuries, the legal system has respected an ancient doctrine giving husbands a "right of chastisement." This rule entitled husbands to punish their wife for disrespectful or disobedient behav-

The London Family Court Clinic, Suite 200, 254 Pall Mall Street, London, Ontario, N6A 5P6 (all authors); Departments of Psychology and Psychiatry, University of Western Ontario (Jaffe); Masters Candidate, University of Western Ontario (Reitzel).

ior (Fleming, 1979). This doctrine was enhanced by the doctrine of "coverture," wherein two persons through marriage become one—that "one" being the male. Upon marriage, women lost their identity and the accompanying legal rights. Legally, women were not allowed to sue their husbands or testify against them (Fleming, 1979). Although laws have changed in the last 150 years, the attitudes that supported the original doctrines have been slower to change (cf. Hilton, this volume). In the 1970s, research relating to arrest patterns of police officers indicated that because of their considerable use of discretion, most officers were still able to avoid making arrests when the offender had physically assaulted his wife (R. E. Dobash & R. Dobash, 1979).

M. Field and H. Field's studies (cited in R. E. Dobash & R. Dobash, 1979) revealed that in Washington, D.C., in 1967, assaults involving strangers resulted in charges 75% of the time, whereas assaults against family members produced charges in only 16% of cases. Studies in Boston and Chicago revealed similar patterns (R. E. Dobash & R. Dobash, 1979). In Canada, women fared no better. Charges for wife assault in the 1970s were rarely laid except in the most extreme instances involving weapons or life-threatening injuries. In London, Ontario, in 1979 police laid charges in only 3% of wife assault calls despite the fact that wives needed medical assistance in 20% of cases (Jaffe & Burris, 1981). At the time, police officers held many erroneous beliefs regarding victims and the system that negatively influenced their decisions regarding charges. Concerns were expressed by police officers that it was difficult to ascertain reasonable and probable grounds that an assault had taken place. In addition, officers tended to believe that victims would not cooperate with the court, leading to most charges being withdrawn or dismissed. Finally, police doubted that laying charges would affect violent behavior in the home (Jaffe & Burris, 1981). Traditionally, police have considered that their primary role in domestic disputes was to restore order; that is, once the officers were able to separate and calm the partners, they believed their job was done.

Policies and Practices

Police inaction has also been promoted by departmental practices in some areas. Telephone screening has been widely used by urban police departments to establish priorities for police dispatch. Starting in the mid-1960s, Detroit police dispatchers were instructed to screen out family disturbance calls unless there were indicators of "excessive" violence. Many female callers have been put on hold, discouraged, or refused help. Calls given low priority have been responded to more slowly, or even worse, completely ignored (R. E. Dobash & R. Dobash, 1979).

In the mid-1970s, police training guides often portrayed battered women as nagging or domineering, and instructed police that removal of an intoxicated and abusive husband in those circumstances would be unreasonable. For example, in 1975, a widely used guide, *The Function of the Police in Crisis Intervention and Conflict Management,* taught officers that they were to avoid arrest at all costs, and if charges appeared inevitable they were advised to explain to the victim the consequences of having to testify in court, potential loss of income, the need to post bail, and so on (cited in Fleming, 1979). Mandates like these would discourage even the most sympathetic officer from meeting the needs of victims.

Factors Influencing Police Response

Victim Injury

U.S. and British police departments traditionally adhered to the informal "stitch" rule, whereby assault charges were laid only if the victim required medical treatment for her wounds. The decision to lay charges when injuries were serious may have been influenced by the fact that another party, usually a hospital, would be involved. Intervening in a family crisis also requires an extraordinarily high level of interpersonal skills, something with which most police officers simply were not adequately equipped. As a result, many officers chose to avoid or minimize intervention in "domestic assaults."

Criminal Justice System Support

In the past, police have also argued that the court response did not support charges, so they were reluctant to waste their time making such arrests (Paterson, 1979). In MacLeod's (1987) study on wife assault in Canada, battered women's advocates reported that very little training existed for lawyers and judges on issues of wife assault. Only 15% of shelter workers surveyed indicated that judges in their area had taken awareness seminars. The lack of understanding of critical issues related to wife assault led to decisions such as that made by an Ontario judge in 1988, reducing a charge of attempted murder to careless use of a firearm for a man who had shot his wife in the head with a .38 caliber handgun during an argument in their home (Smyth, 1988). The judge indicated that the following factors had influenced his decision: (a) the man's judgment had likely been impaired by drinking 12-16 beers that day, (b) the trigger of the gun had been modified to require less pressure to discharge it, (c) the woman was shot through the cheek rather than the temple and her husband only fired once, (d) the man was reported to be upset afterwards, (e) he took his wife to the hospital after the shooting, and (f) he told police it was an accident (although he showed no signs of remorse, the judge interpreted this as an "accidents will happen attitude").

Despite the fact that the accused had a lengthy criminal record, including convictions for breaking and entering, theft, possession of narcotics, and assaulting police, he was sentenced to only 18 months. The judge remarked that most of the charges occurred when the defendant was younger and that he seemed to have led a good life for the past 6 years (Smyth, 1988). Police have understandably been discouraged by court decisions like this that undermine the serious-ness of charges brought before the court. In fact, according to a recent review by Dutton (1988), only 1 out of 250 cases of wife assault actually end up with a report to police, a court conviction, and a serious sentence (jail, probation, or fine).

Police Injury

Police have also been wary of domestic violence cases from the belief that the risk for personal injury is high (A. R. Roberts, 1984). Police intervention in family disputes has long been cited as being particularly dangerous for officers and has been identified as the single most frequent cause of police deaths (A. R. Roberts, 1984; Paterson, 1979). The National Institute of Justice, however, released a research brief in 1986 refuting this view. The institute reported that the risk to officers dealing with wife assault cases was much lower than earlier studies would lead one to believe. The report goes on to say that until 1982, FBI statistics on officer deaths included domestic disturbances with all other types of disturbances. This meant that "family quarrels" were categorized along with bar fights, gang calls, and general disruptions. In 1982, the FBI began separating out domestic disturbance calls, and the reclassification established that these incidents accounted for only 5.7% of police deaths in the preceding 10 years. This was lower than officer deaths due to burglary, other disturbances, traffic, and robbery incidents (Garner & Clemmer, 1986). Unfortunately, this information has not been widely disseminated and many police officers probably still believe that wife assault calls are the most dangerous to respond to (Dutton, 1988). Given their lack of faith in the victims, the system, and the outcome, it is understandable that many police officers may want to minimize their involvement in these cases.

Police Attitudes

Police officers' attitudes toward arrest may also be affected by their identification with the husband and by the notion of the sanctity of the home. Officers who believe that "a man's home is his castle" may be less inclined to pursue criminal charges vigorously for offenders they view as defending male privilege. Edwards refers to police departments themselves as male-dominated institutions that mimic our patriarchal society (cited in DeKeseredy & Hinch, 1991). One recent study of Kansas police officers (Stith, 1990) indicates that police officers' treatment of victims is related to their own approval or use of marital violence. Approval of violence increased an antivictim response, and use of violence at home decreased the officers' use of arrest in hypothetical scenarios (cf. Hilton, this volume).

Still other officers believe that if a battered woman stays with her husband then she either likes the abuse or at least deserves it. This attitude was supported by some judges in the United States who required battered women in the 1970s to pass a "divorce test" before granting legal relief. That is, a woman had to prove that she had filed for divorce and done everything possible to rid herself of her violent partner before she could expect the court to treat the assault seriously (Langley & Levy, 1977).

In keeping with the view that wife assault was a private family matter, police officers in the 1970s instructed women to lay charges privately and apply for civil/restraining orders (Fleming, 1979; Paterson, 1979). Then police often refused to act on restraining orders, maintaining that they were a civil, not a criminal, matter. Few victims followed through with this procedure, feeling that the onus for the charge remained solely with them (Jaffe & Burris, 1981).

Victims' Wishes

In many cases, police have chosen not to lay charges at the victim's request. Many women are reluctant to subject their husband to public humiliation or to risk damaging his reputation or career. Most battered women want the violence to stop but do not necessarily view arrest as the avenue to achieve peace. In fact, many victims are terrified that their spouse will exact revenge if charges are laid. Still others are embarrassed and intimidated by the prospect of appearing in court to testify as a witness against their partner. Practical factors, such as the need to find child care or transportation or to take time off from work in order to pursue criminal charges, are also deterrents for victims. For these reasons, many women will exhort police officers not to lay charges.

Organizational Factors

Some authors (Langley & Levy, 1977) have concluded that police reluctance to lay charges is based on the lack of priority given to wife assault cases. Officers trying to climb the career ladder are more likely to get recognition for arrests on high-profile crimes such as armed robberies or fraud. In the past, police have not been applauded for their efforts to eradicate wife assault.

Police who wanted to intervene, lay charges, and provide safe asylum for victims were often frustrated by the lack of resources (Fleming, 1979). Shelters for battered women were virtually non-existent in most Canadian cities until the late 1970s or early 1980s. Women in rural areas still face difficulty gaining access to shelters and police are often unable to provide transportation from outlying areas. In our experience, officers who have been on the force for a number of years remark that the recent prevalence of shelters has made their job easier and encouraged them to arrest offenders and make appropriate referrals for women in need of safety.

Diversionary Measures

Arrest and jail sentences are not universally accepted as appropriate consequences for wife assault. Most battered women are more interested in their partner's rehabilitation than punishment (Jaffe & Burris, 1981). Women in shelters often wish to continue their marriage, if only the violence would stop. Various attempts have been made to promote treatment for wife assaulters as opposed to incarceration. One of the earliest programs to address the mental health needs of wife assaulters was Project Outreach in Hayward, California, in the early 1970s (Martin, 1978). Special counselors employed by the police department responded to "marital violence" calls with police officers. These therapists stayed with the couple after the police left and began counseling sessions with those who were willing to participate. Up to 10 additional free sessions were provided. In this area, most police forces focused on crisis intervention programs that assured referrals to community agencies and reduced police calls (Jaffe, Finlay, & Wolfe, 1984).

Other police departments where it was considered impractical and expensive to hire and train specialized staff began to offer training for their own officers as to how to handle family dispute calls without laying charges. The focus of officer training was to teach officers to defuse the situation and refer the couple to counseling or civil action. A police crisis intervention training course in San Jose, California, in the early 1970s listed six objectives: (a) to increase officer safety, (b) to decrease the amount of time spent on family disputes, (c) to reduce repeat calls, (d) to decrease citizen injuries in disputes with police involvement, (e) to increase diversions from the criminal justice system, and (f) to provide superior service to citizens in crises (Langley & Levy, 1977). Although referrals for counseling for wife assaulters may have been desirable to some battered women, these policies also had the effect of treating wife assault as a social problem and hence minimized its criminal aspects. This did nothing to help the victim who needed her husband removed and jailed for her own safety.

A serious danger in the police using only a mediation response is the risk of escalating violence. A Kansas City study by Stephens revealed that 85% of women murdered by their spouse had called the police on at least one prior occasion, and 50% had called for help five or more times (cited in Soler, 1987). The notion, then, that wife assault is a private family matter into which law enforcers should not intrude is potentially a deadly one. The use of mediation by police officers also reinforced the attitude that the parties were equally responsible for the violence, rather than clarifying the difference between victim and offender. Battered women were often discouraged, enraged, demeaned, and finally, further jeopardized by this process. At the same time, men got the message that wife assault was not truly considered a crime and that they need not fear the sanctions of the criminal justice system.

Police officers were encouraged by the American Bar Association to divert wife assault cases away from the criminal justice system in order to relieve "harried and overworked judges" (Fleming, 1979). Wife assault was considered appropriate for diversion, along with neighbors squabbling over loud stereos and indiscreet dogs. The Minneapolis Citizens' Dispute Settlement Project in the late 1970s dealt mainly with neighborhood disputes and wife assault. Although guided by a battered women's consortium, the project still operated on the premise that there existed a specific disagreement between spouses that could be mediated and resolved in contract form. This approach also assumed that both parties would respond in a rational, reasonable manner and that violent behavior could be modified through discussion and agreement. This was, at best, a naive assessment of the wife assaulter's motivation and ability to change his behavior.

The Rainbow Family Crisis and Counseling Program in Phoenix, Arizona, offered immediate, 24-hour crisis intervention as well as counseling for domestic violence situations (Fleming, 1979). The project considered some safeguards for victims; for example, wife assaulters who caused their victim injuries severe enough to require hospitalization were excluded.

In Washington, D.C., the Citizen Complaint Center conducted crisis intervention sessions by police referral. A social worker screened cases to determine whether the matter should be prosecuted or referred to counseling. One problem with this project was the long delay (often several weeks) between the incident and the screening appointment. In addition, further delays often ensued if the defendant failed to appear. Another flaw in this system was that prosecution was often based on the victim's wishes, which were frequently influenced by her partner (Fleming, 1979).

A project that focused more on the needs of victims operated out of Milwaukee, Wisconsin. The Battered Women's Project of the Citizen-Victim Complaint Unit worked with local women's groups on behalf of battered women. The project counseled victims and made referrals to other services. Wife assaulters were ordered to meet with the prosecutor and were usually placed on a form of "informal probation." They were cautioned that if probation conditions were violated a formal charge would be laid. This approach was most effective for first-time offenders or for men who for personal or career reasons would choose not to risk a criminal record (Fleming, 1979).

Development of Proarrest Policies

Legislative Changes

In the early 1980s, battered women's advocates began to clamor for more effective responses from police departments. In particular, victims' rights groups lobbied for the recognition of the criminal nature of wife assault. Despite the fact that criminal laws already existed to protect battered women, as we have seen, in practice these laws were rarely enforced. In the United States, one stumbling block to arrest was that officers needed to obtain a criminal arrest warrant unless they witnessed the assault directly. As a result, there was usually a delay between the incident and arrest. In the early 1980s, warrantless arrest provisions were adopted to circumvent this problem. Some states imposed additional responsibilities on police officers, requiring them to ensure the victim's safety if an arrest was not made (Micklow, 1988).

In Canada, feminist lobby groups also demanded that the criminal justice system deal with wife assault appropriately. In 1980, the Canadian Advisory Council on the Status of Women recommended that any direction for change in legislation should be guided by certain principles, which included recognizing that assault is a crime no matter who the victim is, that victims have a right to protection, and that society has an obligation to protect women and promote wife assault prevention (MacLeod, 1987).

The single most powerful action in initiating positive change regarding police intervention in Canada occurred on July 15, 1982. On that date, the federal Ministry of the Solicitor General sent a directive to the executive of the Canadian Association of Chiefs of Police encouraging their cooperation in ensuring that police officers lay charges in all cases in which there were reasonable and probable grounds to believe that an assault had taken place (MacLeod, 1987). The Royal Canadian Mounted Police (R.C.M.P.) subsequently developed a national charging policy in February 1983. Police and prosecutors in the Northwest Territories and in the Yukon were issued similar guidelines in December 1983 (MacLeod, 1987). In addition, two significant legislative changes in Canada occurred. In 1983, sexual assault laws were changed so that a husband could be charged with sexually assaulting his wife. At the same time, the Canada Evidence Act was revised to allow battered women to be compelled to testify against their spouse (MacLeod, 1987).

In 1984, the U.S. Attorney General's Task Force on Family Violence recommended that police departments establish separate statistics for domestic violence arrests. From 1984 to 1986 the percentage of reported assaults resulting in arrests nearly doubled from 24% in 1984 to 47% in 1986 (Cohn, 1987). This means, however, that in 1986 more than half of all urban police departments still did not have a consistent arrest policy in place.

Lawsuits

A number of class action suits filed by victims against police departments was another catalyst for change in arrest policies. In the late 1970s a lawsuit against the New York City police, family court clerks, and probation officers claimed they had failed to protect battered wives. The complaint charged that the police unlawfully refused to arrest wife assaulters and that family court clerks unlawfully refused to allow victims to file for protection orders (Martin, 1978). In a highly publicized case in 1984 in Connecticut, a battered woman received a judgment for $2.3 million after a U.S. district court jury found that police officers had failed to uphold her constitutional rights by not protecting her from a stabbing and beating by her estranged husband. In other jurisdictions, class action suits have been largely settled by consent judgments resulting in negotiated changes in police practices (Micklow, 1988).

Research and Community Models

In 1980, the federally funded San Francisco Family Violence Project was established to change the criminal justice response (Soler, 1987). The police and the district attorney's office were the focus of the project's work. Several significant innovations were adopted by the San Francisco Police Department and the district attorney's office as a result of the project. These included the adoption by police of new policies and procedures designed to reflect the criminal nature of wife assault; specialized training for police personnel; and a data collection system for tracking domestic violence calls, reports, and charges over time. The district attorney's office also restructured its approach to wife assault. This included establishing prosecution protocols, assigning one attorney to handle each case from start to finish, developing victim advocacy units, and providing counseling and education programs for offenders. These guidelines achieved tremendous results within the first year of operation: domestic violence arrests increased by 60%. Likewise, the district attorney's office realized tremendous results from its written protocol for prosecution. By the project's third year, the conviction rate had increased 44% over the preceding year, the number of cases in which charges were filed increased 136% over the first year, and there was a 171% increase in dispositions involving probation, jail, parole, or supervised diversion (Soler, 1987).

In Minnesota, three suburban communities took part in a 2-year project coordinated by the Domestic Abuse Project of Minneapolis (cited in Gamache, Edleson, & Schock, 1984). These community intervention projects were designed to coordinate responses to domestic violence. Like the San Francisco project, these projects assisted police in implementing arrest procedures, helped promote prompt prosecution, and developed mandated counseling programs for assaulters. In each of the three communities, a local battered women's shelter helped coordinate activities. Victim advocacy volunteers and groups for battered women were also established. Once again, these projects demonstrated impressive changes in police and court responses. Sherman and Berk (1984) reported that trends toward an increased number of arrests, successful prosecutions, and court-mandated referrals to men's programs were all significant.

At the same time that community-based projects were forging ahead with innovative approaches, research examining the effects of various police responses was being conducted in Minneapolis. Sherman and Berk (1984) studied three police responses and their effects on future incidents of wife assault. The three responses examined were arrest, counseling, and separation. During a 6-month follow-up period, Sherman and Berk found that men who had been arrested were less likely to assault their wife than men who were separated from their wife for a brief period of time or men who received counseling. These findings were responsible for many U.S. police departments formulating proarrest policies. In a survey of 117 U.S. police forces, over one third indicated that their policy had been influenced by Sherman and Berk's study.

Parallel projects were also under way in Canada in the early 1980s. In London, Ontario, service agencies joined forces to create the Coordinating Committee on Family Violence in 1980 to guide a research project at the London Family Court Clinic (Jaffe & Burris, 1981). The project, funded by the Solicitor General of Canada, was initiated to examine the effectiveness of the criminal justice system's response to wife assault. In the committee's first report several recommendations were made. These included recommendations similar to those in San Francisco that addressed laying of charges, police and court training, advocacy services, and treatment programs for men. In addition, the committee recognized a need for public education regarding wife assault and the need to promote an integrated community response to victims. As a result of the committee's work, in May 1981, London became the first police force in Canada to institute a policy that instructed officers to lay charges of assault in wife assault cases regardless of the wishes of the parties whenever there existed reasonable and probable grounds to believe an assault had taken place.

Another facet of London's response to wife assault is the London Family Consultant Service. This team of social workers was established in 1973 to assist officers in responding to family crises, including wife assault. The service offers crisis intervention and referrals to appropriate agencies, providing a vital link between law enforcement and social services (Jaffe et al., 1984). In 1981, police also began to give out victim information cards to all victims of wife assault at the time of police intervention. The information included the officer's name, number, and plan of action as well as a listing of community supports available. The cards, which gave victims a written summary of police intent regarding charges, may have served to remind and to motivate police to follow the newly issued directive.

Effectiveness of Arrest Policy

Response of the London Police Force

The London Police Force policy to lay charges whenever there were reasonable and probable grounds to believe that an assault had occurred was the first in Canada. At the time of its inception, there had been no prior study of the effectiveness of arrest for wife assault. The London arrest policy spawned a series of studies beginning in 1981. The most recent study, conducted in 1990, examined trends across the decade. The effectiveness of the policy was assessed by interviewing 90 women who had been physically assaulted by their partner and received one of three interventions: (a) police intervention with charges laid, (b) police intervention with no charges laid, and (c) no police intervention and no charges laid. The effectiveness of the policy was assessed by examining police data on the number of charges laid and a survey of police officers' attitudes in regard to the importance and effect of the directive to lay charges in cases of wife assault.

Because of the considerable influence that research into the effectiveness of arrest can have (see above), a full understanding of the research findings is important for both researchers and practitioners affected by the controversy that continues over the effectiveness of arrest. A description of the methods and results of our most recent study follows.

Method

Participants

Participants for the study included 90 women who were victims of "wife" assault in 1988 or 1989 (the "target" incident). Of the 90 participants, 52 had had police intervention and charges laid; 14 had police intervention, but no charges were laid; and 24 had neither police intervention nor charges laid. The participants were recruited in the following manner: 32 responded to written requests from the London Police Force asking for participants for a study investigating the quality of service offered by the London Police Force and other community agencies; 33 responded to newspaper advertisements requesting volunteers for an interview related to their experience with the criminal justice system; 17 were referred by community agencies that provide services for battered women; and a flyer sent to 50,000 randomly chosen London residences requesting volunteers for an interview related to their experience with the criminal justice system recruited 6. One was referred by a family physician who was aware of the study and one referral source was unknown.

Most of the participants (66.7%) were separated from their partner at the time of the interview. At the time of the assault, 57.7% of the women had been legally married and 33.0% were residing in a common-law relationship. The sample was ethnically similar to the population of London, being predominantly Caucasian (95%), with 5% of the participants and 8% of partners representing visible minorities. The average age of the participants was 36 years; the partners averaged 38 years. Both victims and perpetrators were mostly well educated: 45.0% of the women and 50% of partners had attended college or university. The mean family annual income for the participants was $20,000 to $30,000. Thirty-five percent of the participants and 65.0% of the partners were reported to have witnessed wife assault in their family of origin. Thirty-nine percent of the participants' partners had prior police involvement related to a domestic violence incident against the participant. Many women indicated that a previous assault by their partner required them to seek medical treatment (38.3%); almost half had been assaulted during a pregnancy (47.9%).

Of those victims with police contact, 61.0% had called the police themselves, whereas other contacts were made by a neighbor (15.0%), child (5.0%), partner (5.1%), or other person (15.1%).

Procedure

Each participant was screened by telephone to ensure that she met the criteria for inclusion in the study, that is, (a) she was a victim of wife assault by a male partner (married or common law) in 1988 or 1989, (b) she was over the age of 18, (c) she was a resident of London at the time of the assault, and (d) police intervention (if any) involved the London Police Force. Most participants were interviewed in the offices of the London Family Court Clinic (two were interviewed at Women's Community House). The interview lasted 1-2 hours. Three interviews involved a professional interpreter (courtesy of the London Cultural Interpretation Service). Each participant was paid $20.

The three subgroups of participants (i.e., police intervention with charges laid; police intervention with no charges laid; no police intervention and no charges laid) did not differ significantly in income, marital status, or duration of involvement with the partner. The participant profile for the present study is quite similar to the earlier studies (Jaffe & Burris, 1981; Jaffe, Wolfe, Telford, & Austin, 1986).

Measures

The Victim Interview Form formed the basis of a structured interview with participants for the study. It included questions about the woman and her partner such as socioeconomic status, criminal history, and violence in the family of origin and questions about the target incident such as police and court involvement, the assault itself, and the victim's satisfaction with community support and services used following the assault.

The Conflict Tactics Scale is a standardized interview questionnaire that provides an assessment of the form and frequency of verbal and physical aggression between family members (Straus, 1979). It has demonstrated reliability and validity as a measure of parent-to-child and adult-to-adult verbal and physical aggression in a large, representative sample of families (Straus, Gelles, & Steinmetz, 1980). The scale was completed by each participant for the 12-month period preceding and following the target incident.

The Victim Code Sheet was designed as an objective measure of details surrounding the target incident using information from the London Police Force criminal records. This information includes the date of the assault; any related court appearances; the charge laid; who laid the charge; the partner's criminal record; the legal status of the partner prior to sentencing (e.g., in custody); and the charge outcome, including sentence if applicable. This code sheet was also used to record a brief synopsis of the assault incident. The primary purpose of the code sheet was to provide some information to enable the participant to focus on the target incident, but it also provided an objective source of information that was later compared with the participant's testimony during the victim interview. Cases indicating extreme discrepancies in pertinent information when comparing the code sheet to the Victim Interview Form were excluded from the study.

The London Police Force Patrol Operations Branch Survey on Partner Assault (Police Survey) provides an assessment of police officers' attitudes with regard to the policy implemented by the London Police Force in May 1981. The survey was completed by 133 officers of the Uniform Division of the London Police Force. The survey included questions related to police perceptions of the policy's ability to reduce the incidence of wife assault, its effect on the court system and the community, and its potential to prompt negative side effects (such as causing victims to be reluctant to call the police).

Results

Response of the Police to the Charging Policy

In 1979 (prepolicy), London police officers laid charges in only 2.7% of occurrences involving wife assault. By 1983, this figure was 67.3%, and as of 1990, the figure had risen dramatically to 89.3% (see Table 4.1). In contrast, other jurisdictions in Ontario show lower charging rates during this period. For example, R.C.M.P. data indicate a charging rate of 51% between 1985 and 1988 (Williamson & Meredith,

Table 4.1 London Police Force Wife Assault Charges, 1987-1990

	1987	1988	1989	1990
Wife assault occurrence	315	288	335	358
Charges laid by police	205	204	269	320
Charges as a percent of occurrences	65.1%	70.8%	79.1%	89.3%
Officer's reason for no charge related to wishes of victim	18.4%	18.4%	13.6%	3.6%

1990) and a Toronto Police Force study found a 31% charging rate for 1985-1986 (Leighton, 1989). In 1987 and 1988, London police officers laid a higher percentage of charges in wife assault occurrences compared to the provincial average (65.1% vs. 46.6%, and 70.8% vs. 50.8% for 1987 and 1988, respectively). In addition, fewer London police officers are prepared to accept the wishes of the victim not to lay charges (18.4% vs. 32.2%, and 18.4% vs. 29.9%, respectively), reflecting the fact that London Police Force officers are instructed to lay charges when there is reasonable and probable grounds and not to leave the onus on the victim.

Police Attitudes Regarding Mandate

Table 4.2 indicates the changing responses of police to the mandate of laying charges where reasonable and probable grounds exist. Clearly, police officers are more supportive of the policy than in the past. More than half the officers in 1990 felt that the policy was effective, compared with only one third in the previous study. Most important, the majority of officers agree that this policy promotes an important message to the community. More officers believed the policy helps battered women and may be effective in stopping family violence, and that the courts are supportive of this policy. The most

Table 4.2 Police Attitudes Regarding Mandate, 1985 and 1990

Percent responding affirmative to the question, "Do you feel that . . ."	*1985*	*1990*
. . . this policy is effective	33.3	52.3
. . . this policy helps battered women	41.7	48.1
. . . this policy stops family violence	20.5	27.5
. . . this policy promotes an important message to the community	55.0	64.9
. . . the policy has had any negative side effects, such as women hesitant to call the police	31.6	35.4
. . . the policy has had any negative side effects, such as husbands becoming more dangerous	16.4	14.1
. . . the courts support the police policy	26.1	35.3
. . . the victims are more likely to follow through when police lay charges compared to victim laid charges	42.0	77.5

dramatic result is in the area of the police officers' perceptions that victims are more likely to follow through when police lay charges compared to victims laying their own charges: 77.5% of the officers believe victims are more likely to follow through in 1990 compared with 42.0% in 1985.

The data on police attitudes were analyzed according to years of service (under 4 years, 4-10 years, over 10 years) and the differentiation between supervisory police officers (n = 12) and first-class constables (n = 117). Officers with more years of experience hold significantly more progressive views about this policy; that is, a higher percentage of longer serving officers see the policy as effective, as helping battered women, and so on, and a lower percentage see it as having negative effects. The same trend is apparent among supervisory police

Table 4.3 Police Attitudes Regarding Decision to Charge According to
Number of Years in Police Service, 1990

Question: In responding to domestic assault calls, which of the following factors
influence your decision to lay a charge? Rank the three (3) most important factors.

Survey Items	Percent Choosing Item as First Priority			
	Number of Years in Police Service			
	<4	4-10	>10	Overall
Corroborating evidence	27.3	43.3	36.7	35.5
Willingness of victim to testify	39.4	23.3	33.3	32.3
Seriousness of victim's injuries	15.2	16.7	10.0	14.0
Likelihood of conviction	3.0	3.3	10.0	5.4
Willingness of witness to testify	0	3.3	3.3	2.2
Use of alcohol/drugs by victim	3.0	0	3.3	2.2
Police record of domestic violence	6.1	0	0	2.2
Other	0	3.3	3.3	2.2
Presence of children	0	3.3	0	1.1
Composure of victim	3.0	0	0	1.1
Use of alcohol/drugs by offender	0	3.3	0	1.1
Criminal record of offender	3.0	0	0	1.1
Age of victim	0	0	0	0
Age of offender	0	0	0	0
Concurrent civil proceedings	0	0	0	0

NOTE: *N* varies from 89 to 93 due to incomplete surveys.

officers who are significantly more likely than first-class constables to
perceive the policy as effective and helpful.

Table 4.3 outlines police officers' perceptions of the most important
factors that influence their decision to lay an assault charge. Overall,
officers choose corroborating evidence as the Number 1 factor, with
willingness of victim to testify and seriousness of the victim's injuries
as being secondary factors. It is interesting to note that the more junior
officers rely on the willingness of victims to testify more than do the
more senior officers on the force.

Response of Victims of Violence

Overall, the victims participating in the study indicated a high level of satisfaction with police response. Most (74.1%) of the victims indicated that the police responded quickly, and 65.2% indicated that they were satisfied with the advice they received. This figure is in stark contrast to the finding from the 1979 survey that only 48.0% of the victims were satisfied with the police response. Most important, 87.0% of the victims said they would call the police again.

Of those victims who expressed dissatisfaction, 19% suggested that officers should be more understanding (compared with 31% in 1979). Seven victims felt that charges should be laid (11%, compared with 29% in 1979). Six percent of the victims (compared with 3% in 1979) felt that more should be done to protect victims, such as removing the male from the premises. The most common suggestion made for improvements was a general request for more information on court process and community service (28% of victims).

Effect on Violence

The extent and severity of violence used by males against their female partner 12 months before and 12 months after the target incident are summarized in Table 4.4. The violence before the police intervention is consistently at the same level in both studies according to victim reports on the Conflict Tactics Scale. In the majority of cases, there is a statistically significant reduction in the level of violence after the police intervention.

Table 4.5a breaks down the changing pattern of violence according to whether there was a police intervention, and if so, whether this intervention resulted in a charge being laid. As indicated, there were significant differences in the severity of violence used depending whether there was a police intervention and a charge was laid.

Table 4.5b compares the effect of charging to no charging by combining "police intervention/no charges" and "no police inter- vention" into one "no charges" group. This collapse of the no charges groups augmented the sample size from 14 to 51. As indi- cated, charging was associated with a significant reduction in violent behaviors.

Table 4.4 Extent of Violence Used by Males Against Female Partner During 12-Month Periods Before and After Target Incident

Percentage of subjects reporting at least one incident of the following:	1985		1990	
	Before	After	Before	After
Threatened to hit or throw something	78.0	49.1**	65.6	48.0
Threw, smashed, hit, or kicked something	78.0	47.5**	73.9	45.3*
Threw something at the other	54.8	14.8**	45.6	32.0
Pushed, grabbed, or shoved	80.8	54.1**	78.2	52.0**
Hit or tried to hit with something	45.2	18.0**	50.5	24.0**
Beat up the other one	63.0	24.6**	42.9	26.7*
Slapped	71.2	29.5**	60.2	32.3*
Kicked, bit, or hit with fist	57.2	22.9**	46.2	26.7
Threatened with a weapon	24.7	9.8*	20.4	10.8
Used a weapon	4.1	1.6	10.8	6.7

$*p < .05; **p < .01.$

Victims' Experience and Satisfaction With Court Process

The outcomes of assault charges processed by the court by comparison to the previous studies completed in London are summarized in Table 4.6. Only one in nine charges was dismissed or withdrawn (10.9%) compared to 16.4% and 38.4% in 1983 and 1979, respectively. The charges that result in a fine (43.6%), probation (46.2%), or a jail sentence (17.9%) have increased dramatically from previous years.

Victims expressed a higher level of satisfaction with the court process in comparison with previous studies. For example, 65% of the victims who had contact with crown attorneys felt a sense of complete support. In 1979, when a similar question was asked of victims, only 31% were satisfied with the assistance of the crown attorneys. Over half of the victims (53.1%) felt that they spent enough time with crown attorneys, in contrast to 1983 when only 41% of the victims said that they had even spoken to a crown attorney before the first court appearance.

Table 4.5 Severity of Violence Used by Males Against Female Partner During 12-Month Periods Before and After Target Incident

	Mean Violence Severity Score (range 0 = never occurred, to 1 = occurred 1 or more times)					
a.	*No Police*		*Police/No Charges*		*Police/Charges*	
	Before	*After*	*Before*	*After*	*Before*	*After*
Insulted/swore at	0.6	0.7	0.7	0.5	0.7	0.4*
Slapped	0.58	0.47	0.3	0.3	0.64	0.19*
Kicked, bit, or hit with fist	0.5	0.4	0.3	0.4	0.5	0.17*

b.	*No Charges*		*Charges*	
	Before	*After*	*Before*	*After*
Threatened to hit or throw something	0.63	0.63	0.71	0.38*
Pushed, grabbed, or shoved	0.83	0.70	0.80	0.37*
Slapped	0.48	0.41	0.64	0.19*
Kicked, bit, or hit with fist	0.43	0.40	0.50	0.17*

*$p < .05$.

Victims raised some serious questions about the length of the court process. Although London does not face the same problems of backlogged cases as other jurisdictions, 54.3% of the victims were concerned about the time required to reach a final disposition for the charges. Half the victims were worried about their safety during this period and one quarter were actually threatened by their partner. A further 8.9% of victims were assaulted by their partner during the court process (cf. Ford & Regoli, this volume).

Table 4.6 Victims' Court Experience Regarding Wife Assault Charges Laid

	1979[a] %(n)	1983[b] %(n)	1989/90[c] %(n)
Dismissed or withdrawn	38.4(20)	16.4(9)	10.9(5)
Fine	5.8(3)	29.1(16)	43.6(17)
Jail	7.7(4)	7.3(4)	17.9(7)
Probation	26.9(14)	18.2(10)	46.2(18)

a. $N = 52$.
b. $N = 55$.
c. $N = 39$ to 46 due to missing data.

Victims' Perspectives on Community Support

Victims in the study reported utilizing a wide range of supports, ranging from friends to generic social service agencies to specialized services for victims and perpetrators of violence (Table 4.7). Friends, relatives, and family physicians topped the list for supports most commonly utilized. It is important to note that these groups have traditionally been lacking in specialized training regarding wife assault and related community services. These numbers, therefore, highlight the importance of continuing efforts to educate the general public, as well as health and mental health professionals, on the issues surrounding wife assault and services available. Nearly one quarter of respondents also used clergy for assistance, indicating another group that could possibly benefit from additional training and support in this area.

Use of supports increased following the target assault in every case except for hospital services, which remained the same. Over time, it appears that victims either became more aware of services or were more willing to use them. The most dramatic increases in use occurred with the Battered Women's Advocacy Clinic, Women's Community House, and Family Service London, where frequencies virtually doubled. Of particular note is the fact that prior to the target assault, none of the specialized services for victims or perpetrators were among the top five most frequently used supports. In fact, Family Service London and Women's Community House were the least used services prior to

Table 4.7 Community Support to Victims

| Nature of Support | Accessed (Occasionally/Frequently) | | Satisfaction | | |
	Before Assault	After Assault	Not at All Helpful	Somewhat Helpful	Very Helpful
	%	%	%	%	%
Friends	68.1	76.3	7.9	50.0	42.1
Relatives	56.7	73.2	13.5	44.6	41.9
Doctor	42.2	46.9	24.5	35.8	39.6
Individual counseling	30.9	42.5	14.0	14.0	72.0
Battered Women's Advocacy Clinic	17.5	38.7	11.9	26.2	61.9
Clergy	22.6	23.7	29.0	32.3	38.7
Police	19.6	22.4	40.7	18.5	40.7
Women's Community House	11.3	22.4	18.5	18.5	63.0
Hospital	16.5	16.4	19.0	38.1	42.9
Family counseling	14.4	18.4	26.1	17.4	56.5
Police Family Consultant Service	13.4	14.3	31.6	10.5	57.9
Family Service London	7.2	15.3	21.1	10.5	68.4

NOTE: Not represented by this table are services used infrequently by the sample surveyed, including counseling for children, Family and Children's Services, Atenlos, Court Witness Assistance Program, Crisis Telephone Service.

the target assault. Because these are among the primary direct service agencies for victims and perpetrators of wife assault, it is encouraging to see the trend toward higher use of these specialized services following assault. Some victims reported that police referred them to these agencies during intervention (20.4%). Others reported that friends (22.4%), advertising (16.3%), or another agency (13.3%) made them aware of services.

The survey also indicated that victims have continued to contact the police for assistance on successive occasions. The frequency of calls to police increased from 19.6% to 22.4% following the target incident

(Table 4.7). Because charges were laid in the majority of cases involving police intervention in this study, this information is important feedback for officers who have been concerned that the charging policy may discourage women from calling for assistance. Clearly this is not the case; victims are even more likely to call for police intervention on subsequent occasions.

Overall, victims reported positively on community supports utilized. More than 70% rated most services as being somewhat helpful or very helpful. Specialized services such as Battered Women's Advocacy Clinic (61.9% rated it very helpful), Women's Community House (63.0%), and Family Service London (68.4%) were seen to be most helpful (Table 4.7).

Although the London police were seen as helpful by 6 out of 10 victims (59.2% somewhat and very helpful combined), their overall rating was somewhat lower than social services and other helping agencies. This rating is based on victims' global rating of police irrespective of their level of contact and any specific intervention provided. This figure is augmented when victims are asked to specifically rate individual police officers' interventions around the targeted assault incident (65.2% were satisfied with police advice and 87.0% would call the police again).

Several data analyses were completed to examine the interaction between police intervention and level of community support; however, no significant pattern of results was noted.

Comparison With Related Studies

In the United States, the National Institute of Justice has funded six replications of Sherman and Berk's Minneapolis study on police responses. At present, the results of only two are available, and these have not replicated Sherman and Berk's (1984) findings (Dunford, Huizinga, & Elliott, 1990; Hirschel, Hutchison, & Dean, 1992). Data from the other four studies when available will be helpful in closer examination of arrest policies.

Recently, Sherman et al. (1991) completed another study in Milwaukee examining the effects on short- and long-term recidivism of

varying lengths of custody time for males arrested for domestic violence. Alarmingly, short-custody arrests had a deterrent effect lasting
30 days, but showed significantly higher long-term recidivism than no
arrest. Longer custody arrests had no clear long-term effect in either
direction. Short-custody arrest suspects clearly did not view the event
as seriously as long-custody arrests. They were twice as likely to say
they did not care about the arrest, less likely to worry about what
would happen next or to expect the arrest to affect their future
chances of obtaining employment or buying a car, and twice as likely
to expect their friends to be angry at their partner, not them, for the
arrest. The increase in long-term recidivism for these suspects may be
related to their experience that arrest was a minor inconvenience with
few long-term consequences. In addition, only 5% of suspects in the
study were actually charged and only 1% convicted, which would only
serve to reinforce the belief that assault has few, if any, serious
consequences. This does not explain, however, why short-custody
arrests have a stronger immediate deterrent effect than long-custody
arrests. In the London study, suspects were far more likely to be
charged and face conviction with accompanying penalties of jail,
fines, or probation. It may be that the prospect of probable serious
consequences enhances the deterrent effect of arrest in jurisdictions
where a stronger criminal justice system response is the norm.

In addition, it is important to note that this study was conducted
with a population very different from that in the study in London.
Suspects in the Milwaukee study were predominantly unemployed
(55%), never married (64%), and black (76%); only 31% were high
school graduates and 50% had prior arrests. Other studies by Sherman
indicate that there are varying effects of the same length of custody
on different individuals (cited in Sherman et al., 1991). Different types
of perpetrators of violence respond differently to the same treatment.
It may be that although arrest alone is a significant deterrent for some,
consequences need to be escalated to have the same effect on other
individuals.

Although short-custody arrests (under 3 hours) increased long-term
recidivism, long-custody arrests (minimum 12 hours) did not clearly
affect long-term recidivism. This may be an argument for a 12-hour
minimum in custody. The understanding of how other variables inter-

act is critical in determining the usefulness of arrest policies for any given population. Clearly, what works in London may not necessarily hold true for poverty-stricken ghetto areas.

Issues for Future Consideration

Police Education

Police attitudes and training with regard to wife assault have progressed considerably in the last decade. In 1979, the Oakland Police Department's training bulletin indicated that a man should not be arrested for wife assault because he would "lose face" (Paterson, 1979). In those days, training programs for officers relating to assaults in the home emphasized peacekeeping. Although such training can be helpful, it should not preclude or override law enforcement. Arrest and charges send a clear message that our society will no longer tolerate assault. By the mid-1980s, more police officers had been trained to arrest, rather than simply to defuse situations. Still, variations among individual officers and detachments remain significant. Shelter workers are often aware of which municipalities or detachments in their area provide consistently good service and which are known for negative responses. In A. R. Roberts's (1984) national survey, shelter workers indicated wide variance: 34 shelters reported generally positive experiences with the police, 10 reported mostly negative encounters, and 35 described a mixture of productive and nonproductive responses. Some shelter workers indicated that police response had improved as a result of shelter involvement in providing training workshops for officers. Training programs provided by community experts on abuse issues can sensitize police to the nature, etiology, and prevalence of wife assault; provide police with effective intervention skills; and increase their awareness of community supports and services available for victims, perpetrators, and their children.

In Canada, all police education and training centers now include a segment on wife assault in training programs for new recruits. Following the charging policy directive in 1983, a number of courses and training manuals were revised with the input of women's advocacy groups. In Saskatchewan, outside professionals from the R.C.M.P., prosecutors' office, and correctional services are invited to participate in training with the police (MacLeod, 1987). Although the quality and content of training for recruits has improved, there still remains no standardized in-service training for existing members of police forces. Some departments have invited shelter workers to provide workshops, but this is not consistent across the country.

In the United States, police training programs were greatly affected by the Minneapolis Experiment on arrest policies. Changes in training programs included increased time spent on the issue of domestic violence and use of in-service refresher courses on the subject for veteran officers. In 1986, 31% of police departments surveyed in the United States indicated that the Minneapolis study had influenced their training program (Cohn, 1987).

Training programs for police should include information on the social costs of wife assault, statistics on prevalence, information on why victims stay or return, and descriptions of local services. A referral manual of resources should be provided to officers as well as business cards with pertinent phone numbers that can be given to victims. Several excellent videos on wife assault and its effects on child witnesses are now available and are valuable training tools. Police should also be provided with feedback from studies that illustrate how police response can be related to victims' satisfaction and future violence. In essence, Fleming (1979) sums up the need for training to "stress that the police officer's job is not to solve the problem that leads to the incident, nor to save the marriage, but to stop the violence, protect the victim, and enforce the law as he [sic] would in a similar case involving strangers" (p. 10).

Community Interaction

The training of police may necessitate the involvement and cooperation of several agencies. Many areas now have committees composed of representatives from legal, justice, education, health, and social service fields to coordinate the community response to wife assault. These joint efforts have proven to be fruitful and have fostered better understanding and tolerance of each other's roles.

They have also given rise to innovative approaches to maintaining safety for women. In Winnipeg, Manitoba, police, social agencies, and ADT Security Systems Ltd. pioneered a silent alarm system for use by high-risk women. The Domestic Violence Emergency Response System has been pilot-tested in the homes of a dozen women with the only stipulation being that they have to be willing to testify if charges are laid. This program was implemented as a result of Manitoba having the highest rate of female homicide in Canada. Although the system is relatively new, it has been credited with saving the life of at least one woman to date (D. Roberts, 1992).

Despite these types of innovative protection measures, in many situations women are doubly victimized. In January 1992, an Edmonton, Alberta, woman was evicted from her townhouse 2 days after her boyfriend held police at bay for 15 hours. Although police managed to remove the woman safely from the home prior to the standoff, her boyfriend drove through a police roadblock and locked himself in her townhouse, brandishing a semiautomatic assault rifle and a magnum revolver. The woman was held responsible by her landlord for the disturbance and for endangering her neighbors and was evicted on that basis. A newspaper article reported that the victim understood the eviction and that she did not want to further jeopardize herself or anyone else (Staples & Owens, 1992). Clearly, community systems for protecting women fall short in circumstances such as this.

Another common mandate of coordinating committees is to provide public education on awareness and prevention. Subcommittees often take on the task of training hospital personnel, teachers, the judiciary, and lawyers on woman abuse issues. Dissemination of consistent information to service providers helps to facilitate better rapport between providers and better service to victims. All of these efforts combine to make the job of police officers easier and also help to hold them accountable to the community for their actions. In London, Ontario, committee members have written to the Solicitor General praising the London Police Force's charging rates and asking why other communities continue to lag behind. Although London police officers laid charges in 1987-1988 in 2 out of 3 cases, the provincial average was only approximately 1 in 2 cases (law enforcement activity in relation to spouse assault in Ontario for the year 1987 and 1988). Across Ontario, 30% of decisions not to charge were made at the request of the victims, despite the fact that there were grounds to believe an assault had taken place. This is in direct violation of the Solicitor General's directive. Lobbying efforts by coordinating committees can have a substantial effect on police policy and implementation, as was seen in 1983 when police directives were made, and local communities need to maintain their watchdog activities.

Cross-Cultural Issues

Recent studies have suggested that aboriginal women may be at higher risk of being victims of violence (Dumont-Smith & Labelle, 1991; Spero, Doxtator, & George, 1991). In contrast to the usual figures of 1 in 7 or 1 in 10 women in the general population being assaulted, survey results suggest that at least 8 out of 10 aboriginal women may be victims of violence. This violence is rarely reported because of the high level of isolation, community norms, and the serious consequences to the victims for disclosure. Traditionally, aboriginal women lived in a more matriarchal society where violence was not condoned. Many researchers attribute the violence to the effect of racism on the aboriginal people as well as the loss of traditional hunting, fishing, and trapping roles for men. The extent of this problem requires a unique justice system response that is sensitive to the needs of the aboriginal.

As Canada has become a nation of more diverse peoples, difficulties in understanding cultural differences have grown. Language barriers can create significant roadblocks to effective intervention. A recent workshop in Toronto, Ontario, sponsored by the Canadian Council on Muslim women revealed that although wife assault is rampant in Toronto's South Asian community, few victims seek help because mainstream agencies do not meet their needs. Aruna Papp, founder of South Asian Family Support Services, reports that many immigrant women fail to contact the police because of fear of deportation or divorce and that many women are unaware of laws and social services in Canada that could help them. Still other women believe it brings shame to their family to leave or to discuss problems with an outsider. Some have tried Canadian services and suffered negative experiences (Pulling, 1991).

Cultural sensitivity training, information on immigration status and laws, and trained interpreters are all needed in order for police and other service providers to be able to respond appropriately to our growing population of newcomers. Preliminary studies suggest that battered women from minority groups may receive poorer treatment than white women in Canada. In Toronto, it has been reported that black women are less likely to receive police assistance than white women (cited in DeKeseredy & Hinch, 1991). Communities need to begin to strategize now as to how they can best ensure that all battered women receive protection and the services they need.

Primary Prevention

In recent years, shelter workers and others actively working with victims and perpetrators of wife assault have become increasingly alarmed at the effects on children of witnessing violence at home. Several studies have focused on short- and long-term effects on children, such as decreased empathy, increased aggression, tolerance of the use of violence, and victim blaming (Jaffe, Wolfe, & Wilson, 1990). As a result, a current focus has been on providing primary prevention programs at the elementary and secondary school levels (Jaffe, Reitzel, Sudermann, & Killip, 1990). The goal of these programs is to increase awareness of issues, including responsibility for violence, and to provide information on local services. In London, more in-depth programs are beginning to involve students in peer mediation training and conflict resolution skills development. Police involvement can greatly enhance the effect of prevention work; several hundred secondary school students at an assembly were startled to hear from a London police officer that they were sure to be charged if they hit someone and police were called. This information had particular effect because it was delivered firsthand by a police officer rather than relayed through a teacher or other lay person. More and more, police involvement in prevention programs will be seen as highly desirable, and it should be considered an essential part of crime control in the future.

Summary and Conclusions

In this chapter, we have examined the development of police arrest policies related to wife assault. Historically, police response was shaped by popular doctrine, sexist attitudes, and a patriarchal system that discouraged criminal justice system involvement in "family matters." We have seen how feminist groups, research, community pressure, and legislative changes have all substantially affected police policies and practices.

Research on police intervention reveals that although arrest alone does not necessarily decrease violence, the laying of charges appears to be a significant deterrent. Interviews with victims suggest that family and friends are their greatest avenue of support and that police officers and the general public are in need of increased awareness and sensitivity to the issues confronting battered women. Statistics indicate that the enforcement of charging policies varies widely across areas and even within detachments. Community pressure needs to be maintained to assure consistent, effective police responses across the board.

Continuing research such as that described in this chapter is required by police forces to monitor and evaluate the consistency of arrest and charging policies. Although some research controversies appear to dampen the enthusiasm for "wife assault as a crime" policies, it is doubtful that any attempts will be made to decriminalize this behavior. The police response seems vital to communicating to the community that wife assault will no longer be tolerated, similar to campaigns against "drinking and driving."

The research question in the 1990s will not be whether the policy works, but rather how can it work effectively as part of an integrated community response that includes training for judges and prosecutors, support services for victims from the point of police intervention until court dispositions, and resources for wife assaulters and child witnesses to violence. Much of the research to date (Sherman et al., 1991) has been piecemeal in nature rather than focusing on the role of police in the context of an overall justice, social service, and health system response. Future research also needs to focus attention on many victim groups (e.g., aboriginal women, immigrant women) who live with violence without even considering the police as a source of support in ending their suffering.

References

Cohn, E. G. (1987). Changing the domestic violence policies of urban police departments: Impact of the Minneapolis experiment. *Response, 10*(4), 22-25.

DeKeseredy, W. S., & Hinch, R. (1991). *Woman abuse: Sociological perspectives.* Toronto: Thompson Educational.

Dobash, R. E., & Dobash, R. (1979). *Violence against wives: A case against the patriarchy.* New York: Macmillan.

Dumont-Smith, C., & Labelle, P. (1991). *National family violence abuse study.* Ottawa: Indian and Inuit Nurses of Canada.

Dunford, F. W., Huizinga, D., & Elliott, D. S. (1990). The role of arrest in domestic assault: The Omaha Police experiment. *Criminology, 28,* 183-206.

Dutton, D. G. (1988). *The domestic assault of women: Psychological and criminal justice perspectives.* Toronto: Allyn & Bacon.

Fleming, J. B. (1979). *Stopping wife abuse: A guide to the emotional, psychological, and legal implications for the abused woman and those helping her.* Garden City, NY: Anchor.

Gamache, D. J., Edleson, J. L., & Schock, M. D. (1988). Coordinated police, judicial, and social service response to woman battering: A multiple-baseline evaluation across three communities. In G. T. Hotaling, D. Finkelhor, J. T. Kirkpatrick, & M. A. Straus (Eds.), *Coping with family violence: Research and policy perspectives* (pp. 193-209). Newbury Park, CA: Sage.

Garner, J., & Clemmer, E. (1986). *Danger to police in domestic disturbances—A new book.* Washington, DC: U.S. Department of Justice.

Hirschel, J. D., Hutchison, I. W., & Dean, C. W. (1992). The failure of arrest to deter spouse abuse. *Journal of Research in Crime and Delinquency, 20,* 7-33.

Jaffe, P., & Burris, C. A. (1981). *The response of the criminal justice system to wife abuse.* Ottawa: Solicitor General of Canada.

Jaffe, P., Finlay, J., & Wolfe, D. (1984). Evaluating the impact of a specialized civilian family crisis unit within a police force on the resolution of family conflicts. *Journal of Preventive Psychiatry, 2,* 63-183.

Jaffe, P., Reitzel, D., Sudermann, M., & Killip, S. (1990). *The London secondary school intervention project on violence in intimate relationships.* Unpublished research report prepared for the Ontario Ministry of Community and Social Services.

Jaffe, P., Wolfe, D. A., Telford, A., & Austin, G. (1986). The impact of police charges in incidents of wife abuse. *Journal of Family Violence, 1,* 37-49.

Jaffe, P., Wolfe, D. A., & Wilson, S. K. (1990). *Children of battered women.* Newbury Park, CA: Sage.

Langley, R., & Levy, R. C. (1977). *Wife beating: The silent crisis.* New York: Pocket Books.

Leighton, B. (1989). *Spousal Abuse in Metropolitan Toronto: Research Report on the Response of the Criminal Justice System.* Ottawa: Solicitor General of Canada.

MacLeod, L. (1987). *Battered but not beaten . . . Preventing wife battering in Canada.* Ottawa: Canadian Advisory Council on the Status of Women.

Martin, D. (1978). Battered women: Society's problem. In J. R. Chapman & M. Gates (Eds.), *The victimization of women* (pp. 111-141). Beverly Hills, CA: Sage.

Micklow, P. L. (1988). Domestic abuse: The pariah of the legal system. In V. B. Van Hasselt, R. L. Morrison, A. S. Bellack, & M. Hersen (Eds.), *Handbook of family violence* (pp. 407-433). New York: Plenum.

Paterson, E. J. (1979). How the legal system responds to battered women. In D. M. Moore (Ed.), *Battered women* (pp. 79-99). Beverly Hills, CA: Sage.

Pulling, N. (1991, November 19). Wife assault called "epidemic" among S. Asians. *Globe and Mail,* p. A8.

Roberts, A. R. (1984). Police intervention. In A. R. Roberts (Ed.), *Battered women and their families: Intervention strategies and treatment programs* (pp. 116-128). New York: Spring.

Roberts, D. (1992, January 2). Silent alarm guards women. *Globe and Mail,* p. A4.

Sherman, L. W., & Berk, R. A. (1984). The specific deterrent effects of arrest for domestic assault. *American Sociological Review, 49,* 261-272.

Sherman, L. W., Schmidt, J. D., Rogan, D. P., Gartin, P. R., Cohen, E. G., Collins, D. J., & Bacich, A. R. (1991). From initial deterrence to longterm escalation: Short custody arrest for poverty ghetto domestic violence. *Criminology, 29*(4), 821-850.

Smyth, M. (1988, March 22). Shooting verdict upsets Oxford crown. *London Free Press,* p. B1.

Soler, E. (1987). Domestic violence is a crime: A case study—San Francisco Family Violence Project. In D. J. Sonkin (Ed.), *Domestic violence on trial: Psychological and legal dimensions of family violence* (pp. 21-35). New York: Springer.

Spero, M., Doxtator, J., & George, A. (1991). *Native women's needs assessment survey.* London, Ontario: Atenlos.

Staples, D., & Owens, G. (1992, January 24). Woman evicted after standoff between police, boyfriend. *Edmonton Journal,* p. B1.

Stith, S. (1990). Police response to domestic violence: The influence of individual and familial factors. *Violence and Victims, 5*(1), 37-49.

Straus, M. A. (1979). Measuring intrafamily conflict and violence: The Conflict Tactics (CT) scales. *Journal of Marriage and the Family, 41,* 75-88.

Straus, M. A., Gelles, R. J., & Steinmetz, S. K. (1980). *Behind closed doors: Violence in the American family.* Garden City, NY: Anchor.

Williamson, S., & Meredith, C. (1990). *Study to review and analyze R.C.M.P. data on spousal assault from 1985 to 1988.* Ottawa: Solicitor General of Canada.

5

Irreconcilable Differences

Battered Women, Police, and the Law

KATHLEEN J. FERRARO

LUCILLE POPE

The policies of the criminal justice system regarding "domestic violence" have been in the process of reformulation for the past 15 years. The literature describing and examining this process has focused primarily on the effectiveness of interventions. In this chapter, we explore the cultural contexts in which this process is occurring. Specifically, we adopt a critical feminist analysis of law, law enforcement, and the experiences of heterosexual* battered women.** Central to this analysis is the concept of power. We argue that in the contemporary United States, law and law enforcement are elements of a culture of power founded on political liberalism. The content of this culture includes assumptions about universal desires and the appropriate role of the state, which we discuss. When law enforcement is placed in this cultural context, the contradictions between the needs

School of Justice Studies, Arizona State University, Tempe, Arizona, 85287-0403.

*AUTHORS' NOTE: Homophobic legal culture raises questions beyond the scope of this chapter.

**EDITOR'S NOTE: The terms *battering, battered,* and *batterer* are used in this chapter to refer to physical and nonphysical forms of abuse.

of battered women and the orientation of the law become apparent. Our purpose in this chapter is to describe the irreconcilable differences between the cultures of power and of relationships. We draw on an empirical investigation of police responses to battering as an example of the problems inherent in policing battering.

We begin with a brief history of the recent trend toward the criminalization of battering. We then describe the law as a manifestation of the culture of power. The culture of power is then contrasted with relational culture, the context in which battered women make decisions. We next describe the assumptions that police (and all law enforcement officers), as agents of the culture of power, bring to battering situations. These assumptions are contrasted with the lives of battered women and the contingencies that inform their responses to violence. Ferraro's participant observation and interview study of the police is then described to illustrate the cultures discussed earlier. Our conclusion emphasizes that empowering battered women involves recognizing the diversity of needs and the competence of women to identify the most appropriate strategies for their survival. We do not adopt a pro or con stance on mandatory arrest. We attempt to direct attention to the larger context in which policing occurs, rather than focusing on arrest decisions. Our position is that abstracting criminal sanctions from the current social and political context in which they exist detracts from the overall empowerment of women.

Criminalization of Battering

In 1984, the U.S. Attorney General's Task Force on Family Violence recommended that family violence be treated as "a criminal activity" (Hart et al., 1984, p. 10). This recommendation drew on testimony from social science experts, medical and social service professionals, battered women's advocates, and battered women. In the array of data presented, the Minneapolis domestic violence experiment, funded by the National Institute of Justice (NIJ), was highlighted. The Minneapolis study, conducted by Sherman and Berk (1984), employed an experimental model to examine the deterrent effects of arrest, separation, and mediation in the police response to wife battering. Their findings suggested that arrest was significantly superior in deterring future violence relative to the other two interventions (Sherman & Berk, 1984).

These data not only influenced the U.S. Attorney General's Task Force, but also were widely publicized in the popular and police press. Subsequently, the Minneapolis experiment was employed by policy-makers and activists to support legislative and policy changes in policing (Meeker & Binder, 1990; Sherman & Cohn, 1989). Research, lawsuits, and grass roots activism to reduce or eliminate police discretion in responding to domestic violence have been successful in altering state laws and department policies. As of 1987, 30 states had altered their laws to allow misdemeanor arrests based on probable cause. Six states statutorily mandate arrest for domestic violence assaults, and seven mandate arrest for violation of restraining orders (Woods, 1987). Many cities also adopted presumptive or mandatory arrest policies. In 1985, a survey of 140 cities with populations over 100,000 showed that 44 had policies encouraging arrest as the preferred option in domestic violence cases (Crime Control Institute, 1986). The embrace of mandatory and presumptive arrest policies reflects a conviction that discretionary policies result in failure to protect the victim and thus essentially condone male violence.

To test the generalizability of the Minneapolis findings, the NIJ funded six replication studies across the United States. The two replications published in journal form to date have not demonstrated that arrest is significantly more effective than other types of police intervention in deterring future violence (Dunford, Huizinga, & Elliott, 1990; Hirschel, Hutchison, & Dean, 1992). Sherman's analysis of a specific type of offender, inner-city black men, found a short-term deterrent effect for short-term custody, together with long-term criminogenic effects (Sherman, Schmidt, & Rogan, 1991). Long-term custody produced no significant effects. These recent studies suggest the complexity of evaluating police responses to battering. There is no simple answer to the questions revolving around effective protection for battered women.

Although there have been tremendous shifts, reforms, and expansions in domestic violence laws during the last 15 years, there has also been resistance by law enforcement and frustration on the part of battered women and domestic violence service providers (Hanmer, Radford, & Stanko, 1989). We propose that the focus on police response has failed to account fully for the contextual realities of both policing and battering, and the underlying irreconcilable differences between battered women and the law. This absence occludes the complex interconnections among police response, lawyers, child support, courts, family members, child protective services, women, men, and children and the layers of power they represent. The analytical and policy effect of the focus on police response is the disregard of the complex power relations of battering and the promotion of a "cure" that brackets sexism, racism, homophobia, and poverty. An incident of battering has been reduced to an individual pathology for which swift and sure criminal justice sanctions are the remedy.

At the concrete, everyday level of survival, many women require police assistance. For too many women, there is none. When police intervention fails, the larger societal implications are overlooked, attention returning instead to the behavior of police. We argue that the irreconcilable differences in cultural contexts of policing and battering cannot be separated from an analysis of interventions. By cultural context, we mean the everyday behaviors, expectations, and roles, as well as historical and political constructions, of "police" and of "wives." The cultures represented by police and by battered women are necessary domains of inquiry to the development of the most effective strategies to inhibit male violence.

The Law and
The Culture of Power

The culture of power is entrenched in the economic, political, religious, and legal institutions of U.S. society. Although the United States is diverse in cultural characteristics, the values of the culture of power are imposed on all groups, sometimes violently. For example, the emphasis on community and extended family in Pueblo Indian cultures has been attenuated by colonization, genocide, removal of children to boarding schools, and military service of young men. Western European ideology of the privacy of the family and the traditional rights of husbands over other family members remains embedded in the belief systems of policymakers and implementors (Allen, 1986; Red Horse, 1980). The state and national policy responses to battering cannot be separated from the institutional culture in which they exist.

Feminist legal scholars, such as Cain (1991), MacKinnon (1983), Minow (1990), and Scales (1986), critique traditional androcentric jurisprudence for the exclusions created by adherence to liberal philosophy. West (1988) understands traditional liberal jurisprudence as rooted in masculine views of human nature that place individual autonomy first, prior to relationships and "cooperative arrangements with others" (p. 2). Entrenched in an understanding of individuals separate from others, as "physically boundaried" (p. 1), liberal juris-prudence values separation and therefore freedom from others. Anni-hilation is an ever-present source of harm in the struggle for power over scarce resources: "Thus, according to liberal legalism, the subjec-tive experience of physical separation from the other determines both what we value (autonomy) and what we fear (annihilation)" (p. 8).

This philosophical underpinning represents the worldview of a particular group of powerful men and distorts the experiences of many other people. It is especially unrepresentative of the lives of people who give birth, suckle and care for children, and assume responsibility for those outside the competitive marketplace: the sick, the physically or mentally disadvantaged, and the elderly. That is, it is unrepresenta-tive of the life of many women (Jaggar, 1983, p. 45). The centrality of attachment to others in the lives of those women is accompanied by alternative values and fears. For those immersed in a relational culture, the ability to connect, nurture, and maintain intimacy is highly valued. Threats to relationships and the possibility of alienation are feared and guarded against (Gilligan, 1982).

The male bias of U.S. jurisprudence produces a legal structure contradictory to women's needs. Androcentric jurisprudence that values autonomy and fears annihilation collides with the values of women who seek relationship and fear separation. The contradictions can be demonstrated in the continuing conflict between the legal system and battered women seeking orders of protection (OP) (cf. Ford & Regoli, this volume). Judges, committed to traditional liberal legal theory, view the breach of individual rights to due process as justified only by the threat of annihilation and remedied by separation. For some battered women, fearing both invasion and loss of connec-tion, the OP may be seen as a mechanism with the potential to remove the violence by her partner. She may perceive the OP as a technique for ensuring a violence-free marriage, continuing to live with her violent partner and holding the OP as a "guarantee" of protection should he violate his promises that "It will never happen again." For judges, however, a woman's failure to separate from the relationship once an OP is granted is a demonstration of her failure to respect the court and instigation to renewed battering. The disjunction between women's and legal actors' perceptions leads to issuance of mutual OPs, mutual arrests, failure of police to respond to OP violations, denial of subsequent orders, and contempt of court charges against women, all of which can jeopardize women's future safety (see Chadhuri & Daly, 1992).

Although decisions specifically supporting husbands' rights to "moderate chastisement" of wives no longer exist, the de facto acceptance of battering lingers. The examination of the extent of bias in courts by gender bias task forces in 27 states has uncovered stereotyping, devaluation, and "myths and misconceptions about the social and economic realities of women and men's lives" (Schafran, 1989, p. 239). In a study of casebooks to determine how law schools teach about violence against women, the Sex Bias in the Teaching of Criminal Law researchers found that of the "seven most widely used criminal law casebooks . . . only one book even mentioned spousal abuse" (Schafran, 1989, p. 272). The bias against women inherent in U.S. jurisprudence and legal actions militates against the easy solution of mandating alternative police responses.

The Culture of Power and Relational Culture

Two cultures come clashing together when police respond to battering. One is the culture of power, in which decisions are based on rational choice and maximization of profit or benefits. In this culture, manifest in part through the legal system, it is possible to know "the facts" and to determine probable cause, harm, fault, and a calculus of penalties. If a "crime" has been committed, the offender should be processed according to the rules, including the hearing of reliable testimony by victim-witnesses. If there is less than a reasonable doubt of guilt, sanctions equivalent to the degree of harm imposed should be meted out. Rational choice deterrence theory posits that men who

batter will ponder the chance of punitive consequences before inflict-
ing violence on wives or lovers (see Carmody & Williams, 1987, for
empirical refutation of this assumption). This is a culture of clear-cut
boundaries: good/bad; harm/no harm; guilt/innocence.

The "other" culture is relational. We do not mean to suggest that all
battered women are the same or respond to violence in the same ways.
There are, however, features of being physically assaulted by one's
intimate partner that can be generalized (see Browne, 1989; R. E.
Dobash & R. Dobash, 1979, 1992; Ferraro & Johnson, 1983; Kelly,
1988; Russell, 1990; Stanko, 1985; Yllö & Bograd, 1989). The culture
of women abused by their partner is filled with ambiguity, confusion,
and fear. The man who beats, terrorizes, and tortures a woman also
threatens to take her children away, to kill her if she tells the truth, to
kill anyone who helps her, and to institutionalize or abandon her and
her children.

For many women, the relationship and family unit are important.
Women who are battered often say they love their partner. The
meanings of "love" in relationships of terror are not clear and make up
part of the confusion women feel. Supported by romantic ideology,
they share a cultural image of relationships as havens of shared love
and commitment. Occasionally, their abusive partner fulfills some
aspect of the image, adding to the women's hope. Family members
and social service providers kindle this hope, in part to fend off the
intrusion of a dependent woman and her children. In the culture of
relations, decisions are not based on "facts" and a calculation of the
most propitious outcome for the woman. They are more compromises
than decisions—strategies for survival in a confusing, dangerous, unpredictable situation. It is a culture in which boundaries are shifting
and hazy.

In the criminal justice system, it has been common to overlay the
culture of power on strategies for helping women. It is assumed that
this culture provides the resources required for escaping from violent
situations, for redistributing power to the disenfranchised. Too often,
however, the imposition of the culture of power upon women's
problems has not empowered women, but has crushed their self-
determination (see Davis, 1983; Musheno & Seeley, 1986). In an
Omaha study of police response to domestic violence, of 97 victims
whose assailants were arrested, 60% did not want the arrest, 65%

reported that their assailant blamed them for the arrest, and 21% were threatened by the assailant because of the arrest (Dunford et al., 1990). There is an incongruity between the culture of power and relational culture.

The culture of power is not a monolithic institution, but has many levels and is dispersed among agents, institutions, language, and the media (Dreyfus & Rabinow, 1983; Foucault, 1980). Individuals representing state power, such as police, social workers, physicians, and media "experts," communicate the perspective of the culture of power. The desirability of order, profit, rational choice, and a domestic realm of privacy, drawn from liberal theory, defines the parameters of acceptable strategies within this culture for ending violence. We propose that criminal justice intervention in battering is bounded by these assumptions. The realities of living with violence, chaos, and fear in battering relationships challenge these assumptions and exceed the limited responses developed from them.

The Police as Agents
of the Culture of Power

The police, as agents of the law, are bound by certain technical rules and occupational ideals. Police as participants in a patriarchal culture are also bound by personal values, attitudes, and images of marriage. Their daily encounters with battered women provide constant evidence of the contradictions between the law, the police, and battered women.

The police are drawn most often from the same social class as those over whom they are mandated to exercise legal control. They do not unilaterally create the culture of power, but are in dynamic relation to it, and earn their living by enforcing it. There are two distinct yet interconnected ways in which the culture of power influences the police response to battering: through the establishment of technical legal and ideological boundaries and through the reinforcement of the dominant cultural perspective.

First, the police culture reflects the principles of the legal culture. The images of what police are supposed to be doing, who they are protecting from what, and the guidelines for their actions are founded on liberal jurisprudence. The essence of liberal jurisprudence rests in maximizing autonomy and profit while minimizing intervention. The police guard against unlawful intrusion into the maximizing efforts of individuals, focusing on the protection of private property, crime fighting, and maintenance of order (Wilson, 1968).

There are clear boundaries in the statutes that form the basis of police activities, that is, the laws they are empowered to enforce (Littrell, 1979). Standards of evidence, rules of probable cause, jurisdictional boundaries, and laws about search and seizure have been developed through legal decisions dependent on liberal, androcentric jurisprudence. These rules represent efforts to protect the civil rights of individuals against intrusion by the law. They do not reflect the difficulty of women enmeshed in a relational culture or provide officers with authority to alter rules to fit the situation. For example, the first domestic violence laws expanding police powers to arrest were limited to situations involving legally married couples. Officers basing arrest on the probable cause standard could not arbitrarily extend this protection to unmarried cohabitants, even if all other circumstances were identical to a domestic violence assault against a married woman. Of course, officers do employ discretion and discrimination in carrying out their mandate. These choices are generally consistent with the existing hierarchy of power relationships, for example, brutality toward minority group members (see Black, 1976). As we will explore below, the formal rule of law influences police officers' perceptions of the legitimacy of calls by battered women and serves as a resource for conceptualizing the appropriate response.

The second major way in which liberal jurisprudence informs police decision making is in the reinforcement of the acceptance of a particular worldview. This view, as mentioned above, includes clear boundaries between self and other, and between good choices and bad choices. With regard to police work, these boundaries suggest that "normal" citizens do not desire or participate in burglaries of their homes, thefts of their cars, or assaults on their person. Thus, there is an unproblematic assumption of dichotomies between victim and offender, good guys and bad guys, deviant and normal citizens. Police reflect this view in their characterizations of the communities they serve, as they marginalize people living on skid row, in housing projects, or patronizing gay bars or areas of street prostitution. These people are conceptualized by police as a different category of human beings deserving of a different response (Bittner, 1967; Ferraro, 1989a, 1989b; Van Maanen, 1978). They are "others," who constitute the "deviant" because they live outside the boundaries circumscribed by the ideology of rational, self-interested market maximizers or because they threaten such maximizers with theft and corruption. This category is external to the dominant group of law-abiding citizens perceived to constitute the "normal."

The boundaries separating normal and deviant citizens help officers deal with constant encounters with individuals who fail to meet the standards of humanness enmeshed in the ideology of the culture of power. In daily interactions with individuals whose appearance, demeanor, and surroundings contradict the dominant definitions of "normality," police require some mechanism for managing the cognitive dissonance created by the incoherence between the rational model of "man" on which the law is premised and the raw facts of life. Creating a separate category of "others" allows officers to adhere to the ideology of the law and to implement it, even as they face repeated contradictions.

From this perspective, battered women represent individuals who stray from the model of normalcy. They live with men who beat them and their children, become angry at police for trying to help them, and retract accusations of violence after arrests have been made. From the perspective of the culture of power, such actions are irrational and deviant. Women who enact them are, therefore, indistinguishable from their assailants in terms of culpability (see Hilton, this volume, for a review of police attitudes toward victim responsibility). Police stereotypes of battered women are related to their assumptions of "rational" human action and deserving victims. These assumptions are embedded in the law, rules, and procedures that flow from them.

Battered Women and Relational Culture

Violence is an aspect of all women's lives (Stanko, 1990). In that sense, battered women are no different from all other women, although each woman's experience with violence is unique. Yet, repeated physical and emotional abuse by one's husband or lover produces similar emotional reactions in women, including fear, anxiety, depression, and confusion (Blackman, 1989; Kelly, 1988; Pagelow, 1984; Walker, 1979, 1984). In using the language "relational culture," we are not suggesting that all women are inherently more warm, nurturing, and caring than all men. Rather, we use this term to represent the complexity of relationships and concerns that influence battered women.

Battered women are differentiated from most crime victims by their relationship with their assailant. Not only is there a direct emotional bond between the woman and her husband or lover, but they also are tied in the myriad connections created and enforced in a patriarchy in which heterosexual monogamy is compulsory (Rich, 1980). Although the police response to woman battering is influenced by the ideologies of liberal jurisprudence and rational choice, women's responses are located within complex experiential and relational knowledge, as well as the external ideology of romance.

The experience of battering does not occur in isolation from other life circumstances. Some battered women have emotional, social, and economic resources that support escape from violence. Other women do not have access to such resources or face batterers whose persistence makes escape efforts extremely arduous and dangerous. Some women face extraordinary restraints that legally bind them to an abuser, such as court-mandated joint custody and visitation of children, immigration status, or shared financial liabilities.

Responding to physical violence entails a wide repertoire of strategies of survival, some of which are invisible to outsiders. Women approach trusted insiders and external authority figures for assistance in defining experiences, developing strategies for change, providing tangible resources, and intervening in the abuse. Survival strategies involve scrutinizing an array of individuals and institutions for effectiveness. Within the boundaries of her relationship, the woman must evaluate each resource as making a positive or negative contribution to the safety of herself and her children. The demands of maintaining a delicate balance of outside interference add to the complexity of calculating safety. Any resource that upsets that balance threatens her survival.

From this perspective, the police are only one potential resource that must be evaluated within the more complex web of resources making up the larger picture of assistance. Whether the assistance the police offer will prove helpful must be weighed and measured in the shifting and sometimes hazy context of not only the extent of the violence but also the current status of the relationship and the short- and long-term strategies for its maintenance or dissolution. To the extent that any resource, including the police, fails to provide for ultimate safety concerns, it may be abandoned by the woman. The identification and utilization of a given resource can only be framed by the woman's assessment of her needs, a frame that is at once unique and similar to the frames of other women.

The expectations each woman has of helping resources will vary depending on the particular circumstances of the relationship. When women call upon the police they overlay their relational culture, within which they have vast, changeable needs, upon agents of the culture of power operating within limited boundaries with circum-scribed responses. Women's needs are bounded by the culture of relationship; the police response is bounded by the culture of power.

The ideology of romantic love is one of the bulwarks of women's enmeshment in relationships with men who batter. Romantic love is highly regarded in contemporary North American culture, across race and class lines. The culture is saturated with visual, dramatic, auditory, and folkloric imagery of romance, from billboards along the freeway to Disney movies to popular music. It is not unusual or surprising in any way that a woman would hope to establish a romantic relationship with a man. In fact, it is considered quite deviant if she does not. The establishment of romantic relationships is accompanied by high ex-pectations and hopes for fulfillment. When marriage occurs, the state, and state-sanctioned religion, intervene to ensure that both parties take their obligation to matrimony seriously. Even in the case of no-fault divorce, the dissolution of marriage is much slower, more expensive, and more legally complicated than its creation. Informal social control is very clear and strong: Divorce represents failure and should be avoided unless all possible remedies have been exhausted, especially if children are involved.

Most women's first response when hit by a partner is not to leave immediately, file for divorce, and never look back. Rather, a woman will attempt to understand why it happened and how *she* can prevent it from reoccurring. Most women become involved in a process of adaptation and rationalizations, conceptualizing men's violence as a problem they have to deal with and control (Ferraro, 1983; Ferraro & Johnson, 1983). Relational culture is characterized by process and compromise rather than single-point decision making about the best alternatives.

A continuum of adaptations to male violence exists, with initial denial moving to hopes for change and finally to rejection of the relationship (Ferraro, 1983; Ferraro & Johnson, 1983). Women's feelings about violence are neither static nor unidimensional, but instead alternate between levels of rejection of and accommodation to the abuser. The types of help sought and desired vary depending on women's location in the continuum of adaption and on prior help-seeking efforts (Bowker, 1982; R. E. Dobash & R. Dobash, 1979). At any given point of help seeking, women may be broadly grouped as falling into three categories of adaptation: those who have decided to end the relationship; those who still hope for improvement in the relationship; and those who are suicidal, homicidal, or dependent on drugs for alleviation of suffering (Caputo, 1988). Caputo found that a majority of battered women who had called the police for help hoped that the relationship would change (87%). About half of the women said they loved their husband, and 60% said they "didn't know what to do" (p. 503). For a large group of women, help seeking reflects a desire to end the violence, but not necessarily the relationship. These women will have different needs and expectations of police from women who have decided that the violence will not end and desire to terminate the relationship. Variations in women's needs suggest the importance of a police response that is sensitive to the subtleties and complexities of a particular situation and to *women's* evaluations of their needs.

In many cases, a woman calling the police for help with a battering partner is not declaring an end to the relationship. She is asking for help in controlling his violence. At the point of prosecution, many women ask the courts for "help" for their abuser, rather than imprisonment (Ferraro & Boychuk, 1992). Even women who have already ended their relationship and need assistance dealing with the violence that follows that decision may be facing a more complex set of circumstances than a woman assaulted by a stranger. They may know from past experience, for example, that arrest will not end the harassment and abuse, and fear an escalation if they assist in prosecution.

The inability of women to fit into police categories and the common, but *not universal,* feelings of ambivalence toward arrest place battered women at odds with the police. The misfit between battered women's needs and experiences and those of the police results in considerable frustration and ineffectiveness in policing battering. So far in this chapter, we have presented a theoretical account of the cultures of power and relationships. The research that follows serves to illustrate these cultures and how they operate on an everyday level. This study of the adoption of a presumptive arrest policy brings out the complexity of implementing such a policy. The considerations of police officers and battered women's perception of the effectiveness of police intervention provide insight into the clash between the culture of power and relational culture.

Imposition of the Culture of Power: Examination of a Presumptive Arrest Policy

Setting

As part of the national shift toward enhancing the chances for arrests for domestic violence, the Arizona state legislature passed a domestic violence bill in 1980. This legislation prohibited police from citing and releasing domestic violence offenders, expanded police officers' ability to arrest on the basis of probable cause, required officers to provide procedural and service information to victims, and allowed for orders of protection to be obtained independent of a divorce action. By May 1984, the Phoenix, Arizona, Police Department had adopted a presumptive arrest policy that stated: "Officers should arrest domestic violence violators even if the victim does not desire prosecution. When probable cause exists, an arrest should be made even if a misdemeanor offense did not occur in the officer's presence" (Ortega, 1984, p. 1).

Method

To examine the effect of this policy, Ferraro conducted a participant observation study of the police (see Ferraro, 1989a; 1989b). Observations of 44 ten-hour shifts in three precincts were conducted on weekend nights. Observers included one female professor, two male professors, and three female graduate students. The fieldwork began 3 weeks after initiation of the presumptive arrest policy and ended 1 year later.

For purposes of the study, battering was defined as actual or threatened physical violence by one adult against another adult with whom s/he currently or previously had shared an intimate relationship. This definition was more expansive than the domestic violence statute, which was limited to legally or formerly legally married couples. Other criminal statutes, however, were applicable to all incidents coded as "family fights." We chose a more inclusive definition to allow exploration of the range of police responses to cases coded "family fights." Our primary interest was in the application of a presumptive arrest policy in the field to actual cases of domestic violence.

The field notes of 440 hours of field observations were culled for instances of family fights, which were coded for the participants, type of incident, and intervention. After determining these basic data, the notes were analyzed and basic themes regarding police perceptions and actions were extracted. In examining police actions, we attempted to determine whether cases met the legal criteria for arrest, particularly domestic violence arrest, under the new policy.

Results and Discussion

During the researchers' observations, police responded to 69 family fight calls, 49 of which fit our definition of woman battering. Only nine (18%) of these cases resulted in arrest, despite the presumptive arrest policy. All but one of the arrests involved weapons or injury to someone other than a woman.

We discovered that legal criteria were not the only nor the most salient considerations in officers' decision making. Three contextual considerations also emerged. The most prevalent and influential consideration was the background ideological assumptions that police brought to "family fights." Additionally, officers were influenced by the context of daily practical considerations and the politics of police work. These contextual considerations did not operate in isolation, but were intersecting, sometimes dissonant, influences on the officers and their decisions.

It is through exploring these four considerations in police decision making (legal, ideological, practical, political) that we can understand how the irreconcilable differences described above influence the police and battered women. The impact of the differences between the culture of power and the culture of relations can be seen clearly at the point of policy implementation, in the everyday interactions on the street. Each of these considerations and the circumstances in which they were encountered will be described briefly (see Ferraro, 1989a for complete discussion).

Legal Considerations

The nature of police work requires discretionary evaluation of legal criteria. Officers collect information at a crime scene to determine whether an offense has been committed, and if there is probable cause for arrest (Brown, 1981; Littrell, 1979). There are a variety of statutory offenses into which a domestic violence disturbance can be categorized, ranging from disturbing the peace to homicide. For each offense, certain elements must be present for the behavior to fit the legal categorization. In Arizona, for misdemeanor assault, there must be evidence of a physical assault or attempt of an assault, including injuries, weapons, or witnesses. For an officer to make an arrest for misdemeanor assaults against unmarried individuals, the crime must be witnessed.

Domestic violence statutes in Arizona and other states permit arrest on the basis of probable cause, including the above evidence. When the presumptive arrest policy was first adopted in Phoenix, however, domestic violence occurring between cohabiting, unmarried couples was not covered by the statute. Cohabitation was still a crime, so to provide protection to such individuals would support illegal activity. Of the 49 cases of battering observed, 15 involved cohabitants. Three of these, all involving weapons (ball bats and a knife) and injury, resulted in arrests. The identical circumstances between an unmarried couple and a married couple were interpreted differently due to the legal exclusion of cohabitants from the domestic violence statute. The cases where arrests were made involved high levels of violence, which categorized the incident as a felony-level assault, enabling arrest on the basis of probable cause regardless of the couple's relationship. The issue of cohabitation, then, was one legal factor impinging on the construction of probable cause arrest.

At the same time, legal considerations are not immutable forces with which officers must comply, but are resources that can be adapted (Littrell, 1979). For example, the use of citizen's arrest is an option officers can employ when they are unsure of the strength of evidence. If a woman wants an arrest for an assault that only marginally conforms to the legal elements of assault, an officer may assist her in making a citizen's arrest. This legal option was employed in one case of assault by a man against his cohabiting partner, where the assault consisted of spitting. The officer explicitly informed the observer that the use of citizen's arrest would ensure the case would go forward despite the minor nature of the assault. Although this option was available and appropriate, it was not employed on other occasions where the lack of legal marital status was the only barrier to arrest for a misdemeanor assault. Thus the law does impose constraints on decision making, but those constraints are still interpreted in light of other considerations that are more salient to the creation of meaning.

Ideological Considerations

Probably the most influential considerations in police decision making are the background beliefs about battered women and family fights that police bring to specific incidents. These include class, race, and sex stereotypes as well as images of danger and safety. In terms of class, race, and sex, the distinction between normal and deviant citizens described above came into play at domestic disturbances observed in this study. Women from low-income neighborhoods, especially those who did not speak English or were members of racial minorities, were likely to be viewed as enmeshed in a culture of violence. In this context, a specific violent event was understood to be part of a larger pattern of degradation beyond the scope of police intervention. Unless a woman was in the throes of a violent physical assault, such incidents were usually categorized as noncrime. Women were told to call if anything else happened. Even though probable cause already existed, arrests were not made.

The response to domestic violence in the low-income areas reflects the notion that individuals there have fewer rights to privacy and to civil courtesy than middle-class suburban people (Bittner, 1990). In our observations, for example, a woman who spoke only Spanish and lived in a very crowded, poorly maintained housing project was escorted by police to a neighbor's house at 2 a.m., although she wanted her husband arrested. The neighbor was asked to house her and her three small children for the night, while the inebriated, violent husband was left in their house two doors away. It is unimaginable that a similar strategy would be employed in an upper-class neighborhood, where the privacy of each home is sacrosanct.

Anglo-Americans living in the housing projects are not considered part of the "normal" white population, but are grouped with those external to the dominant culture. A young Anglo woman living in the projects was denied any redress although she displayed burn marks around her neck produced by her husband's choke hold. She was informed that no real danger existed and told to call if there was any further trouble. It is not possible to assess whether the lack of responsiveness displayed toward this woman is the result of her class, sex, or status as a battered woman. There were no observations of middle- or upper-income women for comparative purposes. It is possible that any battered woman would fall outside the boundaries of police definitions of "normality."

Officer comments during ride-alongs reflected racist attitudes toward Hispanics, African Americans, and American Indians that then influenced their perceptions of violence. One Anglo male officer expressed the belief that Mexicans were taking over Phoenix, noting that certain parts of Phoenix "look just like old Mexico." Driving by a bar frequented mostly by American Indians, the same officer said, "Yah ta hey! Come down from the reservation to get some firewater. Yeah, going to get a little firewater," and told several stories about drunken Indians, suggesting they were inferior to non-Indians.

Sexist attitudes are expressed in views of battered women as "stupid." They are stupid for "getting themselves into" violent situations and stupid for staying. One officer said that he always asked women why they stayed with abusers. He said one woman told him, "I guess I'm just stupid," and he replied, "I guess you are." He had no sympathy for her because her child was also being abused.

Stith's (1990) analysis of police attitudes toward battered women found that the more traditional their sex-role beliefs and the more conflict officers experienced in their own marriage, the more hostile they were toward battered women. In our study, several officers expressed beliefs that a man's home is his castle where he should be able to control the actions of his wife and children. One officer acknowledged (without remorse) hitting his wife, and another suggested it was better to hit your wife than to destroy your property when angry. Men who destroyed their own property during a battering event were viewed as foolish, but not criminal. In two cases, this property was the wife's car, her only means of escape.

For these officers, the presumptive arrest policy represents a departure from their value system viewing wife battering as a private male prerogative. Evaluations of blame, harm, and danger, which constitute the basis for arrest, are filtered through this value system. The presumption of arrest or probable cause does not override this process.

As Davis (1983) argued, the primary focus of police intervention into domestic violence is the restoration of a "semblance of order." Such a focus does not usually address the private terror experienced by a woman who is threatened by her partner. If the violence has subsided and is no longer visible to outsiders, including the police, officers perceive the situation as "under control." Women who have left the house or who have been left alone by the assailant are perceived as safe by officers. The Anglo woman with burn marks on her neck was told that approaching her abuser would only stir up trouble and that "It will just get him all riled up, and the baby's sleeping. Everything's OK right now."

The focus on "right now" is contrary to women's continuing experiences with violence. The women in our study reported recent use of guns and knives, break-ins, threats, and batterings by their partner, but officers bracketed these incidents as irrelevant to the current search for probable cause. Officers focused on danger and evidence at the specific moment in time and made no attempt to investigate the existence of prior reports. Women were responding to complex biographics of abuse and therefore perceived a higher level of danger. The culture of power, the law, translates battering into an offense that is evaluated in isolation from history and relationships. The relational culture experiences battering as a long-term, escalating process. Even when women attempt to translate their experiences into the language of law by describing prior police contacts, incidents with weapons, and OPs, officers reject information external to the specific incident. The different foci of women and police create disparity in the evaluation of level of danger. As long as a "semblance of order" is restored, police see no need for further action.

Failure to perceive further danger also results in police failure to provide information about social services or legal resources. Information about emergency shelters, counseling, legal aid, and orders of protection was only provided twice without the prompting of the researcher. Several times the researcher acted as a conduit between the officer and the woman seeking resources or referrals. The emphasis on restoring order for the moment leaves battered women and their children in same danger zone after the officer leaves the scene; often, women are left with no phone, car, money, or possibility of police intervention.

The Family Stress Team was available 24 hours a day specifically for counseling battered women. Officers who were questioned about the team said that it did good work and was a valuable resource. Of the 69 cases observed, however, officers made calls to the Family Stress Team only four times, and two of these calls were suggested by the researcher as the officer walked away from the scene. Officers did not see the need for crisis intervention if the couple was separated by arrest or by one person's absence from the home.

Another ideological influence on police perceptions is the belief that battered women are poor witnesses. Police believe that most battered women will not follow through with prosecution and will deny the violence to prosecutors and judges (cf. Ford & Regoli, this volume). Part of the intention of requiring police to arrest by law is to remove the onus of pressing charges from the woman, who is often intimidated by her partner. Theoretically, it is not up to the woman whether she wants to press charges, as the crime is against the state. A crime with a victim who denies its occurrence, however, is difficult to prosecute, especially if there are no visible injuries as a result of the assault. As discussed above, women interact with the criminal justice system at various points in their relationship. Many are not ready to end the relationship and perceive full prosecution as an unacceptable threat to reunification. The range of concerns women face in determining the feasibility of prosecuting assailants is not accessible to police decision makers.

Some officers in our study did express sympathy with women's predicaments, but remained frustrated over energy expended on arrests that resulted in release due to women's decision to drop charges. It is interesting, however, that the proportion of cases dropped from prosecution because of the inadequacy of police reports in documenting evidence (10%) is nearly as great as the proportion dropped because of victim-witness reluctance or refusal to prosecute (13%) (Ferraro & Boychuk, 1992). Police can place blame for dropped cases on battered women and thereby deflect responsibility for failing to handle cases in a manner that would enhance the chances of prosecution.

Officers also tend to rely on the stereotype of the reluctant witness as a model of prediction, reflected in statements such as, "She's mad tonight, but tomorrow they'll be back together." Presumptive arrest is inconsistent with this prediction, leading officers to question the usefulness of arrest. Street-level experience, however, does not reflect knowledge about what happens to women when men are *not* arrested. The continuing danger to women in battering relationships is overshadowed by officers' "street knowledge" of typical patterns of reconciliation.

Practical Considerations

Ideological considerations are linked to considerations of available resources and the practical circumstances facing officers. One major issue overlooked by the presumptive arrest policy is the departure of batterers from the scene when police are called. In 40% of the cases observed, no man was on the scene to be arrested. In such cases, the appropriate procedure is to write a report that can be followed up the next day or to search for the man. The latter option was never followed. It was not always possible to determine whether reports were written by officers, as several cars were called to the same scene. In those cases where the officer being observed was the primary responding officer, observers determined that reports were not written in the majority of cases.

Another practical problem discussed by officers is the issue of "mutual combat." As Berk, Berk, Loseke, & Rauma (1981) and Saunders (1988) have pointed out, "mutual combat" almost always consists of an aggressive male and a defensive female. Women's violence, when it occurs, is an attempt at self-protection. In part because of the decontextualized nature of police intervention, officers who find two violent people at a domestic disturbance find determination of fault problematic. In Washington state, when mandatory arrest was introduced, large numbers of mutual arrests were made on the grounds that officers could not determine who "started it." In response, Washington instituted a "primary aggressor" clause, which requires police to arrest the initiator and the most violent partner (Crane, 1987). In our study, however, the presence of two violent persons translated into no official action, as officers believed it was not possible to build a case when the testimony of either party would be self-incriminatory. This attitude extended to cases where the only "violence" apparent on the part of the woman was yelling and being under the influence of alcohol. The ideological conception of "real danger" structured the perceived practical problems of "mutual combat" in this study.

Time was another consideration that influenced officers' behavior. It takes at least an hour to process an arrest. When officers were nearing the end of their shift, particularly if that shift ended at 4:30 a.m., they were less inclined to initiate lengthy procedures. More important, officers viewed domestic calls as an investment of time that infringed on other police work. Time limits were invoked as rationales for refusing to transport women or to wait and search for an assailant. One officer recounted a situation in which she had been unable to respond to an armed robbery call because she was transporting a woman to a shelter. Such accounts underscore the hierarchy of importance attached to different crimes. Woman battering is low on the hierarchy for police officers.

Other practical considerations we observed included: placing children in foster care in cases of mutual arrest; people who answer the door and insist everything is resolved; wrong addresses, or no response to knocks on the door; and women who request that charges not be brought.

Many of these practical problems are a reflection of the societal emphasis on the privacy of the nuclear family. To protect individual privacy, officers cannot enter private homes without an invitation or a warrant. Women are expected to demonstrate a commitment to prosecution when their husband is the assailant, although the same level of commitment is not expected in the case of stranger assaults. Most significant, police officers do not consider violence against women in their home to be "real police work" equal in importance to crimes committed in public space.

Internal and External Politics

At the same time that police are influenced by legal, ideological, and practical considerations, the politics of the police department and of the community it serves are relevant to officers' actions. In Phoenix, street-level officers doubted the sincerity of administrative fiats, particularly those at odds with the realities of street work. The presumptive arrest policy was viewed by many officers as a political manoeuver by the chief to demonstrate action to battered women's advocates. Although training was provided on the policy, many officers either did not remember it or evaluated it negatively. There were no incentives for following the new policy, nor built-in penalties for failing to follow it. A memo circulated shortly after the introduction of the policy stressed the importance of establishing probable cause. Many officers interpreted the memo as further evidence that the policy was not to be taken seriously, but was merely "for show."

The external politics were perceived by officers as being adversarial and potentially harmful to their career. The low-income, black sections of town were viewed as hostile territory where officers were unwanted and endangered. Police shootings of citizens in the area were recent events and negatively affected the atmosphere of police community relations. Officers believed that housing project committees held considerable power and influence with the police chief. They were therefore reluctant to engage in practices, such as domestic violence arrests with no cooperative witness, in these areas.

At the same time, the community of women activists was not considered large or powerful. There were about a dozen women as part of the Maricopa County Task Force Against Domestic Abuse who fought for greater protection for women. As representatives of the relational culture, however, these women were not adopted into the higher echelons of power at the police or government levels.

Consideration of political influence and community context is important information for advocates working to improve police responses to battered women. In this case, the perception of a weak influence of battered women's advocates and a strong influence of the project committees shaped police officers' perceptions of the consequences of their responses to battering.

Women's Perceptions of
Police Response

Following the observational portion of this study, a small sample of women who had called the police was interviewed. The sample was small because few of the women whose names were given to us by the police department remained at the addresses listed in police files. A number of those who were contacted either did not have time for an interview or did not wish to relive their experiences.

Seventeen open-ended interviews were completed. The women were almost evenly split on whether the police interventions were helpful. Eight women evaluated the police negatively. Two of these women were arrested and spent a night in jail. One of these women was forced out of her home after her husband received an order of protection against her. Other women reported that police promised they would come to the home or would return, but did not. Some were told there was nothing the police could do to help. One woman was "yelled at" for not wanting to press charges, and other women said they were treated rudely. These eight women would not advise other women to call the police if they were battered.

The other nine women evaluated the police positively, but not all believed they were helpful. Women described officers as "professional," or "very nice," but did not necessarily believe the police intervention benefited them. Several women were convinced that their husband's severe alcoholism and "craziness" were uncontrollable through any means. Other women felt that the risks involved in prosecution were greater than in avoiding it. This was true for two women who believed their own or a close relative's immigration status would be jeopardized by police involvement.

Five women were unequivocally positive in their assessments of the police. Four were at the point of ending their relationship and only needed police assistance in persuading their husband to stay away. They were not currently enmeshed in violent situations. Three of these women were divorced following police intervention and had no subsequent problems with their ex-husband. One woman reported that the police intervention was the impetus that led her and her husband to fundamentalist religion and prayer, which she believed had saved their marriage. One woman obtained a second order of protection against her ex-husband and was successful in deterring future violence.

Even with this small sample of women, it is apparent that the needs of women are not identical. Women's needs reflect their current position on the continuum of adaptation to violence. They simultaneously represent various levels of resources, concerns, and knowledge of workable survival strategies. As discussed above, only individual women have access to the range of considerations bearing upon the most appropriate police intervention for their particular situations.

Conclusion

Battering is a serious crime that inflicts suffering on millions of women each year. The empowerment of police, however, is not a substitute for empowerment of women. Any legal or policy changes that increase the power of police without simultaneously striving for the empowerment of women will have the potential to decrease rather than improve the level of women's safety.

Women know their situations and needs, and are capable of developing survival strategies that fit their particular circumstances. When criminal justice agents acknowledge this ability, interventions are more likely to succeed. For example, Ford (1991) found that prosecution of wife batterers was most successful when women were included in the decision-making process. It would be advantageous to follow a similar course in policing. Because the needs of women vary, it seems appropriate to ensure that a full range of options is available. The rapid development of public concern, legislation, and scholarship on battering has accelerated at the expense of a full elaboration of the complexities of emotional and physical violence. The term "battered woman" glosses over the emotional ties, interludes of calm, and shared history that women experience over the course of relationships with violent partners. Extracting physical violence as the pivotal concern, whether for academic or legal purposes, simplifies the intricacies of relationships. This simplified, unidimensional understanding of battering precludes appreciation of the depth of irreconcilable differences between the culture of power and relational culture.

References

Allen, P. G. (1986). *The sacred hoop: Recovering the feminine in American Indian traditions*. Boston: Beacon.

Berk, R. A., Berk, S. F., Loseke, D. R., & Rauma, D. (1981). Mutual combat and other family violence myths. In D. Finkelhor, R. Gelles, G. Hotaling, & M. Straus (Eds.), *The dark side of families: Current family violence research* (pp. 197-212). Beverly Hills, CA: Sage.

Bittner, E. (1967). The police on skid-row: A study of peace keeping. *American Sociological Review, 32,* 699-715.

Bittner, E. (1990). *Aspects of police work*. Boston: Northeastern University Press.

Black, D. J. (1976). *The behavior of law*. New York: Academic Press.

Blackman, J. (1989). *Intimate violence: A study of injustice*. New York: Columbia University Press.

Bowker, L. H. (1982). Police services to battered women: Bad or not so bad? *Criminal Justice and Behavior, 9,* 476-494.

Brown, M. K. (1981). *Working the street: Police discretion and the dilemmas of reform*. New York: Russell Sage Foundation.

Browne, A. (1989). *When battered women kill*. New York: Free Press.

Cain, P. (1991). Feminist jurisprudence: Grounding the theories. In K. Bartlett & R. Kennedy (Eds.), *Feminist legal thought* (pp. 263-280). Boulder, CO: Westview.

Caputo, R. K. (1988). Police response to domestic violence. *Social Casework, 69,* 81-87.

Carmody, D. C., & Williams, K. R. (1987). Wife assault and perceptions of sanctions. *Violence and Victims, 2,* 25-38.

Chadhuri, M., & Daly, K. (1992). Restraining orders: Do they help? In E. Buzawa & C. Buzawa (Eds.), *Domestic violence: The changing criminal justice response* (pp. 227-252). Westport, CT: Greenwood.

Crane, S. W. (1987). Washington's domestic violence prevention act: Mandatory arrest two years later. *Newsletter of the National Center on Women and Family Law, 8,* 1.

Crime Control Institute. (1986). Police domestic violence policy change. *Response, 9,* 16.

Davis, P. W. (1983). Restoring the semblance of order: Police strategies in the domestic disturbance. *Symbolic Interaction, 6,* 261-274.

Dobash, R. E., & Dobash, R. (1979). *Violence against wives.* New York: Free Press.

Dobash, R. E., & Dobash, R. (1992). *Women, violence and social change.* London: Routledge & Kegan Paul.

Dreyfus, H. L., & Rabinow, P. (1983). *Michael Foucault: Beyond structuralism and hermeneutics* (2nd ed.). Chicago: University of Chicago Press.

Dunford, F. W., Huizinga, D., & Elliott, D. S. (1990). The role of arrest in domestic assault: The Omaha police experiment. *Criminology, 28,* 183-206.

Ferraro, K. J. (1983). The rationalization process: How battered women stay. *Victimology, 8,* 203-214.

Ferraro, K. J. (1989a). The legal response to woman battering in the United States. In J. Hanmer, J. Radford, & E. A. Stanko (Eds.), *Women, policing and male violence* (pp. 155-184). London: Routledge.

Ferraro, K. J. (1989b). Policing woman battering. *Social Problems, 36,* 61-74.

Ferraro, K. J., & Boychuk, T. (1992). The court's response to interpersonal violence: A comparison of intimate and nonintimate assault. In E. Buzawa & C. Buzawa (Eds.), *Domestic violence: The changing criminal justice response* (pp. 209-225). Westport, CT: Greenwood.

Ferraro, K. J., & Johnson, J. M. (1983). How women experience battering: The process of victimization. *Social Problems, 30,* 325-339.

Ford, D. A. (1991). Prosecution as a victim power resource: A note on empowering women in violent conjugal relationships. *Law and Society Review, 25,* 313-334.

Foucault, M. (1980). *Power/knowledge: Selected interviews and other writings, 1972-1977.* New York: Pantheon.

Gilligan, C. (1982). *In a different voice.* Cambridge, MA: Harvard University Press.

Hanmer, J., Radford, J., & Stanko, E. A. (Eds.). (1989). *Women, policing, and male violence.* London: Routledge.

Hart, W. J., Ashcroft, J., Burgess, A., Flanagan, N., Meese, C., Milton, C., Narramore, C., Ortega, R., & Seward, F. (1984). *Attorney General's Task Force on Family Violence.* Washington, DC: U.S. Department of Justice.

Hirschel, J., Hutchison, I. W., & Dean, C. W. (1992). The failure of arrest to deter spouse abuse. *Journal of Research in Crime and Delinquency, 20,* 7-33.

Jaggar, A. M. (1983). *Feminist politics and human nature.* Totowa, NJ: Rowman & Allenheld.

Kelly, L. (1988). *Surviving sexual violence.* Cambridge, UK: Polity.

Littrell, W. B. (1979). *Bureaucratic justice: Police, prosecutors, and plea bargaining.* Beverly Hills, CA: Sage.

MacKinnon, C. A. (1983). Feminism, Marxism, method, and the state: Toward feminist jurisprudence. *Signs, 8,* 635-658.

Meeker, J. W., & Binder, A. (1990). Experiments as reforms: The impact of the Minneapolis Experiment on police policy. *Journal of Police Science and Administration, 17,* 147-153.

Minow, M. (1990). *Making all the difference.* Ithaca, NY: Cornell University Press.

Musheno, M., & Seeley, K. (1986). Prostitution policy and the women's movement: Historical analysis of feminist thought and organization. *Contemporary Crisis, 10,* 237-255.

Ortega, R. B. (1984). *Operations Digest,* no. 84-85, pp. 1-2.

Pagelow, M. D. (1984). *Family violence.* New York: Praeger.

Red Horse, J. (1980). *The American Indian family: Strengths and stresses.* Isleta, NM: American Indian Social Research and Development Association.

Rich, A. (1980). *Blood, bread and poetry.* New York: Norton.

Russell, D.E.H. (1990). *Rape in marriage.* Bloomington: Indiana University Press.

Saunders, D. (1988). Other truths about domestic violence: A reply to McNeely and Robinson-Simpson. *Social Work, 33,* 179-183.

Scales, A. (1986). The emergence of feminist jurisprudence. *Yale Law Journal, 95,* 1373-1403.

Schafran, L. H. (1989). Gender bias in the courts: An emerging focus for judicial reform. *Arizona State Law Journal, 21,* 237-273.

Sherman, L. W., & Berk, R. A. (1984). The specific deterrent effects of arrest for domestic assault. *American Sociological Review, 49,* 261-272.

Sherman, L. W., & Cohn, E. G. (1989). The impact of research on legal policy: The Minneapolis domestic violence experiment. *Law and Society Review, 23,* 117-144.

Sherman, L. W., Schmidt, J. D., & Rogan, D. P. (1991). From initial deterrence to long-term escalation: Short custody arrest for poverty ghetto domestic violence. *Criminology, 29,* 821-850.

Stanko, E. A. (1985). *Intimate intrusions: Women's experience of male violence.* London: Routledge & Kegan Paul.

Stanko, E. A. (1990). *Everyday violence: How women and men experience sexual and physical danger.* London: Pandora.

Stith, S. M. (1990). Police response to domestic violence: The influence of individual and familial factors. *Violence and Victims, 5,* 37-49.

Van Maanen, J. (1978). The asshole. In P. Manning & J. Van Maanen (Eds.), *Policing: A view from the street* (pp. 221-238). Santa Monica, CA: Goodyear.

Walker, L.E.A. (1979). *The battered woman.* New York: Harper & Row.

Walker, L.E.A. (1984). *Battered woman syndrome.* New York: Springer.

West, R. (1988). Jurisprudence and gender. *University of Chicago Law Review, 55,* 1-72.

Wilson, J. Q. (1968). *Varieties of police behavior.* Cambridge, MA: Harvard University Press.

Woods, L. (1987). *Arrest in domestic violence cases: A state by state summary.* New York: National Center on Women and Family Law.

Ylló, K., & Bograd, M. (Eds.). (1989). *Feminist perspectives on wife abuse.* Newbury Park, CA: Sage.

PART

III

COURTS

6

The Criminal Prosecution
of Wife Assaulters

Process, Problems, and Effects

DAVID A. FORD

MARY JEAN REGOLI

The prosecution of wife assaulters promises victims security from continuing aggression at the same time that it affirms the state's intolerance of domestic violence. But does prosecution truly prevent violence? Or do currently advocated policies, such as those outlined by the U.S. Attorney General's Task Force on Family Vio-

Indiana University, Department of Sociology, Indianapolis, Indiana (Ford); Indiana University, Bloomington (Regoli). We wish to acknowledge and thank Judge Ruth Reichard of the Marion County (Indiana) Municipal Court and Marion County Deputy Prosecutor Cheryl Hillenberg for contributing invaluable legal expertise and comments to the preparation of this chapter. This chapter includes a report on research conducted under Grant #86-IJ-CX-0012 from the National Institute of Justice. We are grateful for the extraordinary cooperation of the many individuals and agencies who made this research possible. The views expressed are those of the authors and not necessarily those of the funding agencies or of cooperating Marion County criminal justice agencies.

127

lence (1984), represent wishful thinking, inferred from findings on police effects (e.g., Jaffe, Hastings, Reitzel, & Austin, this volume; Sherman & Berk, 1984) and popular notions that punishment deters crime?

Protecting battered women entails preventing their partner from assaulting them. Prosecution may do this by making it known to *all* prospective wife assaulters that the state does not tolerate violence and will punish those who are violent. It has never been demonstrated whether prosecution serves as a general deterrent to wife assaulters, although most would agree that it is at least an effective means of declaring the state's condemnation of violence against women. For a victim who has already suffered a violent assault at the hands of her conjugal partner, prosecution may prevent continuing violence in one of three ways: by punishing him so that he will desist in order to avoid future punishments, by using the power of the court to force him into rehabilitative treatment, or by empowering the woman to take whatever steps she deems appropriate beyond court sanctions to arrange for her own security.

To date, we know very little about the effectiveness of prosecution policies in preventing violence. Controlled studies on the effects of criminal justice have focused on police interventions. Less rigorous studies have examined the effects of judicial outcomes, especially court-mandated treatment for wife assaulters. Only one experiment considers the preventive effects of alternative prosecution policies. As we shall see below, what we do know from limited research findings offers hope that prosecutors may be able to tailor policies to protect individual victims from continuing violence at the hands of a particular offender.

In this chapter, we examine prosecution policies meant to protect battered women. We first introduce general issues concerning the prosecution of wife assault, then describe the process of prosecution, its key players, and its salient problems, in order to establish a context for evaluating and interpreting policy effects. Then, the role of the prosecutor in implementing protective policies is examined, followed by a review of key issues and problems relevant to policies for prosecuting wife assaulters. Findings from evaluations of prosecution policies are then presented. The chapter concludes with a discussion of policy implications.

Background on the
Prosecution of Wife Assault

Laws prohibiting wife assault have a long history in the United States and Canada (Pleck, 1987; cf. Hilton, this volume). Every state and province now has criminal laws prohibiting wife assault. Most offenses are covered under general laws against violence, though some are unique to wife assault (Friedman & Shulman, 1990; Lerman & Livingston, 1983; MacLeod, 1980). Conjugal violence may fall under any number of criminal laws, ranging from murder through simple assault and battery. The laws specify court-imposed sanctions as the principal, intended punishments of criminal justice. But even as sanctions for wife assaulters have become institutionalized in criminal justice, informal punishments incidental to formal processing persist. Starting with arrest and pretrial preparation, the process carries costs that may be more punishing than a formal sentence (Feeley, 1979). For example, to be arrested and jailed, however briefly, is as harrowing an encounter with criminal justice as any citizen would care to experience. The costs are obvious: inconvenience, loss of freedom, expense of posting bail, lost wages, embarrassment, stigmatization, and even loss of employment. In cases of conjugal violence there may be additional punishments unique to the intimate relationship: separation, threatened role relationships, imbalances of power, and loss of trust or respect.

In some states, men who batter habitually may be charged with a more serious offense carrying stiffer punishments. Indiana law provides for charging what normally would be a class-A misdemeanor battery as a D-felony when committed by a man previously convicted of battery against the same victim. Thus, instead of facing up to a year in jail and a $5,000 fine, he could be sentenced to as many as four years in prison with a $10,000 fine. As we shall see later, such a law influences plea agreements and decisions to accept diversion offers.

The recent focus on police responsibility for preventing wife assault overlooks shortcomings in the prosecutor's response. Experiments on the effectiveness of various police interventions (Garner & Visher, 1988) give no insight into the compounding effects of prosecution following arrest. Sherman and Berk (1984) report that only 3 of the 136 suspects arrested in the Minneapolis experiment were subsequently fined or incarcerated. The Milwaukee police experiment also involved arrest with "virtually no prosecution" (Sherman et al., 1991); 5% of arrestees had charges filed against them. A replication experiment in Omaha (Dunford, Huizinga, & Elliott, 1990) found that 64% of suspects arrested were sentenced to fines, probation, jail, or some combination of these. In the absence of controls for prosecution policies, however, one cannot conclude that one sanction is to be preferred to another as a preventive intervention. Another police experiment conducted in Charlotte, North Carolina, found that only 35% of suspects slated for prosecution were in fact prosecuted (Hirschel, Hutchison, & Dean, 1992). As in Omaha, there was no experimental control for prosecution.

The literature on traditional systems of criminal justice paints a bleak picture of prospects for serving victim interests through prosecution. Prosecutors have been reported to be unresponsive to complaints of wife assault, even to the point of further victimizing women (e.g., M. H. Field & H. F. Field, 1973; Ford, 1983; Gayford, 1977; Hilton, 1989; Lerman, 1986). Often women are made to feel responsible for their own victimization through screening questions: "Are you still living with this man?" "Are you married to him?" "Have you filed for divorce?" "Why do you stay with him?" No wonder battered wives feel little support in seeking to prosecute their partner (Walker, 1979). They may be additionally frustrated with the unwillingness of prosecutors to treat their cases seriously or with attempts to discourage them from pursuing criminal justice relief from violence (Ford, 1983; Fromson, 1977). Battered women often misunderstand how the prosecutorial process operates and thus approach it with unrealistic expectations (M. H. Field & H. F. Field, 1973; Ford, 1983; Lerman, 1986). An encounter with a prosecutor leaves many victims with no guarantee of protection.

Prosecution can be a capricious process leaving a victim's fate with the "luck of the draw" (Ford, 1983, p. 467). Her initial wishes may never be realized. The manner in which her charges are pursued depends first on who happens to hear the original complaint (e.g., police, prosecutor, assistant or deputy prosecutor, civilian volunteer). The chance of charges being pursued as expected depends on how officials interpret the crime's seriousness, on perceptions of the victim's commitment to following through, on her demeanor, on her conjugal status, on the degree of assistance she gets in writing her probable cause affidavit, and on how responsibly the paperwork is handled after she leaves the prosecutor's office (cf. Hall, 1975). Battered women are sometimes urged to consider the presumed negative consequences of pressing charges (e.g., Neubauer, 1974). And some prosecutor's offices set up obstacles to prosecuting, such as insisting that the complainant return after "cooling off" or charging fees for filing criminal complaints (Dunford et al., 1990; Hirschel et al., 1992; Steinman, 1991). It is not surprising, then, that some battered women are reluctant to follow through with their complaints.

The problems battered women encounter in pursuing criminal charges may arguably be unique to their "domestic" status. Elliott (1989) found little evidence to support the belief that there are differences in rates of prosecuting domestic violence cases versus others. Citing Brosi (1979) and Boland, Brady, Tyson, and Bassler (1983), however, Elliott (1989) notes that regardless of the type of crime, cases are less likely to be prosecuted when an offender is known to a victim and when prosecuted, they are more likely to result in acquittal than similar crimes between nonintimates. Williams (1976) found that in Washington, D.C., in 1973, in violent conjugal crimes, charges were less likely to be filed, more likely to be dismissed, and more likely to result in acquittal than similar crimes between nonintimates. Friedman and Shulman (1990) cite limited recent evidence showing similarly greater proportions of dismissals in cases of domestic violence and greater leniency when they are pursued. Wasoff (1982) examined case processing in Scottish courts and found that although there was little difference in the handling of cases *within* courts, domestic violence cases were more likely than similar nondomestics to be assigned to the lower district courts, where sanction options are more limited. Dutton (1986, 1987) also reports more lenient sentences for domestic violence. And within the set of domestic violence cases, prosecutors are likely to discriminate against married women in pursuing charges (Ford, 1983; Rauma, 1984).

The literature on recent reforms in prosecutorial policies speaks with confidence of the capacity of prosecution to protect victims by keeping them in the system and using the power of the state to control offenders (Goolkasian, 1986a; Lerman, 1986; U.S. Attorney General's Task Force, 1984). This literature, however, is devoid of rigorous evaluation research to support advocated policies. Later in this chapter, we will look at some efforts to evaluate prosecution policies designed for responding to domestic violence against women. To place our review in context, we first describe the general process of prosecution and the prosecutor's role in that process. Then we describe selected policies that have been evaluated.

The Process of
Prosecuting Wife Assaulters

The term "prosecution" today denotes a process whereby a government attorney responds to an alleged criminal violation by presenting a case for convicting the defendant to a judge and perhaps a jury. In a broader sense, "prosecution" means any action taken by the state to move a case toward adjudication, including such practices as diverting cases from trial into educational or rehabilitative treatments. In this chapter we use the term "prosecutor" to refer to an attorney with responsibility for arguing criminal cases in court on behalf of the government.

Prosecution begins when a prosecutor receives a complaint in the form of a probable cause affidavit or information alleging that a crime has been committed. The complaint may be brought by police officers, either in conjunction with an arrest or in seeking a warrant to enable an arrest. Victims can initiate complaints by filing affidavits with the prosecutor, similarly alleging that someone committed a crime. In some instances, the complainant may have already made a citizen's arrest.

Jurisdictions vary by law, policy, and custom with respect to what determines how a case enters the system. Felony cases generally originate with police investigations of assault or battery with serious injury, or of recklessness with a deadly weapon. By far the most common cases of domestic violence result from a class of misdemeanor offenses, that is, assault and battery, although the same offense may go by different names from one jurisdiction to the next. These cases may begin with either a warrantless police arrest or a victim-initiated complaint. Until reforms permitting warrantless arrests, the only cases of misdemeanor domestic violence brought to a prosecutor's attention were those initiated by a victim, often on advice of police officers. Even today, with proarrest policies in place, jurisdictions with a tradition of serving victim complainants continue to file charges based on victims' affidavits. Elliott asserts that "The vast majority of all family violence cases coming to the attention of the prosecutor involve [on-scene] arrests" (Elliott, 1989, p. 458). In Indianapolis about half of all misdemeanor cases enter the system by virtue of a victim complaint.[1]

Figure 6.1 displays an overview of general steps in the prosecution process, typical especially of misdemeanor cases. Under each mode of entry, a probable cause affidavit is reviewed first by a prosecutor for questions of law and for the prosecutor's willingness to file charges. Later, a judge reviews the allegation to affirm its legality. Cases initiated by warrantless on-scene arrests generally proceed directly to an initial court appearance when the prosecutor's review, judge's review, and arraignment or preliminary hearing occur virtually at the same time. When the police make a warrantless arrest, the defendant is jailed, at least temporarily, and brought before a judge within a day or two. The case can be tracked according to the prosecutor's wishes with little delay. By contrast, victim-initiated complaints do not result in immediate arrest. They follow a more obvious stepwise course, interrupted and often delayed by the need to locate a suspect for his initial court appearance. The prosecutor may recommend to the judge that the man be brought to court either by summons or by warrant arrest. At the preliminary hearing, the judge schedules a pretrial conference or a trial date. Pretrial conferences allow for defendants to appear in court with a lawyer prior to trial for consideration of any legal arguments on the charges and initial plea negotiations, including arrangements for pretrial diversion agreements.

The prosecution process ends with one of the four general outcomes shown in Figure 6.1. These include several typical policy goals toward which cases may be tracked (e.g., pretrial diversion to rehabilitative counseling; adjudicated guilt with counseling as a condition of probation; other sentencing such as fines, probation, and jail time). Details of these outcomes will be described below as objectives of prosecution policy.

We have described the prosecution process as if it followed formal policies. In reality, many prosecutor's offices do not have explicit policies for handling cases of domestic violence. Informal policies that may influence the process (e.g., complainants must be divorced before filing charges) derive principally from the attitudes of prosecutors and the work group norms in both the prosecutor's office and the court. Ultimately, the process is driven by prosecutorial discretion. A victim's control over the process is limited by her ability to influence the prosecutor and by the nature of her testimony and willingness to testify in court (DuBow & Becker, 1976).

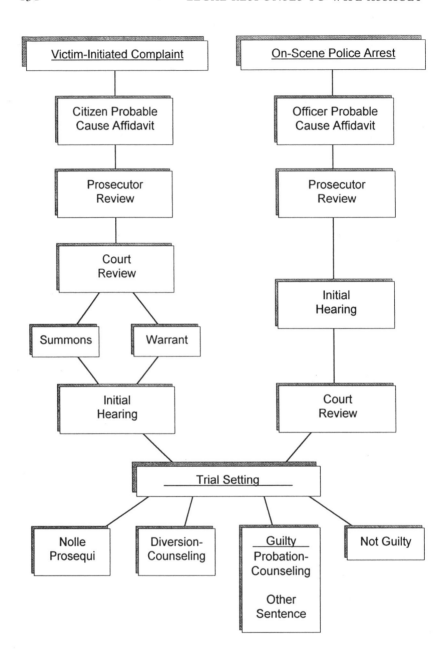

Figure 6.1. Overview of the Prosecution Process

Prosecutor's Role

The prosecutor plays a central and dominant role in the criminal justice response to wife assault. The prosecutor must organize and manage both people and information as a case moves toward adjudication. He or she interacts directly with police, victims, witnesses, defendants and their attorneys, and judges. In exercising broad discretion at various decision points, the prosecutor is most influential in shaping the course of events for *both* victim and defendant.

Prosecutors screen cases to validate police arrests, to verify that charges are consistent with criminal law, and to determine which cases merit further attention in court. They have authority to accept or reject complaints against a defendant in charging decisions. Once a defendant is charged and arraigned the prosecutor may dismiss (nolle prosequi) the case. If the case goes forward, prosecutors filter and shape information for presentation in court at the same time that they interpret laws relevant to victim, police, and even judicial actions. Indeed, their presumed knowledge of cases, apart from legal issues, lends authority to recommendations to the court on matters ranging from bail and protective orders to sentencing.

The prosecutor's discretionary authority enables seemingly arbitrary action consistent with his or her unique interests, sometimes at the expense of the public or specific victims. For example, their screening function allows prosecutors to manage their own work loads. A part-time rural prosecutor may enjoy his or her political position while relying on a private practice for income. To suggest that the prosecutor be more aggressive in encouraging police arrests or victim complaints in domestic cases is to suggest that he or she work harder on a limited budget with low salary. And more important, a rural prosecutor may be voted out of office if he or she starts prosecuting constituents. Without counterincentives, actions to protect victims will not happen.

The ever-expanding domain of prosecutors has usurped many of the traditional functions served by police, judges, defense attorneys, and victim-complainants (McDonald, 1979; McGillivray, 1987). A system that once served to resolve victim-initiated, private disputes today functions to adjudicate crimes at the will of prosecutors in the name of the state (Hilton, 1989; McDonald, 1979; Steinberg, 1984). The prosecutor has the power to define as "problems" actions victims may take in seeking protection through criminal justice. In the next section of this chapter, we discuss a few such "problems" with relevance to the formulation and implementation of prosecution policies meant to protect victims of domestic violence.

Issues and Problems in
Prosecuting Wife Assaulters

Charging Decisions

Regardless of whether a police officer or a victim initiates the complaint, it is the prosecutor who decides if the case will be allowed to continue in the criminal justice system, and if so, what type of charge to file. In making these decisions, the prosecutor ideally balances the need to enforce the law with seeing that justice is served by not prosecuting when evidence is lacking or guilt is in serious doubt (Abadinsky, 1984).

Domestic violence may be charged according to general policies used by prosecutors in charging any criminal complaint (Jacoby, 1979). Within the boundaries of general policies, however, charging decisions in cases of domestic violence are notable for having less to do with legal criteria than with valuations of victims' and defendants' personal attributes. In effect, charging involves selecting suspects and victims worthy of further processing. Research shows that prosecutors are more likely to charge in cases where victims suffer serious injuries and defendants have a record of prior arrests (Rauma, 1984; Schmidt & Steury, 1989). The chance of charges being pursued is all the greater when defendants have "negative" characteristics, suggesting perhaps a generalized guilty status, such as alcohol or other drug use, or failure to comply with directives of the police or courts (Rauma, 1984; Schmidt & Steury, 1989). Conversely, negative victim attributes reduce the chance of filing to the extent that they call into question a woman's status as a "victim" (Rauma, 1984).

Prosecutors are aware that a decision to file charges may bring later hassles associated with the private and emotionally strained nature of victim-offender relations. Cases often hinge on the victim's word against the defendant's with little other evidence. Appearances are likely to carry unwarranted influence. Once in court, the defendant may look respectable, denying any wrongdoing and providing alternative reasons for the victim's injuries (e.g., she was drunk; she fell). In contrast, the victim may not appear credible in court if she is confused or frightened (Lerman, 1986). In deciding which cases to pursue, prosecutors are often encouraged to consider the victim's motivation in filing charges, current relationship with the defendant, and commitment to full prosecution (E. S. Buzawa & C. G. Buzawa, 1990; Ellis, 1984; Ford, 1983; Rauma, 1984).

The differential treatment of wife assault cases is apparent in cases not being treated as felonies although circumstances legally merit a more serious charge. A National Crime Survey found that more than one third of misdemeanor domestic violence cases would have been the felony offenses of rape, robbery, or aggravated assault if committed by strangers (E. S. Buzawa & C. G. Buzawa, 1990).[2] The decision to prosecute is governed by concerns for avoiding uncertainty and is affected by perceptions of what is related to "successful" case prosecution (Albonetti, 1987). In general, felony charges are rejected primarily because of evidence problems, although a systematic investigation of the reasons in domestic cases has not been made (Spohn, Gruhl, & Welch, 1987; see also Myers & Hagan, 1979).

In making charging decisions, prosecutors sometimes miscalculate victim interests and expectations for prosecutorial outcomes. Battered women who contact their prosecutor obviously want protection. Not all victims, however, *expect* protection. They are motivated to seek out the prosecutor for a variety of other reasons. In Indianapolis, for example, only 16% of women seeking charges volunteer "to secure protection" as a primary expected outcome of filing (although protection is top-ranked as "very important" relative to other motivations). Those reasons include personal interests brought to the prosecution process with the hope that they might be fulfilled by filing charges (Ford, 1983). The most frequently mentioned expected outcome (21%) is "to force him to make repayment for damages" (Ford & Burke, 1987). Generally, women hope to secure arrangements enabling them to free themselves from further victimization. But typically, prosecutors make no effort to understand the victim's situation as a whole, nor do they provide the time and resources necessary to enhance the cooperation and commitment of victims. Instead, they find themselves at odds with victims they see as abusing the system, a point we shall elaborate on later.

Pretrial Concerns

Arrests

Although arresting an offender at the scene of a violent incident is the most immediate response the criminal justice system can provide, concerns have been raised that arrest may increase hostilities, especially if the offender is quickly released from custody (e.g., Goolkasian, 1986b; Gottlieb & Johnson, 1983; Women's Law Caucus, 1986; Wright, 1985). The Minneapolis Domestic Violence Experiment did not find this to be the case (Sherman & Berk, 1984). Forty-three percent of those arrested were released from custody within one day, and the victim reported having a new quarrel with the offender within one day in just 6% of those cases. A more recent evaluation of police response to domestic violence incidents in Omaha found that when an arrest was made, 93% of the victims felt the presence of the police stopped the violence (Dunford, Huizinga, & Elliott, 1989). Sixty-five percent of the victims, however, reported that the offender blamed them for the arrest, and 21% said they were threatened by the offender because of the arrest. The offenders in Omaha spent an average of just under 16 hours in custody from the point of booking to release, with under 20% being released in less than 2 hours. In Indianapolis, just 13 of 386 victims claimed any form of violence in retaliation for defendants' entry experiences (on-scene arrest, warrant, or summons). Others may have been assaulted again, but they did not attribute further violence to the initiation of prosecution (Ford, 1991a).

In one study, researchers evaluated differences in the chance of further violence according to the length of time a suspect is held following his warrantless arrest in a sample of impoverished ghetto dwellers (Sherman et al., 1991). Paradoxically, in comparison to a "no arrest" condition, the researchers found evidence that a short-custody arrest (averaging 2.8 hours) resulted in relatively lower rates of violence over the following 30 days but significantly more violence after

1 year. Long-custody arrest (averaging 11.1 hours) neither deterred nor escalated violence for any follow-up period.

Regardless of how long a suspect is held, advocates argue that a wife assaulter should be required to appear in court for arraignment or initial hearing (Goolkasian, 1986a, 1986b). Prosecutors and victims then have an opportunity to inform the court of special circumstances in the case and to give input on the conditions placed upon the suspect when released pending trial. Defendants may be released on their own recognizance or may be required to post bail. Judges have broad discretion to impose additional pretrial release conditions to assure appearance at trial or to prevent intimidation of witnesses (Lerman, 1981). These may include, but are not limited to, requiring the man to stay away from the victim's home or place of employment, to move out of the residence, to refrain from alcohol, to have supervised child visitation, to surrender weapons temporarily, or to participate in a counseling program (Goolkasian, 1986a; Lerman, 1981; Pence, Miletich, Radulovich, & Galaway, 1985). Ordinarily, violations of pretrial release conditions result in a judge either jailing the offender or setting bail at a greater amount.

Victim Complaints

When victims initiate charges at the prosecutor's office, the prosecutor must decide whether to bring the suspect into the process by summons or by warrant. The choice entails weighing possible threats to the victim's security against the realities of system timing and expediency in executing one or the other. Prosecutors and judges sometimes prefer to issue summonses because they can be more reliable in getting suspects to court within a limited time frame. Suspects are less likely to hide or even flee to avoid a summons than to avoid a warrant. Whether a summons or warrant will result in a swifter court appearance is subject to considerable variation depending on how jurisdictions are organized for serving them. The most important concern is whether defendants are more likely to retaliate if arrested by warrant than if summoned to court. In Indianapolis, about one out of four suspects charged subsequent to a victim complaint is "definitely angry" over his entry experience, regardless of whether it was by summons or by warrant. And 25% of those angered commit new violence against their partner before their case is settled in court. Levels of reported anger, however, are related to new violence only for the warrant suspects. Those men brought to court by warrant, but not greatly angered, are less likely than others to assault their victim again prior to case settlement (Ford, 1991a).

Protection Orders

One pretrial strategy for deterring violence is issuing an order of protection (no-contact order), the violation of which constitutes contempt of court, or in some states, a criminal offense. Though traditionally associated with civil proceedings, such as divorce, protective orders are increasingly common as a condition of pretrial release at the beginning of prosecution. It is hoped that a defendant will fear the consequences of assaulting his victim in violation of the order. Formal protection orders can result in stiffer sanctions if their breach constitutes a misdemeanor crime. When properly drafted and consistently enforced, protection orders are presumed by some victims, victim advocates, and judges to be effective in reducing violence (Finn & Colson, 1990; Grau, Fagan, & Wexler, 1984).

On the other hand, several concerns and limitations have been raised about the use of protection orders (E. S. Buzawa & C. G. Buzawa, 1990; Finn & Colson, 1990; Hart, 1988; Lerman, 1980; see also Ferraro & Pope, this volume). Principal among these is the lack of enforcement. The orders cannot protect if violated with impunity. Enforcement can be improved through legislation making violation a criminal offense and authorizing warrantless arrest by police (Finn, 1991). The victim's burden of monitoring compliance to the order can be relieved if court staff or an independent agency review police records and contact victims regularly about possible violations, and if counseling agencies submit reports to the court on compliance (see Pence, 1983, for a description of an innovative enforcement program in Duluth, Minnesota).

Case Attrition

A principal reason prosecutors cite for their unwillingness to accept cases of wife assault is what they consider high rates of victim-caused case attrition. It is well documented that many battered women do seek to withdraw charges after filing. Reports from traditional jurisdictions around the United States indicate that 50%-80% of battered women will drop charges either by requesting dismissal or by failing to appear in court as a witness (Bannon, 1975; M. H. Field & H. F. Field, 1973; Ford, 1983; Parnas, 1970).

The issue of dropped charges is neither new nor unique to cases of wife assault. High rates of dismissal were common under private prosecutor systems. States' attorneys had little discretion in matters of parties using prosecution to secure satisfactory outcomes without adjudication (Steinberg, 1984). What is new is the characterization of dropped charges as a "problem" for criminal justice when battered women are involved (Bard, 1980; R. E. Dobash & R. Dobash, 1979; M. H. Field & H. F. Field, 1973; Ford, 1983; Lerman, 1981; Straus, Gelles, & Steinmetz, 1980). In many respects, victim nonparticipation is a self-fulfilling prophecy attributable to the actions of prosecutors, judges, and defense attorneys.

Prosecutors test victims' commitment to "following through" by asking if they *really* want to prosecute. They may even give battered women reasons for not pursuing charges: for example, that it will cost the defendant money that might be better spent on the family's support; that it will create more stress and conflict in the relationship; that it will anger the defendant to the point of his retaliating; that prosecution cannot guarantee security. And if victims elect to proceed, they may feel that the prosecutor will not support them, as noted above. Judges also talk victims out of pursuing charges. A judge may suggest to a victim that a trial would cause more problems and that if she backs out, the judge will make the defendant promise to leave her alone. If there are further incidents, she need only come back and tell the judge and they will be taken care of. (What the judge does not tell her is that there will be no official record of her current complaint and that the court would have no authority to do anything special on her behalf should she return.)

A defendant's attorney can also contribute to the pressure on a battered woman to drop charges, and in so doing, place her in jeopardy. The best-known strategy is to wear down a victim's resolve to proceed by requesting continuances, thereby forcing multiple trips to court. A more direct strategy is simply to ask the victim to drop charges. Ford and Regoli (1990) describe cases in which defense attorneys engaged their client's victim in negotiations to withdraw charges with assurances that the defendant would leave her alone. In some instances the attorney's efforts bordered on obstruction of justice—a crime—as victims were induced to ignore subpoenas or give false testimony at trial. Victims were persuaded that the lawyers were looking after their interests, as well as the defendants'. Each accepted the word of the lawyer she presumed had some greater control over her assailant's behavior than either she or criminal justice officials. Of course, this was not the case, and when attorneys encourage or facilitate victims dropping charges, they place those victims at greater risk of continuing violence, notwithstanding assurances to the contrary.

Apart from dismissals tacitly encouraged by those with authority in the criminal justice system, victims elect not to go forward to trial for other reasons. For one, the defendant may threaten his victim with more harm if she follows through. Victims who appreciate the inability of police and prosecutors to prevent violence will drop charges out of hopelessness and fear (although we have found relatively few instances of retaliatory violence against women whose cases enter the system; Ford, 1991a).

Finally, some battered women file charges in order to hold the charges over their partner as they bargain for security (Ford, 1983, 1991b). Prosecution is a victim power resource when used in negotiating for security. The bargain may involve simple promises of leaving her alone. Or it may involve agreements for structural arrangements likely to bring longer-term security (e.g., counseling, favorable terms for divorce, support payments, child visitation rights, etc.). Dropping charges fulfills the victim's part of the agreement.

Although dropped charges are neither unique to battered women nor necessarily problematic, recently advocated policies have addressed them as such. For example, Lerman recommends a set of policy changes that "may reduce the likelihood of victim noncooperation in spouse-abuse cases and increase the likelihood that a disposition will be reached" (Lerman, 1981, p. 19). These changes include denying victims' requests to drop charges, avoiding use of extralegal criteria in decisions to file charges, plea bargaining cases where the victim might be traumatized by a trial, sending warning letters to suspected assailants who are not charged, and diverting qualified assailants to treatment programs.

It may be that these policies are effective in reducing case attrition, but until recently, none had been rigorously evaluated to test its effectiveness in controlling assailants and protecting battered women (Center for Women Policy Studies, 1979; Dutton, 1988; Lerman, 1981). The Santa Barbara LEAA (Law Enforcement Assistance Administration) Family Violence Program implemented some of these recommendations (though, notably, not a no-drop policy) in an effort to facilitate prosecution for victims and to make more wife assaulters accountable through criminal justice processing. Evaluation research initially showed that the number of wife assaulters held accountable increased with the introduction of a special unit for domestic cases in the district attorney's office (Berk, Loseke, Berk, & Rauma, 1980). A later evaluation found that with changes in the organization and personnel of the special unit, the earlier gains were lost (Berk, Rauma, Loseke, & Berk, 1982). These findings suggest that whatever policies are put in place, they must be structured for routine administration independent of discretionary or extralegal inclinations of unique officials responsible for their implementation. But the research did not answer the more important question of whether or not the policies serve to protect women from continuing violence.

Prosecutorial Tracking

Once a case is accepted into the system, the prosecutor directs the case toward some outcome specified by policy, custom, or other prosecutor preferences. In this section, we describe several common prosecutorial tracks as implemented in standardized policies. Our model is the system of criminal justice in Marion County, Indiana. Marion County encompasses all of Indianapolis along with a few small townships. In 1985, the county prosecutor's office implemented a demonstration domestic violence program consistent with the U.S. Attorney General's Task Force (1984) recommendations. Structurally, the program called for vertical prosecution[3] with continuing support from victim advocates throughout the prosecution process. A year

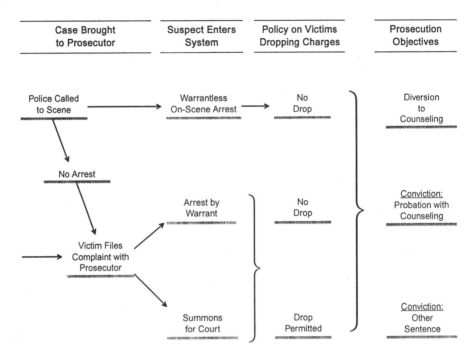

Figure 6.2. Prosecutorial Policy Tracks

later, the office hosted a randomized field experiment to evaluate specific alternative policies for processing cases of domestic violence. Following our description of the policies, we present some findings from that experiment.

Figure 6.2 presents details of prosecutorial tracking from the point a suspect enters the criminal justice system to the point at which his case is scheduled for trial. The first major policy alternative is whether to allow a victim to drop charges. In 1986, the Marion County prosecutor's office maintained a "no-drop" policy consistent with the task force recommendations. "Drop permitted" excepted some victim-complaint cases for purposes of evaluation. Those women were told simply that the prosecutor understood that a victim may have valid reasons for dropping charges and that should she later wish to drop, the prosecutor would oblige following the defendant's preliminary hearing in court. Permission to drop was not given to victims in on-scene arrest cases, which are initiated on the basis of an officer's probable cause affidavit, often without a victim's consent.

Once initiated, a case is tracked toward one of three outcomes: pretrial diversion to counseling for wife assaulters, conviction with counseling recommended as a condition of probation, or conviction with a recommendation for presumptive sentencing not including counseling. These prosecutorial tracks represent alternative courses of prosecution available to a prosecutor for handling a case. They are idealized here as discrete options.

Pretrial diversion programs are commonly offered as alternatives to adjudication, especially for first offenders in misdemeanor cases. In cases of wife assault, diversion is seen as a way of getting an assaulter into rehabilitative treatment without adding further stress to his relationship with the victim. Diversion generally entails continuing a defendant's case to allow time for him to receive counseling. If he successfully completes his treatment, the prosecutor will dismiss charges. At that point, he leaves court without a conviction on his record. The principal difference in diversion agreements from one jurisdiction to another is whether it is conditioned simply on the offender's agreement with the prospect of going to trial if he fails or of being subject to immediate sentencing. Marion County policy follows the former plan.

Any form of rehabilitative counseling could be offered in diversion agreements. The Marion County program uses variations on anger control and values clarification models implemented by local agencies. "Failure" is defined according to the rules of the counseling agencies. In general, a man fails the program if he assaults the original victim while in treatment. He may also fail if he misses sessions, if he is noncooperative, or if, for any reason, he is seen as being unsuitable for treatment. His case is then tracked for adjudication to conviction. Diversion is generally attractive to defendants who risk conviction and want to avoid the threat of any new offense being charged as a felony (see above).

Diversion offers a means of controlling crime through rehabilitation. As with other policies, it has not been rigorously evaluated. Rauma (1984) has presented findings on the nature of prosecutors' decisions to offer diversion under the Santa Barbara program, though not on its rehabilitative effects. His report that prosecutors invoke extralegal criteria in selecting cases for diversion suggests that cases that might otherwise be lost are at least retained under control of the prosecutor with a threat of future prosecution, a consideration apparent in observations of prosecutors in Marion County, Indiana. We discuss the general issue of court-mandated treatment below.

The other two tracks entail the prosecutor winning a conviction and then recommending a particular sentence to the judge. The conviction may follow a trial or it may be a negotiated guilty plea conditioned on the prosecutor's recommended sentence. Marion County's domestic violence prosecutors almost always restrict their plea bargaining to sentencing rather than types of charges. When charges become part of an agreement, however, prosecutors seek to preserve battery charges and give up other misdemeanor offenses. This insures that the wife assaulter has a conviction for battery on record, thus allowing for felony charges should he commit battery again. It also helps get the man into counseling, if recommended.

The second prosecutorial track calls for the same counseling programs used in diversion. Under this option, however, treatment is made a requirement of probation. The sentence typically includes suspended jail time and costs, including fees for probation and counseling. The final track, "other," calls for presumptive sentencing, that is, a recommendation consistent with the basic sentences defined by code. In Indiana, for example, conviction for Class A misdemeanor battery carries a sentence of up to one year in jail and a fine not exceeding $5,000, or if jail time is suspended, probation up to one year, along with court costs and whatever conditions a judge might attach to probation (e.g., restitution, rehabilitative treatment, community service).

Court-mandated counseling by diversion or probation attempts to coerce wife assaulters' participation in programs meant to reduce the chance of continuing violence. Dutton and McGregor (1991) argue that the existence of such treatment options has made criminal justice agencies more receptive to complaints of domestic violence (cf. Sigler, Crowley, & Johnson, 1990). They are willing to hear cases knowing that there is an opportunity for rehabilitation through court action. But the promise of effective treatment (i.e., wife assaulters desisting from habitual violence) has yet to be demonstrated under rigorous research designs. Some evaluations fail to control for possible deterrent effects of criminal justice; some report findings for those who "complete" treatment without consideration for a program's account-ability in keeping clients in treatment; all lack randomized controls for comparing those treated with others receiving comparable criminal justice experiences except for counseling (Dutton & McGregor, 1991; Saunders & Azar, 1989; see also Eisikovits & Edleson, 1989; Hamberger & J. E. Hastings, this volume).

A prosecutor's choice of one policy track over another may be highly constrained by factors beyond his or her control. First, to the extent that the prospect of a conviction rests with a victim's testimony, the prosecutor must consider the victim's willingness and capacity to make a persuasive presentation in court; even under a no-drop policy, victims retain control through their refusal to participate in the pro-ceedings (DuBow & Becker, 1976). And the prosecutor may have to change tracks according to the victim's wishes. Let us assume that office policy calls for seeking executed jail time upon conviction. If the victim does not want the defendant jailed, the prosecutor must prepare for at best a reluctant witness and at worst one willing to perjure herself to realize her interests through prosecution. Often victims want the defendant to get help without suffering the usual criminal sanctions. Perhaps a conviction is still desirable to establish a record for later felony charging. Then the victim might be persuaded to testify with the promise that a request will be made for counseling as a condition of probation, in lieu of jail. Some victims object to their assailant having a criminal conviction on record pursuant to court action. In that case, the prosecutor might seek a diversion agreement, accepting that the lack of a conviction precludes upgrading charges for a new offense.

A final issue in selecting one track over another for misdemeanor offenses is the amount of time each holds a case in the system, both before and after it is settled in court. No one wants cases lingering in the system. For prosecutors and judges, protracted time means pro-longed administrative responsibility. For victims and defendants it brings longer term inconvenience, anguish, and stress. For victims, in particular, extended proceedings may require repeated contacts with their assailant and thus more opportunity for conflict. Diversion gets cases through the process most quickly, provided it is completed successfully. In the Indianapolis experiment reported below, diversion agreements were reached within 122 days of arraignment on average, and treatment completed within 4 months to a year, depending on the counseling agency. Adjudicated guilt cases with counseling or with other sentencing were completed within 168 and 191 days, respectively. Counseling as a condition of probation may take less time to settle because it is more readily agreed to in plea bargaining as an attractive alternative to jail. And defendants can agree to counseling as a demonstration to their victim of their willingness to change. Whatever the sentence, it will keep a defendant in the correctional system for 6 months to a year, depending on the seriousness of the charge.

Evaluations of Prosecution Policies

The prosecution process need achieve no more than conviction to assuage the state's interest in crimes of violence. Advocacy for battered women over the past two decades, however, has sensitized authorities to the responsibility of prosecutors to do what they can to protect victims from continuing violence. In 1984, the protective function of prosecution gained prominence through the U.S. Attorney General's Task Force on Family Violence. In its final report, the task force outlined four specific recommendations for prosecutors with application to wife assault:

- Prosecutors should organize special units to process family violence cases and wherever possible should use vertical prosecution.
- The victim should not be required to sign a formal complaint against the abuser before the prosecutor files charges, unless mandated by state law.
- Whenever possible, prosecutors should not require family violence victims to testify at the preliminary hearing.
- If the defendant does not remain in custody, when it is consistent with the needs of the victim, the prosecutor should request the judge to issue an order restricting the defendant's access to the victim as a condition of setting bail or releasing the assailant on his own recognizance. If the condition is violated, swift and sure enforcement of the order and revocation of release are required.

Each of these recommendations affirms the state's interest in controlling violence, first by organizing prosecutorial activities to insure an effective response to complaints, and then by relieving a victim of the appearance that she is the sole bearer of the charges against her assailant. And with a demonstration of the state's concern and support for the complaining victim, she should have fewer reasons for not participating as the case proceeds to adjudication. The final recommendation additionally promises victims immediate security while the case is in progress.

Underlying these recommendations is the assumption that prosecution ultimately does protect victims from repeated violence, particularly when wife assaulters perceive that the state can respond to alleged criminal conduct apart from victims' complete control. But can the state offer real protection through prosecution? Notwithstanding "enormous reforms in policies and attitudes that reflect a growing consensus on how best to handle family violence" (Friedman & Shulman, 1990, p. 90), we know little with certainty about what best protects victims.

Elliott's (1989) review of the research literature on prosecution effects revealed only one study specifically addressing preventive effects (Fagan, Friedman, Wexler, & Lewis, 1984). And although others have looked at counseling under threat of court sanctions, only one more recent study (Ford & Regoli, 1992) has evaluated the effectiveness of alternative prosecution policies.

Prosecution Versus No Prosecution

Fagan and colleagues (1984) evaluated the prevalence of repeated violence against women served by five federally funded intervention programs. They report findings on the preventive effect of prosecution versus other forms of intervention (police only or social service contacts) based on interviews with 270 battered women who sought help through one of the programs. Twenty-nine percent of these victims reported new incidents of violence within 6 months of intervention. Seventy-four of the defendants were prosecuted, with 18 defendants ultimately convicted and sentenced. Prosecution was not significantly more likely to result in a reduced chance of follow-up violence when compared with other interventions. Similarly, the difference in rates of new violence for those convicted and sentenced versus others was nonsignificant. A closer examination of defendants' prior violence led Fagan (1989) to conclude that criminal justice interventions are most effective in reducing the chance of new violence by defendants with a history of less severe violence. There was no such difference, however, either for those prosecuted versus others or for those convicted and sentenced versus others. In short, the Fagan et al. study suggests that prosecution has *no* preventive effect. Unfortunately, the researchers had too few cases to distinguish the effects of prosecution independent of police actions. A more recent experimental study offers more definitive conclusions on the effectiveness of prosecutorial policies and is described in more detail in the following section.

Alternative Prosecution Policies: The Indianapolis Experiment

The Indianapolis Domestic Violence Prosecution Experiment (Ford & Regoli, 1992) evaluated common policies for processing cases of misdemeanor wife battery initiated either by warrantless, on-scene police arrests (OSA cases) or by victim complaints directly to the prosecutor's office (VC cases). Each victim was told she could not drop charges and that the case involved "a crime against the state." For both entry sets, prosecutors agreed to "track" cases toward one of three court outcomes following randomized recommendations of the experimental team: pretrial diversion to a counseling program for wife assaulters, prosecution to conviction with a recommendation of counseling as a condition of probation, or prosecution to conviction with presumptive sentencing. The victim complaint cases had a fourth randomized condition under which some victims were permitted to drop charges.

The experiments dealt with all men formally charged with a misdemeanor assault against a female conjugal partner between June 1986 and July 1987 who met certain eligibility requirements. A case was rejected if a defendant had previously been prosecuted for an act of violence against the victim, if he had a criminal history of felony violence, or if he posed such a serious threat of imminent danger that the prosecutor took immediate action against the suspect prior to his inclusion in the experiment. The On-Scene Arrest (OSA) experiment involved 198 defendants. The Victim-Initiated Complaint (VC) experiment involved 480 defendants. Within each experiment, tracking recommendations were made to a prosecutor based on randomization of treatments. Researchers then observed cases as they moved through the prosecution process to settlement by dismissal, diversion, or trial. Interviews were conducted 6 months following case settlement with 106 OSA victims and 324 VC victims. Findings on the effectiveness of alternative tracks discussed below are based on victim interview reports of violence in the 6 months prior to the prosecuted charge, violence during the prosecution process, and violence within 6 months following the case being settled in court.

The Indianapolis Experiment was conducted under a model prosecution program designed to support victims as they participate in the criminal justice process. Of course, some victims were permitted to drop charges by experimental design. Others were actively discouraged from trying to drop charges by being informed of the no-drop policy. Even so, about 20% of the OSA cases and 10% of the VC cases were dismissed for lack of a cooperative victim-witness. In most of these cases, the women failed to appear in court despite efforts by victim advocates to locate and encourage them to comply with their subpoena. Thus, under the no-drop policy, the prosecutor could not account for the whereabouts and safety of the victims. On the other hand, 54% of the victims permitted to drop had their case dismissed: 45% by request and 9% by failing to appear. A no-drop policy apparently keeps cases in the system, but forces victims otherwise coerced or determined not to participate to avoid the prosecutor altogether. We will examine its effect on victim security below.

Results

Seventy-five percent of all OSA defendants had battered their victim at least once in the 6 months before the violence resulting in their latest arrest. By 6 months following case settlement, 38% had battered again, a 50% reduction in the chance of new violence based on prior history. Figure 6.3 shows that there is little difference in this

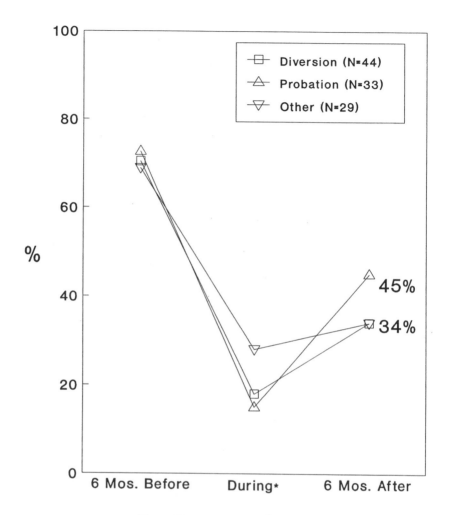

* Mean Process Time (in days):
Diversion 99 Probation 138 Other 137

Figure 6.3. Percentage of Men Violent Before, During, and After Prosecutorial Tracking (On-Scene Police Arrests). Diversion and Probation include Counseling.

pattern according to the prosecutorial track pursued. Although there seems to be some benefit for victims whose assailant is arrested and prosecuted, we cannot say that these victims are better off than if the men had *not* been arrested or had been arrested and not prosecuted. But given arrest with prosecution, one policy is no better than another. Notice, too, that one out of five arrestees commits a new act of violence even before his case is settled. Apparently, whatever punishment is threatened in the prosecution process, it fails to deter this minority of offenders.

Follow-up interviews with OSA victims showed that few attributed new violence to retaliation for arrest. What new violence occurred represented a continuation of an established pattern rather than a criminogenic effect. And despite the percentages reporting new violence, 69% of the victims said they were "satisfied" with the criminal justice system; 75% reported feeling in greater control of their situation as a result of prosecution.

Victims who file charges against their partner have experiences with violence before and after prosecution similar to OSA victims. Seventy-two percent said they were battered at least once prior to the incident on which they filed charges. Twenty-nine percent had been battered again within 6 months following settlement: a 60% reduction in the prevalence of criminal violence. And as with OSA victims, about one out of five VC victims was assaulted while her case awaited settlement. Nevertheless, 65% of the victims said they were "satisfied" with the criminal justice system; 77% reported feeling in greater control of their situation as a result of prosecution.

Also like OSA cases, those initiated by victim complaint show little variation in the chance of new violence among diversion, probation with counseling, and other sentences in preventing further violence, as displayed in Figures 6.4a and 6.4b. Within the warrant arrest track, however, victims who are permitted to drop charges are far less likely to experience new violence either during the process or within the 6-month follow-up period. None of the victims interviewed were assaulted during the process; 13% were battered after settlement.

In Indianapolis, a drop-permitted policy following a warrant arrest reduces the chance of continuing violence more than any other

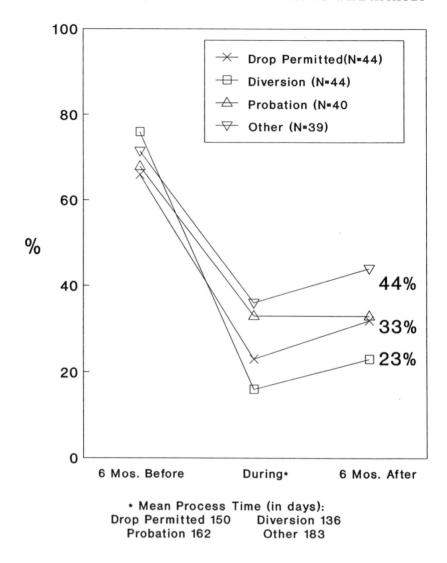

Figure 6.4a. Percentage of Men Violent Before, During, and After Prosecutorial Tracking (Victim-Complainant/Summons Cases). Diversion and Probation include Counseling.

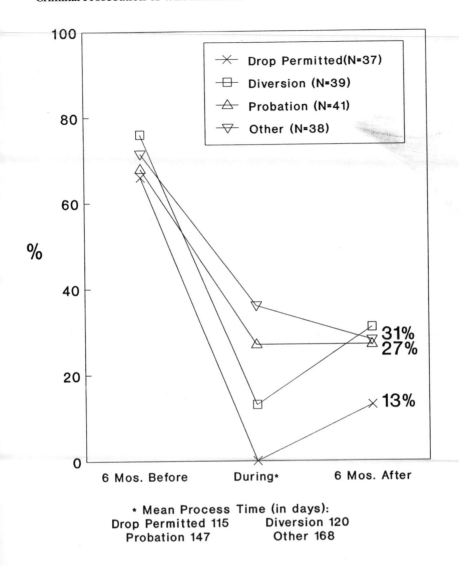

Figure 6.4b. Percentage of Men Violent Before, During, and After Prosecutorial Tracking (Victim-Complainant/Warrant Cases). Diversion and Probation include Counseling.

Table 6.1 Six-Month Follow-up on Violence by Drop Policy and
Case Outcome

	Policy	
	No Drop	Drop Permitted
Case Pursued	30%	7%
	(*n* = 227)	(*n* = 43)
Case Dismissed	33%	41%
	(*n* = 15)	(*n* = 39)

prosecutorial track evaluated. One should bear in mind, however, that all these findings concern prosecutorial tracks—alternative policy options for processing cases—and not necessarily actual prosecution outcomes (see Ford & Regoli, 1992). Victims who were permitted to drop charges did not always drop, and if they did they were not necessarily safer from harm than if they followed through. In fact, among victims interviewed, 48% of victims who were permitted to drop actually did drop, either by request (46%) or by failing to appear for court (2%); only 6% of victims with cases tracked under a no-drop policy had charges dropped (by failing to appear for court or refusing to testify). Table 6.1 summarizes the violent consequence of dropping versus pursuing charges under the drop-permitted and no-drop policies. Although permitting victims to drop charges gives them the best chance for security, clearly, there is danger in actually dropping.

The Indianapolis finding of "no difference" in the follow-up violence of men who were tracked into counseling versus others suggests that rehabilitative treatment has no effect. It is important to note, however, that the experimental track does not necessarily mean that men received treatment. Any number of contingencies might cause the prosecutorial treatments assigned to result in some other treatment delivered. For example, a defendant who is offered diversion might reject it, a judge might ignore the prosecutor's sentencing recommendation, or the man might be found not guilty. In the Indianapolis experiment, including dismissals and not guilty findings, the prosecutor's recommendation was realized in just 58% of the on-scene arrest cases and 65% of the victim complaint cases (Ford & Regoli, 1992). Even so, if we ignore the experimental tracks and look at actual treatment received, a similar finding holds. Mandated counseling appears to be a successful rehabilitative treatment for up to 80% of the assailants in the Indianapolis experiments. Those who received no counseling, however, were equally likely to desist for the 6-month follow-up period. The point, then, is that *any* intervention helps, not necessarily counseling.

Discussion and Policy Implications

The limited evidence on the effectiveness of alternative prosecution policies for preventing wife assault suggests that no single policy commonly advocated is any better than another. The chance of a man assaulting his partner again in the short term is essentially unaffected by whether he is prosecuted under policies calling for harsh punishment or for rehabilitative treatment. What matters is that he faces prosecution. The Indianapolis experiment, however, offers the surprising finding that, contrary to popular advocacy, permitting victims to drop charges significantly reduces their risk of further violence after a suspect has been arrested on a victim-initiated warrant, when compared with usual policies. We believe that under a drop-permitted policy, women are empowered to take control of events in their relationship. Some are empowered through prosecution such that they can use the possibility of abandoning prosecution as a power resource in bargaining for their security (Ford, 1991b). Others are empowered by the alliance they form with more powerful others, such as police, prosecutors, and judges. As long as the alliance is steadfast, a victim can threaten to invoke her allies' power to deter her assailant (Ford & Regoli, 1992). The warrant arrest signifies their attentiveness to her grievance.

Any policy reform based on the Indianapolis findings should recognize that the drop-permitted option was available only to victims who filed charges in person at the prosecutor's office. None of the victims called as witnesses following on-scene arrests of their partner was allowed to drop charges. There is no evidence that some form of drop-permitted policy would be effective in cases initiated by on-scene police arrests. Indeed, such a policy may very well be counterproductive in protecting victims as it could reinforce the prejudices of police officers already predisposed to inaction. The general lesson of victim empowerment might still apply if OSA victims are made to feel secure in alliance with the criminal justice system, and if they are given a voice in determining sanctions for their assailant. Only future research will tell whether this strategy will offer any greater protection.

On the other hand, battered women who initiate complaints with the prosecutor should be told that they may drop charges after the defendant has been arraigned if they are certain that doing so is in their best interests. At the same time, they should be strongly encouraged to follow through with the charges in order to protect themselves. Victims who bargain for security with criminal charges and then drop them are more likely to end up assaulted again than if they proceed to adjudication. It is tempting for some officials to coerce victim cooperation, but the lesson of no-drop policies suggests that any disempowering policy could further jeopardize battered women. Instead, prosecutors can offer incentives to keep victims in the system while reinforcing their power. For example, victims can be given the opportunity to determine the prosecution track for court outcomes. Each victim can be shown respect for making choices that only she is competent to make after receiving good information and reasonable options.

Court-mandated treatment, either by diversion agreement or as a condition of probation, is the most popular of prosecutorial options. Battered women are likely to find men's counseling, when available, consistent with a desire that suspects "get help." Victims, prosecutors, and judges need to recognize that counseling is unlikely to have any greater preventive effect than other alternatives. They need to be vigilant to see that agencies meet their responsibilities to victims. And true to their alliance with victims, criminal justice officials need to insure that men who fail the terms of diversion or probation are vigorously pursued with whatever sanctions were promised in reaching the original agreement or sentence. In anticipation of failure, any description of rehabilitative options presented to victims should include consideration of such issues as the upgrading of charge seriousness following a conviction, a sometimes desirable outcome that is unavailable following failure in pretrial diversion programs.

Prosecutors can further support and perhaps protect victims by attending to victim interests throughout the prosecution process: they can monitor warrants to see that they are served in a timely manner; they can request orders of protection and see that they are aggressively enforced; they can watch for evidence of obstruction of justice in defense attorneys' contacts with victims; and they can make every effort to account for a victim's safety, especially if she fails to appear for scheduled court proceedings. They should not simply let cases slip out of the system without ascertaining that victims are not in danger. An advantage of permitting victims to drop charges is that they can freely express their concerns without avoiding court. Prosecutors can also facilitate the coordination of services for battered women by providing information on shelters and other agencies offering assistance.

We have seen that the criminal prosecution of wife assaulters entails the interaction of police, victims, defendants and their attorneys, prosecutors, judges, and other personnel. Each player in the system carries unique personal motives and institutional perspectives. "Successful" prosecution may be defined differently by each. Policy reforms should acknowledge that institutional definitions of justice may conflict with a particular woman's notions of justice. Policies must be evaluated to insure that prosecutorial action does not place a victim in greater jeopardy than doing nothing at all. And while trying to address the problem of wife assault on a more global scale, prosecutors must not allow their interest in redressing crimes against the state to displace the goal of stopping violence against individual battered women.

The Indianapolis Prosecution Experiment provides evidence that prosecution can prevent violence. It also suggests that empowering the victim by allowing her to make choices in the prosecution process (i.e., whether to drop charges) can increase her security. Policies that exclude the victim from the process must be carefully examined to see whose needs are truly being served: the "system's" or the victim's. The focus should be on providing victims with the information and protection needed so they can make truly free choices. Policy should be directed toward encouraging an alliance between police, prosecutors, and victims with a common goal of breaking the cycle of violence.

Notes

1. The prosecutor may take complaints from victims who never called the police as well as those who called but learned that the police could not arrest for the crime charged. As recently as 1987, 70% of misdemeanor wife battery cases in Marion County, Indiana, were initiated by a victim complaint to the prosecutor, even with a proarrest policy in place among local police agencies. Today, victims file with the prosecutor in about 50% of the cases, an indication perhaps that the arrest policy is taking hold.

2. The decision whether to charge a case as a misdemeanor or as a felony is not trivial. Felonies receive much greater investigative attention from police and, sometimes, grand juries. Felonies are normally handled by more experienced prosecutors with lighter caseloads and greater resources than their counterparts in misdemeanor courts. If available, victim advocates are more likely to be assigned to felony cases. Cases are given much less attention and visibility in misdemeanor courts due to the heavy caseloads. Prosecutorial performance in felony cases is more likely to be subject to community scrutiny (Utz, 1978). Different administrative rules, rights, and sanctions apply to felonies. Felonies are punishable by incarceration for a year or more in a state prison, whereas misdemeanors are punishable by a fine or a term of *up to* one year in a city or county jail. Convicted felons are often subject to other automatic sanctions such as losing the right to vote, to hold public elective office, to carry a weapon, or to hold certain jobs.

3. "Vertical prosecution" is a strategy for closely monitoring cases proceeding through the system. Strictly speaking, it means that the same prosecutor who screens and approves a case tracks it for treatment in court, and ultimately processes the case (by trial, diversion, or nolle prosequi) for disposition.

References

Abadinsky, H. (1984). *Discretionary justice.* Springfield, IL: Charles C. Thomas.

Albonetti, C. A. (1987). Prosecutorial discretion: The effects of uncertainty. *Law & Society Review, 21*, 291-313.

Bannon, J. (1975, August). *Law enforcement problems with intra-family violence.* Speech presented at the annual meeting of the American Bar Association, Montreal, Quebec.

Bard, M. (1980). Functions of the police and the justice system in family violence. In M. R. Green (Ed.), *Violence and the family* (pp. 105-120). Boulder, CO: Westview.

Berk, R. A., Loseke, D. R., Berk, S. F., & Rauma, D. (1980). Bringing the cops back in: A study of efforts to make the criminal justice system more responsive to incidents of family violence. *Social Science Research, 9*, 193-215.

Berk, R. A., Rauma, D., Loseke, D. R., & Berk, S. F. (1982). Throwing the cops back out: The decline of a local program to make the criminal justice system more responsive to incidents of domestic violence. *Social Science Research, 11,* 245-279.

Boland, B., Brady, E., Tyson, H., & Bassler, J. (1983). *The prosecution of felony arrests.* Washington, DC: U.S. Department of Justice, Bureau of Justice Statistics.

Brosi, K. B. (1979). *A cross-city comparison of felony case processing.* Washington, DC: Institute for Law and Social Research.

Buzawa, E. S., & Buzawa, C. G. (1990). *Domestic violence: The criminal justice response.* Newbury Park, CA: Sage.

Center for Women Policy Studies. (1979). *Response to Violence in the Family, 3,* 1-2.

Dobash, R. E., & Dobash, R. (1979). *Violence against wives: A case against the patriarchy.* New York: Free Press.

DuBow, F. L., & Becker, T. M. (1976). Patterns of victim advocacy. In W. F. McDonald (Ed.), *Criminal justice and the victim* (pp. 147-164). Beverly Hills, CA: Sage.

Dunford, F. W., Huizinga, D., & Elliott, D. (1989). *The Omaha domestic violence police experiment: Final report to the National Institute of Justice and the City of Omaha.* Boulder, CO: Institute of Behavioral Science.

Dunford, F. W., Huizinga, D., & Elliott, D. (1990). The role of arrest in domestic assault: The Omaha police experiment. *Criminology, 28,* 183-206.

Dutton, D. G. (1986). The outcome of court mandated treatment for wife assault: A quasi-experimental evaluation. *Violence and Victims, 1,* 163-175.

Dutton, D. G. (1987). The criminal justice response to wife assault. *Law and Human Behavior, 11,* 189-206.

Dutton, D. G. (1988). *The domestic assault of women: Psychological and criminal justice perspectives.* Newton, MA: Allyn & Bacon.

Dutton, D. G., & McGregor, B.M.S. (1991). The symbiosis of arrest and treatment for wife assault: The case for combined intervention. In M. Steinman (Ed.), *Woman battering: Policy responses* (pp. 131-154). Cincinnati, OH: Anderson.

Eisikovits, Z. C., & Edleson, J. L. (1989). Intervening with men who batter: A critical review of the literature. *Social Service Review, 63,* 384-414.

Elliott, D. S. (1989). Criminal justice procedures in family violence crimes. In L. Ohlin & M. Tonry (Eds.), *Family violence* (pp. 65-118). Chicago: University of Chicago Press.

Ellis, J. W. (1984). Prosecutorial discretion to charge in cases of spousal assault: A dialogue. *Journal of Criminal Law & Criminology, 75,* 56-102.

Fagan, J. (1989). Cessation of family violence: Deterrence and dissuasion. In L. Ohlin & M. Tonry (Eds.), *Family Violence* (pp. 377-426). Chicago: University of Chicago Press.

Fagan, J., Friedman, E., Wexler, S., & Lewis, V. L. (1984). *National family violence evaluation: Final report: Vol. 1. Analytic findings.* San Francisco: URSA Institute.

Feeley, M. M. (1979). *The process is the punishment.* New York: Russell Sage Foundation.

Field, M. H., & Field, H. F. (1973). Marital violence and the criminal process: Neither justice nor peace. *Social Service Review, 47,* 221-240.

Finn, P. (1991). State-by-state guide to enforcement of civil protection orders. *Response, 14,* 3-12.

Finn, P., & Colson, S. (1990). *Civil protection orders: Legislation, current court practice, and enforcement.* Washington, DC: National Institute of Justice.

Ford, D. A. (1983). Wife battery and criminal justice: A study of victim decision-making. *Family Relations, 32,* 463-475.

Ford, D. A. (1991a). Preventing and provoking wife battery through criminal sanctioning: A look at the risks. In D. D. Knudsen & J. L. Miller (Eds.), *Abused and battered* (pp. 191-209). New York: Aldine de Gruyter.

Ford, D. A. (1991b). Prosecution as a victim power resource: A note on empowering women in violent conjugal relationships. *Law & Society Review, 25,* 313-334.

Ford, D. A., & Burke, M. J. (1987, July). *Victim-initiated criminal complaints for wife battery: An assessment of motives.* Paper presented at the Third Annual Conference for Family Violence, Durham, NH.

Ford, D. A., & Regoli, M. J. (1990, May). *The effectiveness and impacts of defense counsel in cases of wife battery.* Paper presented at the annual meeting of the Law & Society Association, Berkeley, CA.

Ford, D. A., & Regoli, M. J. (1992). The preventive impacts of policies for prosecuting wife batterers. In E. S. Buzawa & C. G. Buzawa (Eds.), *Domestic violence: The changing criminal justice response* (pp. 181-208). Dover, MA: Auburn House.

Friedman, L. N., & Shulman, M. (1990). Domestic violence: The criminal justice response. In A. J. Lurigio, W. G. Skogan, & R. C. Davis (Eds.), *Victims of crime: Problems, policies, and programs* (pp. 87-103). Newbury Park, CA: Sage.

Fromson, T. L. (1977). The case for legal remedies for abused women. *N.Y.U. Review of Law and Social Change, 6,* 135-174.

Garner, J., & Visher, C. A. (1988). Policy experiments come of age. *NIJ Reports, 21,* 1-6.

Gayford, J. J. (1977). The plight of the battered wife. *International Journal of Environmental Studies, 10,* 283-286.

Goolkasian, G. A. (1986a, May). *Confronting domestic violence: A guide for criminal justice agencies* (National Institute of Justice Issues and Practices Monograph). Washington, DC: U.S. Department of Justice.

Goolkasian, G. A. (1986b). The judicial system and domestic violence: An expanding role. *Response, 9,* 2-7.

Gottlieb, D. J., & Johnson, L. E. (1983). Reform in Kansas domestic violence legislation. *Kansas Law Review, 31,* 527-578.

Grau, J., Fagan, J., & Wexler, S. (1984). Restraining orders for battered women: Issues of access and efficacy. *Women and Politics, 4,* 13-28.

Hall, D. J. (1975). The role of the victim in the prosecution and disposition of a criminal case. *Vanderbilt Law Review, 28,* 931-985.

Hart, B. J. (1988). *Women, violence, and the law* (Statement to the Select Committee on Children, Youth, and Families hearing held September 16, 1987). Washington, DC: U.S. Government Printing Office.

Hilton, N. Z. (1989). One in ten: The struggle and disempowerment of the battered women's movement. *Canadian Journal of Family Law, 7,* 315-335.

Hirschel, J. D., Hutchison, I. W., & Dean, C. W. (1992). The failure of arrest to deter spouse abuse. *Journal of Research in Crime and Delinquency, 29,* 7-33.

Jacoby, J. (1979). The charging policies of prosecutors. In W. F. McDonald (Ed.), *The prosecutor* (pp. 75-97). Beverly Hills, CA: Sage.

Lerman, L. G. (1980). Civil protection orders: Obtaining access to court. *Response to Violence in the Family, 3,* 1-28.

Lerman, L. G. (1981). Criminal prosecution of wife beaters. *Response to Violence in the Family, 4,* 1-19.

Lerman, L. G. (1986). Prosecution of wife beaters: Institutional obstacles and innovations. In M. Lystad (Ed.), *Violence in the home: Interdisciplinary perspectives* (pp. 250-295). New York: Brunner/Mazel.

Lerman, L. G., & Livingston, F. (1983). State legislation on domestic violence. *Response to Violence in the Family, 6,* 1-28.

MacLeod, L. (1980). *Wife battering in Canada: The vicious circle.* Ottawa: Canadian Advisory Council on the Status of Women.

McDonald, W. F. (1979). The prosecutor's domain. In McDonald, W. F. (Ed.), *The prosecutor* (pp. 15-51). Beverly Hills, CA: Sage.

McGillivray, A. (1987). Battered women: Definition, models and prosecutorial policy. *Canadian Journal of Family Law, 6,* 15-45.

Myers, M. A., & Hagan, J. (1979). Private and public trouble: Prosecutors and the allocation of court resources. *Social Problems, 26,* 439-451.

Neubauer, D. W. (1974). *Criminal justice in middle America.* Morristown, NJ: General Learning Press.

Parnas, R. I. (1970). Judicial response to intra-family violence. *Minnesota Law Review, 54,* 585-644.

Pence, E. (1983). The Duluth domestic abuse intervention project. *Hamline Law Review, 6,* 247-275.

Pence, E., Miletich, E., Radulovich, E., & Galaway, B. (1985, August). *A systemic response to spouse abuse.* Paper presented at the Fifth International Symposium on Victimology, Zagreb, Yugoslavia.

Pleck, E. (1987). *Domestic tyranny.* New York: Oxford University Press.

Rauma, D. (1984). Going for the gold: Prosecutorial decision making in cases of wife assault. *Social Science Research, 13,* 321-351.

Saunders, D. G., & Azar, S. T. (1989). Treatment programs for family violence. In L. Ohlin & M. Tonry (Eds.), *Family violence* (pp. 481-546). Chicago: University of Chicago Press.

Schmidt, J., & Steury, E. H. (1989). Prosecutorial discretion in filing charges in domestic violence cases. *Criminology, 27,* 487-510.

Sherman, L. W., & Berk, R. A. (1984). The specific deterrent effects of arrest for domestic assault. *American Sociological Review, 49,* 261-272.

Sherman, L. W., Schmidt, J. D., Rogan, D. P., Gartin, P. R., Cohn, E. G., Collins, D. J., & Bacich, A. R. (1991). From initial deterrence to longterm escalation: Short custody arrest for poverty ghetto domestic violence. *Criminology, 29,* 821-849.

Sigler, R. T., Crowley, J. M., & Johnson, I. (1990). Judicial and prosecutorial endorsement of innovative techniques in the trial of domestic abuse cases. *Journal of Criminal Justice, 18,* 443-453.

Spohn, C., Gruhl, J., & Welch, S. (1987). The impact of the ethnicity and gender of defendants on the decision to reject or dismiss felony charges. *Criminology, 25,* 175-191.

Steinberg, A. (1984) From private prosecution to plea bargaining: Criminal prosecution, the district attorney, and American legal history. *Crime & Delinquency, 30,* 568-592.

Steinman, M. (1991). Coordinated criminal justice interventions and recidivism among batterers. In M. Steinman (Ed.), *Woman battering: Policy responses* (pp. 221-236). Cincinnati, OH: Anderson.

Straus, M. A., Gelles, R. J., & Steinmetz, S. K. (1980). *Behind closed doors: Violence in the American family.* Garden City, NY: Anchor Press/Doubleday.

U.S. Attorney General's Task Force on Family Violence. (1984). *Final report.* Washington, DC: U.S. Department of Justice.

Utz, P. (1978). *Settling the facts.* Lexington, MA: Lexington.

Walker, L. E. (1979). *The battered woman.* New York: Harper & Row.

Wasoff, F. (1982). Legal protection from wifebeating: The processing of domestic assaults by Scottish prosecutors and criminal courts. *International Journal of the Sociology of Law, 10,* 187-204.

Williams, K. M. (1976). The effects of victim characteristics on the disposition of violent crimes. In W. F. McDonald (Ed.), *Criminal justice and the victim* (pp. 177-213). Beverly Hills, CA: Sage.

Women's Law Caucus, University of Montana. (1986). Montana's new domestic abuse statutes: A new response to an old problem. *Montana Law Review, 47,* 403-419.

Wright, C. (1985). Immediate arrest in domestic violence situations: Mandate or alternative. *Capital University Law Review, 14,* 243-268.

7

Family Courts, Marital Conflict Mediation, and Wife Assault

Change, conflict, and conflict management are endemic to society in general and to families in particular (Cain & Kulscar, 1983; Dahrendorf, 1957). Among married couples, intimacy interacts with structural and cultural changes (especially changes in gender relations) to produce variations in the frequency, duration, and severity of marital conflict (Goode, 1969). Frequent, severe, or prolonged marital conflict is strongly associated with separation and divorce (Ellis & Stuckless, 1992). To the conflicts that brought about the end of the marital relationship may now be added conflicts over property, support, and child custody and access. As the relationship conflicts frequently affect the conflicts over separation, the process of managing negotiations between separating spouses in a manner that both protects wives and produces just results is a complicated and difficult endeavor. This is especially true when one of the spouses, usually the wife, has been assaulted by the other. Litigation, lawyer

Department of Sociology, LaMarsh Research Programme on Violence and Conflict Resolution, York University, North York, Ontario, M3J 1P3.

negotiations, and mediation are different means of managing or settling such conflicts.

According to Emery and Wyer (1987), marital conflict (divorce)
mediation differs from litigation (in court) and lawyer negotiations
(out of court) in a number of important ways. Included among them
is client control of the process: "The [cooperating] parties make their
own decisions in mediation" (Emery & Wyer, 1987, p. 472). Based on
the assumption of cooperation between the spouses, then, marital
conflict mediation is a self-help process of settling conflicts that is
facilitated by a third party, the mediator, who is supposed to be
impartial. (For other definitions of mediation, see Carnevale & Pruitt,
1992; Coogler, 1978; Folberg & Taylor, 1984; Gulliver, 1979; Irving,
1980; Rifkin, 1984).

Conceived of in this way, marital conflict mediation may be regarded as "part of the broader movement towards the private ordering
of divorce" (Emery & Wyer, 1987, p. 472). Within this context, the
growth of marital conflict mediation and the reasons for it are discussed in the first half of the chapter. A discussion of the relation
between wife assault and mediation is reserved for the second half.

Marital Conflict (Divorce) Mediation, 1900-1992:
Growth and Rationales

Over 85 years ago, the renowned jurist Roscoe Pound (1906) called
for social experimentation with alternative dispute resolution processes that could more effectively solve human problems involving the
law. Twenty-three years later, in 1939, the seed sown by Pound
blossomed into the Los Angeles Conciliation Court (Payne, 1985). This
court's primary objective was to reconcile spouses through the process of conciliation. It was not until the 1960s that its primary orientation changed to solving conflicts associated with separation and
divorce. In 1963, the Association of Family and Conciliation Courts
was formed.

By 1980, court-based mediation services were available in the major
cities of a growing number of U.S. states and Canadian provinces
(McWhinney, 1985; Payne, 1985). One significant site for the provision of such services was Ontario's first Unified Family Court,

established in Hamilton in 1977. In 1991, this court was selected by the Court Reform Task Force as the test site for a pilot project designed to compare and evaluate comprehensive mediation and lawyer negotiations. In this pilot project, each spouse must have a lawyer for the specific purpose of reviewing the mediation agreement with respect to distribution of marital property and financial matters in general. In sum, not only has there been an increase in the number of U.S. and Canadian courts providing mediation services, but also in at least one court (Unified Family Court, Hamilton) mediation is no longer restricted to custody and access issues. If the pilot project is successful, comprehensive mediation may be implemented throughout the province.

Private mediation was relatively dormant in both the United States and Canada until the mid-1970s. By 1985, private mediation in the United States had become a "major growth industry" (Cain & Kulscar, 1983; Payne, 1985, p. 5). In Canada, a national association, Family Mediation Canada, was formed in 1984. Between 1984 and 1991, membership increased from 275 to 925 members. Nine of the 10 provinces had provincial associations affiliated with Family Mediation Canada. In summary, marital conflict mediation in the United States and Canada has grown markedly during the past 30 years. (For more detailed histories of mediation see Carnevale & Pruitt, 1992; Eekelaar & Katz, 1984; Folberg, 1984; Glendon, 1977; Rheinstein, 1972). There are several reasons or rationales for this development.

1. Rapid increases in the divorce rate during the past 20 years provided increased opportunities for work by all professional workers in the marital dispute settlement industry, family mediators included. Their inclusion was greatly facilitated by relatively slight educational or training requirements. Almost anyone could practice family mediation after a course lasting a weekend or two. Under these circumstances, the supply of mediators could easily be increased as the demand for them increased.

2. Marked increases in the divorce rate have not been accompanied by proportionate increases in resources allocated to family courts. In Canada, the proportion of couples who were divorced increased from one in five in 1971 to one in three in 1987. In 1984, approximately 54,000 marriages ended in divorce. By 1989 this figure had increased to 124,000, an increase of over 120% (Adams & Nagnur, 1990). In the

province of Ontario, budget allocations for all courts during the 5-year period 1984-1989 increased by only 12%. Diverting cases away from litigation was viewed by court authorities and the government as a way of achieving such bureaucratic-judicial goals as reducing caseloads and costs, increasing the speed of processing, and case disposition (Baskin & Sommers, 1990; Lerman, 1984). Lawyer negotiations were encouraged by judges, but these represented only a partial diversion because lawyers in negotiation still made demands on court resources. Mediation makes fewer demands and represents a more economic form of diversion. Hence, in contested cases, mediation could make a greater contribution to the achievement of court-bureaucratic goals than could lawyer negotiations. This conclusion stands without prejudice to many judges who, on the basis of their own experience of adversarial proceedings in divorce cases, their exposure to theory and research on the effects of such proceedings on the welfare of children, and their belief in mediation as a more humane and appropriate method of settling marital conflicts, initiated court-based mediation programs in their courts (Payne, 1985).

3. Judges, whether caring or less caring, prefer to apply determinate standards in reaching their decisions. With respect to child custody, the 18th- and 19th-century predecessors of sitting judges could apply a determinate standard when they applied the paternal, and later the maternal, preference rule. During the 20th century, however, the "best interest" standard became regnant. This standard, which refers to the future welfare of children, is vague and indeterminate (Elster, 1989). Because the outcome is viewed as unpredictable, a premium is placed on the introduction by each spouse's lawyer of any material derogating the other party that may influence the judge. This increases the acrimony of the proceedings. Under these conditions, judges may view the transactional costs of highly acrimonious proceedings to have a more adverse effect on the welfare of children than any decision they make (Eisenberg, 1982; Emery & Wyer, 1987; Mnookin, 1984). Under these circumstances, referring child custody and access cases to a marital conflict resolution process that gets at the underlying causes of conflicts, attempts to resolve indeterminacy through bargaining between the spouses, and is especially appropriate for dealing with the emotional arousal associated with such issues appears to many judges to be a wise decision.

4. Divorce legislation establishing the no-fault ground for divorce had the effect of making the past less important than the present and the future. This effect is uniquely consistent with two important tenets of marital conflict mediation: avoiding blame for past actions and focusing on solving problems with consequences for the future. If mediators themselves were asked to craft legislation designed to promote the mediation of marital conflicts, they would opt for the no-fault ground, such as living apart for a year, as the only criterion of true marriage breakdown.

In some jurisdictions, for example, California, the no-fault ground is the only ground for divorce. Here, however, despite the consistency between the orientation of the divorce legislation and that of mediation, bargaining between spouses in mediation and lawyer negotiations is not facilitated because the "pure no-fault rule of California is uniquely devoid of impetus to negotiation" (Blumberg, 1991, p. 123). Canada's 1986 Divorce Act, on the other hand, establishes two ways of proving that the marriage has truly broken down. The first is the criterion "lived separate and apart" for a year. The second is an offense criterion: a spouse against whom a divorce is sought has since the celebration of the marriage committed adultery or treated the applicant spouse with physical or mental cruelty of such a kind as to render continued cohabitation intolerable (Subsection 8[2]). The inclusion of the offense criterion increases the impetus for bargaining and lawyer negotiations. Other things being equal, the greater the opportunities for bargaining provided by divorce legislation, the greater is the likelihood that contested cases will be settled by lawyer negotiations or marital conflict (divorce) mediation, that is, the more marked the trend toward private ordering.

5. Changes in the relative popularity of psychoanalytic and family systems theory have tended to favor mediation over adversarial processes, including lawyer negotiations. Over the past 30 years, psychoanalytic theory—which supports an adversarial (win/lose) approach—appears to have lost its paradigmatic status to family systems theory, which supports nonadversarial conflict resolution processes such as mediation (Deutch, 1973; Emery & Wyer, 1987; Folberg & Taylor, 1984). Through its effect on judges, legislators, and mental health professionals, family systems theory has influenced the establishment and growth of marital conflict (divorce) mediation.

6. Legislative changes helped legitimate family mediation. In 1986, family mediation in Canada was given legal recognition by the federal Divorce Act. Subsection 9(2) of this act provides:

> It is the duty of every barrister, solicitor, lawyer or advocate who undertakes to act on behalf of a spouse in a divorce proceeding to discuss with the spouse the advisability of negotiating the matters that may be the subject of a support order or a custody order and to inform the spouse of the mediation facilities known to him or her that might be able to assist the spouses in negotiating those matters.

Of greater significance is the Ontario provincial Children's Law Reform Act. Subsection 31(1) of this act states:

> Upon an application for custody of or access to a child, the court, at the request of the parties, by order may appoint a person selected by the parties or any of them to satisfy the needs of the child.

According to Justice Walsh, head of the Family Law Division, Supreme Court of Ontario, "These recent amendments to the Children's Law Reform Act contain the only statutory provision for the resolution of family disputes by mediation" (cited in Payne, 1985, p. 8).

Finally, the growth of private family mediation was facilitated by the fact that models of family mediation already existed in the courts and that mediation as a generic, nonadversarial form of conflict resolution was well established in other industries and businesses, as well as in international relations (McWhinney, 1985).

In the midst of change and growth, there have also been some constants. One is the lack of a professional association with uniform standards and enforceable rules. Another is the apparent lack of interest, until very recently, in the manner in which wife assault is implicated in marital conflict mediation (see Ellis, 1990; Gray, 1992).

Wife Assault and Family Law

To contextualize the discussion that follows, it should be noted that the relative neglect of the crime of wife assault by agents of the family law system is part of the broader pattern of neglect by agents of the criminal justice system (Crawford & Gartner, 1992; The War Against Women, 1991). As participants in the family law system, family mediators participate in a system characterized by legislation that undermines allegations of wife battering (assaults repeated over a period of time) by wives separating from their husbands and that makes wife assault irrelevant to the outcomes of both mediation and lawyer negotiations.

Under the 1968 Divorce Act, marriage breakdown can be established by an applicant if she or he can prove treatment by the spouse "with physical (or mental) cruelty of such a kind as to render continued matrimonial cohabitation intolerable." Here, the case of *Mayberry v. Mayberry* (1941) (as cited by Hackett, 1990) is instructive:

> Her husband had been convicted of assault causing bodily harm on his wife, who had required extensive hospitalization. Further acts of violence by the husband were cited and accepted in evidence. Nevertheless, the judge stated that the cruelty was not of a kind as to render intolerable the continued cohabitation of spouses, but rather a sort of tit-for-tat irritation inflicted on each spouse by the other. (Hackett, 1990, p. 14)

Clearly, wives who are separating from their husbands and who may in the future want to proceed on offense grounds should never hit back, but should remain available and passive victims; however, they should not stay with their assaultive husband for too long, because a judge may interpret this as condoning the violence (cf. Hilton, 1991). Following a review of such cases, Hackett reaches the following conclusion: most wives who petitioned on the basis of physical cruelty that took place over a long period of time while they were cohabiting with their husband discovered that, "Many judges found this alone amounted to 'condonation' and so turned down the petition" (Hackett, 1990, p. 14). These judges either are unaware of research findings that answer the question, "Why does she stay?" by pointing to the economic dependency of wives on their husband, or are aware of the situation but do not consider it relevant.

Wife assault (physical cruelty) is also legally irrelevant to judicial decisions relating to spousal and child support. With respect to these issues, the 1986 Divorce Act directs judges to ignore "any misconduct of a spouse [including wife assault] in relation to the marriage." The act also requires that custody (and access) decisions be made on the basis of the best interests of the child. Wife assault, even repeated wife assault, is legally irrelevant to decisions regarding custody and access (The War Against Women, 1991, p. 45).

Family mediators working in the shadow of the family law system are participants in a system governed by legislation that, if it does not actually condone wife assault, tends to make it irrelevant to the processing of marital separation or divorce via lawyer negotiations or mediation. Under this condition, one might expect both lawyers and mediators to be equally uninterested in wife assault or equally un-able to do much about ensuring the physical safety of their clients. Critics of mediation, however, tend to believe that wives involved in lawyer negotiations are better protected than wives who participate in mediation. There are, they say, factors inherent in the process of marital conflict mediation that make it more dangerous for women participants.

Effect of Mediation on Wife Assault: Theory

In evaluating the effect of mediation on postmediation violence (and other outcomes), it is relevant to note that mediation varies with respect to its scope, format, and procedures. To the extent that outcomes vary systematically with different types of mediation, it is important to specify mediation type when mediation effects are being evaluated (Kressel, Pruitt & Associates, 1989, p. 401). In the critiques of mediation, however, details regarding the specific kinds of media-tion procedures and formats that are alleged to be hazardous for female participants are rarely revealed. Instead, mediation is usually sub-sumed under such general headings as "mandatory," "court based," "private," and so forth.

One of the earliest and most influential analyses linking wife assault with mediation was Lerman's 1984 *Harvard Women's Law Journal* publication. Formulating both "a law enforcement . . . and a femi-nist . . . critique of domestic violence mediation," she contended that "Mediation not only fails to protect women from subsequent vio-lence, but also perpetuates their continued victimization" (p. 61). The assumptions underlying mediation, as well as its primary goals, are primarily responsible for this state of affairs (Lerman, 1984). More specifically, mediators facilitate wife assault and fail to contribute to its prevention because they:

- ignore past marital behavior, including wife assault
- assume that the responsibility for wife assault is shared by the husband and the wife
- assign greater importance to facilitating agreements than to stopping the violence, especially where the latter reduces the likelihood of the former
- facilitate the signing of agreements that legitimate wife abuse
- trivialize violence against wives by using euphemisms to refer to it during the process of mediation and in the agreements spouses sign

Although Lerman did not explicitly formulate a theory, the following thesis does appear to be implicit in her criticisms: the past violence of wife assaulters is associated with their future violence. This association is likely to be stronger for violent husbands whose sense of personal responsibility for their assaultive behavior is muted or deflected by interventions that also attribute responsibility to the wife-victims or legitimate their violence under specified conditions (for examples of such agreements, see Lerman, 1984; Stallone, 1984). Where wife assaulters do not anticipate, and are in fact not subjected to, interventions that deter or treat their violent behavior, the link between past and future violence is strongest. In addition, some husbands who did not assault their wife in the past may now do so, according to Lerman (1984).

The idea that factors inherent in the mediation process indirectly "promote battering" and "perpetuate abuse" has also been advanced by two scholar-activists, Zoe Hilton (1991) and Dianna Stallone (1984). Their explanations, however, can be subsumed under the theory derived from Lerman's critique. The same is true for many of the factors identified by Ellis (1990), including the privacy-plus-self-help combination that tends to inhibit wife assault victims who are participating in divorce mediation from going outside this process and doing something about the violence themselves (e.g., reporting the matter to the police).

An interesting variant of the dual thesis that mediation is more dangerous to women because of factors inherent to mediation and that formal justice does a better job of protecting women than informal justice is presented by Cobb (1992). She analyzed 27 mediation transcripts for the purpose of abstracting "violence stories." These reveal that mediators ignore or "domesticize" violence. Unlike the criminal justice system, which delivers the bodies of violent criminals, including wife assaulters, into "the field of pain and death" (Cover, 1986, p. 1601), mediation facilitates problem solving by ignoring violence and the moral and interpersonal problems it poses (Cobb, 1992, p. 4). Because it constructs a boundary between informal and formal legal settings that "serve[s] to contain and manage conflict" (Cobb, 1992, p. 4), mediation increases the danger to assaulted wives who participate in it. Ignoring violence or dealing with it informally, she implies, neither deters wife assaulters nor teaches them the appropriate moral lesson.

This state of affairs is associated with, and perhaps caused by, "an ideology that simultaneously denies the presence of 'serious' [criminal] violence in informal settings *and* advocates the use of informal settings to deal with violence that occurs between persons who know each other." The mechanism underlying the domestication of violence "is related to the patterned transformation of rights into needs" (Cobb, 1992, p. 3).

The domestication of violence in mediation may be universally present (mediators themselves say they will not mediate violence). Moreover, the antecedent variables identified by Cobb may be included among its most important causes. Cobb, however, provides no research evidence that indicates that recidivist wife assaults occur more frequently to women participating in divorce mediation than to wives whose husband has been delivered "into the field of pain and death." Cobb's rather sanguine evaluation of the effectiveness of the criminal justice system in controlling wife assault and wife homicide is certainly not warranted by the data (Crawford & Gartner, 1992; Dunford, Huizinga, & Elliott, 1991; Farge & Rahder, 1991; Solicitor General of Ontario, 1989; The War Against Women, 1991).

Lawyer negotiators and their supporters appear to be as reluctant as mediators and their supporters are (or were) in acknowledging the possibility of a relationship between marital conflict settlements for separating couples and wife assault. Thus, MacDougall, a supporter of lawyer negotiations, notes that "because . . . of the emotional factors involved in the negotiation of family disputes, aggressive tactics [by lawyers] may produce an unanticipated and undesired response (Mac-Dougall, 1987, p. 37). The possibility that violent personal crimes may be included among these responses is not considered. Surely a great deal of consideration is warranted by the following conjunction of findings: "Most family disputes are resolved by [lawyer] negotiation" (MacDougall, 1984, p. 26) and estranged husbands figure prominently in wife killings (Crawford & Gartner, 1992). The findings referred to here do not indicate whether these husbands actually had their separation negotiated by lawyers. One may infer, however, that most of the homicides were committed by husbands who were separating, separated, or divorced; had children; and were involved in lawyer negotiations with their spouse. Given this possibility, it is difficult to understand how lawyer negotiators and their supporters can remain sanguine about the effect of the negotiation process on postseparation violence.

With respect to the explanations described here, two observations are in order. First, most mediators who participate in marital conflict (divorce) mediation vehemently deny "mediating violence." Many of the criticisms raised relate to mediation programs that deal with wife assaulters who have been diverted from criminal courts. Here, violence is being mediated and the criticisms may be valid.

Second, and partly as a function of their primary focus on mediation within the criminal justice system, critics of mediation have rarely theorized about the effect of lawyer negotiations or litigation on wife assault. These procedures represent alternatives to mediation, alternatives to which adversarial relations are central. Are there not factors inherent in adversarial ways of resolving conflicts that also "promote battering" and "perpetuate wife abuse"? Is a process that assumes cooperation between spouses (mediation) more likely to facilitate wife assault than one that assumes conflict (lawyer negotiations)? It is relevant, though, to note that compared with other specializations, relatively few family law lawyers are outright gladiators. A few are trained as mediators; others adopt a conciliatory approach and in joint meetings (both parties and both lawyers present), act as informal mediators.

Because of systemic gender inequality, power imbalance between male and female mediation participants is an important and relevant concern. Gender-based power imbalance is also implicated in lawyer negotiations. When combined with economic and emotional vulnerability, power imbalance between lawyer and client may become manifest in exploitation, both economic and sexual. The latter type of exploitation has been ignored by most critics of mediation. Lyon (1987), however, contextualizes sexual exploitation of female clients by their male lawyer within a more general critique of uncaring lawyers who emotionally harm their clients. In the present context, it is also relevant to note differences in the structural situation of mediation and negotiation that make sexual exploitation more probable in the latter than in the former.

In the usual mediation arrangement, both the husband and wife are present, forming a triad with the mediator. In the usual lawyer-client relationship, each lawyer and his or her client works as a separate dyad. Given this fundamental structural difference (triads vs. dyads), the process of sexual exploitation and its subtle manifestations in face-to-face interaction are more likely to be visible to the other mediation ex-partners than they are to ex-partners who are clients of other lawyers. The presence of both ex-partners in mediation decreases the likelihood of sexual exploitation by mediators. This specific (structural) source of social control is absent in the case of lawyer-client relationships. Dependence, the major basis of power (Blau, 1964), is inherent in the divorce lawyer-client relationship (Sarat & Felstiner, 1988). Private, separate, dyadic relations set the occasion for the sexual exploitation of female clients by their male lawyer—a lawyer who in his defense may cite "lawyer's prerogative" (Lyon, 1987).

The Effect of Mediation
on Wife Assault: Research

An extensive review of the relevant literature on the effect of mediation on wife assault yields the following conclusion: there isn't much. For example, of the 784 references cited in *Family and Interpersonal Mediation: A Bibliography of the Periodical Literature*,

1980-1989, published by Family Mediation Canada, there was not a single reference to this topic. Scholars and advocates who have provided explanations linking divorce mediation with wife assault routinely fail to cite research findings because such research is so rare. To the extent that wife assault is associated with anger and conflict, the results of a study published by Kelly (1990) do not support critics of mediation. But the study does not support the optimistic predictions of mediators either.

In a self-selected control group design, Kelly's sample consisted of 106 couples who chose mediation and 104 adversarial respondents (including an unidentified number of couples). The effects of mediated and adversarial divorce resolution processes were compared during the divorce processing and at 1 and then 2 years postdivorce.

One of Kelly's major hypotheses was that "divorce mediation intervention would lead to fewer and less intense conflicts in the two years after divorce" (Kelly, 1990, p. 12). This is what she found:

- no difference between mediation and adversarial groups 1 year after divorce
- members of the mediation group reported fewer conflicts about child visitation and payment of debts than did members of the adversarial group
- high anger 2 years after divorce predicted frequency of conflict at this time, but participation in mediation or the adversarial process did not predict high anger 2 years after divorce
- the presence of minor children and noncompliance with financial payments are better predictors of conflict 2 years after divorce than is participation in mediation or the adversarial process

These findings suggest that the effect of mediation (or the adversarial process) on wife assaults associated with conflict will vary with time after divorce. Two years after divorce, wife assault should on the basis of these findings be equally likely among women in the mediated and adversarial groups. During the period of 1 year after divorce, women in the adversarial group are more likely to be assaulted (one may infer) because they report more extreme conflicts on a wide range of issues, including child support. The conflict reported by adversarial women is also more lingering.

In their otherwise excellent study, Wallerstein and Kelly (1980) make scattered observations on violence between separating spouses who participated in their program (not mediation). For example, "Where the latter [husband] was embittered, there was a high likelihood of physical violence and child-napping attempts were not uncommon" (Wallerstein & Kelly, 1980, p. 28). The effect that their program had on postseparation violence, however, was not systematically examined.

To summarize: first, the nature of Kelly's sample and her adversarial sample selection procedures limit the generalizability (external validity) of the findings. Second, her findings suggest that separating women who are involved in adversarial proceedings are at greater risk of conflict-generated assaults than are women involved in mediation. Note that this is an inference. At the time of Kelly's (1990) report, no published study of mediation had included wife assault in the dependent variable measures.

Method

In a study recently published by Ellis and Stuckless (1992), postseparation aggression (physical and verbal) was specifically measured. The findings of this study were based upon two telephone interviews, one before mediation and the other 6 months following mediation. The interviews were conducted on two samples. One consisted of legal aid clients (n = 32) and the other was made up of Family Mediation Service clients at the Hamilton Unified Family Court (n = 41). The 73 separated respondents (46 females and 27 males) who were interviewed constituted a sequential, stratified (by dependent child and contested proceedings) random sample.

It is relevant to note that the legal aid clients participated in only one mediation session. Their participation was experienced by them as being coerced. That is to say, they had failed to resolve matters via lawyer negotiations within a time period and at a cost deemed reasonable by legal aid authorities. They were then told to try to resolve matters through mediation or their legal aid certificate would be withdrawn. Since the publication of our study, Legal Aid (Ontario) no longer makes the retention of a legal aid certificate (Family) contingent

upon mediation. Instead, voluntary settlement conferences have re-
placed mediation.

The court-based sample included participants who on the average
attended five mediation sessions. Mediators in the court-based service
were social workers and accredited mediators. Lawyers who were
accredited mediators conducted the legal aid mediation sessions.
Participants in both legal aid and court-based services volunteered for
the study.

The two telephone interviews administered to the participants took
about 35 minutes to complete. Three dependent variables (hassles,
violence prevention, and emotional and physical aggressions) and one
mediating variable (participants' evaluation of the mediation process)
were measured. The questions measuring these variables are included
in Table 7.1.

Logistic regression was used to predict each of the dependent
variables. This multivariate statistical procedure allowed us to control
for between-subject differences on the three predictor variables.

Results

One of the major, and relevant, findings of this pilot study is that
respondents who reported the mediation process to be "less helpful" were also more likely to report physical or verbal aggression
by their ex-partner after mediation. This finding, however, occurred
only among respondents who felt they had been coerced to participate
in divorce mediation. Had they not participated, their legal aid certifi-
cates, they were told, would be withdrawn. Moreover, they participated in only one mediation session. These two caveats must be kept
in mind in interpreting this finding.

Among respondents who voluntarily chose mediation, evaluations
of the mediation process were positive and no increase or decrease in
postseparation abuse was associated with these evaluations. In other
words, evaluations of the mediation process were unrelated to reported postseparation aggression.

For the sample as a whole, the best predictors of postseparation
aggression were hassles prior to mediation and being frightened of
one's partner (Table 7.2). Signing an affidavit prior to mediation was

Table 7.1 Interview Questions

Hassles (Pre/Post Mediation)

1. Tried to make all important decisions for you?
2. Left you with so little money that you sometimes did not have enough food or rent money?
3. Prevented you from leaving your car, home, or other place?
4. Stole things belonging to you?
5. Destroyed your personal property?
6. Bothered you so much you could not relax or sleep?

Violence Prevention Steps (Pre/Post Mediation)

7. Have you ever had to leave your own home because of your partner's violent behavior and/or threats?
8. Have the police ever come to your home because of your partner's violent behavior and/or threats?
9. Have you ever had to obtain a peace bond or restraining order against your partner?

Emotional and Physical Aggression (Pre/Post Mediation)

10. Called you names or said things that made you feel worthless (stupid; ugly; lazy; a bad parent, lover, and so on)?
11. Threatened to hurt you physically?
12. Threatened to kill you?
13. Physically abused/hurt you (pushed, pulled your hair, bit, kicked, choked, slapped, punched, hit with an object of some kind, stabbed with a knife or sharp instrument, shot with a gun)?
14. Actually injured you physically ever and/or since mediation was completed?
15. If yes, how many times approximately?

Evaluation of the Mediation Process
(Likert Scale: from "strongly agree" to "strongly disagree")

16. Helped me deal with my anger and frustration.
17. Helped me maintain a good relationship with our children.
18. The relationship between me and my ex-partner was much better after mediation than it was before we became involved in mediation sessions.
19. Helped me get my side of the story out, get my points across to my partner.
20. Helped me really listen to what my partner was saying, to the points he/she was trying to get across.
21. Helped me to learn to compromise and cooperate better.

SOURCE: Items selected from Lerman, Kuehl, and Brygger (undated).

Table 7.2 Preseparation Predictor Variables of Aggression After Mediation

Predictors	B	SE	df	Sig.
Hassles prior to separation	.6817	.4693	1	.1463
Frightened of partner	-1.4805	.5487	1	.0070
Affidavit before mediation	.3626	.3814	1	.3418
Constant	.5669	.4516	1	.2093

SOURCE: Ellis and Stuckless (1992). Preseparation abuse, marital conflict and postseparation abuse. *Mediation Quarterly, 9,* 205-226. Reproduced with permission of Jossey-Bass, Inc.

found to be a statistically significant predictor of "calling the police" following mediation. None of these variables is inherent in the mediation process and all of them are only weakly associated with evaluation of the mediation process.

In sum, the results of this study support the following hypothesis: the effect of the mediation process on postmediation abuse varies with the degree to which the decision to participate in mediation is viewed as being voluntary. High-conflict respondents who believe they are being forced to participate in a single mediation session report a relation between satisfaction with mediation and aggression following mediation. Supporters of mediation will contend that this conclusion is spurious because coerced mediation is not really mediation. Supporters and critics of mediation should note that the study described here is a pilot project involving a very small sample. Under these conditions, generalization to other samples or populations is hazardous.

The Effect of Wife Assault
on Mediation: Analysis

In a 1989 report, the Ontario Attorney General's Committee on Mediation in Family Law considered the following question: Should all potential users of mediation be excluded because they have experienced domestic violence? (Attorney General of Ontario, 1989, p. 74).

In attempting to answer this question, they were guided by Sinclair's (1985) definition of domestic violence:

> The intent by a spouse to intimidate, either by threat or by use of physical force on the other spouse's person or property. The purpose of that assault is to control that spouse's behaviour by the inducement of fear. Underlying all abuse is a power imbalance between the victim and the offender. (p. 16)

This gender-neutral definition is more than a definition. Included in the statement is a *conception* of violence as control and a *theory* identifying power imbalance as an underlying cause. Taken together, definition, (instrumental) conception, and theory suggest that pre-mediation violence (that is, violence that occurred during the marital relationship) is likely to have an effect on the mediation process, because separation heightens spousal conflicts and conflict places a premium on the ability of one spouse to control the other. A husband who has in the past used violence to control and intimidate his wife is more likely to sit face to face with a fearful, submissive, or passive wife than a husband who is not a wife assaulter. There is a payoff for past violence in that the more effectively the husband can control his ex-partner, the more likely he is to get the outcomes (e.g., custody, access arrangements, amount of child support) he wants.

From this account, one may infer that wife assault has both direct and indirect effects on the relative positions of male and female ex-partners who participate in mediation. Thus, past violence (wife assault) has direct effects on future violence. As mediation takes place in the future, past violence is a good predictor of violence or abuse during and following mediation. Indirectly, wife assault influences the quality of postseparation life for assaulted wives via its adverse effect on their capacity to effectively state their position and to bargain as an equal. Here, wife assault maintains imbalances in power that are likely to lead to unjust results.

Scholars and activists who emphasize the direct effects of wife assault want all assaulted female partners to be excluded from mediation, even those who have been physically assaulted on only one occasion many years previously (Ontario Association of Interval and

Transition Houses, 1989). Many of those who draw attention to the deleterious direct effects of wife assault also emphasize its indirect effects. Following Sinclair, they contend that wife assaults are invariably associated with power imbalances. Because all assaulted wives have even less power than wives who have not been assaulted, they should be excluded from a process that requires them to bargain with their more powerful expartner. In jurisdictions in which these ideas have become ruling ideas, wife assault has had the following effect on mediation: some divorce mediation programs have closed (e.g., Wilmington, North Carolina) and others have excluded many women who want to have their separation mediated (e.g., Alaska).

In many other jurisdictions, mediators contend that wife assault has no effect on them because they will not mediate acts of violence they are aware of. Nor will they mediate violations of family law legislation that are invoked by women who have been assaulted or who are fearful of being assaulted. In Ontario, this means that violations of restraining orders (under the 1986 Family Law Act) or of an order for exclusive possession of the matrimonial home (under the 1986 Children's Law Reform Act) will not be mediated.

In some jurisdictions, wife assault has influenced mediators to change their role. Mediators in Ontario who read the Attorney General's Advisory Committee's Report will discover that this committee embraces "an enforcement model approach" to acts of domestic violence (Attorney General of Ontario, 1989, p. 74). This implies that mediators should either advise (require?) clients to report acts of criminal violence to the police or report such acts themselves. It is presumed that mediators who are aware of the effects of wife assault on the balance of power should also act as advocates for the wife where imbalances are manifest. Under these conditions, do mediators remain impartial facilitators of a putatively client-controlled process?

As a professional group, mediators reject the notion that all assaulted wives should be excluded from mediation. Some assaulted wives should be excluded. Specifically, cases where violence "has resulted in a serious and unalterable imbalance of power . . . should be denied mediation" (Attorney General of Ontario, 1989, p. 75). Assaulted wives who participate in mediation will, it is assumed, vary greatly with respect to the effect past violence has on their ability to bargain as an equal. The advisory committee wants to exclude only those at the extreme end of the continuum of power imbalance, that is, those rendered "incapable of negotiating with the other spouse" (p. 77). Critics want the cutoff point far, far lower on the power imbalance continuum.

These considerations, and the contention associated with them, have led to the proliferation of power imbalance screening instruments and an increased emphasis on the role of mediators as interpreters, determiners, and screeners of wives who are placed in unequal bargaining positions because of the effects of wife assault (or for any other reason). Wife assault, then, is helping to make the process of divorce mediation more egalitarian, at least with respect to gender relations (see Girdner, 1989; Lerman, Kuehl, & Brygger, undated).

Additional recent developments include the publication of an entire issue of *Mediation Quarterly* (1990) on the topic of domestic violence in divorce mediation, a research grant of $200,000 to the Association of Family and Conciliation Courts (1992) for research "to develop information for the nation's courts on the effective resolution of custody and visitation disputes in divorce and postdivorce civil actions and actions between married partners where there have been instances and/or allegations of domestic abuse" (p. 116), and the Forum on Concerns About Mediation in Cases of Abuse to Women and Children organized by Barbara Landau of the Ontario Association of Family Mediators (May 27-31, 1992, Toronto, Canada). Those who attended included critics from the women's shelter movement and feminist critics of mediation. At this forum, advocates for assaulted wives proposed that these women should not be accepted for divorce mediation unless the mediator can provide good reasons for their participation (e.g., the woman feels safe, she has undergone therapy, the violence occurred a long time before).

Finally, wife assault is also having an effect on the training of mediators. They are being advised to attend training sessions on domestic violence and its relation to gender inequality. University-based, 2-year certificate courses in mediation now include the topic of gender inequality and violence against women in their curriculum.

Summary and Conclusions

Concerns about the effects of wife assault are warranted primarily on the grounds of caring and also on theoretical and empirical grounds. Probability surveys indicate that rates of wife assault are highest among the separated and divorced (Smith, 1987). Preliminary data collected by Ellis and Stuckless (1992) indicate that 47% of wives involved in lawyer negotiations report being physically hurt by their partner during the marriage. The comparable figure for wives participating in mediation is 45%. When almost one out of two separating couples report physical assault, it is certainly time to investigate systematically, and if necessary to do something about, the effect of mediation and lawyer negotiations on wife assault and vice versa.

References

Adams, O., & Nagnur, D. (1990). Marrying and divorcing: A status report for Canada. In C. Mekie & K. Thompson (Eds.), *Canadian Social Trends* (pp. 142-145). Toronto: Thompson Educational Publishing.

Association of Family and Conciliation Courts. (1992). *Newsletter, 11*(1).

Attorney General of Ontario (1989). *Advisory Committee Report on Mediation in Family Law.* Toronto: Ministry of the Attorney General.

Baskin, D., & Sommers, I. (1990). Ideology and discourse: Some differences between state planned and community-based justice. *Law and Human Behaviour, 14,* 249-270.

Blau, P. (1964). Differentiation of power. In P. Blau (Ed.), *Exchange and power in social life* (pp. 115-142). New York: John Wiley.

Blumberg, C. G. (1991). Reworking the past: Imagining the future: On Jacob's silent revolution. *Law and Social Inquiry, 16,* 115-159.

Cain, M., & Kulscar, K. (1983). Introduction. In Cain, M., & Kulscar, K. (Eds.), *Disputes and the law.* Budapest: Adcademiai Kiado.

Carnevale, P. J., & Pruitt, D. (1992). Negotiation and mediation. *Annual Review of Psychology, 43,* 531-582.

Cobb, S. (1992, May). *The domestication of violence in mediation: The social construction of disciplinary power in law.* Paper presented at the Law and Society Conference, Philadelphia.

Coogler, O. J. (1978). *Structured mediation in divorce settlements.* Lexington, MA: D. C. Heath.

Cover, R. (1986). Violence and the word. *Yale Law Journal, 95,* 1601-1629.

Crawford, M., & Gartner, R. (1992). *Woman killing: Intimate femicide in Ontario, 1974-1990* (Report prepared for the Women We Honour Action Committee, Toronto).

Dahrendorf, R. (1957). *Class and class conflict in industrial society.* Stanford, CA: Stanford University Press.

Deutch, M. (1973). *The resolution of conflict.* New Haven, CT: Yale University Press.

Dunford, F. W., Huizinga, D., & Elliott, D. (1990). The role of arrest in domestic assault: The Omaha police experiment. *Criminology, 28,* 183-206.

Eekelaar, J. M., & Katz, S. N. (1981). *Marriage and cohabitation in contemporary societies.* Toronto: Butterworths.

Eisenberg, D. (1982). The bargaining principle and its limits. *Harvard Law Review, 95,* 741-763.

Ellis, D. (1990). Marital conflict mediation and post-separation wife-abuse. *Law and Inequality, 8,* 317-339.

Ellis, D., & Stuckless, N. (1992). Preseparation abuse, marital conflict mediation and postseparation abuse. *Mediation Quarterly, 9,* 205-226.

Elster, J. (1989). Solomonic judgments: Against the best interests of the child. In J. Elster (Ed.), *Solomonic judgments: Studies in the limitations of rationality* (pp. 123-173). Cambridge, UK: Cambridge University Press.

Emery, R. E., & Wyer, M. M. (1987). Divorce mediation. *American Psychologist, 42,* 472-480.

Farge, B., & Rahder, B. (1991). *Police response to incidents of wife assault* (Report prepared for the Assaulted Women's Helpline and the Metro Toronto Committee Against Wife Assault, Toronto).

Folberg, H. J. (1984). Divorce mediation: The emerging American model. In J. M. Eekelaar & S. N. Katz (Eds.), *The resolution of family conflict: Comparative legal perspectives* (pp. 193-210). Toronto: Butterworths.

Folberg, H. J., & Taylor, A. (1984). *Mediation: A comprehensive guide to resolving conflicts without litigation.* San Francisco: Jossey-Bass.

Girdner, L. (1989). *Dealing with spouse abuse: Recommendations for divorce mediators.* Presented at Family Mediator's Conference, New York.

Glendon, M. A. (1977). *State, law and family.* London: North Holland.

Goode, W. (1969). Violence among intimates. In D. Mulvihill & M. Tumin (Eds.), *Crimes of violence* (pp. 941-947). Washington, DC: National Commission on the Causes and Prevention of Violence.

Gray, E. (1992). *Marital conflict resolution: A review of research and theory.* Unpublished manuscript, LaMarsh Research Programme on Violence and Conflict Resolution, York University, Toronto.

Gulliver, P. H. (1979). *Disputes and negotiations.* New York: Academic Press.

Hackett, D. (1990). *Gender equality* (Produced by the Canadian Judicial Centre [Ottawa] for the Education Committee of the Canadian Judicial Council).

Hilton, N. Z. (1991). Mediating wife assault: Battered women and the new family. *Canadian Journal of Family Law, 9,* 29-53.

Irving, H. (1980). *Divorce mediation.* Toronto: Personal Library.

Kelly, J. (1990). *Mediated and adversarial divorce resolution processes: An analysis of post-divorce outcomes* (Final report). Washington, DC: Fund for Research in Dispute Resolution.

Kressel, K., Pruitt, D., & Associates (1989). *Mediation research: The process and effectiveness of third-party intervention.* San Francisco: Jossey-Bass.

Lerman, L. (1984). Mediation of wife abuse cases: The adverse impact of informal dispute resolution on women. *Harvard Women's Law Journal, 7,* 57-113.

Lerman, L., Kuehl, S. J., & Brygger, M. P. (undated). *Mediators' response to battered women and abusive men: Guidelines for policy makers and mediators* (Unpublished report). Washington, DC: National Abuse Prevention Project.

Lyon, T. (1987). Sexual exploitation of divorce clients: The lawyer's prerogative? *Harvard Women's Law Journal, 10,* 159-201.

MacDougall, D. J. (1984). Negotiated settlement of family disputes. In J. M. Eekelaar & S. N. Katz (Eds.), *The resolution of family conflict: Comparative legal perspectives* (pp. 26-40). Toronto: Butterworths.

McWhinney, R. L. (1985). Family mediation in Ontario: Origins and development. *Therapy Now, 11,* 18-19.

Mnookin, R. (1984). Divorce bargaining: The limits on private ordering. In J. M. Eekelaar & S. N. Katz (Eds.), *The resolution of family conflict: Comparative legal perspectives* (pp. 364-385). Toronto: Butterworths.

Ontario Association of Interval and Transition Houses. (1989). *Mediation and violence against women.* Presentation to Standing Committee on Alternative Dispute Resolution, Queens Park, Toronto.

Payne, J. (1985). Aspects of mediation: Mediation in Canada and the United States. *Therapy Now, 11,* 4-6.

Pound, R. (1906). The causes of popular dissatisfaction with the administration of justice. *American Bar Association Reports, 29,* 395.

Rheinstein, M. (1972). *Marriage, stability, divorce and the law.* Chicago: University of Chicago Press.

Rifkin, J. (1984). Mediation from a feminist perspective: Promise and problems. *Law and Inequality, 21,* 330-342.

Sarat, A., & Felstiner, W. (1988). Law and social relations: Vocabularies of motives in lawyer/client interaction. *Law and Society Review, 22,* 738-769.

Sinclair, D. (1985). *Understanding wife assault. A training manual for counsellors and advocates.* Toronto: Ontario Ministry of Community and Social Services.

Smith, M. (1987). The incidence and prevalence of wife abuse in Toronto. *Violence and Victims, 2,* 33-47.

Solicitor General of Ontario. (1989). *Law enforcement activity in relation to spousal assault in Ontario.* Toronto: Queen's Park.

Stallone, D. (1984). Decriminalization of violence in the home: Mediation in wife battering cases. *Law and Inequality, 2,* 493-519.

Wallerstein, J., & Kelly, J. B. (1980). *Surviving the breakup: How children and parents cope with divorce.* New York: Harper Torchbooks.

The War Against Women. (1991, June). *First Report of the Standing Committee on Health & Welfare, Social Affairs, Seniors and the Status of Women.* House of Commons, Ottawa.

8

Court-Mandated Treatment of Men Who Assault Their Partner

Issues, Controversies, and Outcomes

L. KEVIN HAMBERGER

JAMES E. HASTINGS

The primary purpose of this chapter is to review issues related to perpetrator treatment and outcome, particularly when court mandated. When wife assault is called a crime, several forces come to bear. First, the criminal justice system responds, as society's representative, to hold the wife assaulter unequivocally responsible for the violence. By mandating treatment for the offender, the criminal justice system and the treatment community are simultaneously giving him an opportunity to change and telling him that he is responsible for stopping his violence. Hence, there is good reason to coordinate criminal justice, social service, and treatment components to respond to partner

Department of Family Medicine, Medical College of Wisconsin, Tallent Hall, P.O. Box 598, Kenosha, Wisconsin, 53141 (Hamberger); Psychology Service, Zablocki V.A. Medical Center, Milwaukee, Wisconsin, 53295 (Hastings).

violence. Together, such components form a united force to confront domestic violence, to hold the perpetrator accountable, and, it is hoped, to stop the violence, both within individual relationships and on a community level (Pence, 1989). Of particular interest in the present chapter are questions related to mandatory treatment of wife assaulters. Such questions include: (a) What role does court mandating play in facilitating treatment? (b) What are the most effective treatments for wife assaulters? (c) What is the research on treatment outcome with wife assaulters?

Why Mandate Wife Assaulters to Treatment?

Several treatment authorities have called for greater reliance on the courts to require treatment following arrest for wife assault. Reasons vary, but have a common theme of holding the assailant accountable to acknowledge and change his violent behavior (Ganley, 1987; Pence, 1989). Also, as elucidated by Soler (1987), the offender often has a continuing relationship with the victim, thus necessitating a different criminal justice disposition from that used for a stranger assault. When a victim has no relationship to the offender, the goal of prosecution is primarily punishment. In partner violence, however, the victim often wishes to continue the relationship. Further, there may be reasons, such as sharing of children, that necessitate continuing a relationship. In such cases, although the victim wants justice, an equally strong desire to end the violence also exists. Hence, rehabilitation to end the violence is an appropriate criminal justice goal (Ganley, 1987; Pence, 1989; Soler, 1987). Moreover, although probation may inhibit violence by monitoring a perpetrator's behavior over time, treatment may be necessary to teach new, nonviolent behaviors. Further, wife assaulters exhibit characteristics that generally require formal intervention to stop the violence (Ganley, 1987), such as a tendency to minimize or deny their violence or to attribute responsibility to sources outside of themselves. This view is also consistent with findings by Hamberger and Hastings (1988a) that many domestically violent men exhibit a variety of personality disorders, which often include patterns of conflict with authority and manipulation, particularly in ambiguous situations. Many wife assaulters are not internally motivated to stop their violence (Ganley, 1987; Sonkin, Martin, & Walker, 1985). Indeed, Hamberger and Hastings (1986) showed that even when treatment was offered at no cost, only about 16% of men followed through with treatment. In another study (Hamberger & Hastings, 1989), it was found that wife assaulters court-ordered to treatment were less likely to drop out of treatment than were men not court mandated. Hence, the criminal justice system may provide the needed leverage to compel a wife assaulter to seek treatment, monitor compliance, and administer sanctions for failure to comply. Despite the many good reasons for mandating treatment for perpetrators of partner assault, little has been written about what a "court mandate" is and how it works.

Types of Court Mandates

Sonkin et al. (1985) define two types of mandates from the criminal justice system. The first involves pretrial diversion or deferred prose-cution, whereby the wife assaulter can have his arrest record cleared or the charge reduced upon successful completion of treatment (see also Ford & Regoli, this volume). Ganley (1987) reports on potential shortcomings of pretrial diversion. In many diversion programs, the perpetrator is not required to enter a guilty plea. He enters counseling without having assumed responsibility for his violence, which can affect his behavior in counseling. For example, he may continue to insist on his innocence, participating in counseling only to get his charges dropped. In the program reported by Hamberger and Hastings (1990), admission to a deferred prosecution agreement requires that the man enter a plea of guilty. Program completion results in reduction of charges from criminal to ordinance violation and a reduced fine. Failure to complete treatment results in full prosecution of the battery charge.

Another type of mandate is a direct court order to participate in counseling as part of the sentence imposed following a conviction. Such an order can include jail time with release privileges to attend counseling or to be served prior to counseling participation (Pence, 1989). The order could also include a requirement of formal probation supervision, with treatment as a condition of probation or parole. One exception to this occurs when the man is on probation or parole for another offense, but in the course of his supervision, the agent learns about current domestic violence. In such cases, mandated counseling referrals can occur without the men necessarily going to court first. Failure to comply with treatment can result in temporary incarceration or probation/parole revocation and incarceration for the duration of the sentence.

A third type of mandate occurs in municipal court for ordinance violations not rising to the level of a misdemeanor. In the Kenosha Domestic Abuse Intervention Project (Hamberger, 1984), when an assault does not meet criteria for a criminal arrest, the man is issued a municipal citation with bond set at the maximum allowable of $625, and if possible, he is held overnight in the city jail. If he agrees to plead guilty or no contest, he can either pay the fine ($625) or complete the treatment program and pay a reduced fine ($85). With the treatment option, a series of court proceedings is scheduled to monitor participation, as well as compliance with any other required referrals, for example, alcohol and drug counseling. In some municipalities, the civil courts may also require a man to complete counseling (Ganley, 1987). Such an order may be a condition of a restraining order or related to child visitation.

Given that courts may rely on treatment for wife assaulters to serve a variety of purposes at the pretrial, sentencing, and supervision stages, information about the efficacy of court-mandated treatment is of great importance. Research that provides such information is the subject of the remainder of this chapter.

Research on Compliance
With Court-Mandated Treatment

There are two main areas of research on the efficacy of court-mandated treatment for wife assaulters. One involves the effectiveness of court-mandated treatment on reducing recidivism. This will be addressed in a later section. Another area of research concerns attrition (drop out) from treatment, and how well the criminal justice system holds wife assaulters accountable when they fail in treatment. Surprisingly little research has been done in this area, and in contrast to studies of the effects of arrest, no studies employing randomized experimental designs have been conducted on the effects of court mandates on treatment compliance. Some studies of men in treatment constituting a "convenience" sample have been studied, but without a comparison group.

In general, treatment dropouts have been found to be younger, less well educated, and with lower employment and income levels than treatment completers (Gruznski & Carillo, 1988; Hamberger & Hastings, 1989; Saunders & Parker, 1989). Other variables, including childhood exposure to violence (Gruznski & Carillo, 1988) and personality characteristics (Hamberger & Hastings, 1989), also appear related to compliance. In a study of court-mandated treatment, Hamberger and Hastings (1989) found that completers were also significantly more likely to have been court ordered. About two thirds of court ordered men completed treatment, compared with 42% of men not court ordered. The type of court order was not specified, so it is not known whether different types of mandates had differential effects on treatment completion. Saunders and Parker (1989) meanwhile reported that among men who were older than 25, were college educated, and perpetrated less severe violence, voluntary referral was related to treatment completion. In contrast, younger, less well educated offenders were more likely to complete treatment if they were court ordered.

The question of whether criminal justice mandates are effective in getting wife assaulters into and compliant with treatment is important and has begun to receive research attention. Equally important but rarely studied questions are: (a) Whether different types of mandates are differentially effective in achieving their goals and (b) To what degree do mandating systems actually deliver negative consequences to men who fail to enter or complete treatment? Saunders and Parker (1989) compared probation/parole and deferred prosecution referrals. Significant differences in attrition were not found, although a trend suggested greater completion rates for deferred prosecution referrals. Deferred prosecution subjects were more often first offenders and had higher rates of employment. Hamberger and Hastings (1990) evaluated three criminal justice mandates: municipal court; circuit court/deferred prosecution; and probation/parole. All men referred through any of these court systems over a one-year period were studied. The three court systems did not differ significantly in the proportion of dropouts, nor in the rates with which dropouts received negative consequences. Municipal court, however, was found to have significantly more no-shows. Forty-eight percent of men originally referred by municipal court failed to make or keep a first appointment, compared with 22% for circuit court and 23% for probation/parole. Moreover, no-shows from municipal court were less likely to receive negative consequences; about two thirds of municipal court no-shows avoided negative consequences, compared with 25% of men from each of the other two referral sources.

The Hamberger and Hastings (1990) study suffers from many of the methodological flaws that are typical of this area of research. First, group assignment was not random. The average index offense of municipal court referrals was less severe than index offenses of deferred prosecution and probation/parole referrals, and the men had fewer violent offenses on their police record than did circuit court/ deferred prosecution referrals. Hence, it could be that less violent offenders in a lower court system are less likely to view treatment as useful and more likely to view the sanctions for failure (fine, brief jail sentence) as insufficient to compel compliance. Municipal court referrals were also better educated than men from the other two groups, a variable found by Saunders and Parker (1989) to be related to higher dropout rates among mandated men. This research does suggest that not all mandating systems are alike in their effectiveness to compel wife assaulters to seek treatment. Nor are the systems alike in the consistency with which no-shows are actively penalized for failing to comply with orders to attend treatment. It may be, however, that offender characteristics, as found by Saunders and Parker (1989), interact with system characteristics to predict mandate compliance. Because of the paucity of research in this area, firm conclusions cannot be drawn.

At this point, empirical evidence supporting the use of court mandates is mixed. Some studies have failed to find an overall effect (e.g., Lund, Larsen, & Schultz, 1982; Saunders & Parker, 1989). One study did find a clear positive relationship between criminal justice mandating and remaining in treatment (Hamberger & Hastings, 1989), and one study found an interaction effect between being mandated and demographic factors such as age, education, employment, and violence severity (Saunders & Parker, 1989). The most pessimistic interpretation of this research would be that mandating treatment for offenders is not worth the effort as research to date has not produced a resounding endorsement. But as Saunders and Parker (1989) observed, "Even if further research does not support the use of criminal justice sanctions to maintain clients in treatment, the criminal justice involvement of the mandated client may have a deterrent effect that lowers recidivism in spite of, or with the help of, treatment" (p. 28). Furthermore, even if criminal justice mandates are not entirely effective in keeping an offender in treatment, the goal of forcing accountability for noncompliance can still be achieved through administration of sanctions, that is, jail term, criminal record, and so forth. The preliminary research in this area reported by Hamberger and Hastings (1990) suggests that the stronger criminal justice components such as criminal court and probation/parole monitoring may be the most effective in achieving these goals.

Finally, despite the imperfections of the various mandating sources in compelling treatment participation (Hamberger & Hastings, 1990), more mandated men (about 40%) continue to enter and complete treatment than nonmandated men. Hamberger and Hastings (1986) reported very low rates (16%) of nonmandated men entering and completing wife assault treatment. Gondolf and Foster (1991) have reported on a study of factors related to attrition by wife assaulters. They found an attrition rate of 93% between pretreatment inquiry and completion of at least 12 sessions of counseling. Although "informal referrals" (i.e., by partner or shelter) had the lowest attrition rates, overall attrition rates were extremely high. Therefore, the role of criminal justice mandating is still relatively unknown and deserves further study.

Recommendations for Research

Research in this area has been characterized by a number of methodological shortcomings that should be attended to in future studies. First, mandate variables should be clearly defined, because different types of court mandates may have different effects, either generally or with different types of offenders. Second, many studies in this area have focused primarily on main effects (e.g., whether certain mandates improve treatment compliance) that may mask important interactions (e.g., whether some types of mandate work best for men of different ages or educational levels) and consequently lead to inaccurate and misleading results and policy recommendations. Another problem in this area of research is generalizability of findings. In general, research on mandate effects has been carried out on convenience samples of small to moderate size, usually from a specific program in a specific locale. Among the studies reviewed, only one (Hamberger & Hastings, 1990) included a replication effort even within the same program. Therefore, it will be important to develop research programs that attempt to replicate studies conducted to date, both within programs and using multiple site designs.

Much of the research to date has provided potentially useful descriptive information about completers of and dropouts from court-mandated treatment. These studies, however, do not appear to have been based on theory and therefore do not allow for inferences about possible underlying mechanisms. Furthermore, no experimental studies utilizing randomized group assignment to mandated treatment or nonmandated treatment conditions have been conducted. Although a potentially controversial research approach with this violent population, experimental studies of the effects of mandating on treatment attendance should be done. Studies on the effects of arrest (e.g., Dunford, Huizinga, & Elliott, 1990; Sherman & Berk, 1984) and treatment effectiveness (Edleson & Syers, 1990) can serve as models for designing such experiments, including appropriate safety and monitoring provisions.

Different Treatment Approaches: Issues and Controversies

The review above suggests that although court mandating is viewed as an important tool, there is still no firm conclusion on its overall efficacy as an external motivator for facilitating entry and retention in domestic violence treatment. Preliminary indications are that certain types of mandates are at least somewhat effective with certain types of offenders and that no type of mandate is universally effective in accomplishing the goals listed above. The next question is, "To what type of treatment are these offenders being mandated?" This question has sparked considerable controversy. The main debates center around issues of format, content, and theoretical orientation. In this section, we will summarize some of the major points. A number of detailed analyses are available for the reader who wishes more detail (Adams, 1988; Caesar & Hamberger, 1989; Eisikovits & Edleson, 1989; Sonkin et al., 1985).

Theoretical Issues

Adams (1988) identified five primary theoretical orientations in the area of treatment of domestically violent men. First, the *ventilation* model views partner violence as symptomatic of suppressed anger that needs to be expressed through some other cathartic means. According to Adams (1988), because of this perspective, proponents of ventilation therapy approaches have not developed programs specifically for the treatment of domestically violent men. Instead, such men, and often their partners, are seen in groups with a variety of other couples to work on developing honest communication. Both partners are viewed as culpable for "playing games," and there is often little or no distinction between perpetrators and victims of the violence. Counseling approaches may include learning to "fight fairly" and can also include such "cathartic" exercises as hitting each other with styrofoam bats.

There are several aspects of a ventilation approach that discourage adoption in a court-mandated program. If the overall goal of integrating the criminal justice and mental health fields is to provide a united front to hold the assailant responsible to change (Ganley, 1987), it makes little sense to refer a man to a nonspecialized program that does not emphasize the primacy of the violence and the man's responsibility to stop it. Further, viewing both partners as culpable for the violence is contrary to the criminological notion of culpability on the part of the perpetrator only. Finally, although cathartic methods such as hitting with foam bats or verbally "blowing up" to get the anger out may reduce tension temporarily, that very tension reduction constitutes negative reinforcement, increasing rather than reducing the likelihood that aggression will be repeated in subsequent situations (e.g., Feshbach, 1956; Hartmann, 1969).

The basic premise of *insight-oriented* therapy approaches is that the violent behavior is symptomatic of some other, underlying conflict, often stemming from the perpetrator's background or childhood (e.g., parental abuse, rejection, overdependency or unmet dependency needs, or resulting fear or anger toward parents). The nature of such conflict is thought to be unconscious and the energy generated by the conflict motivates the behavior. As described by Kado (1985), for example, the wife assaulter may unconsciously select partners who play roles that stimulate the conflict, which he then attempts to master. Therapy is aimed at identifying the conflict through analysis of both inner-life experiences and historical and present-day inter-actions with the world. Theoretically, once the conflict has been made conscious, insight into the root causes of the violence has also been accomplished and the aggression should cease. Kado (1985) proposes that insight-oriented approaches may be important in facilitating deep insights necessary for insuring long-term treatment gains and decreas-ing relapse. Kado suggests that failing to address the unresolved emotional trauma could make treatment "too superficial" to support long-term change.

Such approaches are not without controversy and criticism. For example, Adams (1988) points out that factors described as *char-acteristic* of wife assaulters (e.g., low self-esteem) are often used tautologically as *explanations* for the violence. A focus on intraper-sonal characteristics and dynamics diminishes wife assaulters' direct responsibility for their violence. Adams asserts that by looking to intrapsychic factors, valid as they may be in the life of many wife assaulters, the functional nature of the man's violence in controlling and dominating his partner is overlooked and therefore at least tacitly supported. Also, focusing on "underlying causes" avoids directly confronting the violence and the more proximal causes of the so-called underlying problems (Adams, 1988). Sonkin et al. (1985) view wife assault as a crisis analogous to suicidal feelings and behavior. Both are serious problems in their own right, but once the behavior has been brought under control through direct intervention, it may be desirable to do further therapy to address many of the underlying issues.

Proponents of a *systems* or *interactional* approach to partner vio-lence are numerous (e.g., Deschner, 1984; Geffner, Mantooth, Franks,

& Rao, 1989; Geller & Wasserstrom, 1984; Lane & T. Russell, 1989; Neidig, 1984; Neidig, Friedman, & Collins, 1985). This approach views violence as a culmination of an interaction process in which each partner attempts to dominate and control the other. In the early stages of the interaction, strategies employed are primarily verbal and emotional. As both partners escalate in an effort to succeed, one of them may resort to violence. The violence may function to preserve homeostatic balance when the partners are locked into a relationship based on certain complementary relationship structures. Neidig et al. (1985) have clearly stated the system/interactional position: "Abusive behavior is a relationship issue. Both parties participate in abusive behavior, although not necessarily equally" (p. 196). There is no clear "perpetrator" or "victim," and such terms are often eschewed in favor of terms such as "abusive couple." Interventions are focused on helping each partner identify and appreciate his or her role in the violence and in bringing the violence to an end. Partners are usually seen together or in couples' groups. Treatment emphasizes enhancement of communication skills and modification of rigid, complementary structures in the relationship.

These approaches have been the subject of much controversy among researchers, clinicians, and advocates in the field of partner violence. A recent ruling by the state of Colorado (1989) that requires certification for domestic violence counselors for court-ordered perpetrators effectively prohibits the use of conjoint counseling models. This has resulted in heated reaction from systems therapists who maintain that the attempt "to fit all abusive men, abused women and dysfunctional relationships into a Procrustean treatment bed is ineffective and potentially damaging" (Goldman, 1989, p. 13). Goldman (1991) further characterizes the result of the certification rule as currently structured as a war in which "rhetoric became reality and shots against generalists were fired" (p. 15).

From a feminist perspective (e.g., Adams, 1988; Bograd, 1984), the notion that both partners share responsibility for the man's violence is particularly dangerous. As stated by Adams (1988), "When a woman's 'precipitating' behavior becomes the object of focus . . . therapists implicitly reinforce men's attempts to divert attention away from their own choices" (p. 187). Further, encouraging battered women to change their behavior so that men will not be violent denies them the right to function autonomously. Some interactional proponents do make clear statements about the sole responsibility of the assailant for his violence (e.g., Geffner et al., 1989). A feminist critique (e.g., Adams, 1988; Bograd, 1984; Edleson, 1984), however, concludes that any attention to the victim's role in the violence and in subsequent therapy sends mixed messages about her culpability. Furthermore, as pointed out by Hamberger and Lohr (1989), a man's partner need neither be physically present nor actively interacting with him in order to be subsequently assaulted. A man may talk himself into anger and violence against his partner when she is not present or while she is sleeping. An interactional theory is inadequate to account for such a phenomenon or to intervene with it therapeutically in a couples context.

From a criminal justice perspective, systems/interactional approaches seem to fall short. For example, Lane and T. Russell (1989) described a systems-based program in which clients are accepted under a court mandate for only one session. Any subsequent sessions are considered voluntary and not subject to monitoring by the court. Furthermore, because wife assaulters are often required by the courts to have no contact with their victim-partner for a period of time, theoretical approaches that emphasize interactional therapies would be impossible. Even without official no-contact orders, it would be improbable for a court to order a victim to accompany to therapy the man who battered her.

Perhaps the most widely used theoretical formulation in wife assault treatment is the *cognitive-behavioral* approach. Cognitive-behavioral approaches are based on social learning theories such as that of Bandura (1977) and Staats (1975). Wife assault is construed as behavior learned via direct observation of role models (especially in the family of origin), indirect observation (as through film and other media), and direct "trial and error" learning experiences. In the cognitive-behavioral framework, the violence, per se, is the problem. Violent behavior develops into a repetitive pattern because it has functional value to the perpetrator. Such functional value differs across perpetrators and across situations. Examples of such functions include tension release, avoidance of unpleasant tasks and situations, and enforced victim compliance. To understand a perpetrator's violence, therefore, it is necessary to conduct a functional analysis of the violent behavior, including overt behaviors (what is said and done) and covert behaviors (physical arousal, imagery, attributions and "self-talk"). Once critical behaviors have been identified, interventions can target problems in the man's behavior. Such interventions can include conflict abeyance techniques (i.e., time-outs), verbal interactional skills such as assertiveness, relaxation skills for reducing physiological arousal, and cognitive strategies for self-instructing in nonviolence and for reevaluating threat-oriented, anger-producing thoughts to more task-oriented interpretations. These intervention strategies, together with the social learning analysis of violence in a variety of settings, center the behavioral responsibility for the violence within the perpetrator (Hamberger & Lohr, 1989). Only the perpetrator learned and committed the behavior. Further, only the perpetrator need learn and perform new, nonviolent behaviors in similar situations in the future.

The cognitive-behavioral approaches are not without critics. According to Adams (1988), such approaches are value neutral. By failing to incorporate gender/power issues, cognitive-behavioral approaches risk viewing wife assault as a purely skills deficit or stress management problem, and not part of a broader societal oppression of women (Hamberger & Lohr, 1989). Devoid of a gender-political analysis, such approaches cannot easily account for why many men assault only their female partner, and why many stressed and skill-deficient men are not violent (Adams, 1988). From a criminal justice perspective, the focus of cognitive-behavioral perspectives on the violence and on learning nonviolent strategies has important advantages. First, the specific behavior for which the perpetrator is being held accountable is also the specific target of intervention from a cognitive-behavioral perspective. Second, the cognitive-behavioral approach of holding the perpetrator solely responsible for his violence and for changing it also appears consistent with the intent of criminalizing partner violence and requiring the perpetrator to change.

Another issue that has generated controversy in treating wife assaulters is whether they should be taught "*anger management* skills" or whether therapy should involve strategies facilitating deeper level resocialization through "long-term reeducation and monitoring" (Gondolf & D. Russell, 1986, p. 5). Anger management emphasizes short-term intervention to help the assailant become more aware of anger cues through monitoring and then to employ some type of behavioral strategy to reduce arousal, modulate the anger, and "short-circuit" a potential violent episode. According to Gondolf and D. Russell (1986), there are several problems with such an approach. First, the apparent superficial level of changes facilitated constitutes a "quick fix." Although anger levels and even physical violence may be reduced, more subtle forms of violence and control may be inadvertently reinforced as the man learns to tone down his anger while manipulating, and therefore appear less obvious in his abuse. Gondolf and D. Russell (1986) list other "shortcomings" of anger management approaches: (a) principles of anger control imply that victims provoke the violence rather than view male perpetrators as relentlessly attempting to dominate and control women; (b) the emphasis on a provocation-reaction focus ignores the intent often observed in men's attempts at control; (c) because anger management training is based in large part on a stress model (e.g., Novaco, 1975), responsibility for the wife assaulter's behavior is too easily diffused to external sources such as "stress" or other provocation; and (d) focusing on teaching men only self-management skills individualizes the problem, failing to acknowledge its sociopolitical roots or challenge societal norms and practices that promote wife assault. In short, the assailant is "treated," leaving no need for the larger community to change. As an antidote, Gondolf and D. Russell (1986) propose a more broad-ranging intervention including detailed, gender-power analyses of wife assaulters' behaviors and how such behaviors also reinforce the larger patriarchal social structures. Organizing sessions around relevant themes and assigning antisexist social action projects to clients are examples of such approaches.

In rebuttal, Tolman and Saunders (1988) state that most programs with cognitive-behavioral bases do integrate skills training with broader, gender-power analyses. Furthermore, such approaches are based on empirically supported techniques. The highly problem-focused nature of cognitive-behavioral approaches also allows for rapid intervention in a highly dangerous, potentially lethal behavior problem; yet the cognitive-behavioral techniques are not necessarily quickly mastered and therefore should not be considered a "quick fix." Tolman and Saunders point out that cognitive-behavioral approaches do place behavioral responsibility on the perpetrator and focus on changing perpetrator behaviors, not environmental (e.g., victim) factors. Finally, Tolman and Saunders repeat that the first goal of intervention is to stop the acute violent behavior. A treatment approach to accomplish such a goal might best be one component of a broader community response.

Perhaps the oldest and most widely held beliefs about the causes of male-to-female violence are the *profeminist* perspectives (Pence, 1985): that most simply, male-to-female violence is a sociopolitical issue, rooted in men's power granted by patriarchal social systems that subordinate and oppress women in a myriad of ways, including physical violence. Men are understood as being more powerful than their female partner, both physically and politically. Not only are men therefore more likely to terrorize, injure, disable, or kill their female partner than vice versa, but also by virtue of their gender alone, in a patriarchal society, their violence is likely to be reinforced and empowered. Reinforcing mechanisms have historically included the criminal justice system (Eisenberg & Micklow, 1977), as well as other societal structures such as social service, mental health, economic, religious, and medical agencies (Ganley, 1989). Profeminist intervention is viewed as part of a larger goal of transforming societal norms and practices with respect to gender power. Counseling therefore cannot take place outside the context of a broader community response (e.g., Pence, 1989).

Although profeminist perspectives have predominated in the wife assault field for many years, there are criticisms. Neidig et al. (1985), for example, claim that the approach is biased, based only on perspectives provided by battered women, leading to overgeneralized concepts of "victim" and "abuser" and to counterproductive blaming. Conversely, Island and Letellier (1991) argue that to view men's violence as caused by societal structures is to suggest that an assaultive male has no choice in his violence and unwittingly exonerates him of responsibility for his behavior.

Lane and T. Russell (1989) view the feminist emphasis on power and control, together with its emphasis on utilizing court-ordered treatment to compel change, as itself a hierarchical form of power and control. They assert that compelling someone to treatment inhibits the curiosity that is necessary to facilitate self-exploration and change. Seeing clients under a court mandate also places the therapist in the role of social control agent, no different from a probation officer (Lane

& T. Russell, 1989). Hence, therapy becomes a type of punishment wherein even the clientele fail to discriminate between the therapist and the system.

From a criminal justice perspective, the profeminist view appears to be a compatible alternative insofar as both perspectives call for clearly identifying perpetrators and victims (Ganley, 1989) and active community involvement to stop the violence. Moreover, although in theory feminism may target social forces over individual dynamics, in practice wife assaulters are viewed as responsible both for their behavior and for changing it. Hence, programs that incorporate feminist theory work well within a criminal justice system framework.

Treatment Format Issues

Other controversies in the treatment of domestically violent men include *how* treatment is conducted and *what* constitute the optimal elements of such treatment. Should wife assaulters be seen for treatment individually, in men's groups, with their partner, or in couples' groups?

The question of *group versus individual* treatment has not been highly controversial. In general, the standard mode of treatment is some form of group intervention. This preference has both practical and philosophical bases. First, from a practical position, a relatively large number of referrals at any one time would quickly overtax the resources of any care delivery system. It is simply more economical to see the men in groups. Wife assaulters are typically viewed as having learned their sexist, power-driven strategies in a social/cultural setting, with social groups of men reinforcing their woman-dominating behaviors. It follows that the most effective setting for confronting old habits and receiving feedback and support for development of nonviolent behaviors is in groups of like-minded men struggling toward similar goals (Adams & McCormick, 1982; Ganley, 1989). Indeed, as pointed out by Jennings (1987) and witnessed by anyone who has ever facilitated a group for domestically violent men, the experience of the group, getting feedback and support and finding out "I am not alone" are some of the most beneficial aspects of treatment reported by men. Geffner et al. (1989) report similar practical and philosophical reasons for conducting conjoint therapy in a couples' group, rather than with individual couples. Although groups are the dominant and preferred format for treatment, individual therapy may have a role, as some men may be inappropriate for group treatment for a variety of reasons.

Although there is little debate about the preference for group treatment, there is debate about the relative value and effectiveness of *structured versus unstructured* programs (Jennings, 1987, 1990; Lane & T. Russell, 1989). Jennings (1987, 1990) maintains that development of structured programs was based on biased, distorted views of wife assaulters as incapable of functioning outside the strict limits of structured therapy programs. Jennings argues further that although some men are extremely dangerous and in need of close monitoring, most wife assaulters, when given the chance, are capable of insightful exploration in an unstructured group setting. Moreover, Jennings believes that in the unstructured approach, most of the material dispensed in structured programs eventually emerges anyway—and at a time directed more by client readiness than by therapist fiat. According to Jennings, structured approaches are rigid, with steps locked into a progression and little or no room for spontaneity, and proponents of structured programs assume that wife assaulters are incapable of insight and "must be carefully controlled . . . and . . . socially 're-strained' to behave like 'normal' people" (1987, p. 204).

Such a draconian characterization of structured approaches undoubtedly obscures the human and humane aspects of the process in any well-run therapy group. For example, discussing clinical behavior therapy, Goldfried and Davison (1976) state, "Any behavior therapist who maintains that principles of learning and social influence are all one needs to know in order to bring about behavior change is out of contact with clinical reality" (p. 55); they go on to discuss the importance of the therapist's ability to translate structured principles into language understandable to the client and relate to the client in a warm and empathic manner. A number of authors have echoed these sentiments (e.g., Saunders, 1981; Sonkin et al., 1985). Until comparative studies of actual process in structured and unstructured programs are done, it would be best to view preferences for one or the other approach in the context of the background, skills, and interests of the therapist conducting the particular program (Feazell, Mayers, & Deschner, 1984).

The debate about whether to treat wife assaulters *conjointly* with their victim-partner was discussed in some detail in the previous section on theoretical issues. There are, however, a number of practical issues that enter the debate. Proponents of couples' counseling maintain that couples often express a strong desire to stay together and request couples' counseling to stop the violence (Geffner et al., 1989). Many battered women's advocates nevertheless express concern that to include the victim in the therapy and to encourage her to be honest and open about the relationship places her in great danger should she report on issues deemed off limits by her partner (Adams, 1988). Conjoint proponents such as Geffner et al. (1989) argue that steps can be taken to enhance safety and forestall violence during treatment. For example, prior to each session, Geffner et al. (1989) have each partner separately and independently report on critical incidents in the past week. If violence is reported, other steps, including getting the woman to a shelter, are taken to further enhance safety. Geffner has pointed out that men in men-only treatment groups have also been violent. Separation of partners for treatment is no guarantee that violence will not recur during treatment. As in other areas of domestic violence intervention, this appears to be an empirical question awaiting research. Useful information may be forthcoming in the next few years with the completion of a large-scale, randomized study of conjoint versus gender-specific counseling (Dunford, 1992).

In general, the issues presented in this section, like those in the preceding sections, often lack sufficient empirical bases to resolve them effectively at this time. Discussion is nevertheless important to clarify the issues and lead to better research questions. The ultimate research question in the area of wife assaulter rehabilitation, of course, is how effective such programs are and with what types of clients. This question is addressed in the following section.

Treatment Outcome

In this final section of the chapter, we include a review of most of the major research studies and presentations that have evaluated treatment outcome in the area of domestic violence. Twenty-eight studies, reviews, and surveys from 1984 to 1990 are summarized. The concluding pages address the major methodological issues affecting this research and suggest strategies for improvement.

Early Surveys on Treatment Outcome

A number of the studies reviewed below are evaluations of specific programs from specific locales. National surveys have also been conducted to assess treatment. In these surveys, researchers have attempted to provide descriptions of various treatment approaches used and estimate how well the programs work to stop violence against women.

Feazell, Mayers, and Deschner (1984)

Of 187 survey questionnaires mailed, 90 were completed sufficiently for inclusion in a summary study. Fifty of the programs surveyed were specifically for the treatment of wife assault, whereas the other service agencies, typically over 3 years old, offered multiple services including wife assault treatment. Of the clients surveyed who stayed in treatment for a given program's duration, 90% remained nonviolent during treatment. At follow-up contacts on the average at 1 year, nonviolence rates were 66% to 75%. Many of the programs gathered data in methodologically incomplete fashion, that is, with small samples, varied definitions of recidivism, client self-report, and so forth. The results are interesting, but must be interpreted with caution.

Pirog-Good and Stets (1986)

Of 211 programs contacted, 72 completed a lengthy questionnaire. The programs were of many and diverse formats, including group, couples' and individual treatment, alone or in combination. Many of these programs collected no formal data on their efforts and had to estimate the information requested. Estimates of recidivism, which was defined arbitrarily and differently across programs, varied from approximately 10% to 30% at 1 year. An average attrition rate of 40% was also reported. Greater attrition was found among Caucasians, blue-collar workers, the unemployed, and nonmandated participants and in programs that were longer or were not free of charge to participants. Not all of these findings have been replicated and they must be viewed as no more than hypotheses for further research.

Treatment Outcome Studies

See also Table 8.1.

Deschner (1984)

Couples, as well as individual men, were treated. Positive changes on the Taylor-Johnson Temperament Analysis and a nonsignificant decrease in self-reported violence were observed in a sample of 12 men. At an 8-month follow-up of a somewhat larger sample, only half of the group could be reached. Recidivism was reported at about 15%, but because the data are self-reported, with a small, select sample of men, some of whom were no longer living with their abused spouse, the actual rate of recidivism is unclear.

Halpern (1984)

This article describes a program consisting of intake, assessment, and orientation sessions, followed by 16 weekly 3-hour treatment sessions. Session content included education and cognitive-behavior modification methods aimed at anger management, conflict avoidance, problem solving, and conflict resolution. Concurrent spouse groups, a coed group, and a maintenance group were also offered. An outcome study provided follow-up data on 39 program completers and 45 dropouts. Follow-up was conducted at 3, 6, 12, and 24 months after treatment, using the Conflict Tactics Scale and partner report whenever possible. Eighty-five percent of the treated men were reported nonviolent at (presumably) 3-month follow-up. Of 45 men assessed but not treated, 82% were reported nonviolent. Seventeen of the treated nonviolent group were living with their partner, as were 20 of the untreated nonviolent men. These were rather small samples, with no inferential statistics.

Table 8.1 Summary of Outcome Studies

	N	Control	Court Referral[d]	Attrition	Treatment Mode[f]	Duration[i]	Data Source	Recidivism[j]
Deschner (1984)	12	No	Unknown	About 50%	Anger[g]	10	Self, Testing	15% (0)
Halpern (1984)	39	45 dropouts[a]	No	82%	Anger, Education	16	Self, Partner	15% (3-24 mo)
Stacey and Shupe (1984)	244	No	Unknown	37%	Unknown	Unknown	Self, Partner	25%-50% (variable)
Edleson, Miller, Stone, and Chapman (1985)	9	No	No	0%	Cog-Beh	12	Self	22% (7-21 wks)
Hawkins and Beauvais (1985)	106	No	Yes	14%	Anger, Self, Communication, Problem, "Traditional"[h]	22	Police	18% (6 mo)
Kelso and Personette (1985)	94	No	Yes	72%	Cog-Beh, Anger, Assertion, Exercise, Relaxation	26	Self	4% (0)
Neidig, Friedman, and Collins (1985)	Unknown	No	Yes	Unknown	Cog-Beh, Anger, Problem	10	Self, Partner, Police	13% (4 mo)
Dutton (1986)	100	Yes[a]	Yes	0%	Cog-Beh, Anger, Assertion	16	Self, Partner, Police	4%-16% treated 16%-40% untreated (6-36 mo)
Rosenbaum (1986)	11	No	No	18%	Education	6	Self	11% (6-24 mo)

Study	N	Comparison	Random	Completion	Treatment	Sessions	Outcome Source	Recidivism
Saunders and Hanusa (1986)	113	No	Yes	19%	Assertion, Relaxation, "Traditional"	20	Self, Partner, Testing	0% (0)
DeMaris and Jackson (1987)	414	No	Yes	83%	Education, Anger, Communication, Stress	4 (avg.)	Self	35% (20 mo)
Leong, Coates, and Hoskins (1987)	67	No	Yes	76%	Cog-Beh, Conflict	24-36	Partner, Police	15%-19% (3 mo)
Maiuro, Cahn, Vitaliano, and Zegree (1987)	65	25 Waitlist[b]	Yes	75%	Education, Cog-Beh, Anger	18-20	Self, Partner, Police, Testing	Unknown
Shepard (1987)	92	No	Yes	25% 50%[c]	Education, Cog-Beh	24	Self, Partner	30%-39% (14 mo)
Tolman, Beeman, and Mendoza (1987)	48	No	No	68%	Cog-Beh, Anger, Conflict, Education	26 weeks	Self, Partner	47% (6 mo-4 yrs)
Edleson and Gruznski (1988)	202	66 dropouts[a]	Yes	31% 49%	Cog-Beh, Self	16	Partner, CTS	33%-41% completers 46%-48% dropouts (5-9 mo)
Hamberger and Hastings (1988b)	35	36 dropouts[a]	Yes	51%	Cog-Beh, Anger, Problem	12	Self, Partner, Police	28% completers 47% dropouts (1 yr)

(Continued)

Table 8.1 (Continued)

	N	Control	Court Referral[d]	Attrition	Treatment Mode[f]	Duration[i]	Data Source	Recidivism[j]
Hamberger and Hastings (1990)	106	No	Yes	16%	Cog-Beh, Anger, Problem	12	Self, Partner, Police	30% (1 yr)
Tolman (1988)	98	No	Yes	Unknown	Cog-Beh, Education, Conflict	26	Partner	Unknown
Chen, Bersani, Myers, and Denton (1989)	120	101[a]	Yes	37%	Education, Self, Conflict	2 sets of 4 2-hour meetings	Police	5% Treated 10% Untreated (14 mo)
Edleson and Syers (1990, 1991)	283	No[c]	Yes	68%[e]	Education vs. Self	12 vs. 16	Self, Partner	33% Education 50% Self-help
Johnson and Kanzler (1990)	687	No	Yes	30%	Education, Cog-Beh, Anger	12	Self	7% (5 mo)
Meredith & Burns (1990)	125	No	No	53%	Education	9-24	Self, Partner	Unknown

a. Control group membership not randomized.
b. Control group membership randomized (waiting list minimal intervention).
c. Treatment randomized.
d. Some or all subjects court referred.
e. At follow-up.
f. Anger—Anger management; Assertion—Assertion training; Cog-Beh—Cognitive Behavior; Communication; Conflict—Conflict resolution; Education; Exercise; Problem—Problem solving; Relaxation—Relaxation training; Self—Self-help/self-management; Stress—Stress management; "Traditional." All treatment in men's groups except where specified.
g. Couples' groups.
h. Men's groups and couples' groups.
i. In weeks.
j. Duration of follow-up interval in parentheses.

Stacey and Shupe (1984)

The authors combined data from three programs in Texas, including the one reviewed by Deschner (1984). Most of the follow-up clients were from one of the three programs. Of the original sample, 63% of the men and 41% of the partners were located and agreed to follow-up interviews. The follow-up intervals varied from a few months to a few years. Approximately three quarters of the men and half of the women reported no repeat violence. These figures were smaller for men who did not complete their treatment program.

Edleson, Miller, Stone, and Chapman (1985)

The authors studied men who volunteered for treatment after admitting acts of physical or sexual assault on their partner. They were treated in several small groups (a multiple baseline design) in a 12-week, cognitive-behavioral program. At follow-up, 7 to 21 weeks later, seven of the nine clients (78%) reported no new violence. The small sample, short follow-up period, and exclusive reliance on self-reports limit the usefulness of the study conclusions.

Hawkins and Beauvais (1985)

The authors reported on a treatment program consisting of twelve 2-hour groups focusing on anger control, stress management, family problems, and communication skills. These were followed by six 2-hour individual or couple therapy sessions tailored to the specific needs of the patient and spouse. Subjects were 106 men, nearly 75% court referred to treatment. Police records were studied for the 6 months prior to treatment, during the treatment interval, and for 6 months after treatment. The authors report an 18% recidivism rate, defined as renewed police contact for domestic violence in the post-treatment interval. Recidivism rates were not different for program completers versus dropouts, nor were they different for court-referred versus self-referred clients. As there was no control group of any sort, the observed phenomena cannot be said to be a treatment effect.

Kelso and Personette (1985)

The authors studied a 6-month treatment program. Treatment components included cognitive-behavioral approaches to anger management and assertiveness training, as well as physical exercise and relaxation training for stress management. Many of the clients were seen in individual as well as group treatment. Only 28% of the sample "completed" the treatment; the average treatment duration was $4\frac{1}{2}$ months. There was no posttreatment follow-up, but the men were reassessed monthly during treatment to determine the effect of the therapy on psychological as well as physical violence. Only about half of the participants agreed to be assessed, and the data are all from self-reports. The number of men reporting each month varied substantially. As might be expected, violence was often reported to be quite low (as low as 4%) and tended to decline over the course of treatment. One interpretation of this finding is that men who continued to be violent dropped out of treatment.

Neidig, Friedman, and Collins (1985)

The report covers a U.S. Marine Corps program that provides mandatory early intervention in domestic abuse among Marine personnel. Violence is viewed as a skill deficit rather than as an expression of "man's right to beat a woman." Group treatment focuses on accepting responsibility, committing to change, use of time-outs, anger management, and other conflict containment and resolution skills. Although the focus is on the male assailant, both partners participate in treatment. The authors report 80% of their cohort to be violence free at a 4-month follow-up, a relatively short interval. As the military might be expected to be able to retain more control and surveillance over its members than can occur in the civilian community, the generalizability of the findings seems unnecessarily limited. It is noted that alcoholism and severe violence were not reliable predictors of poor prognosis; however, sociopathy, poor reality testing, and a resistive attitude late in treatment were related to recidivism.

Dutton (1986)

Dutton compared 50 treated wife assaulters with 50 "untreated" controls. Treatment was a 16-week court-mandated program that included assertion training, anger management training, and other cognitively oriented behavior management skills. Outcome measures included police records of recidivism, as well as client and spouse reports on the Conflict Tactics Scale at intervals varying from 6 months to 3 years after treatment. Rearrest rates were a stable 4% across the follow-up interval for the treated men. In the untreated sample, rearrest increased from an initial 16% to 40% over the same interval. Spouse reports of recidivism in the treatment group were 16%. Although methodologically superior to other studies in this area, this study is marred by the nonrandom assignment to treatment versus control group. Some of the control group were men who lived too far away to attend the program and thus were in effect assigned to the no-treatment condition. Others had been deemed "unsuitable" for treatment by probation officers or the therapist, and some were treatment dropouts.

Rosenbaum (1986)

In an early report of a brief (6-week) psychoeducational group treatment of nine men who volunteered for treatment after admitting to at least one incident of violence against their spouse, clients were interviewed on the phone every 3 months from 6 to 24 months after treatment. Self-reports provided the only data, and eight of the nine men (89%) reported no further violence. This is, of course, a very brief therapy, and very small sample, using a notoriously unreliable data source (self-report).

Saunders and Hanusa (1986)

The authors studied 92 men who had completed a 20-session cognitive-behavioral treatment program. Men with serious psychiatric or substance abuse problems were screened out in initial interviews.

Treatment included 12 structured sessions (assertion training, relaxation training, cognitive restructuring, etc.) and 8 more traditional
"group therapy" sessions. Collectively, the men showed improvements
in attitudes toward women, jealousy, anger, and depression. The study
did not, however, measure changes in violent behavior. In correlating
men's self-reports with scores on the Marlowe-Crowne Social Desirability Scale, it was noted that there was a substantial correlation
between underreporting negative qualities and high scores on the
social desirability measure.

DeMaris and Jackson (1987)

The authors attempted to contact 414 men who had been treated.
Only 312 could be reached, and of those only 53 (17%) responded to
the survey. A modified Conflict Tactics Scale was used. Recidivism,
however, was simply the answer to a yes-no question. By this criterion,
35% of the respondents were identified as recidivists. Predictors of
recidivism were alcohol abuse problems and having witnessed parental violence. High versus low attendance in treatment was not related
to outcome. Comparing respondents to nonrespondents, it emerged
that those less likely to respond were Protestants, men with alcohol
problems, men who had witnessed parental violence, and those who
had actually "beat up" their partner. The fact that the data are based
on such a small proportion of the total treatment sample, plus the
observation that three of the four predictors of nonresponding were
empirically or intuitively related to recidivism, suggests that the 35%
figure is an underestimate of the actual level of recidivism.

Leong, Coates, and Hoskins (1987)

Data are presented on 47 men (of 67 who started the program). Only
23 of these completed a court-mandated treatment, and at the follow-
up, only 16 partners could be located. Of these, only three (19%)
reported continued violence. The rearrest rate for the larger, original
sample was 15%. The meaning of these findings, given the large (76%)
attrition rate, is unclear.

Maiuro, Cahn, Vitaliano, and Zegree (1987)

The authors studied an 18- to 20-week structured group treatment that included a psychoeducational component as well as cognitive-behavioral skills training (including the Novaco anger management program), and featured the use of videotaping. A group of 65 men who began the program were compared with 25 waiting list controls. Pre- and posttreatment assessment included scales for the measurement of depression, hostility, and coping methods. At the end of treatment, the treated group showed diminished anger and depression and improved coping methods (on paper), whereas there were no significant changes in the untreated group. Spouses also reported "improvement." At a one-year follow-up, 16 partners (25%) of the treated group were located and reported that the improvement was maintained.

Shepard (1987)

Shepard studied the Duluth Domestic Abuse Intervention Program (DAIP). Treatment was organized into a two-phase program: 12 weeks of group counseling in anger management with other, similar cognitive-behavioral treatment; and a 12-week course of education about abusive attitudes and behaviors. Outcome evaluation was also a two-phase process, including all men who had completed one or both phases of treatment up to (a) 3 months before and (b) 14 months after completing the program. The first outcome evaluation included the men ($n = 92$) and the partners of some of them ($n = 77$). The second evaluation included only the partners still available ($n = 33$). Estimates of nonviolence increased from 61% after Phase 1, to 69% after Phase 2, to 70% after 14 months. These findings must be tempered by the observation that 25% of men dropped out after the intake interview and less than half of the partners were still available for follow-up at 14 months. It is also noted that 60% of the couples were no longer living together, which has a likely influence on repeat violence. Partners' reports routinely indicated more violence than the men themselves reported and also showed that the incidence of psychological abuse did not change with treatment.

Tolman, Beeman, and Mendoza (1987)

The authors studied treatment offered to volunteers, sponsored by a women's shelter. Treatment consisted of 26 sessions and included training in anger management and other conflict resolution strategies, as well as discussion of sexist attitudes underlying wife assault. Follow-up after 6 months included a questionnaire and modified CTS, as well as a phone interview with both client and partner. Of the original sample, only 32% were included in the follow-up. Partners reported that nearly 47% of the men had committed violent acts and 51% had engaged in threats or property violence. Clients had completed varying numbers of treatment sessions, and there was a nonsignificant trend toward more recidivism with more treatment. There was no control group, but the findings, if valid, are certainly discouraging, especially as the "worst" candidates, those with obvious psychiatric and substance abuse problems, were screened out of the program before treatment.

Edleson and Gruznski (1988)

Three studies concerned the Minneapolis Domestic Abuse Program (DAP). Study 1 compared 32 completers with 31 dropouts in an 8-week, cognitive-behavioral group treatment program. Partner reports at intervals of 5 to 9 months showed 64% nonviolence in the completers, as opposed to only 54% for the dropouts.

Study 2 included 8 weeks of "structured" group therapy, plus at least 16 weeks of a less structured treatment group. Of the 86 men entering the study, only 42 partners could be reached at the 9-month follow-up interval. Sixty-seven percent of them reported no recurrent violence, although threats of violence remained common (43%).

The third study compared a different group of completers (n = 84) with dropouts (n = 37) in the treatment program described in Study 2. In contrast to the earlier findings, completers were not significantly less violent at follow-up than dropouts (59% vs. 52%), and threats of violence were common in both groups. The authors report that the men in Study 3 had more unemployment and substance abuse, as well as histories of prior treatment, suggesting a more "hard-core" group. It should also be noted that in all studies, follow-up interviews included spouses no longer living with the partner, thereby possibly inflating the estimates of nonviolence in all samples.

Hamberger and Hastings (1988b, 1990)

Two studies derived from a violence abatement program that includes intake assessment sessions, an orientation meeting, and 12 weekly group treatment sessions emphasizing cognitive-behavioral skills training. One-year follow-up includes client and partner report (interview and Conflict Tactics Scale), as well as police records of recurrent violence, domestic or otherwise.

In Study 1, the data from 35 program completers were compared with 36 program dropouts. At one year follow-up, completers showed a 28% recidivism rate (per self-, partner, or police report), whereas dropouts showed a 47% rate. There were significant decreases in CTS scores as well as self-rated depression and anger in the completer group, but no change in basic personality as assessed by the Millon Clinical Multiaxial Inventory (MCMI). Evidence of continued psychological abuse was apparent, despite treatment.

The second study focused on 106 men, either self- or court referred for treatment. In the year after treatment, four follow-up contacts were made with each client and his partner to assess recidivism. There were 32 recidivists (30%). The reports of 58 of the nonrecidivists were validated by partner report; as the remaining 16 partners could not be reached, the recidivism rate may be higher. Chemical dependency and sociopathic personality were related to recidivism.

Tolman (1988)

Tolman investigated the effect of the criminal justice system on recidivism after one of a number of different treatments. The patients (n = 98) were either mandated, recommended, or self-referred into treatment programs. Aggressive behavior, as measured by the Conflict Tactics Scale, was related to several factors, including time since treatment and chronicity of pretreatment violence. The men who were "recommended" to treatment showed diminished recidivism at 6 months and 4 years. Type of treatment was not related to outcome, nor was number of treatment sessions. The meaning of these findings is not intuitively obvious. It must also be noted that the sample was not randomly assigned: criminal justice system personnel decided whom to "mandate" to treatment, and whom to merely recommend, and not all clients recommended to treatment chose to accept that recommendation. Thus, it is both a court-selected and self-selected sample.

Chen, Bersani, Myers, and Denton (1989)

The authors reported on the effectiveness of a court-mandated treatment program. Treatment was a two-phase program: four 2-hour informational sessions and four 2-hour interactive group sessions focusing on self-esteem, stress reduction, and conflict avoidance strategies. Participants were 120 convicted wife assaulters for whom treatment was mandated and a retroactively selected sample of 101 cases not referred for treatment, drawn from the municipal court files. Recidivism was based on court records and included both wife assault and other violent crime.

Compared with the control group, recidivism was lower in the 63% of the treatment group who had attended 75% or more of the treatment sessions. Recidivism was higher in men with a history of more frequent or severe violence, and it increased across the follow-up period. The authors note that "about 5%" of the treatment group were charged with subsequent domestic violence; "about 10%" of the controls were so charged. An effort was made to identify the characteristics of men whom the judges "selected" for treatment and a marked lack of consistency across the six judges was noted (p. 317).

Edleson and Syers (1990, 1991)

A somewhat more complicated study evaluated treatment effectiveness at 6-month and 18-month follow-ups. There were three types of treatment: a structured, psychoeducational group; a less structured "self-help" group; and a combination of the two. Treatments were offered at two levels of intensity: 12 or 32 sessions. In the initial follow-up, 92 clients and/or their partner were interviewed (80 partner report, 12 client self-report only). The more structured treatments (Groups 1 and 3) had the strongest effect, with reports of approximately two thirds of these groups nonviolent at 6 months, compared to less than half of the self-help group. Regardless of type of treatment, nonviolence was more prevalent among participants in the 12-session versus the 32-session group. This reverse dose-dependent effect was not predicted, seems counterintuitive, and is not readily interpreted. It is understandable that more sessions might not necessarily add to the effect of the initial 12, but why additional treatment should actually detract from the efficacy is problematic. Even more confusing is the observation that at the 18-month follow-up, a significantly greater proportion of the men in the self-help condition were nonviolent. This finding was also not predicted and would need cross-validation before being accepted as other than chance.

Johnson and Kanzler (1990)

The report concerns a program that offers treatment as an alternative to incarceration for first-arrest domestic violence offenders. The program is a 12-week, small group format, targeting the resocialization of sexist stereotypes, as well as teaching anger management and other cognitive-behavioral skills. Follow-up interviews were attempted with partners 3 to 5 months posttreatment. Of the original sample of 687, 515 (75%) could be contacted. Of these, only 485 responded (70% of the original total). Four hundred and fifty (66%) reported no further violence in the 3- to 5-month period. Only 35 (7.2% of the respondents, but 5% of the original sample) reported recidivism. These estimates seem at the low end of the spectrum observed in this area. It is possible that the "first-arrest" criterion skewed the sample away from older, more "hard-core" assailants, although the authors point out that many of the clients reported previous violence for which they had not been arrested. It is also not clear what proportion of the partners were still living with their violent spouse.

Meredith and Burns (1990)

Ontario Correctional Services sponsored a survey of nine treatment programs, all based on the services model psychoeducational group program. As applied by the nine centers, program duration varied from 9 to 24 weeks. A structured interview was used to gather data on physical, verbal, and emotional aggression. Conclusions were based on reports from 125 clients and 81 partners, although the authors report a 53% dropout rate from that starting sample. All forms of aggression are reported to have declined; however, no inferential statistics are provided, nor is it clear whether the reported statistics represent all clients at each assessment, or (more appropriately) only those available for pre- and posttests and 3-month follow-up.

Summary of Problems With Outcome Research

After reviewing much of the research literature, what do we "know" about the short- and long-term effects of treatment on wife assault? The answer, unfortunately, is "Not much." "Recidivism," however measured in the studies reviewed here, varied from: (a) not reported, to (b) 4%-5% (rearrests), to (c) up to 50%. We cannot confidently say whether "Treatment works." We should be well beyond that question, asking instead, "What treatment works best on which types of client, and under what conditions?" We are, however, also unprepared to provide even partial answers to those questions. Amid some moderately good studies, many have one or more significant methodological or conceptual flaws that render them at best unhelpful and at worst misleading. Taken together, these studies are so varied in their makeup, process, and reporting as to make cross-study generalizations impossible. If we are to make progress in this area, studies must be conducted that are scientifically sound, and they must be conducted in a manner that makes it possible to pool the results with those of other studies over time to allow solid generalizations to be made. Some of the important shortcomings include the following:

1. Small Sample Size

Some studies are based on a very small number of clients. One started with as few as nine; some others were not a great deal larger and with attrition ended up being almost as small by the time of follow-up. Results of such studies cannot be considered reliable standing alone, and researchers who are required to work with such small numbers need to be especially mindful of the factors outlined below that may facilitate the grouping of their data with the results of other studies.

2. Nonrandom Assignment to Treatment

If subjects are not randomly assigned to treatment (and control) conditions, then treatment is by definition confounded with the assignment criteria. Any observed effects, however "intuitively obvious," cannot validly be ascribed to the effects of treatment.

3. No Control Groups

In the complete absence of a control group, no observed effects can be validly ascribed to treatment. Any behavior changes that are noted may be related to multiple other specific and nonspecific factors surrounding treatment, that is, arrest, other criminal justice system involvement, spouse leaving or threatening to leave home, and so forth. Clearly, there would be ethical concerns about not offering a demonstratedly effective treatment to a violent and dangerous wife assaulter. At this point, however, we have no treatment programs that we unequivocally know to be effective. Further, there are many venues wherein wife assaulters, even when they are brought to police or court attention, do not receive treatment. Rather, they may be served with restraining orders or given probation on condition of nonviolence. Given the expense and the labor-intensive nature of treatment programs, comparisons with "no-treatment" conditions need to be made. Waiting lists are common in treatment programs for other, equally dangerous behavior, particularly in the context of court involvement and probation, and their use should be considered. It can be argued that offering treatment in the absence of evidence of its efficacy is itself unethical. It is expensive, is often paid for by third-party payers or tax dollars, and may mislead the victim-partner to expect more safety in the relationship than actually exists. We need control groups.

4. Attrition

Loss of participants before, during, and after treatment is very common in the studies reviewed here. In an ideal situation, agencies (such as perhaps the criminal justice system) would effectively require continued participation from clients considering dropping out. The reality is that this is usually not possible. Police and court systems are swamped with crime and criminals, and nonlethal wife assault simply has not been assigned sufficient priority to be followed that closely. Therefore, attrition, even from "mandated" treatment, remains a fact of life. In trying to provide data that will be most useful to the research and treatment community, it will be very important to specify the apparent trends in outcome findings that are actually attributable to artifacts of attrition. For example, observed recidivism rates of 30%, 25%, and 20%, measured at 3-, 6-, and 12-month intervals, might seem to suggest a diminished recidivism over time. If, however, the results are based on 75%, 50%, and 25% of the original sample, respectively, with recidivists gradually self-selecting out of the follow-up sample, then the apparent trend is not meaningful. Recidivism statistics must reflect only the members of the sample present for both measurement periods for the percentages to be meaningful.

5. Inadequate Specification

As noted above, we need to move beyond the crude question of whether "treatment works," and ask what treatments work best for what clients and under what conditions. Few (or no) agencies have a sufficient variety of treatments, adequately large client samples, or assortment of conditions to tease out these issues. It becomes important that all treatment agencies specify what they are doing with sufficient clarity that cross-study comparisons (meta-analyses) can be done. Specificity is needed in several areas. The characteristics of the treatment sample is one major area. The research reviewed here suggests that a number of demographic and other characteristics may be pertinent: age, race, educational level, employment status, prior violent and nonviolent offenses, severity of previous violence, psychiatric illness, personality disorder, and substance abuse. We would urge the development and use of a standardized data form for subject description, as well as the use of well-validated psychological assessment devices, such as the MMPI or the MCMI.

The context of the "referral" may also be important and should be noted, with the data analyzed separately. Was the client self-referred, urged or threatened into treatment by the victim-partner, given the suggestion by police, or forced by court/probation/parole authorities? The nature of any continuing relationship between client and partner is also important. Are they continuing to live together, separated but continuing a relationship, or separated or divorced and no longer maintaining a relationship? Are there children from the relationship?

The particulars of the treatment should be specified, both the structural variables (number, frequency, and timing of meetings; number of persons in each group; number, sex, and perhaps race of therapists; etc.) as well as the content of the sessions. This would include the specific "psychoeducational" content, as well as the content and method of any "cognitive-behavioral" skills training.

6. Follow-Up Interval

Some "follow-ups" in the studies reviewed here were evaluations or "re-evaluations" immediately following treatment. Other instances referred to assessments at 3, 6, 12, 24, and even 48 months. Clearly, for a treatment to be deemed valuable or effective, it must have a demonstrable effect quickly and maintain that effect beyond the immediate end of treatment. We would suggest one year as a standard. It may also be the case that factors related to immediate outcome are not the same as those correlated with longer term effects. Outcome analyses should be conducted with that possibility in mind.

7. Outcome Measures

The main focus in the research, and appropriately so, has been on repeat violence against the partner. The source of that information has varied. Reliance on reports from the criminal justice system alone (police, probation/parole, court records, etc.) has yielded the lowest estimates of recidivism. Obviously, much recurrent violence goes unreported to the authorities. Likewise, client self-reports of recidivism routinely provide a lower estimate than partner reports. The best estimates are perhaps yielded using all these sources in combination.

Structuring the data collection, using such instruments as the Conflict Tactics Scale, offers the best hope of subsequent cross-study outcome comparison. Several studies, although reporting diminished physical violence against the partner, noted continued threats, property violence, and other forms of intimidation. The use of this scale, or some similar tool, would facilitate the collection of that important data as well.

Many studies reported here included a "psychoeducational" component, the implication being that a good grasp of this information would facilitate subsequent behavior change. Yet none of the studies reported anything about pre- and posttests to validate that the information presented had been learned. This would seem to be an important component of any outcome study.

A few studies reported changes in scores on various psychological tests (Beck Depression Inventory, Novaco Anger Scale, etc.). Although interesting and potentially useful, these scores of course need to be interpreted against changes in the same tests administered to control group subjects. Diminished depression, anger, or anxiety may be the result of passage of time (without disaster) since arrest, rather than any effect of treatment. It would perhaps also be useful to view such changes within the context of a broader understanding of the client's personality or psychopathology.

One final aspect of outcome measurement deserves mention: the status of the client and partner's relationship at the termination of treatment and at follow-up. It is not surprising that a man shows decreased violence toward his partner if they have separated or divorced and he does not see her anymore. Yet several studies noted only as an afterthought that various proportions of the treatment sample were living alone, or at least not with their original victim-partner, at the time of the reported reassessment.

8. Statistics

Given an otherwise sound study, the results are not useful if appropriate inferential statistics are not included, as was the case in several studies reviewed here. Merely stating the percentages in various outcome categories is not sufficient, nor is referring to "improvement" in various measures without presenting numbers with statistics showing that the change is unlikely to have occurred by chance.

9. Anomalous Findings

A few studies included one or more outcomes that do not make intuitive sense, for example, greater recidivism associated with more therapy sessions, or one treatment approach being associated with superior results at one interval and another approach showing a greater effect at a different interval. Such findings may, of course, reflect an underlying reality. If so, the effect will be observed in replications. More likely, however, such findings are the result of random chance and will "wash out" with replications. To avoid misleading the methodologically unsophisticated reader, it is important that such anomalous results be described as random chance and viewed, at most, as hypotheses for future research. This is especially true for observations that cannot be fitted reasonably into a sensible theoretical framework.

Conclusion

It is discouraging that all of the effort and expense of the treatments themselves, as well as the research on them, have yielded so few conclusions, none of them firm. It is hoped that the present review and critique will help in the development and implementation of improved individual research studies in the future. More important, however, we hope that by specifying the needs, we will facilitate an attitude of cooperation among research groups. The accomplishment of definitive research in this area will require sufficient commonalities in the structure, process, and focus of individual studies as to allow meta-analyses of the "pooled" research data.

References

Adams, D. (1988). Counseling men who batter: A profeminist analysis of five treatment models. In M. Bograd & K. Yllö (Eds.), *Feminist perspectives on wife abuse* (pp. 176-199). Beverly Hills, CA: Sage.

Adams, D., & McCormick, A. (1982). Men unlearning violence: A group approach. In M. Roy (Ed.), *The abusive partner: An analysis of domestic battering* (pp. 170-197). New York: Van Nostrand Reinhold.

Bandura, A. (1977). *Social learning theory.* Englewood Cliffs, NJ: Prentice-Hall.

Bograd, M. (1984). Family systems approaches to wife battering: A feminist critique. *American Journal of Orthopsychiatry, 54,* 558-568.

Caesar, P. L., & Hamberger, L. K. (Eds.). (1989). *Treating men who batter: Theory, practice and programs.* New York: Springer.

Chen, H., Bersani, L., Myers, S. C., & Denton, R. (1989). Evaluating the effectiveness of a court-sponsored abuser treatment program. *Journal of Family Violence, 4,* 309-322.

Colorado. (1989, April). *The manual of standards for the treatment of domestic violence perpetrators.*

DeMaris, A., & Jackson, J. K. (1987). Batterers' reports of recidivism after counseling. *Social Casework, 68,* 458-465.

Deschner, J. (1984). *The hitting habit: Anger control for battering couples.* New York: Free Press.

Dunford, F. W. (1992). *San Diego Navy Spouse Assault Treatment Experiment* (Contract #5BCM-I 2B01-MH 45080-02). Washington, DC: National Institute of Mental Health.

Dunford, F. W., Huizinga, D., & Elliott, D. S. (1990). The role of arrest in domestic assault: The Omaha police experiment. *Criminology, 28,* 183-206.

Dutton, D. G. (1986). The outcome of court-mandated treatment for wife assault: A quasi-experimental evaluation. *Violence and Victims, 1,* 163-175.

Edleson, J. L. (1984). Violence is the issue: A critique of Neidig's assumptions. *Victimology: An International Journal, 9,* 483-489.

Edleson, J. L., & Gruznski, R. J. (1988). Treating men who batter: Four years of outcome data from the Domestic Abuse Project. *Journal of Social Service Research, 12,* 3-22.

Edleson, J. L., Miller, D. M., Stone, G. W., & Chapman, D. G. (1985). Group treatment for men who batter. *Social Work Research and Abstracts, 21,* 18-21.

Edleson, J. L., & Syers, M. (1990). Relative effectiveness of group treatments for men who batter. *Social Work Research and Abstracts, 26,* 10-17.

Edleson, J. L., & Syers, M. (1991). The effects of group treatment for men who batter: An 18-month follow-up study. *Research in Social Work Practice, 1,* 227-243.

Eisenberg, S. E., & Micklow, P. L. (1977). The assaulted wife: "Catch 22" revisited. *Women's Law Reporter, 3,* 138-161.

Eisikovits, Z. C., & Edleson, J. L. (1989, September). Intervening with men who batter: A critical review of the literature. *Social Service Review,* pp. 384-414.

Feazell, C. S., Mayers, R. S., & Deschner, J. P. (1984). Services for men who batter: Implications for programs and policies. *Family Relations, 33,* 217-223.

Feshbach, S. (1956). The catharsis hypothesis and some consequences of interaction with aggressive and neutral play objects. *Journal of Personality, 24,* 449-462.

Ganley, A. (1987). Perpetrators of domestic violence: An overview of counseling the court-mandated client. In D. J. Sonkin (Ed.), *Domestic violence on trial: Psychological and legal dimensions of family violence* (pp. 155-173). New York: Springer.

Ganley, A. (1989). Integrating feminist and social learning analyses of aggression: Creating multiple models for intervention with men who batter. In P. L. Caesar & L. K. Hamberger (Eds.), *Treating men who batter: Theory, practice and programs* (pp. 196-235). New York: Springer.

Geffner, R. A., Mantooth, C., Franks, D., & Rao, L. (1989). A psychoeducational, conjoint therapy approach to reducing family violence. In P. L. Caesar & L. K. Hamberger (Eds.), *Treating men who batter: Theory, practice, and programs* (pp. 103-133). New York: Springer.

Geller, J. A., & Wasserstrom, J. (1984). Conjoint therapy for the treatment of domestic violence. In A. R. Roberts (Ed.), *Battered women and their families: Intervention strategies and treatment programs* (pp. 33-48). New York: Springer.

Goldfried, M. R., & Davison, G. C. (1976). *Clinical behavior therapy.* New York: Holt, Rinehart & Winston.

Goldman, J. (1989). Treating couples: An alternative approach. *Family Violence Bulletin, 5,* 13-14.

Goldman, J. (1991). Protect us from the protectors. *Family Violence Bulletin, 7,* 15-17.

Gondolf, E. W., & Foster, R. A. (1991). Pre-program attrition in batterer programs. *Journal of Family Violence, 6,* 337-350.

Gondolf, E. W., & Russell, D. (1986). The case against anger control treatment programs for batterers. *Response, 9,* 2-5.

Gruznski, R. J., & Carillo, T. P. (1988). Who completes batterer treatment groups? An empirical investigation. *Journal of Family Violence, 3,* 141-150.

Halpern, M. (1984, August). *Battered women's alternatives: The men's program component.* Paper presented at the meeting of the American Psychological Association, Toronto.

Hamberger, L. K. (1984, August). *Helping men who batter: A two-stage community intervention program.* Paper presented at the meeting of the American Psychological Association, Toronto.

Hamberger, L. K., & Hastings, J. E. (1986). Characteristics of spouse abusers: Predictors of treatment acceptance. *Journal of Interpersonal Violence, 1,* 363-373.

Hamberger, L. K., & Hastings, J. E. (1988a). Characteristics of male spouse abusers consistent with personality disorders. *Hospital and Community Psychiatry, 39,* 763-770.

Hamberger, L. K., & Hastings, J. E. (1988b). Skills training for treatment of spouse abusers: An outcome study. *Journal of Family Violence, 3,* 121-130.

Hamberger, L. K., & Hastings, J. E. (1989). Counseling male spouse abusers: Characteristics of treatment completers and dropouts. *Violence and Victims, 4,* 275-286.

Hamberger, L. K., & Hastings, J. E. (1990, November). Different routes to mandated spouse abuser counseling II: A cross validation study. In C. Rasche (Chair), *Current Studies of Perpetrators and Victims of Spousal Violence.* Symposium presented at the meeting of the American Society of Criminology, Baltimore, MD.

Hamberger, L. K., & Lohr, J. M. (1989). Proximal causes of spouse abuse: Cognitive and behavioral factors. In P. L. Caesar & L. K. Hamberger (Eds.), *Treating men who batter: Theory, practice and programs* (pp. 53-76). New York: Springer.

Hartmann, D. (1969). Influence of symbolically modeled instrumental aggression and pain cues on aggressive behavior. *Journal of Personality and Social Psychology, 11,* 280-288.

Hawkins, R., & Beauvais, C. (1985, August). *Evaluation of group therapy with abusive men: The police record.* Paper presented at the meeting of the American Psychological Association, Los Angeles.

Island, D., & Letellier, P. (1991). *Men who beat the men who love them: Battered gay men and domestic violence.* New York: Harrington Park.

Jennings, J. L. (1987). History and issues in the treatment of battering men: A case for unstructured group therapy. *Journal of Family Violence, 2,* 193-213.

Jennings, J. L. (1990). Preventing relapse versus "stopping" domestic violence: Do we expect too much too soon from battering men? *Journal of Family Violence, 5,* 43-60.

Johnson, J. M., & Kanzler, D. J. (1990, November). *Treating domestic violence: Evaluating the effectiveness of a domestic violence diversion program.* Paper presented at the meeting of the American Society of Criminology, Baltimore, MD.

Kado, R. (1985, August). *Treatment of the male batterer: A brief overview.* Paper presented at the meeting of the American Psychological Association, Los Angeles.

Kelso, D., & Personette, L. (1985). *Domestic violence and treatment services for victims and abusers: An analysis of violent behavior of abusers and victims in relation to AWAIC treatment service.* Unpublished report available from Abused Women's Aid in Crisis, 100 W. 13th Avenue, Anchorage, AK 99501.

Lane, G., & Russell, T. (1989). Second-order systemic work with violent couples. In P. L. Caesar & L. K. Hamberger (Eds.), *Treating men who batter: Theory, practice and programs* (pp. 134-162). New York: Springer.

Leong, D. J., Coates, C. J., & Hoskins, J. (1987, July). *Follow-up of batterers treated in a court-ordered treatment program.* Paper presented at the Third National Conference for Family Violence Researchers, Durham, NH.

Lund, S. H., Larsen, N. E., & Schultz, S. K. (1982). *Exploratory evaluation of the Domestic Abuse Project.* Unpublished report, Program Evaluation Center, Minneapolis, MN.

Maiuro, R. D., Cahn, T. S., Vitaliano, P. P., & Zegree, J. B. (1987, August). *Treatment for domestically violent men: Outcome and follow-up data.* Paper presented at the meeting of the American Psychological Association, New York.

Meredith, C., & Burns, N. (1990). *Evaluation of batterer's treatment programs.* Ottawa: ABT Associates of Canada.

Neidig, P. H. (1984). Women's shelters, men's collectives and other issues in the field of spouse abuse. *Victimology: An International Journal, 9,* 3-4.

Neidig, P. H., Friedman, D. H., & Collins, B. S. (1985). Domestic conflict containment: A spouse abuse treatment program. *Social Casework: The Journal of Contemporary Social Work, 66,* 195-204.

Novaco, R. (1975). *Anger control.* Lexington, MA: Lexington.

Pence, E. (1985). Response to Peter Neidig's article: "Women's shelters, men's collectives, and other issues in the field of spouse abuse." *Victimology: An International Journal, 9,* 477-482.

Pence, E. (1989). Batterer programs: Shifting from community collusion to community confrontation. In P. L. Caesar & L. K. Hamberger (Eds.), *Treating men who batter: Theory, practice and programs* (pp. 24-50). New York: Springer.

Pirog-Good, M., & Stets, J. (1986). Programs for abusers: Who drops out and what can be done? *Response, 2,* 17-19.

Rosenbaum, A. (1986). Group treatment of wife abusers: Process and outcomes. *Psychotherapy, 23,* 607-612.

Saunders, D. G. (1981). Treatment and value issues in helping battered women. In A. S. Gurman (Ed.), *Questions and answers in the practice of family therapy* (pp. 493-496). New York: Bruner/Mazel.

Saunders, D. G., & Hanusa, D. (1986). Cognitive behavioral treatment for men who batter: The short-term effects of group therapy. *Journal of Family Violence, 1,* 357-372.

Saunders, D. G., & Parker, J. C. (1989, September). Legal sanctions and treatment follow-through among men who batter: A multivariate analysis. *Social Work Research and Abstracts,* pp. 21-29.

Shepard, M. (1987, July). *Intervention with men who batter: An evaluation of a domestic abuse program.* Paper presented at the Third National Conference for Family Violence Researchers, Durham, NH.

Sherman, L. W., & Berk, R. A. (1984). The specific deterrent effects of arrest for domestic assault. *American Sociological Review, 49,* 261-272.

Soler, E. (1987). Domestic violence is a crime: A case study—San Francisco Family Violence Project. In D. J. Sonkin (Ed.), *Domestic violence on trial: Psychological and legal dimensions of family violence* (pp. 21-28). New York: Springer.

Sonkin, D. J., Martin, D., & Walker, L. E. A. (1985). *The male batterer: A treatment approach.* New York: Springer.

Staats, A. (1975). *Social behaviorism.* Homewood, IL: Dorsey.

Stacey, W. A., & Shupe, A. (1984). *The family secret: Family violence in America.* Boston: Beacon.

Tolman, R. M. (1988, November). *The impact of court involvement on the effectiveness of intervention with men who batter.* Paper presented at the meeting of the American Society of Criminology, Chicago, IL.

Tolman, R. M., Beeman, S., & Mendoza, C. (1987, July). *The effectiveness of a shelter-sponsored program for men who batter: Preliminary result.* Paper presented at the Third National Conference for Family Violence Researchers, Durham, NH.

Tolman, R. M., & Saunders, D. G. (1988). The case for the cautious use of anger control with men who batter. *Response, 11,* 15-20.

PART
IV

VICTIMS

9

Battered Women as Defendants

LENORE E. A. WALKER

The possibility that battered women could also be defendants in the legal system was not even discussed until the late 1970s in the United States, when it became apparent that some women who killed their violent partner did so out of desperation and in self-defense. Eventually, as attention became focused on the assaulted woman's state of mind, the fact that other crimes were committed by battered women under fear and duress of violence became more evident, too. Today, an understanding of the dynamics of wife assault and its psychological effect on women's behavior has been presented by a psychologist expert witness as part of a woman's defense in at least 500 trials in the United States. Such testimony is beginning to be introduced in trials in other countries with as broad a variety of legal systems as Canada, Great Britain, France, Greece, Belize, and Costa Rica.

My own work as an expert witness in almost 300 U.S. trials began in 1977 when I was asked to evaluate Miriam Griegg, a Billings, Montana, woman who had been seriously assaulted during most of her marriage. One night, she shot and killed her husband with six hollow-point bullets from his own magnum .357 gun. During an argument, he threw the gun at her and ordered her to shoot him, or else, he threatened, he would shoot and kill her. When the police arrived,

Walker & Associates, 50 South Steele, Suite 850, Denver, Colorado, 80209.

Miriam Griegg warned them to be careful as she knew her husband would be very angry. Obviously, her emotional state caused her to be unaware that he was dead; any one of the six bullets would have killed him instantly. She made it perfectly clear, however, that she had shot him because she had believed that he would have killed her otherwise, a straightforward self-defense argument. After listening to her testimony and mine—I explained the context of the relationship and how Miriam Griegg knew in her own mind that she would die if she did not do what her husband ordered her to do—the jury agreed that she was not guilty (Walker, 1989a).

Only a small number of battered women ever reach the point at which they believe that killing is the only way for them to stay alive (Walker, 1992). In fact, only 12% of the homicides in the United States are committed by women (Browne & Williams, 1989; Jones, 1981); most of these are women killing their violent partner. Wife assault victims make up the largest percentage of women who are incarcerated for attempted and completed homicides (Bauschard, 1986). Commission of other crimes by women, such as assault, burglary, robbery, theft, check and other fraud, and drug offenses, often have some component of physical or sexual abuse if they involve a male codefendant. My own work, together with that of investigative reporters, indicates that most of the approximately 30 women on death row in the United States are also abuse victims (Walker, 1991).

The fact that these women have been assaulted is of course not sufficient for them to gain special treatment in the criminal justice system. It is the effect of abuse on their state of mind and how that influences the level of responsibility to which they are held that merits attention. The British common-law system, and to a lesser degree, the Napoleonic legal system provide the basis for the laws in most countries in the world today. Both systems require a determination of what is in the mind of the actor and an assignment of a level of responsibility for the illegal behavior. Understanding what is in someone's mind at the time he or she commits any particular behavior, then, is as critical when judging the legal responsibility for behavior as is the act itself.

Morally, some people may believe that killing another human being is always murder, even though most people believe some exceptions are justified, such as a police officer who kills while trying to stop a crime or soldiers who kill during war. Legally, self-defense has always been considered to justify homicide if the danger appears of reasonable magnitude to those judging the action. Historical precedent created a standard based on men defending themselves and their family against other men. The problem has been to judge self-defense by a standard that included women's reasonable perception of danger, particularly when based upon years of suffering physical, sexual, and psychological aggression. Thus, the specialty areas of clinical, social, and forensic psychology, which provide empirical and clinical research about human behavior, can assist the triers of fact (the judge or jury) in deciding the effects of violence on a person's state of mind when a criminal act is committed. Such education can be done through expert witness testimony at several phases of legal proceedings.

The introduction of psychologists as expert witnesses has been debated in the literature. Faigman (1986) and Faust and Ziskin (1988) argue that such testimony biases the jury because of the prominence given to psychologists, whereas others (Fowler & Matarazzo, 1988; Monahan, 1980; Monahan & Walker, 1986) find it more helpful than prejudicial. A new field of feminist jurisprudence (MacKinnon, 1983) has developed because of the documented gender bias in U.S. courts (Shaffran, 1990) and the need for more equitable consideration of women's rights under the law (Bunch, 1991; McConnell, 1991). The criminalization of domestic violence in the early 1980s has created a need to sensitize the criminal justice system to women's ways of knowing and reacting to the world (cf. Edwards, 1989; Goolkasian, 1986; U.S. Attorney General's Task Force on Family Violence, 1984). An understanding of the secondary victimization of women under the law (Ryan, 1971) resulted in policy changes to admit testimony about wife assault and the battered woman syndrome when women become defendants (Blackman, 1986, 1989; Bocknak, 1981; Browne, 1987; Browne, Thyfault, & Walker, 1987; Ewing, 1987; Ewing & Aubrey, 1987; Maguigan, 1991; Mahoney, 1991, Price, 1985; Rosewater, 1987a; Saunders, 1986; Schneider, 1986; Sonkin, 1987; Walker, 1984b; 1989a, 1989b, 1989c, 1991, 1992).

Levels of Responsibility

Prior to the late 1970s, most battered women who killed their partner were told by their attorney to plead guilty. They were then sentenced to long prison terms (often 25 years to life) without a trial in which to present evidence about how being assaulted affected their state of mind and caused a reasonable belief of imminent danger at the time of the homicide (Bauschard, 1986; Jones, 1981). In some cases, particularly where the battered woman was considered a good member of the community or perhaps even a "lady" who unfortunately was involved with a "horrible brute of a man," the woman was permitted to plead not guilty by reason of insanity and received an indeterminate term in the state mental hospital's forensic unit or was not even charged (Jones, 1981).

The familiar case of Francine Hughes, played by Farrah Fawcett in the movie version of *The Burning Bed,* is an example of such a defense (although in this case, the attorney argued that the insanity was temporary and healed upon the death of her tormentor so that she was released upon the jury's findings). Although the discussion of defenses in this case applied only to the United States and indeed varies from state to state, the arguments can be adapted and applied to murder defenses in other legal systems.

The difference between the self-defense and insanity defenses to murder rests on the level of responsibility involved: a self-defense argument states that the woman had a reasonable perception of imminent danger and therefore was *justified* in using lethal force, whereas an insanity defense states that the woman was unable to tell the difference between right and wrong because she was mentally incompetent (perhaps harmed by head injuries or driven crazy by the behavior of her husband) and therefore should be *excused* from any culpability.

A justification defense uses the regular justice system; an excuse defense relies on psychiatric or psychological testimony concerning competency and the effect of abuse on the woman's fear and belief in her ability to protect herself (cf. Blackman, 1989; Bochnak, 1981; Browne, 1987; Ewing, 1987; Maguigan, 1991; Schneider, 1986; Walker, 1989a, 1992).

Murder Charges

Charges are filed against those suspected of having or known to have killed someone according to what they did, how they did it, and what was in their mind at the time the homicide occurred. In most state and federal courts, there are several levels of responsibility, which carry a range of penalties depending upon how much forethought and planning went into the action. Murder charges are usually divided into two groups, equivalent to first- and second-degree murder. Although there may be different labels, first-degree, or the highest level murder charges, usually involve premeditation of the homicide. A first-degree murder conviction carries the most serious consequences, such as 25 years to life in prison without the chance of parole. Sentencing guidelines usually permit deviation from the recommended range of punishment for extenuating circumstances, and of course, wife assault is one of a number of such circumstances. In many states, however, there is no freedom to deviate from life imprisonment (except for the possibility of parole).

Although most battered women who kill are initially charged with first-degree murder, they are rarely convicted at such a high level of responsibility if evidence of the wife assault and its effect on the woman's state of mind is presented during trial or sentencing. Yet even today, with more enlightened defense attorneys, evidence about the woman being assaulted may be presented at trial without any explanation of how the violence affected her ability to premeditate or plan a crime. Obviously, this critical omission frequently results in confusing jurors rather than helping them to understand the defendant's state of mind at the time of the incident.

Few battered women actually premeditate their assaulter's death, although almost every battered woman wishes for him to die at some time during their relationship (Walker, 1984a). Some may even tell a friend about that death wish, still without ever intending to kill. Others may even plan a killing as a way to protect their mind from being destroyed by the continued abuse, but they are not serious about carrying the plan out until the partner hurts them again. Still others come to believe that the man is so dangerous that he will only stop terrorizing them when he is dead—and these men often beg the woman to kill them, feeling their lack of control of their own behavior (Walker, 1989a). These women, too, may think about how to kill the man, but rarely carry out a prearranged plan (Walker, 1984a). Those few who do plan the event in advance with certainty can be distinguished from the typical premeditated killer by the insufficient thought given to the details and the concern for not hurting the man too much. For example, Clara Hess put a mattress over her husband's dead body before she covered it with dirt so he would not be hurt by the falling earth! The goal of the battered woman who kills is to stop the abuse, not to kill the man (Walker, 1989a).

Second-degree murder is the next most serious level of responsibility for killing someone. Usual definitions here exclude any conscious intent to plan to kill the man; instead, the woman is held responsible for using deadly force when she should have known that it could result in the man's death. It is often difficult to distinguish between the battered woman who threatens with a weapon to try to stop the man from using further violence and someone who uses a weapon when its dangerousness should have been known. A battered woman rarely thinks about killing a man when she picks up a weapon; rather, she is more likely see the weapon as a power equalizer or a way to grab the man's attention and persuade him to stop his cruel treatment of her. This is not second-degree murder. At most, if there is no apparent reasonable perception of imminent danger, it may be considered manslaughter: either the danger is honestly but incorrectly perceived or the wife assaulter causes the woman to reach her breaking point through his mental torture.

Voluntary and Involuntary Manslaughter

Manslaughter is the term given to a lower level of responsibility for a homicide that occurs for several legally defined reasons, for example, provocation by the victim, extreme emotional distress of the defendant, "heat of passion" when the defendant is enraged and cannot use appropriate judgment to evaluate the situation, and similar reasons that tend to lessen the responsibility necessary for first- or second-degree murder. Some states still have a diminished capacity defense at this level, although this form of mental distress, somewhere between insanity and justification, is rarely available anymore. "Diminished capacity" means the person may not be insane but his or her judgment is impaired sufficiently to mitigate the responsibility for the act. Other states have something known as imperfect self-defense, where there is an unreasonable but honest perception of danger by the defendant. This defense is usually used when there is no reasonable evidence that the man will harm the woman at that very moment, but the woman has an honest belief that harm is about to happen based on other information, such as his previous violence toward her. Voluntary and involuntary manslaughter often are differentiated by the same intent and nonintent issues as for first- and second-degree murder. Ewing (1987), Maguigan (1991), Mahoney (1991), McConnell (1991), and Schneider (1986) provide further discussion of these legal distinctions.

Other factors that influence the charges include the use of a weapon leading to additional charges and aggravation of the offense such as killing a police officer even if he is acting in his private capacity as a woman's violent husband. There is a basic unfairness in penalizing a woman for needing to pick up a weapon to defend herself against a man's fists when he has been socialized to use his fists as a weapon and she has not been so trained. This issue of fairness has been addressed by several courts, including the Washington State Supreme Court in the *Wanrow* decision (see *State v. Wanrow,* 1977, in Bochnak, 1981). Most states, however, add an additional charge if a gun or other weapon is used by the woman to defend herself. Also, if the man was killed while the woman was committing another criminal act, she could receive a steeper sentence or even the death penalty in some states. Rarely do attorneys even try to see to it that the jury is provided with instructions that account for gender differences in sex-role socialization.

Duress Defenses

Many other crimes committed by women are done under the instructions of a male codefendant, although sometimes the woman takes the entire blame and the existence of a partner is not known to the legal system. If the woman does commit the act because she fears further harm to herself or others (usually her children, family, or the victim of the crime), then her actions may be defended on the grounds that she was coerced. U.S. federal laws on duress state that her fear must reach a certain magnitude, such as from a threat to her life; serious bodily harm or death is usually required under state standards. The belief of many battered women that the wife assaulter could or would kill them at some time if he becomes angry enough with them usually suffices, although some courts do require evidence that threats to kill the woman or someone else were indeed made. Duress defenses usually do not completely remove the woman's responsibility for what she did (i.e., the property or other crime), but they can be used to mitigate the sentence. This use is especially important now that many U.S. jurisdictions have introduced mandatory sentencing, leaving judges only limited discretion in the length of prison time they can impose for a particular conviction. Battered women often plead guilty to these types of crimes because they cannot stand the tension of trial preparation, feel guilty, believe that their lawyers do not or will not believe them, or are still so afraid of their partner that they are sure he will continue to place them in danger unless they just plead guilty and do the time without exposing him.

Mental Health Defenses

The standard for mental health or excuse defenses for battered women in each state is the insanity definition. Most of these definitions have been revised following the *Hinkley* case (Bochnak, 1981) in the early 1980s, and they are now extremely difficult to meet. Some states, including Idaho and Nevada, have abolished the insanity defense, substituting a "guilty but mentally ill" defense that results in a woman's incarceration in a mental institution until she is competent to complete her sentence in prison. Most current standards for insanity date back to the mid-19th-century British common-law standard called the M'Naghten Rule, which states that someone is not culpable if he or she is so mentally diseased or disordered as to be unable to know the difference between right and wrong at the time the act is committed. Many battered women know that difference, but cannot conform their behavior to that knowledge because they believe they will be seriously hurt or killed if they do. Other battered women have been so seriously damaged by abuse that they do indeed fit the traditional insanity standard. Some battered women lose the ability to make appropriate judgments because of organic brain damage from head injuries or because they have become psychotic, perhaps as a way to escape from the terrible psychological abuse that accompanies physical and sexual violence. Many battered women, particularly those who are also survivors of incest or other child abuse, have learned to dissociate their mind from their body and to operate on "automatic pilot," without any ability to think about right and wrong (Krystal et al., 1989; Spiegel, 1990; van der Kolk, 1988). These women also fit the justification defense, as it is the perception of serious bodily harm or death that caused them to go into the dissociative state. Often, they have no memory of what precipitated the dissociation (Herman, 1992; Herman & Schatzow, 1987). Thus, it is entirely possible for a battered woman who kills in self-defense to use the insanity defense legitimately (cf. Walker, 1989a).

Despite the legitimacy of this defense, it is very difficult both to get mental health professionals to diagnose battered women properly, assigning causation for their psychological symptomology to living in a violent environment, and to persuade lay juries to excuse someone for committing a violent crime, especially a woman who may spontaneously recover once the danger has passed and who may appear quite "normal" by the time she is placed on trial.

Practically, then, although the insanity defense is available in many cases, it is rarely successful and therefore is only used in a few cases. Furthermore, many battered women advocates believe that it is demeaning for a woman to be declared insane for acting to save her own life; this feminist political perspective has also contributed to the unpopularity of the insanity defense.

Battered Woman Self-Defense Standard

As discussed above, the legal standards may be very different from what actually is the battered woman's state of mind at the time she attempts to defend herself (and perhaps her children or others) against what she perceives to be further violence and ultimately death. It is for this reason that an expert witness who is trained in the psychology of battered women is so important. The two issues that appear to differ for battered women and other defendants are the timing and reasonableness of the perception of danger. The legal standard for self-defense calls for a reasonable perception of imminent danger.

Reasonableness

The standard of the "reasonable person" is often objectively defined as reasonable man rather than reasonable woman or even reasonable battered woman (cf. Tomkins, Kenning, Greenwald, & Johnson, this volume). Take the case of a sleeping man. A man or even a nonbattered woman would have a very different perception of whether a sleeping man is dangerous than would be expected of a battered woman, particularly if she has experienced him waking up unpredictably and assaulting her. Some people argue that the typical wife assaulter's rapid mood swings from happy and contented to angry, hostile, and aggressive make it a reasonable perception of any battered woman to fear even a sleeping man, the length of whose quiet period is unpredictable by definition (Blackman, 1991; Browne, 1987; Ewing, 1987; Schneider, 1986; Sonkin, 1987; Walker, 1989a). Only when the dynamics of wife assault are truly understood does such a concept become plausible.

Alternatively, take the example of the battered woman who reports being terrified of the following scene: the man begins to argue with the woman, his anger appears to escalate, his words begin to come faster, he pushes her, his facial features appear to change, and his eyes get darker and empty looking. Another man probably would ignore this man, thinking he was just "blowing off steam"; or if the observer had some concern about the rapid escalation of the anger, he might try to do something to settle the argument. A nonbattered woman may be frightened by the man's loud argument and may even define the behavior as menacing and threatening, but may simply choose to leave the scene. A battered woman, however, may pick up a gun and shoot the man, particularly if he previously seriously hurt her following similar escalating arguments when he had the same look in his eyes that perhaps only she or another battered woman could recognize as dangerous.

Is this a reasonable perception of danger? The psychological research on battered woman syndrome and post traumatic stress disorders says, "yes!" Most women who are repeatedly assaulted recognize danger more quickly and accurately than do others, even though sometimes they block such information from their awareness (Blackman, 1989; Browne, 1987; Ewing, 1987; Pagelow, 1984; Walker,

1984a, 1989a). Thus, small cues and similarity of situation should be expected to constitute a battered woman's reasonable perception of danger.

Reasonableness of the perception does not necessarily mean that it is accurate. In a Wyoming case, a woman thought a flash of silver light was a gun when in reality it turned out to be a cigarette lighter (Walker, 1989a); however, the man had threatened to kill her and said he was going to get his gun, adding to the reasonableness of her perception. The same could also be true for a man with a gun in his hand who is watching television. For example, one woman thought that her part-ner would shoot her at the end of the show he was watching and so before the last commercial was over, she went and got her gun and shot him in the head. The Texas jury hearing this information found her not guilty (Walker, 1989a).

Imminent Danger

The question of imminent danger has caused difficulties in the courts, because imminent is often confused with "immediate" despite the usual statutory definition suggesting "about to occur." Considering the research that demonstrates that one of the psychological effects of violence is that the victim becomes hypervigilant to any cues of impending danger, a battered woman's concept of imminence may be different from that of a man or a woman who has not been threatened by violence. Behavioral principles support this conclusion; classical and operant conditioning theories and learning theories explain the process in detail (Cotton, 1990; Seligman, 1975, 1990).

The various state courts have been trying to understand the ques-tions of imminence of danger for assault victims, beginning with *State of California v. Garcia* (Bochnak, 1981) in the mid-1970s. Inez Garcia was raped by two men in her neighborhood who threatened to come back and do it again. She went home, got a gun, and after several hours had passed, chased down one of the men and shot and killed him. She was acquitted after her second trial, in which the court permitted evidence of self-defense even though there was an intervening time period between the actual danger and her protective actions. The court decided that the threat of further violence was sufficient for her perception of danger to meet the imminence standard (see

Bochnak, 1981; Schneider, 1986; Walker, 1989a, for a more complete discussion).

In battered women cases, however, the woman is usually living with the man and it may be difficult to argue that she is always afraid of him, especially when the research on wife assault suggests that there is a period of loving-kindness and contrition following each episode of violence. This cycle has been subjected to both empirical and clinical research and has been clearly found in over two thirds of the 1,600 battering incidents (not cases as erroneously reported in other reviews, such as Faigman, 1986) studied (Walker, 1984a). The nature of wife assault, however, and its effect on the victim's perceptions, demonstrate clearly that battered women live their life always having an underlying fear of the man's violent potential, even when they learn to adopt various coping mechanisms to protect this information from causing them to be depressed constantly. Stories of battered women who kill in self-defense tell of the variety of ways that these women try to live a normal life and cover up this fear on the outside (Blackman, 1989; Browne, 1987; Ewing, 1987; Walker, 1989a). In my research, almost 85% of the 400 battered women interviewed felt that they could or would be killed at some time by their assailant. Most wished at some time that he would die, although their fantasies were usually of natural causes or accidents (Walker, 1984a).

Assessment

It is important to find ways to measure cognitive judgment, affect, and behavior when analyzing whether a woman has been assaulted, whether she developed battered woman syndrome, and whether her state of mind was affected at the time of the act. For example, Dutton (1992) and Rosewater (1985a, 1985b) have published research data on the several clinical personality patterns that are observable in large samples of battered women. It is not enough to have been assaulted, although sometimes proof of violence has been substituted for further proof of an effect on the defendant's state of mind. A clinician can evaluate a defendant, prepare a report, and testify on her behalf. If the findings of a psychological assessment support the use of battered woman syndrome in a self-defense or duress defense, then it would be important for the woman to obtain trial testimony to that effect. Use of psychological test data to diagnose battered women appropriately has been a recent innovation (Rosewater, 1987a).

Dynamics of Violent Relationships

The Cycle Theory of Violence

My research (Walker, 1979, 1984a) demonstrates that violence does not take place at all times in a relationship, but neither is it as random as those involved perceive it to be. There was a definite pattern seen in two thirds of the 1,600 battering incidents reported by 400 women interviewed (Walker, 1984a). This pattern included three phases of the cycle of violence: Phase 1 was the period of *tension building,* Phase 2 was the *acute battering incident,* and Phase 3 was the period of *loving-contrition,* or absence of tension. In some cases where the violence had reached dangerous proportions all or most of the time, Phase 3 was not readily perceived, and although there was some lessening of the tension, the woman never felt out of danger.

Development of Learned Helplessness

The theory of learned helplessness helps to demonstrate how a seemingly normally functioning woman loses the ability to predict that her actions will affect her safety. Although the originator of the term *learned helplessness* (Seligman, 1975) was looking for a theory to explain the process of exogenous depression in animals and people exposed to unpredictable and uncontrollable aversive stimulation, I believe he really produced a laboratory version of post traumatic stress disorder. Sometimes the participants' behavioral responses made a difference to what happened (i.e., outcomes were controllable), whereas other times they did not, creating the condition of noncontingency between response and outcome that then taught the participants not to trust in their own responses when under threat of danger.

In my research, we administered many of the same assessment instruments to battered women that Seligman administered in pre- and posttests to his research participants. We then attempted to find other factors that influenced the effect of the violence on the participants' life experiences. We found that there were five childhood factors that yielded strong correlations with the learned helplessness scores on the tests and seven factors related to wife assault (Walker, 1984a).

The five childhood learned helplessness factors found were (a) the woman witnessing or experiencing violence in her childhood home; (b) sexual molestation or abuse as a child or adolescent; (c) critical experiences as a child that were perceived as uncontrollable, including early parent loss through death or divorce, frequent moves, alcoholism in one or both parents, sibling problems, poverty; (d) rigid traditional sex-role stereotyped behavior; and (e) chronic or serious illness as a child.

The seven factors that predicted the development of learned helplessness from a violent adult relationship were (a) violence occurring in a pattern of escalation over time and the cycle of violence; (b) sexual assault within the relationship; (c) power and control variables such as the wife assaulter's intrusiveness, overpossessiveness, isolation, and jealousy; (d) threats to kill the woman or others; (e) psychological torture by the assaulter, including waking the woman in the middle of the night or not letting her sleep (by forcing her listen to long harangues), verbal degradation, humiliation, and put-downs, monopolizing her perceptions, isolation, and attempts at mind control, combined with occasional indulgences; (f) other acts of violence that the woman knows about, particularly fights between the wife assaulter and other people, child abuse, destruction of objects, or hurting of pets and other living things; (g) alcohol and/or drug abuse.

These factors are important especially in light of Seligman's (1990) latest work, which demonstrates a link between optimism and reversal of or even inoculation against the development of learned helplessness attitudes.

Termination of the Violent Relationship

Perhaps the most often asked question about battered women, including those who kill in self-defense, is "Why didn't she leave?" Asking this question assumes that leaving will stop the violence. Over a decade of working with battered women and their children, however, has taught us that simply ending the relationship does not stop the violence. The point of separation, and the 2 years following, is the most dangerous period in a violent relationship. Browne and Williams (1989) found that in 35 U.S. states the number of women killed by *former* partners is increasing even as the number of women who kill their partner in self-defense is decreasing. This decrease is mostly accounted for in areas where women are offered the most resources to assist them in leaving their partner.

In the United States, it has been found that many wife assaulters continue their need for power and control over the women by obsessional thoughts, harassment, and stalking. Many homicides against women occur when stalkers become so emotionally enraged that they kill the woman. Often this occurs around visitation and custody issues with children (Liss & Stahly, 1993). Often sexual assault is involved (Finkelhor & Yllö, 1985; Margolin, Moran, & Miller, 1989). In the United States, 21 states have passed antistalking laws directly aimed at making the external consequences serious enough to deter these men. Battered women who kill in self-defense often describe the continued harassment they experienced by the assaulter's stalking behavior (Walker, 1989a).

Battered Woman Syndrome

Battered woman syndrome is considered a subcategory of the post traumatic stress disorder diagnosis (PTSD) in the revised third edition of the *Diagnostic and Statistical Manual of Mental Disorders* (DSM-III-R) (American Psychiatric Association, 1987). The syndrome is a collection of thoughts, feelings, and actions that logically follow a frightening experience that one expects could be repeated. This fight or flight response is one that has long been documented in the literature, but only recently used to describe the psychological effect of trauma (Figley, 1985; Ochberg, 1988; van der Kolk, 1987). There are three major symptom clusters that are measured to determine whether or not a person who has been exposed to trauma has developed a PTSD: cognitive disturbances, high arousal symptoms, and high avoidance symptoms.

Cognitive disturbances seem to be clustered around disturbances in memory, including (a) repetitive intrusive memories, with or without exposure to stimuli that serve as reminders; and (b) loss of memory, accompanied by denial, minimization, and repression of violent incidents. Van der Kolk (1988) suggests that there are neurochemical changes in brain pathways that facilitate these memory distortions.

Cognitive confusion, attention deficits, and lack of concentration are also reported by trauma victims, especially battered women. Battered women who have experienced multiple forms of abuse, particularly from other partners and in their childhood home, are especially likely to confuse their experiences. When placed in another frightening situation, these women often have flashbacks that cause them to reexperience fragments of previous abusive incidents, increasing their perception of danger. A carefully detailed abuse history will often help sort out which symptoms come from which experience, although sometimes it is impossible to separate them.

High arousal symptoms, or high anxiety, is the second major area of symptoms experienced by trauma victims. Here, the woman is prepared to fight and her preparedness is augmented by physical and neurochemical changes. She becomes hypervigilant to cues of potential danger; recognizes the little things that signal an impending incident; and often appears nervous, jumpy, and highly anxious. Sometimes panic attacks and phobic responses are also evidenced (Fodor, 1992). Eating and sleep disorders may accompany this set of symptoms (Root, 1991). Physiological reactivity is also present, often with impulsive decision making and little insight into long-term consequences. Obsessive rumination and intrusive thinking, along with compulsive repetitive behavior, may also be observed in some women, particularly those who believe that they are the only ones who can calm down the man. If the woman has also been sexually assaulted, some type of sexual dysfunction may also be described (Finkelhor & Yllö, 1985; Margolin et al., 1989).

Avoidance symptoms, including depression, are the third major constellation in this syndrome. Denial, minimization, and repression are the major techniques used to avoid having to deal with the dangerousness of the situation. Battered women become more isolated over time, especially as the wife assaulter exerts his power and control over her. They lose interest in activities they used to enjoy, are less likely to go to places they want to go to but which the wife assaulter disapproves of, become less involved with family and friends, and often hide the fact that they are being hurt. Victimization has been found to be a leading cause of depression in women (McGrath, Keita, Strickland, & Russo, 1990). Sometimes they keep themselves so busy that they do not have time to think about what is happening to them.

Often, they suppress their feelings so that they do not get too excited or too disappointed about things that used to have meaning to them.

Although battered women may appear to outsiders to be fiercely loyal to their partner, in fact they may maintain this stance in order to keep the man as calm as possible. When separated from the man, and if they perceive some safety, they are more likely to admit to their feelings of fear and distress. Interviewing techniques that avoid victim blaming and accusations about what motivates victims' behavior will often elicit expression of those underlying feelings that have been shut off (Walker, in press). Eventually, mild to moderate depression sets in and the women may even be misdiagnosed as having a bipolar affective disorder, especially when the alternating arousal and avoidance symptoms are observed. Certainly, diagnoses other than PTSD should be reserved for at least 6 months after the initial diagnosis has been confirmed.

Diagnosis and Legal Issues

Diagnosis

Appropriate diagnosis of battered women and others who have experienced trauma that causes PTSD has been difficult. Most mental health professionals minimize women's reports of family violence (Hansen, Harway, & Cervantes, 1991) and even those charged with creating diagnostic categories have permitted gender bias to get in the way of their research. The controversy over the American Psychiatric Association's attempts to add a category for Masochistic Personality Disorder to its official nosology system, the DSM-III-R (American Psychiatric Association, 1987) in the mid-1980s is an example of such gender bias (cf. Caplan, 1985, 1991; Pantony & Caplan, 1991; Rosewater, 1987b; Walker, 1987). Such controversies have stimulated feminist psychologists to conduct research that has contributed to a better understanding of the effect of violence on women. Brown and Root (1990) examine the effect of diversity on mental health issues, Dutton-Douglas and Walker (1988) and Brown and Ballou (1992) look at the effect of feminist theory on all therapy systems, Leidig (1981) presents a theoretical continuum for all violence against women to be considered, and Koss (1990) describes the women's mental health research agenda. Personality disorders, often confused with post traumatic stress reactions, have been more closely examined by accounting for victimization responses (Brown, 1992; Herman, 1992; Howard, 1984; Janoff-Bulman, 1979; Janoff-Bulman & Lang-Gun, 1988; Root, 1992). Post traumatic stress disorders have been studied in battered women (Walker, 1991, 1992), children who witness domestic violence (Jaffe, Wolfe, & Wilson, 1990), sexually assaulted children (Walker, 1990), victims of violence (Herman, 1992), rape victims (Koss & Harvey, 1991), battered women who are accused of crimes (Walker, 1992), crime victims in general (Kilpatrick et al., 1989), and children who kill in self-defense (Mones, 1991). Mas, Alexander, and Turner (1991) found differences in those who were traumatized and those who exhibited delinquent behavior. Most PTSDs do not satisfy insanity standards, although some certainly do, as in the case of war veterans (Figley, 1985).

Most battered women easily meet the DSM-III-R PTSD criteria, usually with more symptoms than necessary for the diagnosis. Some people have objected to using the battered woman syndrome diagnostic category, for fear that women who are responding naturally to potential or actual violence will be misclassified as being mentally ill (Blackman, 1986; Maguigan, 1991; Mahoney, 1991; McConnell, 1991; Schneider, 1986). Many battered women themselves fear that the assailant's taunts that no one will believe them because they are crazy will come true. Thus, the caution about misdiagnosis and overclinicalizing the victims of wife assault is one that should be paid serious attention.

Root (1992) has suggested that assessment for all PTSD subcategories should consider the additional stressors caused by indirect trauma such as cultural oppression, racism, religious discrimination, gender bias, and other insidious forms of daily harassments. She suggests that the effect of battered woman syndrome or any of the other subcategories (e.g., rape trauma syndrome, battered child syndrome, child sexual abuse accommodation syndrome, post sexual abuse syndrome) can depend upon the other stressors to which the individual is exposed. It is important to note that in my own work with battered women who kill in self-defense, those who were African American and killed African American partners still were twice as likely to be convicted of murder and were sentenced to longer periods in prison than those who were Caucasian or from other minority groups. Green (1990) presents a cogent argument for how this injustice can happen to African-American women, as does Ho (1990) for Asian-American women. Women who were poor and less educated appeared to be subject to a similar bias in the courts.

Effect on State of Mind

Forensic diagnosis includes not only clinical diagnosis of the woman's current state, but also her state of mind at the time of the incident. This diagnosis involves collecting many samples of the woman's cognition, affect, and behavior over the years; comparing them with her current state; and then making comparisons with the information about the act for which she is before the court. Information including police statements about the crime scene; physical evidence of the crime; witness statements; any statement the woman may have made at the time of the incident; and any previous records of witnesses, doctors, police, or others who might corroborate the woman's stories of violence can be most helpful. In the end, however, the diagnosis is based on the expert's professional opinions of the woman's mental state and on knowledge about battered women, *not* on the descriptions of whatever it is the woman is said to have done.

Presentation in Courts of Law

The rules of evidence that govern what information can be presented at a trial usually do not permit the regular witnesses to testify to anything other than facts about which they have direct knowledge. Those who created these rules of evidence believed these limitations would make testimony more reliable and valid. This result has not occurred, however, in the case of explaining women's behavior, which is frequently motivated by a combination of facts and the context in which they occur. Opinions about why these factual experiences occurred or testimony about even the context during which they happened is rarely permitted, even though excluding this information skews the evidence the judge or jury does get to hear (Blackman, 1986; Bochnak, 1981). A mental health expert can, however, testify to her or his opinion and can add context to the explanations, provided it is part of the expert opinion. Expert witness testimony to explain the battered woman's state of mind at the time of an incident, then, may be the only time the judge or jury hears much relevant evidence.

Presentation of the dynamics of wife assault, including power and control, the cycle of violence, and evidence that leaving her assaulter may make his killing her more likely, is critical to the jury's judging the defendant's actions. Information about psychological effects—battered woman syndrome and PTSD—may be the only way a jury gets to hear about the entire context of the act. Battered women often cannot tell their story as effective witnesses; a lifetime of violence may have caused them to be fearful of talking in a courtroom, memory difficulties may make it impossible for them to recite the facts required of nonexpert witnesses, and confusion about what happened may cause them to sound less credible. Thus, an expert witness who can describe both the general situation of battered women and the specifics of this particular woman's situation, including her state of mind from the effects of violence, may be the only way justice can in fact be accomplished.

There are few trained mental health professionals competent to give expert witness testimony in these cases. The expert must be thoroughly familiar with the literature on battered women, wife assaulters, and children who live with domestic violence. A clear understanding about how wife assault affects the woman's state of mind is also necessary. Battered women understand that wife assaulters are willing and able to carry out even the most outrageous threat. Presentation of psychological effects of violence, such as those found in battered woman syndrome, is also important. Having been assaulted is not a sufficient defense to the criminal charges described in this article; it is the effect of violence on the woman's state of mind that is relevant to the legal issues discussed here.

Summary and Conclusions

In summary, battered women, whom we typically think of as victims, often find themselves as defendants in criminal proceedings for committing acts that they say were done in order to protect themselves and their loved ones from further violence or even death. The introduction of psychological information about both the dynamics of wife assault and its psychological effect on a battered woman's state of mind is critical to her actions being fairly judged in a court of law. Many of these dynamics defy our logic, such as why a battered woman might perceive a man's behavior as dangerous when others who have not experienced violence may not understand it in the same way. It is often believed that terminating a relationship is the best way to stop the violence; yet the research described here suggests that leaving might actually place the woman in greater danger of further harm or death. Saying "no" to the wife assaulter, who expects his woman to do exactly what he tells her to do, may indeed be more dangerous than committing a felony for which there may be serious consequences. All of these factors must be understood by those trying to comprehend and judge the battered woman defendant's actions.

Most U.S. states now permit the expert testimony of psychologists and others who can explain both the dynamics of wife assault and the battered woman syndrome. In 1992, Congresswoman Connie Morella from Maryland introduced federal legislation that would encourage all states to change their laws to mandate such testimony when a woman claims she has been assaulted. If this legislation passes, it will also provide funding to develop resources to assist mental health professionals and attorneys to provide such expert witness testimony. This legislation is appropriately titled *The Fair Justice Acts*.

References

American Psychiatric Association. (1987). *Diagnostic and Statistical Manual of Mental Disorders* (3rd ed., rev. DSM-III-R). Washington, DC: Author.

Bauschard, L. (1986). *Voices set free: Battered women speak from prison.* St. Louis, MO: Women's Self Help Center.

Blackman, J. (1986). Potential uses for expert testimony: Ideas toward the representation of battered women who kill. *Women's Rights Law Reporter, 9,* 227-238.

Blackman, J. (1989). *Intimate violence.* New York: Columbia University Press.

Bochnak, E. (Ed.). (1981). *Women's self defense cases: Theory and practice.* Charlottesville, VA: Michie.

Brown, L. (1992). A feminist critique of personality disorders. In L. Brown & M. Ballow (Eds.), *Personality and psychopathology* (pp. 206-228). New York: Guilford.

Brown, L., & Ballou, M. (Eds.). (1992). *Personality and psychopathology. New York: Guilford.*

Brown, L., & Root, M.P.P. (Eds.). (1990). *Diversity and complexity in feminist therapy.* New York: Haworth.

Browne, A. (1987). *When battered women kill.* New York: Free Press.

Browne, A., Thyfault, R., & Walker, L.E.A. (1987). When battered women kill: Evaluation and expert witness techniques. In D. J. Sonkin (Ed.), *Domestic violence on trial* (pp. 71-85). New York: Springer.

Browne, A., & Williams, K. (1989). Resource availability for women at risk and partner homicide. *Law and Society Review, 23,* 75.

Bunch, C. (1991). Recognizing women's rights as human rights. *Response, 13,* 13-16.

Caplan, P. (1985). *The myth of women's masochism.* New York: Dutton.

Caplan, P. (1991). How DO they decide what is normal? The bizarre, but true, tale of the DSM process. *Canadian Psychologist, 32,* 162-170.

Cotton, D.G.H. (1990). *Stress management: An integrated approach to therapy.* New York: Brunner/Mazel.

Dutton, M. A. (1992). *Empowering the battered woman.* New York: Springer.

Dutton, M. A., & Walker, L.E.A. (Eds.). (1988). *Feminist psychotherapies: An integration of therapeutic and feminist systems.* Norwood, NJ: Ablex.

Edwards, S.S.M. (1989). *Policing domestic violence: Women, the law and the state.* London: Sage.

Ewing, C. P. (1987). *Battered women who kill.* New York: Lexington.

Ewing, C. P., & Aubrey, M. (1987). Battered women and public opinion: Some realities about the myths. *Journal of Family Violence, 2,* 257-264.

Faigman, D. (1986). The battered woman syndrome and self-defense: A legal and empirical dissent. *Virginia Law Review, 72,* 619-647.

Faust, D., & Ziskin, J. (1988). The expert witness in psychology and psychiatry. *Science, 241,* 31-35.

Figley, C. (1985). *Trauma and its wake.* New York: Brunner/Mazel.

Finkelhor, D., & Yllö, K. (1985). *License to rape: Sexual abuse of wives.* New York: Holt, Rinehart & Winston.

Fodor, I. G. (1992). The agoraphobic syndrome: From anxiety neurosis to panic disorder. In L. S. Brown & M. Ballou (Eds.), *Personality and Psychopathology: Feminist reappraisals* (pp. 177-205). New York: Guilford.

Fowler, R. D., & Matarazzo, J.D. (1988). Psychologists and psychiatrists as expert witnesses: Comment. *Science, 241,* 1143-1144.

Goolkasian, G. A. (1986). *Confronting domestic violence: A guide for criminal justice agencies.* Washington, DC: U.S. Department of Justice.

Green, B. (1990). What has gone before: The legacy of racism and sexism in the lives of Black mothers and daughters. In L. S. Brown & M.P.P. Root (Eds.), *Diversity and complexity in feminist therapy* (pp. 207-230). New York: Haworth.

Hansen, M., Harway, M., & Cervantes, N. (1991). Therapists' perceptions of severity in cases of family violence. *Violence and Victims, 6,* 225-235.

Herman, J. L. (1992). *Trauma and recovery.* New York: Basic Books.

Herman, J. L., & Schatzow, E. (1987). Recovery and verification of memories of childhood sexual trauma. *Psychoanalytic Psychology, 4,* 1-4.

Ho, C. K. (1990). An analysis of domestic violence in Asian American communities: A multicultural approach to counseling. In L. S. Brown & M.P.P. Roots (Eds.), *Diversity and complexity in feminist therapy* (pp. 129-150). New York: Haworth.

Howard, J. (1984). Societal influences on attribution: Blaming some victims more than others. *Journal of Personality and Social Psychology, 47,* 494-505.

Jaffe, P. G., Wolfe, D. A., & Wilson, S. K. (1990). *Children of battered women.* Newbury Park, CA: Sage.

Janoff-Bulman, R. (1979). Characterological versus behavioral self-blame: Inquiries into depression and rape. *Journal of Personality and Social Psychology, 37,* 1798-1809.

Janoff-Bulman, R., & Lang-Gun, L. (1988). Coping with disease, crime, and accidents: The role of self-blame attributions. In L. Y. Abramson (Ed.), *Social cognition and clinical psychology* (pp. 116-147). New York: Guilford.

Jones, A. (1981). *Women who kill.* New York: Holt Rinehart.

Kilpatrick, D. G., Saunders, B. E., Amick-Mullen, A., Best, C. L., Veronen, L. J., & Resick, H. S. (1989). Victim and crime factors associated with the development of crime-related post-traumatic stress disorders. *Behavior Therapy, 20,* 199-214.

Koss, M. P. (1990). The women's mental health research agenda: Violence against women. *American Psychologist, 45,* 374-380.

Koss, M. P., & Harvey, M. R. (1991). *The rape victim: Clinical and community interventions* (2nd ed.). Newbury Park, CA: Sage.

Krystal, J. H., Kosten, T. R., Southwick, S., Mason, J. W., Perry, B. D., & Giller, E. L. (1989). Neurobiological aspects of Post Traumatic Stress Disorder: Review of clinical and preclinical studies. *Behavior Therapy, 20,* 177-198.

Leidig, M. W. (1981). Violence against women: A feminist-psychological analysis. In S. Cox (Ed.), *Female psychology: The emerging self* (2nd ed., pp. 190-205). New York: St. Martins.

Liss, M., & Stahly, G. (1993). Domestic violence and child custody. In M. Hansen & M. Harway (Eds.), *Recovering from battering: Family therapy and feminism.* Newbury Park, CA: Sage.

MacKinnon, C. A. (1983). Feminism, marxism, method and the state: Towards feminist jurisprudence. *Signs: Journal of Women in Culture and Society, 8,* 635-658.

Maguigan, H. (1991). Battered women and self-defense: Myths and misconceptions in current reform proposals. *University of Pennsylvania Law Review, 140,* 379-486.

Mahoney, M. R. (1991). Legal images of battered women: Redefining the issue of separation. *Michigan Law Review, 90,* 1-94.

Margolin, G., Moran, P., & Miller, M. (1989). Social approval for violations of sexual consent in marriage and dating. *Violence and Victims, 4,* 45-55.

Mas, C. H., Alexander, J. F., & Turner, C. W. (1991). Dispositional attributions and defensive behavior in high and low conflict delinquent families. *Journal of Family Psychology, 5,* 176-191.

McConnell, J. E. (1991, May). *Beyond metaphor: Battered women, involuntary servitude and the Thirteenth Amendment.* Paper presented in International Victimology Conference, Institute for Sociology and the Law, Onati, Spain.

McGrath, E., Keita, G. P., Strickland, B., & Russo, N. F. (Eds.). (1990). *Women and depression: Risk factors and treatment issues. Final report of the APA National Task Force on Women and Depression.* Washington, DC: APA.

Monahan, J. (Ed.). (1980). *Who is the client?* Washington, DC: American Psychological Association.

Monahan, J., & Walker, L.E.A. (1986). Social authority: Obtaining evaluating, and establishing social science in law. *University of Pennsylvania Law Review, 134,* 477-517.

Mones, P. (1991). *When a child kills: Abused children who kill their parents.* New York: Simon & Schuster Pocket Books.

Ochberg, F. (Ed.). (1988). *Post-traumatic therapy.* New York: Brunner/Mazel.

Pagelow, M. D. (1984). *Family violence.* New York: Praeger.

Pantony, K., & Caplan, P. (1991). Delusional dominating personality disorder: A modest proposal for identifying some consequences of rigid masculine socialization. *Canadian Psychologist, 32,* 120-133.

Price, R. L. (1985). Battered woman syndrome: A defense beginning to emerge. *New York Law Journal, 194,* 104.

Root, M. P. (1991). Persistent disordered eating as a gender specific form of Post Traumatic Stress Response to sexual assault. *Psychotherapy: Theory, Research and Practice, 28,* 96-102.

Root, M. P. (1992). Reconstructing the impact of trauma on personality. In L. Brown & M. Dallou (Eds.), *Personality and psychopathology: Feminist reappraisals.* New York: Guilford.

Rosewater, L. B. (1985a). Feminist interpretations of traditional testing. In L. B. Rosewater & L.E.A. Walker (Eds.), *Handbook on feminist therapy: Psychotherapy for women* (pp. 266-273). New York: Springer.

Rosewater, L. B. (1985b). Schizophrenic, borderline or battered? In L. B. Rosewater & L.E.A. Walker (Eds.), *Handbook on feminist therapy: Psychotherapy for women* (pp. 215-225). New York: Springer.

Rosewater, L. B. (1987a). The clinical and courtroom application of battered women's personality assessments. In D. J. Sonkin (Ed.), *Domestic violence on trial* (pp. 86-94). New York: Springer.

Rosewater, L. B. (1987b). A critical analysis of the proposed self-defeating personality disorder. *Journal of Personality Disorders, 1,* 190-195.

Ryan, W. (1971). *Blaming the victim.* New York: Pantheon.

Saunders, D. (1986). When battered women use violence: Husband abuse or self-defense? *Violence and Victims, 1,* 47-60.

Schafran, L. H. (1990). Overwhelming evidence: Reports on gender bias in the courts. *Trial, 26,* 28-35.

Schneider, E. M. (1986). Describing and changing: Women's self-defense work and the problem of expert testimony on battering. *Women's Rights Law Reporter, 9,* 195-222.

Seligman, M.E.P. (1975). *Helplessness: On depression, development and death.* New York: W. H. Freeman.

Seligman, M.E.P. (1990). *Learned optimism: The skill to conquer life's obstacles, large and small.* New York: Random House.

Sonkin, D. (Ed.). (1970). *Domestic violence on trial.* New York: Springer.

Spiegel, D. (1990). Hypnosis, dissociation and trauma. In J. L. Singer (Ed.), *Repression and dissociation: Implications for personality theory, psychopathology, and health.* Chicago: University of Chicago Press.

U.S. Attorney General's Task Force on Family Violence (1984). *Final report.* Washington, DC: U.S. Department of Justice.

van der Kolk, B. (1987). The psychological consequences of overwhelming life experiences. In B. van der Kolk (Ed.), *Psychological trauma* (pp. 1-30). Washington, DC: American Psychiatric Press.

van der Kolk, B. (1988). The trauma spectrum: The interaction of biological and social events in the genesis of the trauma response. *Journal of Traumatic Stress, 1,* 273-290.

Walker, L.E.A. (1979). *The battered woman.* New York: Harper & Row.

Walker, L.E.A. (1984a). *The battered woman syndrome.* New York: Springer.

Walker, L.E.A. (1984b). Battered women, psychology and public policy. *American Psychologist, 29,* 1179-1182.

Walker, L.E.A. (1987). Inadequacies of the masochistic personality disorder diagnosis for women. *Journal of Personality Disorders, 1,* 183-189.

Walker, L.E.A. (1989a). *Terrifying love: Why battered women kill and how society responds.* New York: Harper & Row.

Walker, L.E.A. (1989b). Psychology and violence against women. *American Psychologist, 44,* 695-702.

Walker, L.E.A. (1989c). When the battered woman becomes the defendant. In E. Viano (Ed.), *Crime and its victims: International research and public policy* (pp. 57-70). New York: Hemisphere.

Walker, L.E.A. (1990). Psychological assessment of sexually abused children for legal evaluation and expert witness testimony. *Professional Psychology: Research and Practice, 21,* 344-353.

Walker, L.E.A. (1991). Post-Traumatic Stress Disorder in women: Diagnosis and treatment of battered woman syndrome. *Psychotherapy, 28,* 21-29.

Walker, L.E.A. (1992). Battered woman syndrome and self-defense. *Notre Dame Journal of Law, Ethics, & Public Policy, 6,* 321-334.

Walker, L.E.A. (in press). *The abused woman and survivor therapy: Assessment and treatment.* Washington, DC: American Psychological Association.

10

Self-Defense Jury Instructions in Trials of Battered Women Who Kill Their Partner

ALAN J. TOMKINS

MARY K. KENNING

JESSICA P. GREENWALD

GREGORY R. JOHNSON

When a family is terrorized by a stranger who intrudes into its residence, there seems to be an intuitive understanding that it is sensible to confront the assailant and that someone who kills the intruder in protection of the family deserves legal exculpation. One does not need to have a degree in law to understand that we would like the protector to be absolved of legal blameworthiness for the homicide on the grounds that the action was *justified* or that the protector is legally *excused* for the action taken.

University of Nebraska-Lincoln (Tomkins and Johnson); Psychological Services, Hennepin County Court, Minneapolis, MN (Kenning); Victims of Violence Program, Cambridge Hospital, MA (Greenwald).

By *justification,* the law typically means that although one's actions are ordinarily deemed to be wrongful criminal conduct, the particular circumstances surrounding the specific act are such that it is "socially acceptable," warranting "neither criminal liability nor even censure" (Note, 1975, p. 916). Some would even argue that the act was socially desirable, under the circumstances, because it prevented an even greater harm from occurring (see, e.g., Morse, 1990). In contrast to justification, the doctrine of *excuse* focuses on the actor, not the act. Excuse addresses the issue of whether the actor lacks legal culpability because s/he "is not morally to blame for committing an unjustified act" (Dressler, 1987b, p. 177). An actor is not legally blameworthy when s/he "is not fully responsible for his or her conduct" (Morse, 1990, p. 602). An excused act is one that was not socially desirable, but is morally understandable.

Thus, it is easy to imagine that there would be little dispute over whether it was legally *justifiable* for a mother to kill the intruder if she did so because she reasonably believed that she was going to be raped in front of her children (e.g., the intruder specifically commands, as her children stand trembling nearby, "Undress, I am going to rape you"). The homicide of the intruder is the less undesirable outcome, and the justification defense of self-defense (or perhaps the defense of others; see Dressler, 1987b, pp. 190-217; LaFave & Scott, 1986, pp. 454-465; P. H. Robinson, 1984, chap. 4) would be applicable. Justification defenses are true defenses, which means that if proved by the defendant (and the proof standard is ordinarily "preponderance of the evidence"), then the defendant is acquitted as a matter of law even though the prosecutor may have proved all the elements of the crime beyond a reasonable doubt (Dressler, 1987b, pp. 175-176).

At a minimum, even if we change the hypothetical scenario to eliminate the risk of rape (e.g., assume the intruder simply stated "I will not hurt you, I just want to take your valuable Picasso painting"), but the mother nonetheless perceived a risk because she had been sexually assaulted in similar circumstances in the past, then we might still subscribe to the proposition that she is not morally blameworthy for her actions and should be *excused* for the homicide. As a general matter, excuse defenses, like justification defenses, are true defenses and if successfully proved by the defendant, serve to acquit the accused of the charged crime (although they may not relieve defendants of all criminal liability; see, e.g., Dressler, 1987b, p. 175). Excuse defenses focus on whether the defendant is fully responsible for his or her behavior, and include examinations of whether the defendant's actions are compelled rather than voluntary (see, e.g., Morse, 1990). (For more information on the excuse doctrine, see generally Dressler, 1987b, pp. 175-190; P. H. Robinson, 1984, chapter 5. See also Dressler, 1987a; Fletcher, 1979; Greenwalt, 1984, 1986; Moore, 1984, 1985; Morse, 1984, 1986, 1990; Schopp, 1991.)

In contrast to the family intruder scenario, there is much less consensus concerning the proper legal response to take and which legal theory to use in the case of a battered woman who kills her partner (e.g., compare Ewing, 1990, with Morse, 1990; Rosen, 1986). Although most commentators acknowledge that wife assault is a major problem in our society, there are disputes over whether battered women are treated appropriately and fairly by the legal system (cf. Walker, this volume). A principal concern is the belief that battered women who kill their tormentor are less likely to have their behavior legally exculpated than would a person terrorized by a stranger who responds to the encroachment by killing the intruder. The view that women are disadvantaged by existing legal rules and doctrines has led some advocates to suggest changing the law to correspond better to the realities of the battered woman's psychosocial predicament and her response (Browne, 1987; Crocker, 1985; Ewing, 1987, 1990; Gillespie, 1989; Kinports, 1988; Schneider, 1980).

In this chapter, we will address issues relevant to the plight of the battered woman who becomes a criminal defendant because she has killed her partner. The perspective adopted in this chapter is the perspective of those who are concerned about the fact that there appear to be numerous battered women who are convicted for such killings. Although we are concerned about unnecessarily reforming the law in a lame attempt to address underlying unfairness (Maguigan, 1991; Morse, 1990), we are also concerned about the symbolic values inherent in legal doctrines and practices in battered woman exculpatory doctrines and practices (e.g., Ewing, 1990). As an overall aspiration, we hope this review stimulates further, and even more effective, efforts to aid battered women who are subject to criminal prosecution for their actions.

We begin with a brief discussion of the debate concerning whether a battered woman should be legally culpable for killing her partner.

Although resolving this debate is beyond our scope in this chapter, this debate has led some to suggest that one way for the law to address the psychosocial complexities and realities of women killing their assailant is to reform the traditional self-defense rules that are available to counter prosecutions for murder. In this chapter, we discuss an especially interesting and controversial reform proposed by Professor Charles Ewing (1987, 1990), which he terms "psychological self-defense." After we describe psychological self-defense, we review the sparse empirical literature that would shed light on whether there would be any practical effect if the self-defense doctrine was changed to embrace a psychological self-defense. Finally, we suggest future directions for self-defense research.

Legal Perspectives Relevant to Battered Women Who Kill Their Partner

Straus (1991), among others (e.g., Dutton & McGregor, 1992; Elliott, 1989; Martin, 1978), notes that differences in defining what constitutes "battering" engender a plethora of practical problems for documenting and researching the phenomenon. A myriad of differences, in definitions, in perceptions of the severity of the problem, in assessments of the propriety of "taking the law into your own hands," in the appraisal of the value and accuracy of social science being used to change basic criminal law, and so on, seems to have resulted in reasonable (and sometimes similarly minded) people vehemently arguing over whether the law should exculpate women who kill their partner. Some commentators are sympathetic to the social and political plight of battered women, but believe that some of the recent legal attempts to address the problem have been misguided (Faigman, 1987; Kinports, 1988; Maguigan, 1991; Morse, 1990; Note, 1986; Rosen, 1986; see also Jenkins & Davidson, 1990).

Limitations to Traditional Self-Defense

As noted earlier, legal exculpatory doctrines relevant to a battered woman who kills her partner are those of justification and excuse (Dressler, 1987a; LaFave & Scott, 1986; P. H. Robinson, 1984). The distinction between justification and excuse, although once an important distinction in the law, has "blurred over time" (Dressler, 1987b, p. 179). As Dressler notes:

> Today, justified and excused actors are treated the same by the criminal courts: each is acquitted of the offense and neither is punished for her conduct. As a result, many courts, legislatures, and commentators have become inattentive to the inherent differences between the two classes of defenses, even to the point of using the terms "justification" and "excuse" interchangeably. (Dressler, 1987b, p. 179, footnote omitted)

Nonetheless, the distinction can be important not only legally (Dressler, 1987a; Morse, 1990; Rosen, 1986), but also politically and socially. Given the historical sociopolitical context in which wife assault was tolerated in the past (e.g., Gordon, 1988; Pleck, 1987), which continues to exist today (e.g., Dutton, 1988; Frieze & Browne, 1989; Gelles & Straus, 1988; Margolin, Sibner, & Gleberman, 1988; Straus, 1979; Straus, Gelles, & Steinmetz, 1980; cf. Hilton, this volume), the law should allow the defendant to focus on her reactions to the violence (justification) rather than require her to focus on herself as a victim or survivor of abuse (excuse). Thus, the understandable focus of exculpation for battered women has been on justification principles as asserted through self-defense claims (e.g., Ewing, 1987; Gillespie, 1989; Kinports, 1988; Rosen, 1986) rather than resorting to sociopolitically repugnant excuse principles embodied in temporary insanity arguments (e.g., Comment, 1987).

The problem has been that the traditional legal doctrine of self-defense is a weak ally for battered woman defendants (e.g., Browne, 1987; Ewing, 1987; Gillespie, 1989; Kinports, 1988; Schneider, 1980; Walker, this volume). Self-defense law requires that a person who kills to protect herself must have acted on a reasonable belief that her actions were necessary to prevent imminent harm (Dressler, 1987b, p. 191; LaFave & Scott, 1986, p. 454).[1] The weakness of traditional self-defense doctrine as applied in many battered women cases, argues Ewing, is that "Battered women who kill their batterers do not do so in response to what reasonably appears to be a threat of imminent death or serious bodily injury" (Ewing, 1990, pp. 585-586; see also LaFave & Scott, 1986, pp. 458-459). Consequently, their claim of self-defense either is not being allowed by the courts or is deemed inapplicable by juries.

We will take a detailed look at the North Carolina case of *State v. Norman* (1988, 1989). An examination of this case is helpful because it epitomizes the problems that several commentators (e.g., Browne, 1987; Ewing, 1987, 1990; Gillespie, 1989) claim exist for battered women defendants who ought to have the protection of a self-defense claim that will provide the possibility of an acquittal. The homicide in *Norman* clearly reflected an intentional killing. The killing was the culmination of a relationship that had been characterized by 20 years of physical, mental, and sexual assault of Judy Norman by her husband, J. T. Norman, during their marriage of nearly 25 years. The following provides a brief summary of the ordeals endured by the defendant, Judy Norman, as recounted in the state supreme court opinion (*State v. Norman*, 1989, pp. 9-11) and in the earlier opinion in the case issued by the state court of appeals (*State v. Norman*, 1988, pp. 587-589).

The defendant had been victimized by Mr. Norman since his abuse of alcohol began approximately 5 years after they were wed. His violence was extensive; it included slapping, punching, kicking, and striking Mrs. Norman with various objects (e.g., glasses, beer bottles, ashtrays, and other objects). Mr. Norman extinguished cigarettes on Mrs. Norman's neck, splashed her with hot coffee, smashed glass in her face, and crushed food on her face. He frequently made his wife bark like a dog, with the penalty for not barking being more beatings. She was constantly verbally demeaned by him; he often called her a bitch, a dog, and a whore. She was even made to eat dog or cat food out of the dog's or cat's bowl and to sleep on the concrete floor. At times, Mr. Norman would prohibit Mrs. Norman from shopping for food for the family (including five children, four of whom were still residing with the couple at the time of his killing) or from eating food herself. She carried several scars on her face caused by her husband's violence.

Mrs. Norman was forced to work as a prostitute to support herself and her husband (who did not usually work). If she resisted prostituting herself, or if Mr. Norman was not pleased with the amount of money she made (she was supposed to reach a minimum quota of $100/day), he would assault her. Finally, he made frequent threats to kill his wife. He not only made these threats directly to her, but also would tell others of his plans. The appellate court noted that

Mr. Norman "also threatened to cut her heart out" (*State v. Norman,* 1988, p. 587).

Because the particulars are so arresting, we rely on the language of the two North Carolina appellate courts (*State v. Norman,* 1988, pp. 587-589; 1989, pp. 9-11) to detail the last days of the couple:

[In the early morning hours of] 10 June 1985, [J. T.] Norman forced [Judy Norman] to go to a truck stop . . . in order to prostitute [herself. Mrs. Norman]'s daughter and [Mrs. Norman]'s daughter's boyfriend accompanied [her there]. Later that day, [J. T. returned] to the truck stop, apparently drunk, and began hitting defendant in the face with his fist and slamming the car door into her. He also threw hot coffee on [Mrs. Norman.] While driving home, he was stopped by a patrolman and jailed on a charge of driving while impaired.

[Mr. Norman] seemed angrier than ever after he was released from jail [the next morning, June 11]. His abuse of defendant was more frequent. That evening, sheriff's deputies were called to the Norman residence. . . . The officer responding to the call testified that [Mrs. Norman] was bruised and crying and that she stated she could not take it any longer. [Mrs. Norman] was advised to file a complaint, but she said she was afraid her husband would kill her if she had him arrested.

[The deputy left but returned] less than an hour later after [Mrs. Norman] had taken a bottle of pills. [When the deputy sheriff arrived back at the scene, he found Mr. Norman] was interfering with emergency personnel who were trying to treat [Judy. J. T.] was drunk and was making statements such as, "If you want to die, you deserve to die. I'll give you more pills," and "Let the bitch die. . . . She ain't nothing but a dog. She don't deserve to live." [In front of both the officer and the paramedics, J. T.] also threatened to kill [his wife. The] sheriff's deputy finally chased him back into the house as [Mrs. Norman] was put into an ambulance [and transported to the hospital where her stomach was pumped].

While in the hospital, [Mrs. Norman discussed her situation with the on-call therapist. Mrs. Norman told the therapist that] she was angry and depressed and that she felt her situation was hopeless. [She threatened several times during her conversation to kill her husband] "because of the things he had done to her."

The next day, 12 June 1985, the day of [J. T.] Norman's death, [J. T.] was angrier and more violent with [Judy] than usual. [During the course of the day, Mrs. Norman went to the local mental health center, where she discussed the possibility of filing charges against her husband and having him committed for treatment, and to the social services office, where she was inquiring about obtaining welfare benefits. At the social services office, her husband] interrupted her interview and made her go home with him. [At some point during the day, Mrs. Norman drove her husband and his best friend to a nearby town. During the drive, J. T.] slapped [Judy] for following a truck too closely and poured a beer on her head. [J. T.] kicked [his wife] in the side of the head while she was driving and told her he would "cut her breast off and shove it up her rear end."

[During the course of the day, Judy's mother was informed by one of Judy's daughters about the frightful abuse Judy was experiencing. Judy]'s mother called the sheriff's department, but no help arrived at that time. Witnesses stated that back at the Norman residence, [J. T.] threatened to cut [Judy]'s throat, threatened to kill her, and threatened to cut off her breast. [J. T.] also smashed a doughnut on [Judy]'s face and put out a cigarette on her chest [which caused] a small burn on her upper torso. He would not let her eat or bring food into the house for their children.

[By the late afternoon or evening, Mrs. Norman] and her husband went into their bedroom to lie down, and he called her a "dog" and made her lie on the floor when he lay down on the bed. Their daughter brought in her baby to leave with [Judy, and J. T.] agreed to let her baby-sit. After [J. T.] fell asleep, the baby started crying and [Judy] took it to her mother's house so it would not wake up her husband.

[Mrs. Norman] took a pistol from her mother's purse and walked the short distance back to her home. She pointed the pistol at the back of her sleeping husband's head, but it jammed the first time she tried to shoot him. She fixed the gun and then shot her husband in the back of the head as he lay sleeping. After one shot, she felt her husband's chest and determined that he was still breathing and making sounds. She then shot him twice more in the back of the head. . . .

[Mrs. Norman] testified at trial that she was too afraid of her husband to press charges against him or to leave him. She said that she had temporarily left their home on several occasions, but he had always found her, brought her home and beaten her. Asked why she killed her husband, [Mrs. Norman] replied, "Because I was scared of him and I knowed when he woke up, it was going to be the same thing, and I was scared when he took me to the truck stop that night it was going to be worse than he had ever been. I just couldn't take it no more. There ain't no way, even if it means going to prison. It's better than living in that. That's worse hell than anything."

Mrs. Norman was charged with first-degree murder. The trial judge instructed the jury that they had the option of finding the defendant guilty of first-degree murder or voluntary manslaughter, or if they had a reasonable doubt as to her guilt, they could acquit her. The jury convicted Mrs. Norman of voluntary manslaughter. Mrs. Norman was sentenced to 6 years imprisonment.

Although it was requested by the defense, the jury was not instructed about the possibility, under the North Carolina self-defense law, of an acquittal verdict by reason of the self-defense justification for homicide. The refusal to provide Mrs. Norman with an opportunity to exculpate herself on self-defense grounds was appealed. The North Carolina Court of Appeals held that the defendant was entitled to an instruction to the jury on North Carolina law of self-defense, which allows the jury to acquit if they believe "there is a reasonable doubt as to the unlawfulness of defendant's conduct" (*State v. Norman,* 1988, p. 592).

The State appealed the decision of the Court of Appeals to the North Carolina Supreme Court. The majority of the state supreme court concluded that the defendant was not entitled as a matter of law to a jury instruction that would require the jury to determine whether the homicide was justifiably committed in self-defense.

The *Norman* opinion underscores the concern of those who argue that battered women who kill are not able to avail themselves of legitimate self-defense claims. Relying heavily on the word "imminent" in the self-defense doctrine, the North Carolina Supreme Court found that the circumstances did not establish an "immediate danger, such as must be instantly met, such as cannot be guarded against by calling for the assistance of other or the protection of the law" (*State v. Norman,* 1989, p. 13, quoting *Black's Law Dictionary,* 1979). The court determined that no harm was "imminent" when the defendant killed her husband because she:

> was not faced with an instantaneous choice between killing her husband or being killed or seriously injured. Instead, *all* of the evidence tended to show that the defendant had ample time and opportunity to resort to other means of preventing further abuse by her husband. There was no action underway by the decedent from which the jury could have found that the defendant had reasonable grounds to believe either

that a felonious assault was imminent or that it might result in her death or great bodily injury. Additionally, no such action by the decedent had been underway immediately prior to his falling asleep. (*State v. Norman*, 1989, p. 13, emphasis in original)

Also, the court felt that allowing the jury instruction of self-defense would involve a broadening of the "established law of self-defense," and would give the term "imminent" a meaning substantially more indefinite and all-encompassing than its present meaning. Without such imminence, a defendant's belief that her act was "necessary" to avoid harm was deemed unreasonable. The court was concerned that a "relaxation" of these requirements for self-defense:

would tend to categorically legalize the opportune killing of abusive husbands by their wives solely on the testimony concerning their subjective speculation as to the probability of future felonious assaults by their husbands. Homicidal self-help would then become a lawful solution, and perhaps the easiest and most effective solution to this problem. (*State v. Norman*, 1989, p. 15)

The *Norman* opinion presents a classic example of the treatment of battered women defendants who want to use the traditional self-defense doctrine to refute the charge of nonjustifiable homicide.[2] The court was clearly reluctant to give the jury any opportunity to acquit the defendant completely. The jury did mitigate in this case, convicting Mrs. Norman of voluntary manslaughter. There was a dissenting justice who believed that the evidence was sufficient to allow a self-defense instruction under the current doctrine of self-defense. He argued that "imminent" is a term that must be grasped from the defendant's point of view and that "the battered wife is constantly in a heightened state of terror because she is certain that one day her husband will kill her during the course of a beating" (*State v. Norman*, 1989, p. 18, quoting Eber, 1981, pp. 928-929). His view, however, did not attract any of the other justices. Under North Carolina law, as is true for other jurisdictions (including California [*People v. Aris*, 1989]; Kansas [*State v. Stewart*, 1988]; and Pennsylvania [*Commonwealth v. Grove*, 1987]), there is no right for a defendant such as Mrs. Norman to have the jury instructed as to her self-defense theory. (Other jurisdictions do give battered women defendants the right to pursue a self-defense claim, including Illinois [*People v. Scott,* 1981]; Minnesota [*State v. Hennum,* 1989]; New Mexico [*State v. Gallegos,* 1986]; New York [*People v. Emick,* 1984]; North Dakota [*State v. Leidholm,* 1983]; and Washington [*State v. Allery,* 1984].) A battered woman's right to self-defense protection is undermined, as noted by the North Carolina Supreme Court in *Norman,* because the case facts do not comport with traditional, self-defense criteria. As in *Norman,* there are questions about the immediacy of the woman's peril. There are questions about the necessity of the homicide. There are questions about the reasonableness of using lethal force to protect herself from imminent, bodily harm (cf. Walker, this volume).

Ewing's Psychological Self-Defense Proposal

In response to these perceived weaknesses in the law of self-defense, Ewing (1987) proposed a reform of self-defense doctrine to allow for a *psychological self-defense.* Battered women, argues Ewing (1987, 1990), are in psychological danger as well as physical danger. The homicide is more understandable if the psychological peril is considered in addition to the physical peril. Ewing's proposal is to modify self-defense law so that a person may respond with reasonable force to avert a serious and immediate threat to protect one's psychological well-being. There must be the risk of a "gross and enduring impairment of one's psychological functioning which significantly limits the meaning and value of one's physical existence" (Ewing, 1987, p. 79). Akin to physical self-defense, the danger to the psychological self cannot be minor: there must be the risk of "extremely serious psychological injury" (Ewing, 1990, p. 587). Ewing (1990) contends that the law needs to recognize:

> that the value of human life lies not in mere physical existence but rather in the capacity to experience that existence in a psychologically and meaningful and rewarding fashion. When, as in the experience of some battered women, victimization becomes so severe that the capacity to function as an autonomous (psychologically integrated and self-directed) individual is lost, severely impaired, or threatened with loss

or severe impairment, physical existence ("life") loses much if not most of its meaning and value.

To justify taking a life to prevent such loss or severe impairment of one's essential selfhood in no way denigrates respect for life. Indeed, such justification expresses a respect for human life even greater than that implicit in current self-defense doctrine. Unlike current self-defense law, which generally gives priority only to mere physical existence, the proposed doctrine of psychological self-defense would give equal priority to those vital aspects of human functioning that give meaning and value to such existence—in other words, those psychological attributes that make life worth living (Ewing, 1990, pp. 589-590).

In other words, if the North Carolina Supreme Court had considered the psychological dimensions of Judy Norman's existence and not simply whether she might be in physical danger at the moment of the shooting, then they might have been better able to translate Mrs. Norman's description of her experience ("I was scared of him and I knowed when he woke up, it was going to be the same thing . . . I just couldn't take it no more. There ain't no way, even if it means going to prison. It's better than living in that. That's worse hell than anything") into appropriate legal doctrine.[3]

Empirical Research on Psychological Self-Defense

Although we concede that there are weaknesses in Ewing's psychological self-defense proposal on grounds of not only legal theory and public policy but also its purported social science rationale (Morse, 1990; see also Faigman, 1987; Kinports, 1988; Maguigan, 1991), we nonetheless believe that Ewing, as well as others (e.g., Browne, 1987; Gillespie, 1989), has aptly identified a sociopolitical concern that should be rectified. Ultimately, we are less concerned with whether psychological self-defense itself becomes part of the legal lexicon than whether battered women like Mrs. Norman may have all of their circumstances and options considered in their plea for justification and may be seen to be legally justified in their acts if their pleas are supported by a preponderance of the evidence.

Frankly, insofar as fairness is concerned, we believe that the North Carolina Supreme Court's decision in *Norman* was clearly erroneous. It is beyond dispute that more women than men are in a disadvantaged position in intimate relationships and that for some women this disadvantage means being subject to the most brutal physical and psychological degradation. Simply put, the reality is that too many women are being battered and killed (U.S. Department of Justice, 1990, p. 379) by their male partner (e.g., Gelles & Straus, 1988; Straus et al., 1980). Although it is possible that a battered woman who kills her partner will not be charged by the state (Maguigan, 1991, p. 395 & n. 56; Comment, 1989), basic considerations of justice require fair treatment within the legal system for the majority of such women who do face prosecution.[4] At a minimum, to decide that a battered woman defendant is not entitled to a self-defense instruction "usurps the jury's function and deprives the battered woman defendant of her right to a trial by a jury of her peers by removing from the jury's consideration the factual determination of whether her actions constituted reasonable self-defense" (Comment, 1989, p. 181, footnote omitted; see especially Maguigan, 1991). It goes too far in protecting against the possibility that because the jury sympathized with her plight, the jury would nullify the law (see Comment, 1989) by erroneously acquitting a defendant who, if we could know the "truth," actually committed an unjustified homicide.

These are our beliefs. An important addition to the debate surrounding the intricacies of criminal defense doctrine, however, is an examination of the empirical realities and implications. Consequently, the primary question with which we are concerned, as we have detailed elsewhere (Greenwald, Tomkins, Kenning, & Zavodny, 1990), is whether a psychological self-defense option would provide any practical relief for battered women if it were adopted by a court or legislature. The research and discussion that follow are intended to shed some light on this aspect of the self-defense debate.

Method

To examine whether having a psychological self-defense option would have any significance for a battered woman defendant, we

(Greenwald et al., 1990) asked 196 undergraduate psychology students to read a vignette depicting a battered woman who killed her partner. The vignette was described as "an excerpt from a court case in which Kathy Bender (DEFENDANT) is on trial for killing her husband. At this time she is on the witness stand giving her testimony. Her lawyer (DEFENSE ATTORNEY) is questioning her."

Two different forms of a partial "transcript" from the direct examination of Kathy Bender were used. (No statistical difference was found between the two vignette/transcripts.) The vignettes, through Kathy Bender's "testimony," describe how the couple met, how a nonabusive relationship evolved into a violent one that was characterized by cycles of violence and reconciliation, and how a violent incident ended in the killing of Larry Bender by his wife.

Following the transcript vignette, subjects were provided with jury instructions (adapted from Michigan and Ohio) that, depending upon the condition, were 9 to 11 pages. The instructions began by asking participants to respond as if they were actual jurors in the case. They instructed the mock juror subjects to consider only evidence presented in the case, and they explained that the prosecution had to convince the juror of guilt beyond a reasonable doubt. The instructions informed the subjects about the elements of first-degree murder, second-degree murder, and voluntary manslaughter, and they also explained how to choose among them if the juror thought the defendant was indeed guilty. Finally, jurors were given one of four self-defense options and informed that the self-defense claim (if applicable) must be established by the defendant by a preponderance of the evidence. There was one NO SELF-DEFENSE condition (n = 48) and three self-defense instruction conditions: PHYSICAL SELF-DEFENSE (n = 50), PSYCHOLOGICAL SELF-DEFENSE (adapted from Ewing, 1987; n = 48), and both PHYSICAL AND PSYCHOLOGICAL SELF-DEFENSE (n = 50). After reading the vignette and jury instructions, jurors provided one of four verdict options (Guilty of First-Degree Murder, Guilty of Second-Degree Murder, Voluntary Manslaughter, Not Guilty) and then responded to various questions concerning their decision making (Greenwald et al., 1990, pp. 172-174).

Table 10.1 Frequency and Percentage of Verdicts by Jury Instruction Condition

Jury Instruction/ Condition	Verdict				
	First Degree	Second Degree	Voluntary Manslaughter	Not Guilty	Totals
Physical only	1 0.51%	14 7.18%	24 12.31%	10 5.13%	49 25.13%
Psychological only	1 0.51%	8 4.10%	18 9.23%	21 10.77%	48 24.62%
Psychological and physical	2 1.03%	12 6.15%	13 6.67%	23 11.79%	50 25.64%
Control	4 2.05%	11 5.64%	28 14.36%	5 2.56%	48 24.62%
Totals	8 4.10%	45 23.08%	83 42.56%	59 30.26%	195 100.00%

SOURCE: Greenwald, Tomkins, Kenning, and Zavodny (1990). Psychological self-defense jury instructions: Influence on verdicts for battered women defendants. *Behavioral Sciences and the Law*, 8, 171-180, p. 175. © 1990 John Wiley & Sons, Ltd. Reproduced by permission of John Wiley & Sons, Ltd.

Results

Our results suggested that psychological self-defense instructions promoted acquittals at the expense of convictions on the lesser crime of voluntary manslaughter (see Table 10.1). First, we found that the proportion of participants who issued a First- or Second-Degree Murder verdict remained fairly constant across all four conditions: NO SELF-DEFENSE (30.6%), PHYSICAL SELF-DEFENSE (30.6%), PSYCHOLOGICAL SELF-DEFENSE (18.8%), and PHYSICAL AND PSYCHO-LOGICAL SELF-DEFENSE (28.0%). The proportion of acquittals varied significantly and substantially across conditions: NO SELF-DEFENSE (10.4%), PHYSICAL SELF-DEFENSE (20.4%), PSYCHOLOGICAL SELF-DEFENSE (43.8%), and PHYSICAL AND PSYCHOLOGICAL SELF-DEFENSE (46.0%). To put it another way, when a psychological self-defense instruction (either alone or in combination with a physical self-defense instruction) was offered to our subjects, nearly half (44 out of 98 subjects, 44.9%) chose to acquit the battered woman defendant. An acquittal was virtually three times more likely in a psychological self-defense condition than when no psychological self-defense instruction was offered (only 15 out of 97 subjects, 15.5%; Table 10.1). Although PHYSICAL SELF-DEFENSE instructions resulted in almost twice as many acquittals (10 out of 49 subjects, 20.4%) as in the NO SELF-DEFENSE condition (5 out of 48 subjects, 10.4%), the proportion of acquittals was twice as high in both of the two psychological self-defense conditions: the PSYCHOLOGICAL SELF-DEFENSE condition contained 21 out of 48 juror acquittals (43.8%), and the PSYCHOLOGICAL AND PHYSICAL SELF-DEFENSE condition contained 23 out of 50 acquittals (46.0%).

Related Research

Does the psychological self-defense instruction prompt jurors to focus on the exculpatory context of the defendant's behavior? Another study, conducted by Finkel, Meister, and Lightfoot (1991), examined the psychological self-defense variable; however, they did not provide psychological self-defense information through jury instructions. Instead, Finkel et al. used expert testimony to deliver the information to mock jurors because, they argue, psychological self-defense is "much more likely to appear in expert testimony than in jury instructions" (Finkel et al., 1991, p. 589, citing Kinports, 1988). Thus, their study differed from ours on the dimension of how the psychological self-defense concept was presented to the juror. In addition, they used more elaborate stimuli and more varied verdict options (GUILTY: First-Degree Murder, Second-Degree Murder, Voluntary Manslaughter, and Guilty But Mentally Ill; NOT GUILTY: Not Guilty by Reason of Self-Defense and Not Guilty by Reason of Insanity) than we used. They also used a nonstudent, adult group in addition to a student group (Finkel et al., 1991). Finally, the researchers not only had their participants consider the case of a battered woman who kills her violent husband, they also had them consider the case of a homicide defendant who protects herself against an attempted robbery in a subway and the case of a homicide defendant who claims she was raped. Each of these three case types were administered to each participant. For each of the case types, there also were between-group factors.

In the case of interest here, the battered woman case, Finkel et al. (1991) used a 5×3 between-group design. The first variable was the SERIOUSNESS/IMMINENCE to which the defendant responded or did not respond. Three confrontational circumstances (the husband approaches the defendant with a GUN, the husband approaches with a KNIFE and the defendant kills him with a gun, or the husband approaches with his FISTS and the defendant kills him with her gun) and two nonconfrontational circumstances (the husband is AWAKE watching television after assaulting the defendant and threatening future violence, or the husband is ASLEEP in front of the television after assaulting the defendant and threatening future violence) were studied. The second variable involved EXPERT TESTIMONY in the trial. There was a NO EXPERT level, an EXPERT DIAGNOSIS level (in which the expert testifies generally about battered woman syndrome), and an EXPERT PSYCHOLOGICAL TESTIMONY condition in which the expert testifies about battered woman syndrome and about psychological self-defense, opining "that the syndrome sensitized the defendant 'such that she thought that she was in immediate danger of attack,' and that acting 'on her sense of immediate danger, she believed that she was acting in self-defense'" (Finkel et al., 1991, p. 590).

Of the 86 participants in the Finkel et al. study who were exposed to the expert PSYCHOLOGICAL testimony, 60% offered a verdict of Not Guilty by Reason of Self-Defense. Although we would be interested in comparing the findings of our study to the condition in which the EXPERT testified about a battered woman who killed her husband when he was ASLEEP, the researchers did not report their results in such a way that we can directly examine that particular condition. We do know from their report, however, that 45% of the 55 subjects who read about the defendant who killed her sleeping husband thought that the defendant was not guilty by reason of self-defense. Moreover, we also know that for the battered woman case, there were no overall significant effects of having expert testimony, nor were there significant effects between the two types of expert testimony for the battered woman cases in general or for the AWAKE and ASLEEP cases in particular. Thus, it seems reasonable to conclude that the 45% not guilty by reason of self-defense rate found in the ASLEEP condition overall cannot be very different for the particular comparison of interest to us. This conclusion is of considerable importance because it suggests that Finkel et al. found what we found, that is, providing information about psychological self-defense results in roughly 40% of mock jurors voting to acquit the battered woman defendant on grounds of self-defense.

Thus, in response to our previous question, "Does the psychological self-defense instruction prompt jurors to focus on the exculpatory context of the defendant's behavior?" we can now provide a more interesting reply. It seems that psychological self-defense information, whether emanating from instructions or from experts, influences a sizable proportion of mock jurors (approximately 40%) to indicate that a battered woman defendant is not guilty of first- or second-degree murder nor of voluntary manslaughter.

Other researchers have conducted studies on the effect of expert testimony on battered woman syndrome in homicide cases (Follingstad et al., 1989; Schuller, 1990; cf. Walker, this volume). Unfortunately for purposes of this chapter, Schuller's vignette involved a confrontation situation and the Follingstad et al. study used the nonconfrontational, victim asleep scenario as only one of three conditions and did not report the data in such a way as to allow us to determine the proportion of subjects who acquitted the defendant in the asleep scenario. Nonetheless, the conclusion reached by Vidmar and Schuller (1989) concerning the effect of expert testimony, based upon their review of the Schuller and Follingstad et al. research, seems apropos to both expert testimony and jury instructions regarding what we might expect for psychological self-defense information: it "causes the jurors to give more attention to the social and psychological context within which the defendant claimed to be afraid and helpless, rather than causing them to reinterpret her character or misinterpret the law" (Vidmar & Schuller, 1989, pp. 154-155, footnote omitted).

Current Status
of Psychological Self-Defense

Given that the research described above indicates that psychological self-defense information can influence mock juror decisions, we can now ask, has psychological self-defense had an effect on the law itself? In other words, are there cases in which a battered woman defendant has attempted to use a psychological self-defense? We have uncovered only one, unsuccessful, attempt to do so. The case was a New York homicide trial that "apparently was the first time such a claim has been raised in a New York court" (Adams, 1991, p. 1). The case involved a daughter, Mary Anderson, who was charged with second-degree murder for killing her father by stabbing him with an ice pick. The daughter explained that her father had sexually and verbally abused her, and that she killed him to protect herself from further psychological injury. A psychologist testified that in response to her father's "curs[ing] her in front of his friends and accus[ing] her of stealing money," Mary Anderson "relived her experiences with physical and sexual abuse and felt that her psychological well-being was under such devastating attack that she was compelled to protect herself from further psychological injury" (Adams, 1991, p. 1). The trial judge rejected the defendant's psychological self-defense claim, in part because there was no physical threat to the defendant. Mary Anderson was convicted of criminally negligent homicide because her testimony "raise[d] a reasonable doubt as to any culpable mental state higher than criminal negligence" (Adams, 1991, p. 1).

We uncovered one other case in which a psychological self-defense claim was presented to the court. In *People v. Yates* (1990), a Vietnam War veteran, suffering from post traumatic stress disorder (cf. Walker, this volume), killed a young woman with whom he had just engaged in sexual relations because she threatened to blackmail him for having sex with a minor. A psychiatrist testified that the defendant, upon being threatened with blackmail, responded in "psychological self-defense" in which he "entered into a survival mode which caused him to view the victim's threat as seriously as a threat to his physical self" (*People v. Yates,* 1990, p. 1000). The trial judge refused to instruct the jury about self-defense, and the appellate court upheld his refusal, stating that self-defense "does not cover circumstances where a mental disorder causes the defendant to overreact to a nonphysical threat" (*People v. Yates,* 1990, p. 1001).

These cases underscore the practical problem with the psychological self-defense notion. It is unlikely to be embraced by a court until after it receives a societal "imprimatur" through the enactment of appropriate legislation (see Note, 1988). Until the law acknowledges the need for a person to act in psychological self-defense, however, we can anticipate that many battered women who kill their partner in nonconfrontational contexts are not going to find relief in psychological self-defense claims nor in other forms of self-defense claims (but see Maguigan, 1991), although they may be able to reduce their conviction to the less serious charge of criminally negligent homicide (e.g., *People v. Anderson,* reported in Adams, 1991) or manslaughter (e.g., *State v. Norman,* 1989; see also *People v. Aris,* 1989).

Empirical research to date supports the assumption that the reformation of traditional self-defense doctrine to embrace the notion of *psychological* self-defense could result in more battered women being acquitted of the homicides they commit. The research does not address whether the notion is warranted (e.g, Maguigan, 1991) or whether it is a sound legal idea (e.g., Faigman, 1987; Kinports, 1988; Morse, 1990). Nonetheless, Ewing's (1987, 1990) proposal for a psychological self-defense is one idea to address the inherent inequities that exist for battered woman defendants (e.g., Browne, 1987; Crocker, 1985; Ewing, 1987; Kinports, 1988; O'Donovan, 1991; Schneider, 1980), and it is an idea as worthy of further debate as are other solutions that have been attempted (e.g., R. Sherman, 1991, describing Ohio Governor Richard Celeste's grant of clemency to 25 battered women who were in prison after having been found guilty of killing their partner). Moreover, the debate over the acceptability and the advisability of psychological self-defense may serve as a stimulus for change in those jurisdictions that restrict a battered woman defendant in nonconfrontational cases (as in *Norman*) from instructing the jury about a *traditional* self-defense. The warning to the legal system could be this: if self-defense doctrine is interpreted such that nonconfrontational incidents involving a chronically battered woman defendant are not properly included under the self-defense umbrella, then legislative change to make provisions for a psychological self-defense may be in order. For the majority of jurisdictions, however, the better solution might be to have trial courts follow the prevailing self-defense law rather than to advocate for the psychological self-defense reform (Maguigan, 1991).

Women who have been chronically battered and who ultimately kill their partner deserve the law's sympathy, not its punishment. A trial is itself an ordeal. To handicap the battered woman defendant from focusing the jury's attention on the legal relevance of her claims of self-protection is unconscionable. Ewing (1987) found that in 18 cases in which battered women were not denied by the court the right to present battered woman syndrome evidence, all were convicted. Not all women deserve to be acquitted, of course; but battered women do deserve the right to present evidence or to have the court present instructions that focus the fact finder on the psychological realities they faced (see, e.g., Estrich, 1990) as long as threshold evidentiary criteria are met (Maguigan, 1991).

Recommendations for Future Research

Future research needs to become more sophisticated so that we can investigate whether Ewing's psychological self-defense notion is even necessary. Studies need to be conducted that control for strength of psychologically relevant evidence while varying self-defense instructions. In addition, it will be valuable to examine specifically whether there are meaningful differences between providing psychological self-defense information through expert testimony versus jury instructions. Interestingly, research on eyewitness testimony indicates that in this domain expert testimony is more influential than jury instructions (Vidmar & Schuller, 1989).

Also, research needs to be more methodologically sound and varied (cf. Vidmar & Schuller, 1989). More heterogeneous pools of participants should be employed (as was done by Finkel et al., 1991) instead of relying solely on college student populations. Clearly, deliberations should also be encouraged (as was done by Schuller, 1990). Although there are bases to believe that sample heterogeneity and jury deliberations will not substantially alter the main thrust of findings gleaned from college student, mock juror studies, it would be preferable to expand the data base using deliberating, jury-eligible subjects who reflect the demographic characteristics of actual jurors and who respond to more textured, more complex, and otherwise more ecologically valid case stimuli than can be achieved using vignette descriptions. Other methods, such as interviewing jurors after they have served in these types of cases (Vidmar & Schuller, 1989), will also provide valuable data that can confirm or contradict findings obtained from simulation research.

It would be useful to know not only the actual, annual number of homicides committed by battered women against their partner, but also what proportion of these women killed in a nonconfrontational context and how many claim they were acting in self-defense (physical or psychological). It also would be helpful if we knew the number of women each year who were unable to present relevant justification evidence and/or who are unable to get the trial court to present justification instructions to the jury. Present estimates indicate that each year about 750 men are killed by wives, girlfriends, lovers, and so on, and that "most female homicide defendants had been battered by the men whom they killed" (Maguigan, 1991, p. 397). Sue Ostfoff, executive director of the Philadelphia-based, public interest law firm the National Clearinghouse for the Defense of Battered Women, estimates that wife assault in the United States continues at the rate of 3-4 million women each year (cf. Straus et al., 1980) and that "there are about 1,000 'battered woman' cases a year" (R. Sherman, 1991, p. 3). Maguigan (1991) reviewed the available studies and law enforcement data and concluded that about 10% of the women who kill commit the homicide in nonconfrontational contexts.

Finally, as O'Donovan (1991) indicates, a useful methodological technique would be for researchers to talk directly to battered women who have killed their tormentor and to battered women who have not, in order to learn more about their experiences, their perceptions, their rationales for their actions, and so on. Although some evidence on these issues is available (see especially Browne, 1987, 1988, and Walker, 1984, for examples of this type of approach; an epidemiological approach to domestic violence is taken by Stark & Flitcraft, 1988), much more research is needed.

Conclusion

It is hard to know quite what to do when we are presented with a battered woman who has just killed her partner. It would be optimal to rely on research evidence to garner our social and legal resources to intervene (e.g., Sedlak, 1988; see also L. W. Sherman & Cohn, 1989) before the violence escalates into the death of either party. Indeed, early intervention could also benefit child witnesses to the violence (Jaffe, Wolfe, & Wilson, 1990; Kenning, Merchant, & Tomkins, 1991). Until we develop policies and practices that effectively address this and other types of family violence, however, concerned social scientists are resigned to conducting further research intended to prevent additional injustices from being perpetrated against women like Judy Norman, who have been brutally victimized for intolerably long periods of time.

Notes

1. One commentator succinctly summarizes the classic formulation of the doctrine of self-defense found in §.5.7 of the authoritative treatise by LaFave and Scott (1986):

> The elements of the justification of self-defense are, generally, that a defendant may use *physical force* when and to the extent that he or she reasonably believes necessary to prevent the imminent (or immediate) use of unlawful physical force against the defendant. A defendant may not use physical force in self-defense if he or she provoked the encounter by unlawful conduct or was the initial aggressor.
>
> Most jurisdictions impose additional requirements that must be satisfied before the use of *deadly physical force* is justified to repel an attack. The defendant must reasonably believe that the attacker is using or is about to use deadly physical force. Some jurisdictions require that, before resorting to deadly force, the defendant retreat from the encounter, if safe retreat is possible. Most of those jurisdictions exempt a defendant who is attacked in his or her home from the retreat requirement. (Maguigan, 1991, p. 392 n. 34, emphases in original, citations omitted)

2. Maguigan (1991) argues that nonconfrontational homicides like that committed in *Norman* are in fact not as frequent as commentators such as Ewing (1987, 1990) suggest. In her review of all U.S. appellate decisions, reported and unreported, issued between 1902 and 1991, Maguigan found 270 opinions, representing 233 incidents: "in cases where (1) the defendant was a woman, (2) the defendant was accused of killing her spouse or lover, (3) there was evidence of a history of abuse of the woman by the man, (4) the defendant claimed to have acted in self-defense, and (5) the defendant was convicted" (Maguigan, 1991, p. 394, footnotes omitted). Her review revealed that the

vast majority (75%) of the 233 incidents involved some type of confrontation between the defendant and the decedent and only 16% were the *Norman*-like sleeping man cases (8%) or cases in which the defendant killed her partner after a "lull in the violence" (also 8%). The remaining 9% of the cases were either contract killing cases (4%) or cases in which the incident facts were not reported in the appellate opinion (5%).

Before we accept Maguigan's conclusion that nonconfrontational homicides are an insubstantial proportion of the homicides committed by battered women against their partner (and 37 battered women convicted of nonconfrontational homicides even over the last 25 years is a small number), it is important to note that Maguigan omitted cases in which no self-defense claim was made by the defendant. It would seem logical (almost tautological) that nonconfrontational homicides are those that are least likely to result in a self-defense claim because, among other reasons, (a) these are the battered woman cases that least comport with the traditional self-defense requirements of imminence, necessity, and so on; and (b) beliefs (perhaps myths), which admittedly could be based on faulty evidence of a nonsystematic nature (see, e.g., Ewing, 1987), could lead attorneys to believe in the uselessness of self-defense claims resulting in either plea bargains or alternative defense strategies (meaning that any appeal of the case would not include a discussion of the self-defense issue). The consequence is that we might expect comparatively fewer nonconfrontational cases to be appealed than confrontational cases. Thus, Maguigan's reliance on appeals to identify nonconfrontational cases may severely *underestimate* the actual incidence rate. Even if her study does not underestimate the reality, the nonconfrontational cases that commentators have documented are typically so striking in their face unfairness (the *Norman* case, it seems to us, is exemplary) to warrant serious consideration of how to address appropriately the needs and interests of these select, few women who ought to have their justification claim addressed by the fact finder. Finally, it should be noted that our view is not at all inconsistent with Maguigan's. After serious consideration of the dilemma, Maguigan concludes that the solution lies with appropriate application of existing self-defense doctrine by trial court judges. Although this solution may address many of the issues associated with self-defense and the battered woman, it does not address the needs of battered women defendants in jurisdictions such as North Carolina where the state law is currently interpreted as not entitling a battered woman defendant to a right to a self-defense instruction.

3. An example of an expanded notion of self-defense doctrine based on the totality of the circumstances is found in the decision by the Supreme Court of Washington in *State v. Wanrow* (1977). In *Wanrow,* the court held that "the justification of self-defense is to be evaluated in light of *all* the facts and circumstances known to the defendant, including those known substantially before the killing" (*State v. Wanrow,* 1977, p. 234, emphasis in original). *Wanrow* was not a case involving a battered woman defendant, but it did involve the use of deadly force by a small woman against a man. In cases involving battered woman defendants, the issue typically arises in the context of whether expert testimony concerning battered woman syndrome is admissible to explain the defendant's perceptions of the situations (see, e.g., *State v. Kelly,* 1984; see generally P. H. Robinson, 1984, p. 412 & n. 48; see also J. G. Robinson, 1988, pp. 56-57, n. 48). As a general matter, testimony on battered woman syndrome is admissible in most U.S. jurisdictions (see, e.g., the concurring opinion of Justice Cappy in *Commonwealth*

v. Dillon, 1991, p. *5, n. 2, citing both reported and unreported cases that have held such testimony admissible; see generally Maguigan, 1991).

4. As Professor Faigman (1987) argues:

> The challenge for battered women defendants and their advocates lies in explaining the actual reasonableness of the particular conduct in question; and the challenge for courts lies in understanding the battered woman's plight within a societal context in which her options may be few. The use of deadly force, although departing from traditional notions of self-defense, in some cases may be readily understood as justified. Where the pattern of violence is unambiguous, and the woman's unique position in the relationship allows her to recognize and predict her tormentor's violence, the justness of her defensive action is obvious. (Faigman, 1987, p. 224)

Professor Faigman's view, which nicely articulates our view, is not held by all. For example, in a recent California appellate case, the court wrote that

> Batterers of women, even though they deserve punishment for their acts of battery, nevertheless are entitled to the same protection of their lives by the law that is afforded to everyone. That protection is the deterrence to would-be killers afforded by the knowledge that a killing with malice aforethought will be punished as a murder unless the killer actually perceived an imminent danger of death or serious bodily injury at the hands of the deceased.
>
> While we recognize that applying such a rule in cases such as this one is difficult because of our sympathy for the plight of a battered woman and disgust for the batterer, it is fundamental to our concept of law that there be no discrimination between sinner and saint solely on moral grounds. Any less exacting definition of imminence fails to protect every person's right to live. (*People v. Aris,* 1989, p. 174, footnote omitted)

References

Adams, E. A. (1991, March 14). "Psychological self-defense" rejected in murder case. *New York Law Journal,* p. 1.

Black's Law Dictionary (5th ed.). (1979). St. Paul, MN: West.

Browne, A. (1987). *When battered women kill.* New York: Macmillan.

Browne, A. (1988). Family homicide: When victimized women kill. In V. B. Van Hasselt, R. L. Morrison, A. S. Bellack, & M. Hersen (Eds.), *Handbook of family violence* (pp. 271-289). New York: Plenum.

Comment. (1987). The defense of battered women who kill. *University of Pennsylvania Law Review, 135,* 427-452.

Comment. (1989). Rendering each woman her due: Can a battered woman claim self-defense when she kills her sleeping batterer? *Kansas Law Review, 38,* 169-192.

Commonwealth v. Dillon, 1991 WL 222827 (Pa., October 31, 1991) (WESTLAW).

Commonwealth v. Grove, 363 Pa.Super. 328, 526 A.2d 369, *appeal denied,* 517 Pa. 630, 539 A.2d 810 (1987).

Crocker, P. L. (1985). The meaning of equality for battered women who kill men in self-defense. *Harvard Women's Law Review, 8,* 121-153.

Dressler, J. (1987a). Justifications and excuses: A brief review of the concepts and the literature. *Wayne Law Review, 33,* 1155-1175.

Dressler, J. (1987b). *Understanding criminal law.* New York: Matthew Bender.

Dutton, D. G. (1988). *The domestic assault of women: Psychological and criminal justice perspectives.* Boston: Allyn & Bacon.

Dutton, D. G., & McGregor, B.M.S. (1992). Psychological and legal dimensions of family violence. In D. K. Kagehiro & W. S. Laufer (Eds.), *Handbook of psychology and law* (pp. 318-340). New York: Springer-Verlag.

Eber, L. P. (1981). The battered wife's dilemma: To kill or to be killed. *Hastings Law Journal, 32,* 895-931.

Elliott, D. S. (1989). Criminal justice procedures in family violence crimes. In L. Ohlin & M. Tonry (Eds.), *Family violence* (pp. 427-480). Chicago: University of Chicago Press.

Estrich, S. (1990). Defending women [Review of *Justifiable homicide: Battered women, self-defense, and the law*]. *Michigan Law Review, 88,* 1430-1439.

Ewing, C. P. (1987). *Battered women who kill: Psychological self-defense as legal justification.* Lexington, MA: D. C. Heath.

Ewing, C. P. (1990). Psychological self-defense: A proposed justification for battered women who kill. *Law and Human Behavior, 14,* 579-594.

Faigman, D. L. (1987). Discerning justice when battered women kill [Review of *Battered women who kill: Psychological self-defense as legal justification*]. *Hastings Law Journal, 39,* 207-227.

Finkel, N. J., Meister, K. H., & Lightfoot, D. M. (1991). The self-defense defense and community sentiment. *Law and Human Behavior, 15,* 585-602.

Fletcher, G. (1979). Should intolerable prison conditions generate a justification or excuse for escape? *U.C.L.A. Law Review, 26,* 1355-1369.

Follingstad, D. R., Polek, D. S., Hause, E. S., Deaton, L. H., Bulger, M. W., & Conway, Z. D. (1989). Factors predicting verdicts in cases where battered women kill their husbands. *Law and Human Behavior, 13,* 253-269.

Frieze, I. H., & Browne, A. (1989). Violence in marriage. In L. Ohlin & M. Tonry (Eds.), *Family violence* (pp. 163-218). Chicago: University of Chicago Press.

Gelles, R. J., & Straus, M. A. (1988). *Intimate violence.* New York: Simon & Schuster.

Gillespie, C. K. (1989). *Justifiable homicide: Battered women, self-defense, and the law.* Columbus: Ohio State University Press.

Gordon, L. (1988). *Heroes of their own lives: The politics and history of family violence.* New York: Penguin.

Greenwald, J. P., Tomkins, A. J., Kenning, M. K., & Zavodny, D. (1990). Psychological self-defense jury instruction: Influence on verdicts for battered women defendants. *Behavioral Sciences and the Law, 8,* 171-180.

Greenwalt, K. (1984). The perplexing borders of justification and excuse. *Columbia Law Review, 84,* 1897-1927.

Greenwalt, K. (1986, Summer). Distinguishing justifications from excuses. *Law and Contemporary Problems, 49,* 89-126.

Jaffe, P., Wolfe, D., & Wilson, S. K. (1990). *Children of battered women.* Newbury Park, CA: Sage.

Jenkins, P., & Davidson, B. (1990). Battered women in the criminal justice system: An analysis of gender stereotypes. *Behavioral Sciences and the Law, 8,* 161-170.

Kenning, M., Merchant, A., & Tomkins, A. (1991). Research on the effects of witnessing parental battering: Clinical and legal policy implications. In M. Steinman (Ed.), *Woman battering: Policy responses* (pp. 237-261). Cincinnati, OH: Anderson.

Kinports, K. (1988). Defending battered women's self-defense claims. *Oregon Law Review, 67,* 393-465.

LaFave, W. R., & Scott, A. W., Jr. (1986). *Criminal Law* (2nd ed.). St. Paul, MN: West.

Maguigan, H. (1991). Battered women and self-defense: Myths and misconceptions in current reform proposals. *University of Pennsylvania Law Review, 140,* 379-486.

Margolin, G., Sibner, L. G., & Gleberman, L. (1988). Wife battering. In V. B. Van Hasselt, R. L. Morrison, A. S. Bellack, & M. Hersen (Eds.), *Handbook of family violence* (pp. 89-117). New York: Plenum.

Martin, D. (1978). Overview: The scope of the problem. In U.S. Commission on Civil Rights, *Battered women: Issues of public policy* (pp. 3-19). Washington, DC: U.S. Government Printing Office.

Moore, M. S. (1984). *Law and psychiatry: Rethinking the relationship.* New York: Cambridge University Press.

Moore, M. S. (1985). Causation and the excuses. *California Law Review, 73,* 1091-1149.

Morse, S. J. (1984). Undiminished confusion in diminished capacity. *Journal of Criminal Law & Criminology, 75,* 1-55.

Morse, S. J. (1986). Psychology, determinism, and legal responsibility. In G. B. Melton (Ed.), *The law as a behavioral instrument: Nebraska Symposium on Motivation, 1985* (pp. 35-85). Lincoln: University of Nebraska Press.

Morse, S. J. (1990). The misbegotten marriage of soft psychology and bad law: Psychological self-defense as a justification for homicide. *Law and Human Behavior, 14,* 595-618.

Note. (1975). Justification: The impact of the Model Penal Code on statutory reform. *Columbia Law Review, 75,* 914-962.

Note. (1986). The battered woman syndrome and self-defense: A legal and empirical dissent. *Virginia Law Review, 72,* 619-647.

Note. (1988). Is "psychological self-defense" a solution to the problem of defending battered women who kill? *Washington and Lee Law Review, 45,* 1527-1547.

O'Donovan, K. (1991). Defences for battered women who kill. *Journal of Law and Society, 18,* 219-240.

People v. Aris, 215 Cal. App. 3d 1178, 264 Cal. Rptr. 167 (Cal. App. 4th Dist. 1989).

People v. Emick, 103 A.D.2d 643, 481 N.Y.S.2d 552 (1984).

People v. Scott, 97 Ill. App. 3d 899, 424 N.E.2d 70 (1981).

People v. Yates, 195 Ill. App. 3d 66, 551 N.E.2d 999 (1990).

Pleck, E. (1987). *Domestic tyranny: The making of American social policy against family violence from colonial times to the present.* New York: Oxford University Press.

Robinson, J. G. (1988). *Pocket part to P. H. Robinson's Criminal Law Defenses.* St. Paul, MN: West.

Robinson, P. H. (1984). *Criminal law defenses* (vol. 2). St. Paul, MN: West.

Rosen, C. J. (1986). The excuse of self-defense: Correcting a historical accident on behalf of battered women. *American University Law Review, 36,* 11-56.

Schneider, E. M. (1980). Equal rights to trial for women: Sex bias in the law of self-defense. *Harvard Civil Rights Law Review, 15,* 623-647.

Schopp, R. F. (1991). *Automatism, insanity, and the psychology of criminal responsibility: A philosophical inquiry.* New York: Cambridge University Press.

Schuller, R. A. (1990). *The impact of expert testimony pertaining to the "battered woman syndrome" on jurors' information processing and decisions.* Unpublished doctoral dissertation, University of Western Ontario.

Sedlak, A. J. (1988). Prevention of wife abuse. In V. B. Van Hasselt, R. L. Morrison, A. S. Bellack, & M. Hersen (Eds.), *Handbook of family violence* (pp. 319-358). New York: Plenum.

Sherman, L. W., & Cohn, E. G. (1989). The impact of research on legal policy: The Minneapolis domestic violence experiment. *Law and Society Review, 22,* 118-144.

Sherman, R. (1991, February 4). Acceptance of defense is up. *National Law Review,* pp. 3, 28.

Stark, E., & Flitcraft, A. (1988). Violence among intimates: An epidemiological review. In V. B. Van Hasselt, R. L. Morrison, A. S. Bellack, & M. Hersen (Eds.), *Handbook of family violence* (pp. 293-317). New York: Plenum.

State v. Allery, 101 Wash. 2d 591, 682 P.2d 312 (App. Div. 1984).

State v. Gallegos, 104 N.M. 247, 719 P.2d 1268 (N.M. Ct. App. 1986).

State v. Hennum, 441 N.W.2d 793 (Minn. 1989).

State v. Kelly, 97 N.J. 178, 478 A.2d 364 (1984).

State v. Leidholm, 334 N.W.2d 811 (N.D. 1983).

State v. Norman, 89 N.C.App. 384, 366 S.E.2d 586 (1988), *rev'd,* 324 N.C. 253, 378 S.E.2d 8 (1989).

State v. Norman, 324 N.C. 253, 378 S.E.2d 8 (1989).

State v. Stewart, 243 Kan. 639, 763 P.2d 572 (1988).

State v. Wanrow, 88 Wash.2d 221, 559 P.2d 548 (1977) (en banc).

Straus, M. A. (1979). Measuring family conflict and violence: The Conflict Tactics (CT) Scale. *Journal of Marriage and the Family, 41,* 75-88.

Straus, M. A. (1991). Conceptualization and measurement of battering: Implications for public policy. In M. Steinman (Ed.), *Woman battering: Policy responses* (pp. 19-47). Cincinnati, OH: Anderson.

Straus, M. A., Gelles, R. J., & Steinmetz, S. K. (1980). *Behind closed doors: Violence in the American family.* New York: Anchor.

U.S. Department of Justice. (1990). *Sourcebook of criminal justice statistics—1990.* Washington, DC: U.S. Government Printing Office.

Vidmar, N. J., & Schuller, R. A. (1989). Juries and expert evidence: Social framework testimony. *Law and Contemporary Problems, 52*(4), 133-176.

Walker, L.E.A. (1984). *The battered woman syndrome.* New York: Springer.

PART
V

SUMMARY

11

Legal Responses to Wife Assault

Future Prospects for Intervention and Evaluation

RONALD ROESCH

STEPHEN D. HART

LAURENE J. WILSON

The other contributors to this volume have discussed several major topics in the area of wife assault. In this final chapter, we begin by reviewing the previous contributions in order to identify crucial research issues and knowledge gaps. Second, we will attempt to summarize recent trends in research on wife assault and to make recommendations for the future. We should emphasize that this chapter is not intended to give a thorough description of the "state of the art"; rather, we make comments that we hope will stimulate the interest and imagination of researchers.

Simon Fraser University, Burnaby, British Columbia, V5A 1S6.

Review of Previous Chapters

Daniel Saunders reviews the literature on "risk markers" for wife assault and makes the important point that wife assaulters should not be considered a homogeneous group, as they vary on a number of sociodemographic and personality characteristics. The risk marker literature is of questionable theoretical relevance because, as Saunders recognizes, the factors identified do not necessarily play a causal role in wife assault; they merely discriminate between men who assault their partner and those who do not. Saunders makes a strong argument, however, that identified risk markers and heterogeneity among assaulters may have important practical implications with respect to treatment and management. Saunders describes a three-part typology of wife assaulters based on his own research and experience, a typology that appears to be consistent with those developed by other leading experts in the area (e.g., Dutton, 1988; Gondolf, 1988b). Unfortunately, there is no research at present that supports the usefulness of the typology in treatment planning, although Saunders offers some conjectures that could serve as a useful starting point. As we discuss later in our review of Hamberger and J. E. Hastings' contribution, researchers working in the area of wife assault may be able to build on the efforts of those who have investigated the effectiveness of psychotherapy; the latter have spent considerable time and effort attempting to devise appropriate methods for detecting programmatic, client, and therapist variables that impact on treatment success (see Kazdin, 1992).

The editor of this volume, N. Zoe Hilton, provides a brief review of public and police opinions about wife assault and then presents data from her own study of 240 subjects who read one of four scenarios in which type of assault (wife or stranger) and prior record (first offender or recidivist) were varied. She finds that the majority of respondents felt that the offender should be charged, although they saw this option as most useful for cases of repeat offenses by strangers. In cases of wife assault, respondents were more likely to recommend alternative services for the victims. This type of research is important because of the influence that public attitudes have on social and legal policy regarding wife assault, as Hilton discusses in her overview of the literature. Collecting data of this sort in a more systematic way (for example, using probability sampling) could also provide a "yardstick" by which to measure changes in public attitudes over time; time series analysis of such data would allow us to determine the effect of new public education programs, media coverage, or policies.

Peter Jaffe, Elaine Hastings, Deborah Reitzel, and Gary Austin review police arrest policies regarding wife assault. They note that police practices have changed considerably in the past decade, particularly in an increased use of arrest. These changes have been influenced by a number of research projects as well as by activist groups. Future research needs to address how the changing policy can be incorporated as part of an integrated community response to dealing with violence against women, including support services for women, and treatment and resources for wife assaulters and child witnesses to violence. Jaffe et al. raise two issues worthy of special consideration by researchers and policymakers. One, they comment on the importance of understanding cross-cultural issues, pointing to the higher risk of victimization among certain groups, such as aboriginal women. Two, they comment on the need for primary prevention programs to help children who have witnessed violence in the home. As we will discuss later in this chapter, these kinds of prevention programs may be essential in breaking the cycle of violence.

Kathleen Ferraro and Lucille Pope raise a number of important issues for researchers in their chapter on the relationship among battered women, the police, and the law. They focus on police responses to domestic violence and identify cultural, attitudinal, and other differences between police and battered women that influence the behavior of both groups. Most interventions, including presumptive arrest policies, pay little attention to differences of this sort; consequently, research tends to ignore them as well. Ferraro and Pope identify a number of possible causes of the failure of the legal system to respond adequately to wife assault. They conclude that "Any legal or policy changes which increase the power of police without simultaneously striving for the empowerment of women will have the potential to decrease rather than improve the level of women's safety." We agree wholeheartedly with this position. Later in this chapter, we review some prior research and recommend some new approaches that we believe are much more sensitive to the needs and desires of battered women. For example, one line of study, which could be labeled "consumer satisfaction" evaluation, surveys battered women's perceptions of the various services (legal, medical, mental health, etc.) that they receive.

David Ford and Mary Jean Regoli look at the role of the prosecutor in criminal cases involving wife assault. They argue that this role is a crucial one, at least in the United States, and describe numerous legal and extralegal factors that may affect prosecutorial decision making. They also describe the results of a study in which researchers evaluated the effect of various prosecution policies in one U.S. jurisdiction. As was the case with the chapter on mediation, there is an almost total lack of basic research in this area. Although interesting, the study described by the authors needs replication and extension. It might also be informative to survey a random sample of prosecutors in urban and rural counties to see how interested, knowledgeable, and experienced they are with respect to wife assault. It would also be useful to know what they perceive to be the biggest impediments to successful prosecution.

Desmond Ellis contrasts mediational and adversarial approaches to conflict resolution with wife assault victims and offenders. He discusses the pros and cons of both approaches, including the possibility that mediation "promotes battering" or "perpetuates abuse," and notes that there is a lack of substantial empirical evidence to support any opinion. He describes two studies in the area, both of which suffer from methodological shortcomings (small samples, nonrandom assignment). This is an area that cries out for basic research. Many battered women are potential consumers of mediation services, including a large number whose partner was never charged with nor convicted of criminal offenses; we need to know how best to protect the rights and interests of these women and their family. Should we attempt to conduct evaluative research where couples are randomly assigned to mediational or adversarial approaches, or would this be unethical? Are there alternative approaches, for example, the use of a control jurisdiction (where mediation is not available) together with statistical controls for important variables (e.g., couple's income, severity of violence)? Also, does the nature of the dispute between wife and husband make a difference (e.g., custody/access, maintenance/alimony, separation/divorce)?

Kevin Hamberger and James Hastings discuss court-mandated treatment for men who assault their partner. They outline a number of individual and group approaches to treatment, but the primary focus of the chapter is on whether the research literature can inform us about the effectiveness of treatment for wife assaulters. They complete their chapter with a synopsis of some 28 outcome studies conducted during the 1980s. Their conclusions are not encouraging. Hamberger and J. E. Hastings believe that we have learned very little about treatment effects, pointing to a number of crucial methodological flaws in the research (high attrition rates, lack of statistical evaluation, failure to include control groups, nonrandom assignment to groups). Furthermore, the authors argue that the question, "Does treatment work?" is simplistic and should be abandoned in favor of, "What treatment works best for which type of client?" These conclusions are very distressing. It appears that treatment outcome research in the area of wife assault lags about 30 years behind the more general research literature on the effectiveness of psychotherapy, which has long recognized the need for focused research questions, random assignment to treatment or control groups, and appropriate statistics to assess change and to control for the effects of attrition (Eysenck, 1952; Kazdin, 1992; Keisler, 1971; Paul, 1967).

Lenore Walker introduces the subject of battered women who kill their partner. She discusses the various defenses that are available to these women, who may be charged with murder, manslaughter, or some other violent crime. Walker argues that the experience of being assaulted alters a woman's perception of the imminence of danger from her partner. She bases her argument on the battered woman syndrome and its relation to post traumatic stress disorder (PTSD), which she claims can affect the state of the mind as seen in the eyes of the law (mens rea). The battered woman syndrome, however, has been controversial (e.g., Frieze & Browne, 1989), and research into PTSD among battered women is still needed. Walker, an expert witness herself, believes that expert testimony is important in conveying to judges and jurors the psychological effect of violence on the battered woman defendant.

Alan Tomkins, Mary Kenning, Jessica Greenwald, and Gregory Johnson discuss the use of self-defense jury instructions, another way of conveying this information in cases where battered women kill their partner. They note that battered women who kill their assailant are frequently unable to claim self-defense, as the threat of physical harm is not imminent. Alternatives to traditional self-defense options have been put forward, including one suggested by Ewing (1990), who favors broadening the concept of self-defense to include threats of serious psychological harm. Although Tomkins and his colleagues recognize that Ewing's proposal has weaknesses (e.g., Morse, 1990), they believe that changes to the doctrine of self-defense could help the law to demonstrate greater respect for human life and to recognize the disadvantaged position of women in intimate relationships. They present the results of their own research to show that the use of psychological self-defense instructions may lead to more acquittals. The authors correctly point out that the generalizability of this result to actual court cases is unknown. They uncovered only two actual cases in which psychological self-defense was used, and in both instances the defense was rejected by the trial judge. Tomkins et al. conclude their chapter with an overview of directions for future research, including more sophisticated studies looking at the necessity of psychological self-defense and at the effect of expert testimony as compared with jury instructions. They also call for greater ecological validity in such research; for example, the use of subjects who better reflect the demographics of actual jurors and who deliberate like a true jury. In addition, basic information is required concerning the scope of the issue, for example, the annual number of occurrences of battered women killing their partner, the context or situation in which these killings occur, and what proportion of women claim self-defense as a motive. Finally, interviewing battered women who have and have not killed their partner may provide additional insight as to their experiences, perceptions, and decision-making processes. We suggest that researchers and policymakers refer to a Canadian case, *R. v. Lavallee* (1990). In this case, which involved a battered woman who killed her common-law husband, the Supreme Court of Canada affirmed the extension of self-defense to cases in which the threat of violence is not necessarily imminent. This might eliminate the need for a psychological self-defense, yet still provide jurors with an alternative to conviction in those cases where it seemed appropriate.

Recent Trends and
New Directions in Research

Let us now turn from the individual chapters to the content of the volume as a whole. After reading the various contributions, the present authors met on several occasions for discussion. We found that several major issues dominated our conversation. Some of the issues concerned material that was included in this book, and because it is impossible for any single volume to give proper coverage to all the facets of an issue as complex as wife assault, some concerned material that was excluded. These issues are outlined below.

What Are the Goals of Intervention?

It is clear from reading the chapters that there is no general consensus on how to define "success" when evaluating the various legal responses to wife assault. In fact, as embarrassing as it is to admit, it appears that we as a society have not made the goals of our interventions sufficiently explicit. This is a question of fundamental importance that has rarely received attention from researchers.

To make this point, let us turn once again to the issue of court-mandated treatment for wife assaulters. Surely, any evaluation of this intervention must take into account the courts' sentencing goals. These goals probably include general deterrence, specific deterrence (desistence), rehabilitation, and to a lesser extent, retribution. Desistence of criminal behavior is probably the primary goal (would a judge perceive an offender's treatment to have been effective when he assaults his wife again, even if the offender's self-esteem had improved or he had incorporated some profeminist ideals into his value system?), but we simply don't know. This is a crucial issue, as one of the biggest criticisms leveled against court-mandated treatment is that it focuses on physical violence and places less emphasis on other forms of abuse, such as verbal abuse. Verbal abuse, however, is not a crime (except for threats of physical harm). Does the court have a right to control an offender's verbal behavior, as long as it conforms to the law? Civil libertarians might construe that as censorship, as a violation of Charter or Constitutional rights. In any event, verbal abuse (by both women and men) probably occurs to a limited extent in all intimate relationships; is it realistic or even appropriate to expect that, say, 16 weeks of group therapy should not only stop an offender from being violent but also make him less verbally abusive than the average, nonassaultive man?

There is a clear need for research on the goals of wife assault interventions as perceived by various players in the criminal justice system: police, prosecutors, judges, victims, and assaulters. Once we know the goals, we can develop appropriate outcome measures. (We use the plural form here because it is doubtful that a single measure can assess progress toward a goal, and because it is almost certain that multiple goals will be identified by research.) This approach avoids any presupposition that the police or the courts know what is best for battered women and would allow us to interpret intervention evaluations from a number of different perspectives.

Needed: A Few Good Studies . . .

One point made frequently in the previous chapters is the need for increased methodological rigor in research on wife assault. In social science, all three of the following serve primarily to raise questions: research ideas stimulated by case reports; clinical anecdotes; and small, uncontrolled studies. In order to answer these questions, however, the procedures used to gather data must evolve into more complex and sophisticated forms.

It appears that research on wife assault interventions has reached an impasse of sorts. For example, as a number of reviewers have noted (Hamberger & Hastings, this volume; Rosenfeld, 1992; Tolman & Bennet, 1990), after a decade of asking, "Is court-mandated treatment for wife assaulters effective?" we still have no satisfactory answer to this question. We support the use of court-mandated and voluntary treatment of wife assaulters at the present time; society should take any reasonable measures to protect women's safety in the short term. A proper evaluation, however, must be done. Our view is that it is unethical for mental health professionals to provide services of unknown effectiveness, as long as proper evaluation is scientifically possible (e.g., Webster & Hilton, 1990). For all we know, we may be treating the people who are least likely to recidivate or using treatment components that are inappropriate given the psychological characteristics of assaulters; worse still, treatment may actually be increasing the likelihood of violence against women.

We hope that a call for increased methodological rigor is not seen as putting the whims of academic journal reviewers or doctoral committee members ahead of the needs of battered women. Rather, we believe that a small number of good (i.e., methodologically sound) studies can do more to better the circumstances of battered women than dozens of poor-quality studies, by (a) increasing the effectiveness of services and (b) providing excellent ammunition with which to lobby public officials for increased funding. As an illustration, take the example of research on the prevalence of wife assault. Prompted by clinical anecdotes and observations, the initial surveys, now about two decades old (e.g., Straus, Gelles, & Steinmetz, 1980), used standard epidemiological methods. They produced dramatic results that were replicated across North America (e.g., Kennedy & Dutton, 1989; Straus & Gelles, 1986). The findings stimulated research on aspects of wife assault, gave the study of family violence a high profile in the scientific community, and most important, seized the attention of public officials. In some respects, one could argue that research on prevalence has been too good, as, probably because they yield "definitive" findings, governments seem to favor funding prevalence studies over intervention studies. Another example is the original Sherman and Berk (1984) study looking at the deterrent effect of arrest, which had a substantial influence on arrest policy despite the study's methodological limitations.

Poor studies are generally ignored by credible scientists and may lead to frustration among policymakers, making them less willing to devote needed funds to research and evaluation. Researchers need to be reminded that studies using random assignment to interventions can be ethically justified in certain circumstances. For example, as noted above, there is no consensus in the literature that court-mandated treatment for wife assault is any more effective than criminal justice monitoring (i.e., close supervision), and most jurisdictions do not have sufficient resources to treat all convicted wife assaulters. Thus, convicted wife assaulters could be randomly assigned to treatment or to supervision. If treatment is responsible for changing attitudes and behavior, then treatment should be better than supervision;

otherwise, the active component of treatment is probably just super-vision! Even in those instances where random assignment is not possible, more sophisticated quasi-experimental designs can be em-ployed. For example, the effectiveness of various prosecutorial policies probably cannot be examined using true random assignment; judges may see this as arbitrary justice. Changes in case dispositions within a jurisdiction pre- and post-policy change, however, could be exam-ined using time series analysis or by comparing the trends with those from similar jurisdictions that had no change in policy. We need to provide public officials with a viable alternative to funding yet another series of prevalence studies.

Cumulative Research

It is not possible for most researchers to conduct systematic research that examines different facets of wife assault, because they typically have direct access to only a single population of interest (e.g., women in shelters, or men arrested for wife assault). This limitation is unfor-tunate, as research is most influential when it is cumulative and programmatic, and the results of a study constitute one piece of a larger puzzle. We need to know, for instance, whether men who are arrested for wife assault differ systematically from wife assaulters as a whole, whether those convicted and ordered into treatment differ from those arrested; and whether those who drop out of treatment differ from those who complete it. If a single research team cannot provide the answers, then researchers must link together in a coop-erative network. As an example, in our home province of British Columbia, an agency that treats primarily voluntary wife assaulters (the Victoria Family Violence Project, under the direction of Alayne Hamilton) has joined forces with another that treats primarily court-mandated men (the Vancouver Assaultive Husbands Project, under the direction of Don Dutton) in order to collect evaluative information that will directly benefit both programs. The research findings will also be more generalizable than those based on data from a single program. (For readers interested in a model of programmatic interven-tion research, we recommend the one developed by Gottman and Markman, 1978).

Battered Women as Service Consumers

As we foreshadowed earlier, one fascinating area of research, addressed only briefly by Jaffe et al. (this volume), looks at battered women's perceptions of the services they receive from various social service agencies. Part of our enthusiasm for consumer satisfaction research is that it explicitly recognizes the importance of the consumer and her beliefs and attitudes, which is consistent with the more general philosophy of empowering battered women. Also, such research has direct relevance for the improvement of service delivery, as recommended changes can be incorporated into practice almost immediately. Topics studied previously in this area include the following: battered women's health care needs and their evaluation of the effectiveness of health care received from physicians (Bowker & Maurer, 1987; McFarlane, 1989; Rodriguez, 1989); satisfaction with services received from shelters and the effect of these services on battered women's decisions regarding postshelter residence and marital status, and factors associated with readmission to shelters (Compton, Michael, Krasavage-Hopkins, Schneiderman, & Bickman, 1989; Gondolf, 1988a; Russell, 1990; Stone, 1984; Wilson, Baglioni, & Downing, 1989); a comparative evaluation of pastoral, mental health, and self-help counseling programs (Bowker & Maurer, 1986); and satisfaction with legal services (Bowker, 1987; Horton, K. M. Simonidis, & L. L. Simonidis, 1987).

Prevention

This is an area excluded from the current volume that has important implications for intervention. We recognize the need for interventions that are reactive in nature, that deal with women and their violent partner after an assault has occurred. Reactive programs, however, are necessarily limited in their scope. To use a medical analogy, if wife assault is an illness, this book is all about treating sick patients once they come into hospital; it does not tell us what causes the illness, how to prevent patients catching it in the first place, or how to identify those affected before they require hospitalization. (In some respects, this is like responding to an outbreak of cholera by building more hospitals and morgues rather than by vaccinating those at risk.) We must keep in mind that only a small proportion of wife assaults (Dutton, 1988, estimates about 15%) is reported to the police in the first place, and the proportion resulting in arrest is smaller still (a measly 1.2%). Thus, the vast majority of wife assault may never be officially detected by criminal justice or social service agencies, even though it may have a profound negative effect on the physical and psychological well-being of battered women and their children. Other than to encourage the reporting of assaults through public education and awareness, the only thing we can do for these "unknown victims" is to prevent assaults occurring in the first place.

Of course, before we begin large-scale prevention programs, we need to know how to identify people at risk for perpetrating violence or being assaulted, and also what factors are causally related to wife assault. This may not be as difficult to find out as it may seem. Perhaps the single most robust finding in the family violence literature is that children who experience or witness violence appear to be at a significantly increased risk for assaulting others or becoming victims as adults (e.g., Hotaling & Sugarman, 1986; Widom, 1989). There is some evidence that this "cycle of violence" operates through a social learning mechanism, whereby children are reinforced for using instrumental violence in situations of conflict, incorporate social values that justify or excuse violence, or fail to learn alternative psychological coping skills (Christopoulous et al., 1987; Dutton & Hart, 1992b; Jaffe, Wilson, & Wolfe, 1988; Stagg, Wills, & Howell, 1989; Suh & Abel, 1990). Programs for children at risk of violence have already been piloted. One program provided 10 weekly 1½-hour groups that dealt with issues such as feelings, anger, safety skills, social support, social competence and self-concept, and understanding family violence (Jaffe et al., 1988). Mothers perceived improvement in the children, and the children themselves reported more safety skill strategies and had more positive perceptions of both parents; however, the children's behavior was not measurably improved on the Child Behavior Checklist. Another potential mode of intervention attempted for children of battered women has been a reception classroom to provide continuity in education during the time of stay at a shelter. Kates and Pepler (1989) described a secure, confidential setting with peers of a similar background where a great deal of individualized educational and socially and emotionally supportive assistance was given.

Attempts to address concerns such as problem-solving difficulties were also considered. Programs such as these might benefit from research looking at why many, perhaps even most, children who witness wife assault avoid violence as adults (children who could be characterized as "hardy").

There is also some need for more general prevention programs that target children with no obvious risk factors. For example, Walther (1986) described an education program designed to change the attitudes of high school boys that led them to excuse some aspects of wife assault and to place partial blame on the victim. She found that viewing a film about battered women and the myths surrounding wife assault did not significantly change attitudes. One possible explanation is that the instrument used to assess attitudes may not have been sufficiently sensitive to detect change, but it is also likely that a more potent intervention is required. This might include a more in-depth discussion of sex roles, social stereotypes, gender equality, and interpersonal problem-solving skills (Walther, 1986). Unfortunately, it is difficult to assess the effect of such prevention programs on actual wife assault, as a long follow-up period is required; researchers could instead broaden the nature of the dependent variable to include dating violence or other forms of violence against women, which may have appreciable base rates in high school boys (e.g., Jaffe & Reitzel, 1990). Future attempts at prevention could target young adult couples, who have appreciable rates of wife assault even over relatively short periods of time (O'Leary & Arias, 1985).

Training of Service Providers

Research indicates that many professionals, including lawyers, physicians, nurses, police, and counselors, may hold inaccurate, stereotyped, or negative attitudes concerning battered women and their needs (Bowker, 1987; Bowker & Maurer, 1987; Kurz, 1987; Lavoie, Jacob, Hardy, & Martin, 1989; Saunders & Size, 1986; Trute, Sarsfield, & MacKenzie, 1988; Walker, 1981). These attitudes may adversely affect the quality of services they provide to battered women. For example, given that many urban police forces devote some portion of their recruit training and continuing education programs to the topic of wife assault, researchers have an opportunity to evaluate various training models (e.g., didactic versus experiential, presentations by battered women) and their effect on attitudes and behavior (Stith, 1990). In a similar vein, Trute, Sarsfield, & Mackenzie (1988) suggest implementing (and evaluating) wife assault awareness programs for physicians. They believe that physicians must be encouraged to inquire directly about assault when they examine women with suspicious injuries, to take an extensive history once a case of wife assault has been identified, and to refer victims to the appropriate community agencies.

Another neglected area is training programs for probation and parole officers. Recent research conducted in British Columbia indicates that a high proportion of the caseload of probation officers consists of men who can be considered "wife assaulters" (i.e., who have an official record of actual, attempted, or threatened wife assault). For example, Dutton and Hart (1992a, 1992b), using a file review procedure, found that about 20% of men incarcerated in Canadian federal prisons have a history of physical violence against family members; the vast majority of these offenders had assaulted intimate partners. In another study conducted by the Mental Health, Law, and Policy Institute (1992), a probability sample consisting of 10% of all adult offenders (men and women) on bail, probation, and parole in one region of the British Columbia Corrections Branch was surveyed using a file review procedure to determine the prevalence of spouse assault. Interestingly, all the recorded incidents involved wife assault—no women had a history of husband assault. Of the men, 17.6% had a current charge or conviction for spouse assault; when past offenses were also included, the figure rose to 21.5%. Given the large number of wife assaulters and their psychological characteristics (such as minimization and denial), corrections agencies may need to develop specialized training to help probation officers identify and manage wife assaulters, as well as to develop strategies for protecting battered women and referring them to the appropriate service agencies.

Conclusion

Wife assault is a problem that has tremendous costs both for battered women and for society at large. Past research has played an important role in forcing society to accept that this problem exists; now, we must redouble our efforts to demonstrate conclusively that appropriate intervention is possible. The previous chapters in this book represent the first steps toward this goal, and the contributors should be congratulated for their work. We hope that our comments may motivate other researchers to join in the search for solutions.

References

Bowker, L. H. (1987). Battered women as consumers of legal services: Reports from a national survey. *Response, 10,* 10-17.

Bowker, L. H., & Maurer, L. (1986). The effectiveness of counseling services utilized by battered women. *Women and Therapy, 5,* 65-82.

Bowker, L. H., & Maurer, L. (1987). The medical treatment of battered wives. *Women and Health, 12,* 25-45.

Christopoulos, C., Cohn, D. A., Shaw, D. S., Joyce, S., Sullivan-Hanson, J., Kraft, S. P., & Emery, R. E. (1987). Children of abused women: I. Adjustment at time of shelter residence. *Journal of Marriage and the Family, 49,* 611-619.

Compton, W. C., Michael, J. R., Krasavage-Hopkins, E. M., Schneiderman, L. S., & Bickman, L. (1989). Intentions for postshelter living in battered women. *Journal of Community Psychology, 17,* 126-128.

Dutton, D. G. (1988). Profiling of wife assaulters: Preliminary evidence for a trimodal analysis. *Violence and Victims, 3,* 5-29.

Dutton, D. G., & Hart, S. D. (1992a). Evidence for long-term, specific effects of childhood abuse on criminal behavior in men. *International Journal of Offender Therapy and Comparative Criminology, 36,* 129-137.

Dutton, D. G., & Hart, S. D. (1992b). Risk markers for family violence in a federally incarcerated population. *International Journal of Law and Psychiatry, 15,* 101-112.

Ewing, C. P. (1990). Psychological self-defense: A proposed justification for battered women who kill. *Law and Human Behavior, 14,* 579-594.

Eysenck, H. J. (1952). The effects of psychotherapy: An evaluation. *Journal of Consulting Psychology, 16,* 319-324.

Frieze, I. H., & Browne, A. (1989). Violence in marriage. In L. Ohlin & M. Tonry (Eds.), *Family violence* (pp. 163-218). Chicago: University of Chicago Press.

Gondolf, E. W. (1988a). The effect of batterer counseling on shelter outcome. *Journal of Interpersonal Violence, 3,* 275-289.

Gondolf, E. W. (1988b). Who are those guys? Toward a behavioral typology of batterers. *Violence and Victims, 3,* 187-203.

Gottman, J., & Markman, H. J. (1978). Experimental designs in psychotherapy research. In S. L. Garfield & A. E. Bergin (Eds.), *Handbook of psychotherapy and behavior change* (pp. 23-62). New York: John Wiley.

Horton, A. L., Simonidis, K. M., & Simonidis, L. L. (1987). Legal remedies for spousal abuse: Victim characteristics, expectations, and satisfaction. *Journal of Family Violence, 2,* 265-279.

Hotaling, G. T., & Sugarman, D. B. (1986). An analysis of risk markers in husband to wife violence: The current state of knowledge. *Violence and Victims, 1,* 101-124.

Jaffe, P., & Reitzel, D. (1990). Adolescents' views on how to reduce family violence. In R. Roesch, D. G. Dutton, & V. F. Sacco (Eds.), *Family violence: Perspectives on treatment, research, and policy* (pp. 51-66). Burnaby: British Columbia Institute on Family Violence.

Jaffe, P., Wilson, S. K., & Wolfe, D. (1988). Specific assessment and intervention strategies for children exposed to wife battering: Preliminary empirical investigations. *Canadian Journal of Community Mental Health, 7,* 157-163.

Kates, M., & Pepler, D. (1989, September). A reception classroom for children of battered women in emergency shelters. *Canada's Mental Health,* pp. 7-10.

Kazdin, A. E. (Ed.). (1992). *Methodological issues and strategies in clinical research.* Washington, DC: American Psychological Association.

Keisler, D. J. (1971). Experimental designs in psychotherapy research. In A. E. Bergin & S. L. Garfield (Eds.), *Handbook of psychotherapy and behavior change* (pp. 36-74). New York: John Wiley.

Kennedy, L. W., & Dutton, D. G. (1989). The incidence of wife assault in Alberta. *Canadian Journal of Behavioral Science, 21,* 40-54.

Kurz, D. (1987). Emergency department responses to battered women: Resistance to medicalization. *Social Problems, 34,* 69-81.

Lavoie, F., Jacob, M., Hardy, J., & Martin, G. (1989). Police attitudes in assigning responsibility for wife abuse. *Journal of Family Violence, 4,* 369-388.

McFarlane, J. (1989). Battering during pregnancy: Tip of an iceberg revealed. *Women and Health, 15,* 69-84.

Mental Health, Law, and Policy Institute. (1992). *Spousal assault: Prevalence and service delivery in the Fraser Region of the British Columbia Corrections Branch.* Unpublished report available from Simon Fraser University, Burnaby, BC, Canada, V5A 1S6.

Morse, S. J. (1990). The misbegotten marriage of soft psychology and bad law: Psychological self-defense as a justification for homicide. *Law and Human Behavior, 14,* 595-618.

O'Leary, K. D., & Arias, I. (1985). Prevalence, correlates, and development of spouse abuse. In J. McMahon (Ed.), *Marriage and famiilies: Behavioral treatments and processes* (pp. 112-143). New York: Brunner/Mazel.

Paul, G. L. (1967). Strategy of outcome research in psychotherapy. *Journal of Consulting Psychology, 31,* 109-118.

R. v. Lavallee, 4 W.W.R. 1 (S.C.C., 1990).

Rodriguez, R. (1989). Perception of health needs by battered women. *Response, 12,* 22-23.

Rosenfeld, B. D. (1992). Court-ordered treatment of spouse abuse. *Clinical Psychology Review, 12,* 205-226.

Russell, M. (1990, June/September). Second stage shelters: A consumer's report. *Canada's Mental Health,* pp. 24-26.

Saunders, D. G., & Size, P. B. (1986). Attitudes about woman abuse among police officers, victims, and victim advocates. *Journal of Interpersonal Problems, 1,* 25-42.

Sherman, L. W., & Berk, R. A. (1984). The specific deterrent effects of arrest for domestic assault. *American Sociological Review, 49,* 261-272.

Stagg, V., Wills, G. D., & Howell, M. (1989). Psychopathology in early childhood witnesses of family violence. *Topics in Early Childhood Special Education, 9,* 73-87.

Stith, S. M. (1990). Police response to domestic violence: The influence of individual and familial factors. *Violence and Victims, 5,* 37-49.

Stone, L. H. (1984). Shelters for battered women: A temporary escape from danger or the first step toward divorce? *Victimology: An International Journal, 9,* 284-289.

Straus, M. A., & Gelles, R. J. (1986). Societal change in family violence from 1975 to 1985 as revealed by two national surveys. *Journal of Marriage and the Family, 48,* 465-479.

Straus, M. A., Gelles, R. J., & Steinmetz, S. (1980). *Behind closed doors: Violence in the American family.* New York: Anchor.

Suh, E. K., & Abel, E. M. (1990). The impact of spousal violence on the children of the abused. *Journal of Independent Social Work, 4,* 27-34.

Tolman, R. M., & Bennett, L. W. (1990). A review of quantitative research on men who batter. *Journal of Interpersonal Violence, 5,* 87-118.

Trute, B., Sarsfield, P., & MacKenzie, D. A. (1988). Medical response to wife abuse: A survey of physicians' attitudes and practices. *Canadian Journal of Community Mental Health, 7,* 61-71.

Walker, L.E.A. (1981). Battered women: Sex roles and clinical issues. *Professional Psychology, 12,* 81-91.

Walther, D. J. (1986). Wife abuse prevention: Effects of information on attitudes of high school boys. *Journal of Primary Prevention, 7,* 84-90.

Webster, C. D., & Hilton, N. Z. (1990). Violence in the family institution: The future of research and practice. In R. Roesch, D. G. Dutton, & V. F. Sacco (Eds.), *Family violence: Perspectives on treatment, research, and policy* (pp. 173-182). Burnaby, British Columbia Institute on Family Violence.

Widom, C. S. (1989). Does violence beget violence? A critical examination of the literature. *Psychological Bulletin, 106,* 3-28.

Wilson, M. N., Baglioni, A. J., Jr., & Downing, D. (1989). Analyzing factors influencing readmission to a battered women's shelter. *Journal of Family Violence, 4,* 275-284.

Author Index

Abadinsky, H., 136
Abel, E. M., 300
Adams, D., 196, 197, 198, 199, 200, 203, 205
Adams, E. A., 276, 277
Adams, O., 167
Albonetti, C. A., 137
Alexander, J. F., 250
Allen, C. M., 17
Allen, P. G., 99
Almeida, R. V., 26
American Psychiatric Association, 247, 249
Amick-Mullen, A., 250
Anglin, K., 14
Arias, I., 301
Ashcroft, J., 97
Association of Family and Conciliation Courts, 184
Attorney General of Ontario, 181, 183
Aubrey, M., 235
Austin, G., 38, 42, 44, 76
Azar, S. T., 26, 147

Bacich, A. R., 86, 87, 93, 129, 138
Baglioni, A. J., Jr., 299

Ballou, M., 249
Bandura, A., 199
Bannon, J., 141
Bard, M., 44, 141
Barling, J., 15
Baskin, D., 168
Bassler, J., 131
Bauschard, L., 234, 236
Beauvais, C., 208, 211
Becker, T. M., 133, 147
Beeman, S., 209, 216
Bennett, L. W., 11, 13, 15, 296
Berg, B. J., 6
Berk, R. A., 4, 25, 44, 45, 73, 86, 97, 117, 128, 129, 138, 143, 195, 297
Berk, S. F., 117, 143
Bernard, J. L., 14
Bernard, M. L., 14
Bersani, L., 210, 218
Best, C. L., 250
Bhosley, G., 26
Bickman, L., 299
Binder, A., 98
Bittner, E., 105, 113
Black, D. J., 104
Blackman, J., 106, 235, 236, 242, 244, 250, 251

Black's Law Dictionary, 266
Blau, P., 176
Blood, R. E., 20
Blumberg, C. G., 169
Bochnak, E., 235, 236, 239, 240, 243, 244, 251
Bograd, M., 26, 102, 198, 199
Boland, B., 131
Bowker, L. H., 24, 108, 299, 301
Boychuk, T., 108, 116
Brady, E., 131
Brisson, N., 18, 27
Brosi, K. B., 131
Brown, L., 249, 250
Brown, M. K., 111
Browne, A., 17, 40, 102, 234, 235, 236, 242, 244, 246, 260, 262, 263, 269, 277, 279, 293
Brygger, M. P., 180, 184
Bulger, M. W., 275
Bunch, C., 235
Burgess, A., 97
Burke, M. J., 137
Burns, N., 210, 219-220
Burris, C. A., 3, 38, 63, 67, 68, 73, 76
Buzawa, C. G., 4, 38, 42, 44, 45, 137, 140
Buzawa, E. S., 4, 38, 42, 44, 45, 137, 140
Byles, J. A., 44

Caesar, P. L., 3, 18, 19, 196
Cahn, T. S., 14, 209, 215
Cain, M., 165, 167
Cain, P., 100
Campbell, A., 54
Caplan, P., 249
Caputo, R. K., 108
Carillo, T. P., 192
Carmody, D. C., 102
Carnevale, P. J., 166, 167
Carrillo, T. P., 25
Center for Women Policy Studies, 143
Cervantes, N., 249
Chadhuri, M., 101
Chapman, D. G., 208, 211

Chatterton, M. R., 44
Chen, H., 210, 218
Christopoulos, C., 300
Clairmont, D., 38
Clemmer, E., 66
Coates, C. J., 14, 209, 214
Cobb, S., 174
Cohen, E. G., 86, 87, 93
Cohn, D. A., 300
Cohn, E. G., 71, 89, 98, 129, 138, 280
Coleman, D. H., 17
Collins, B. S., 16, 198, 202, 208, 212
Collins, D. J., 86, 87, 93, 129, 138
Collins, J. J., 13
Colson, S. 140
Comment, 262, 270
Commonwealth v. Dillon, 281-282
Commonwealth v. Grove, 267
Compton, W. C., 299
Conway, Z. D., 275
Coogler, O. J., 166
Cotton, D.G.H., 243
Cover, R., 174
Crane, S. W., 117
Crawford, M., 171, 174, 175
Crime Control Institute, 98
Crocker, P. L., 260, 277
Crowley, J. M., 146
Cullen, F. T., 39, 40

Dahrendorf, R., 165
Daly, K., 101
Das Gupta, B., 48
Davidson, B., 261
Davis, P. W., 102, 114
Davison, G. C., 204
Dean, C. W., 4, 25, 44, 45, 86, 98, 130, 131
Deaton, L. H., 275
DeKeseredy, W. S., 66, 92
DeMaris, A., 25, 26, 27, 209, 214
Denton, R., 210, 218
Deschner, J. P., 197, 204, 206, 207, 208, 211
Deutch, M., 169

Dobash, R., 38, 39, 45, 63, 64, 102, 108, 141
Dobash, R. E., 38, 39, 45, 63, 64, 102, 108, 141
Doob, A. N., 48
Dow, M., 44
Downing, D., 299
Doxtator, J., 91
Dressler, J., 259, 260, 261, 262
Dreyfus, H. L., 103
DuBow, F. L., 133, 147
Dumont-Smith, C., 91
Dunford, F. W., 4, 25, 86, 98, 103, 130, 131, 138, 174, 195, 205
Dutton, D. G., 14, 15, 38, 44, 65, 66, 131, 143, 146, 147, 208, 213, 261, 262, 290, 297, 300, 302
Dutton, M. A., 244, 249

Eber, L. P., 267
Edleson, J. L., 72, 147, 195, 196, 199, 208, 209, 210, 211, 216, 218-219
Edwards, S.S.M., 38, 235
Eekelaar, J. M., 167
Eisenberg, D., 168
Eisenberg, S. E., 202
Eisikovits, Z. C., 147, 196
Elliott, D. S., 4, 25, 42, 43, 44, 86, 98, 103, 130, 131, 132, 138, 149, 174, 195, 261
Ellis, D., 44, 165, 170, 173, 178, 181, 185
Ellis, J. W., 137
Elster, J., 168
Emery, R. E., 166, 168, 169, 300
Endicott, T. A., 3
Estrich, S., 278
Ewing, C. P., 4, 235, 236, 239, 242, 244, 260, 261, 262, 263, 268, 269, 277, 278, 280, 281, 294
Eysenck, H. J., 293

Fagan, J. A., 18, 25, 38, 140, 149, 150
Faigman, D., 235, 244
Faigman, D. L., 261, 269, 277, 282

Faragher, T., 38, 44
Farge, B., 174
Faulk, M., 17
Faust, D., 235
Feazell, C. S., 204, 206
Feeley, M. M., 129
Felstiner, W., 176
Ferraro, K. J., 45, 102, 105, 108, 110, 111, 116
Feshbach, S., 196
Field, H. F., 130, 141
Field, M. H., 130, 141
Figley, C., 247, 250
Figlio, R. M., 39, 40
Finkel, N. J., 273, 274, 275, 278
Finkelhor, D., 6, 10, 247, 248
Finlay, J., 68, 74
Finn, P., 140
Flanagan, N., 97
Fleming, J. B., 63, 64, 67, 69, 70, 89
Fletcher, G., 260
Flitcraft, A., 279
Fodor, I. G., 248
Folberg, H. J., 166, 167, 169
Follingstad, D. R., 6, 275
Ford, D. A., 120, 130, 131, 137, 138, 140, 141, 142, 149, 150, 156, 157
Foster, R. A., 194
Foucault, M., 103
Fowler, R. D., 235
Franks, D., 197, 199, 203, 205
Friedman, D. H., 16, 198, 202, 208, 212
Friedman, E., 149, 150
Friedman, L. N., 129, 131, 149
Frieze, I. H., 17, 40, 262, 293
Fromson, T. L., 130
Fruchtman, L. A., 24

Galaway, B., 139
Gamache, D. J., 72
Ganley, A., 189, 190, 191, 196, 202, 203
Garner, J., 66, 129
Gartin, P. R., 86, 87, 93, 129, 138
Gartner, R., 171, 174, 175
Gaudreault, A., 56

Gayford, J. J., 130
Gebotys, R. J., 48
Geffner, R. A., 197, 199, 203, 205
Geller, J. A., 198
Gelles, R. J., 10, 11, 12, 13, 16, 17, 20,
    39, 76, 141, 262, 270, 279, 297
Gentemann, K. M., 39, 40
George, A., 91
Giller, E. L., 241
Gillespie, C. K., 260, 262, 263, 269
Gilligan, C., 100
Girdner, L., 184
Gleberman, L., 14, 262
Glendon, M. A., 167
Goldfried, M. R., 204
Goldman, J., 198
Gondolf, E. W., 16, 18, 19, 194, 200,
    201, 290, 299
Goode, W., 165
Goolkasian, G. A., 131, 138, 139, 235
Gordon, L., 46, 262
Gottfredson, M., 13
Gottlieb, D. J., 138
Gottman, J., 298
Grau, J., 25, 140
Gray, E., 170
Green, B., 251
Greenblat, C. S., 39, 40
Greene, J. R., 39
Greenwald, H. J., 20
Greenwald, J. P., 270, 271, 272
Greenwalt, K., 260
Gruhl, J., 137
Grusznki, R. J., 25, 192, 209, 216
Gulliver, P. H., 166

Hackett, D., 171
Hagan, J., 137
Hall, D. J., 130
Halpern, M., 207, 208
Hamberger, L. K., 3, 14, 16, 19, 26,
    189, 190, 191, 192, 193, 194,
    195, 196, 199, 200, 209, 210, 217
Hanmer, J., 98
Hanneke, C. R., 16, 18
Hansen, K. V., 18

Hansen, M., 249
Hanusa, D. R., 15, 209, 213-214
Hardy, J., 41, 42, 59, 301
Harris, M. B., 54
Hart, B. J., 140
Hart, S. D., 300, 302
Hart, W. J., 97
Hartmann, D., 196
Harvey, M. R., 250
Harway, M., 249
Hastings, J. E., 14, 16, 19, 26, 189,
    190, 192, 193, 194, 195, 209,
    210, 217
Hause, E. S., 6, 275
Hawkins, R., 208, 211
Helmreich, R. L., 20
Herman, J. L., 241, 250
Hershorn, M., 19
Hilton, N. Z., 5, 45, 46, 130, 135, 171,
    173, 296
Hinch, R., 66, 92
Hirschel, J. D., 4, 25, 44, 45, 86, 98,
    130, 131
Hirschi, T., 13
Ho, C. K., 251
Hofeller, K. H., 18, 19
Holtzworth-Munroe, A., 14
Horton, A. L., 299
Hoskins, J., 209, 214
Hotaling, G. T., 11, 12, 16, 17, 300
Howard, J., 250
Howell, M., 300
Huizinga, D., 4, 25, 86, 98, 103, 130,
    131, 138, 174, 195
Humphreys, J. C., 44
Humphreys, W. O., 44
Hutchison, I. W., 4, 25, 44, 45, 86, 98,
    130, 131

Irving, H., 166
Island, D., 202

Jackson, J. K., 26, 27, 209, 214
Jacob, M., 41, 42, 59, 301
Jacoby, J., 136

Jaffe, P. G., 3, 15, 38, 42, 44, 63, 67, 68, 73, 74, 76, 92, 250, 280, 300, 301
Jaggar, A. M., 100
Janoff-Bulman, R., 250
Jenkins, P., 261
Jennings, J. L., 203, 204
John, R. S., 14
Johnson, I., 146
Johnson, J. M., 102, 108, 210, 219
Johnson, L. E., 138
Jones, A., 234, 236
Joyce, S., 300

Kado, R., 197
Kanzler, D. J., 210, 219
Kates, M., 300
Katz, S. N., 167
Kazdin, A. E., 290, 293
Keisler, D. J., 293
Keita, G. P., 248
Kelly, J., 177, 178
Kelly, J. B., 178
Kelly, L., 102, 106
Kelso, D., 208, 212
Kennedy, L. W., 297
Kenning, M. K., 270, 271, 272, 280
Killip, S., 92
Kilpatrick, D. G., 250
Kinports, K., 260, 261, 262, 269, 273, 277
Koss, M. P., 250
Kosten, T. R., 241
Kraft, S. P., 300
Krasavage-Hopkins, E. M., 299
Kressel, K., 172
Krystal, J. H., 241
Kuehl, S. J., 180, 184
Kulscar, K., 165, 167
Kurz, D., 301

Labelle, P., 91
LaFave, W. R., 259, 261, 262, 280
Lane, G., 198, 199, 202, 204
Lang-Gun, L., 250

Langley, R., 67, 68
Larsen, N. E., 193
Lavoie, F., 41, 42, 59, 301
Leidig, M. W., 249
Leighton, B. N., 39, 76
Leong, D. J., 14, 209, 214
Lerman, L. G., 129, 130, 131, 137, 139, 140, 141, 142, 143, 168, 172, 173, 180, 184
Letellier, P., 202
Levens, B. R., 44
Levinson, D., 17
Levy, R. C., 67, 68
Lewis, V. L., 149, 150
Lightfoot, D. M., 273, 274, 275, 278
Lindquist, C. U., 16
Lindsey, M., 14
Link, B. G., 39, 40
Liss, M., 247
Littrell, W. B., 104, 111, 112
Livingston, F., 129
Loeber, R., 53
Lohr, J. M., 14, 199, 200
Loseke, D. R., 117, 143
Lund, S. H., 193
Lyon, T., 176

MacDougall, D. J., 175
MacKenzie, D. A., 301, 302
MacKinnon, C. A., 100, 235
MacLeod, L., 3, 4, 5, 44, 64, 71, 89, 129
Maguigan, H., 235, 236, 239, 250, 260, 261, 269, 270, 277, 278, 279, 280, 282
Mahoney, M. R., 235, 239, 250
Maiuro, R. D., 14, 209, 215
Mantooth, C., 197, 199, 203, 205
Margolin, G., 14, 247, 248, 262
Marin, G., 41, 42, 59
Markman, H. J., 298
Martin, D., 29, 68, 71, 190, 196, 197, 204, 261
Martin, G., 301
Mas, C. H., 250
Mason, J. W., 241
Mastrofski, S. D., 39

Matarazzo, J. D., 235
Maurer, L., 299, 301
Mayers, R. S., 204, 206
McCall, G. J., 18
McConnell, J. E., 235, 239, 250
McCormick, A., 203
McDonald, W. F., 135
McEvoy, J., 40
McFarlane, J., 299
McGillivray, A., 4, 135
McGrath, E., 248
McGregor, B.M.S., 146, 147, 261
McWhinney, R. L., 166, 170
Meeker, J. W., 98
Meese, C., 97
Meister, K. H., 273, 274, 275, 278
Mendoza, C., 209, 216
Mental Health, Law, and Policy Institute, 302
Merchant, A., 280
Meredith, C., 77, 210, 219-220
Michael, J. R., 299
Micklow, P. L., 70, 72, 202
Miletich, E., 139
Miller, D. M., 208, 211
Miller, M., 247, 248
Milton, C., 97
Minow, M., 100
Mnookin, R., 168
Monahan, J., 235
Mones, P., 250
Moore, M. S., 260
Moran, P., 247, 248
Morse, S. J., 259, 260, 261, 262, 269, 277, 294
Muncer, S., 54
Murphy, C., 17
Musheno, M., 102
Myers, M. A., 137
Myers, S. C., 210, 218

Nagnur, D., 167
Narramore, C., 97
Neidig, P. H., 16, 198, 202, 208, 212
Neubauer, D. W., 131
Nordholt, E., 38

Note, 259, 261, 277
Novaco, R. W., 20, 201

Ochberg, F., 247
O'Donovan, K., 277, 279
O'Leary, K. D., 16, 17, 301
Ontario Association of Interval and Transition Houses, 182
Oppenlander, N., 44
Ortega, R., 97
Ortega, R. B., 109
Owens, G., 90

Pagelow, M. D., 106, 242
Pantony, K., 249
Parker, J. C., 26, 192, 193, 194
Parnas, R. I., 141
Paterson, E. J., 64, 65, 67, 88
Paul, G. L., 293
Payne, J., 166, 167, 168, 170
Pence, E., 3, 139, 140, 189, 190, 202
People v. Aris, 267, 277, 282
People v. Emick, 268
People v. Scott, 268
People v. Yates, 276, 277
Pepler, D., 300
Perry, B. D., 241
Personette, L., 208, 212
Pillemer, K., 13
Pirog-Good, M., 206-207
Pizzey, E., 38
Pleck, E., 45, 46, 129, 262
Polanzi, C. W., 39, 40
Polek, D. S., 6, 275
Pound, R., 166
Price, R. L., 235
Pruitt, D., 166, 167, 172
Ptacek, J., 5
Pulling, N., 91

R. v. Lavallee, 294
Rabinow, P., 103
Radford, J., 98

Radulovich, E., 139
Rahder, B., 174
Rao, L., 197, 199, 203, 205
Rauma, D., 117, 131, 136, 137, 143, 145
Red Horse, J., 99
Regoli, M. J., 142, 149, 150, 156, 157
Reitzel, D., 92, 301
Resick, H. S., 250
Rheinstein, M., 167
Rich, A., 106
Rifkin, J., 166
Roberts, A. R., 65, 88
Roberts, D., 90
Roberts, D. V., 48
Roberts, J. V., 48
Robinson, J. G., 281
Robinson, P. H., 259, 260, 261, 281
Rochon, C., 38, 39, 57
Rodriguez, R., 299
Rogan, D. P., 86, 87, 93, 98, 129, 138
Root, M.P.P., 248, 249, 250
Rosen, C. J., 260, 261, 262
Rosenbaum, A., 15, 19, 208, 213
Rosenfeld, B. D., 296
Rosenfeldt, G., 5
Rosewater, L. B., 235, 244, 245, 249
Russell, D., 200, 201
Russell, D.E.H., 6, 102
Russell, M., 299
Russell, T., 198, 199, 202, 203, 204
Russo, N. F., 248
Rutledge, L. L., 6
Ryan, W., 235

Sarat, A., 176
Sarsfield, P., 301, 302
Satow, Y., 20
Saunders, B. E., 250
Saunders, D. G., 12, 15, 19, 21, 26, 29, 40, 41, 42, 58, 117, 147, 192, 193, 194, 201, 202, 204, 209, 213-214, 235, 301
Scales, A., 100
Schafran, L. H., 101, 235
Schatzow, E., 241

Schechter, S., 3, 4
Schmidt, J. D., 86, 87, 93, 98, 129, 136, 138
Schneider, E. M., 235, 236, 239, 242, 244, 250, 260, 262, 277
Schneiderman, L. S., 299
Schock, M. D., 72
Schopp, R. F., 260
Schuller, R. A., 275, 278, 279
Schultz, S. K., 193
Scott, A. W., Jr., 259, 261, 262, 280
Sedlak, A. J., 280
Seeley, K., 102
Seligman, M.E.P., 243, 245, 246
Seward, F., 97
Shaw, D. S., 300
Shepard, M., 209, 215
Sherman, L. W., 4, 25, 44, 45, 73, 86, 87, 93, 97, 98, 128, 130, 138, 195, 280, 297
Sherman, R., 277, 279
Shields, N. M., 16, 18
Shulman, M., 129, 131, 149
Shupe, A., 208, 211
Sibner, L. G., 262
Sigler, R. T., 146
Simonidis, K. M., 299
Simonidis, L. L., 299
Sinclair, D., 182
Singer, S. I., 39, 40
Size, P. B., 40, 41, 58, 301
Smith, C., 12, 27
Smith, M., 185
Smith, M. D., 17
Smith, T. W., 54
Smyth, M., 65
Snyder, D. K., 24
Soler, E., 69, 72, 189
Solicitor General of Ontario, 174
Sommers, I., 168
Sonkin, D. J., 29, 190, 196, 197, 204, 235, 242
Southwick, S., 241
Spence, J. T., 20
Spero, M., 91
Spiegel, D., 241
Spohn, C., 137

Staats, A., 199
Stacey, W. A., 208, 211
Stagg, V., 300
Stahly, G., 247
Stallone, D., 173
Stanko, E. A., 98, 102, 105
Staples, D., 90
Stark, E., 279
Stark, R., 40
State v. Allery, 268
State v. Gallegos, 268
State v. Hennum, 268
State v. Kelly, 281
State v. Leidholm, 268
State v. Norman, 263, 264, 266, 267,
    268, 270, 277, 281
State v. Stewart, 267
State v. Wanrow, 239, 281
Steinberg, A., 135, 141
Steinfeld, G. J., 29
Steinman, M., 131
Steinmetz, S. K., 10, 11, 12, 13, 16, 17,
    20, 39, 76, 141, 262, 270, 279,
    297
Stets, J., 206-207
Steury, E. H., 136
Stewart, D. K., 18
Stille, R., 29
Stith, S. M., 42, 66, 114, 302
Stone, G. W., 208, 211
Stone, L. H., 299
Stordeur, R. A., 29
Strachan, C. E., 14
Straus, M. A., 5, 10, 11, 12, 13, 15, 16,
    17, 20, 27, 39, 76, 141, 261, 262,
    270, 279, 297
Straver, R., 38
Strickland, B., 248
Stuckless, N., 165, 178, 181, 185
Sudermann, M., 92
Sugarman, D. B., 11, 12, 16, 17, 300
Suh, E. K., 300
Suitor, J. J., 13
Sullivan-Hanson, J., 300
Syers, M., 195, 210, 218-219

Taylor, A., 166, 169
Taylor, R. B., 39
Telch, C. F., 16
Telford, A., 38, 42, 44, 76
Thyfault, R., 235
Tolman, R. M., 11, 13, 15, 26, 201, 202,
    209, 210, 216, 217-218, 296
Tomkins, A. J., 270, 271, 272, 280
Tracy, P. E., 39, 40
Tremblay, P., 38, 39, 57
Trute, B., 301, 302
Turner, C. W., 250
Tyson, H., 131

U.S. Attorney General's Task Force on
    Family Violence, 127-128, 131,
    143, 148, 235
U.S. Department of Justice, 270
Utz, P., 160

van der Kolk, B. A., 23, 241, 247
Van Maanen, J., 105
Veronen, L. J., 250
Vidmar, N. J., 275, 278, 279
Visher, C. A., 129
Vitaliano, P. P., 14, 209, 215
Vivian, D., 16

Walker, L.E.A., 17, 29, 106, 190, 196,
    197, 204, 234, 235, 236, 237,
    238, 241, 242, 243, 244, 245,
    246, 247, 249, 250, 279, 301
Walker, L. W., 130
Wallerstein, J., 178
Walther, D. J., 301
War Against Women, The, 171, 172,
    174
Wasoff, F., 131
Wasserstrom, J., 198
Webster, C. D., 296
Welch, S., 137
West, R., 100

Wexler, S., 25, 140, 149, 150
White, G. L., 20
Widom, C. S., 300
Williams, K., 234, 246
Williams, K. M., 131
Williams, K. R., 102
Williamson, S., 77
Wills, G. D., 300
Wilson, J. Q., 104
Wilson, M. N., 299
Wilson, S. K., 15, 92, 250, 280, 300
Wolfe, D., 68, 74, 280, 300
Wolfe, D. A., 15, 38, 42, 44, 76, 92, 250
Wolfe, D. M., 20

Wolfgang, M. E., 39, 40
Women's Law Caucus, University of Montana, 138
Woods, L., 98
Wright, C., 138
Wright, J., 27
Wyer, M. M., 166, 168, 169

Ylló, K., 6, 10, 17, 102, 247, 248

Zavodny, D., 270, 271, 272
Zegree, J. B., 209, 215
Ziskin, J., 235

Subject Index

Aboriginal women:
  as victims of violence, 91, 94, 291
African Americans:
  wife assault among, 12, 250
Age:
  and assaultive behavior, 13
Alcohol consumption:
  and assaultive behavior, 13, 14, 18,
    27, 246
American Bar Association, 69
American Psychiatric Association, 249
Anderson, M., 276
Antistalking laws, 247
Arizona:
  domestic violence of, 111
Arizona state legislature:
  domestic violence bill of, 109
Arrest policy effectiveness:
  of London Police Force, 74
Assaultive behavior:
  age and, 13
  alcohol consumption and, 13, 14,
    18, 27
  behavioral deficits and, 13-14, 18
  child abuse and, 15, 18
  childhood violence and, 11, 18, 27
  class and, 11-13

decision-making power and, 17
depression and, 16
education level and, 12
patriarchal attitudes and, 17, 18
power imbalance and, 17, 18
psychopathology and, 14, 18
relationship conflict and, 16, 18,
  165
risk markers for, 10-18, 290
self-esteem and, 16, 18
sexual assault and, 16, 18
stress and, 15-16
violent crime and, 17
Assaults:
  frequency of, 24
  severity of, 23-24
Association of Family and Conciliation
    Courts, 166
Attitudes Toward Women Scale, 20

Battered child movement, 46
Battered child syndrome, 250
Battered woman self-defense standard,
    241-245
  assessment and, 244-245
  imminent danger and, 243-244, 293

standard of reasonableness and, 242-243
Battered woman syndrome, 244, 247-249, 293
    and PTSD, 247, 252, 293
    and women who kill their partners, 4
    diagnosis of, 249-251
    effect of on state of mind, 251, 252
    presentation of in courts of law, 251-252
    use of as defense in trials, 233
Battered women:
    as defendants, 233-253
    as service consumers, 299
    levels of responsibility of defendant, 236-241
    major symptom clusters of, 248
    manslaughter charges against, 238-239
    murder charges against, 237-238
    PTSD in, 250
Battered Women's Advocacy Clinic (London, Ontario), 84, 86
Battered women's movement, 46, 70
Battered Women's Project (Milwaukee), 70, 86-87
Battered women trials (for women who kill partners):
    current status of psychological self-defense in, 276-278
    duress defenses in, 239-240, 244
    empirical research on psychological self-defense in, 269-270
    excuse defense in, 236, 259, 260, 261, 262
    expert witnesses in, 235, 252, 253, 293
    justification defense in, 236, 259, 261, 262
    limitations to traditional self-defense in, 261-268
    mental health defenses in, 240-241
    psychological self-defense in, 261, 268-269, 278-279, 294
    self-defense jury instructions in, 258-280, 293

Beck Depression Inventory, 20, 224
Behavioral deficits:
    and assaultive behavior, 13-14, 18
Blue-collar workers:
    and wife assault, 12
Boston, 63
British Columbia, 198, 302
British Columbia Corrections Branch, 302
Buss-Durkee Hostility Inventory, 15

California:
    as no-fault divorce state, 169
    no self-defense jury instructions in, 267
Canada Evidence Act, 71
Canadian Advisory Council on the Status of Women, 70
Canadian Association of Chiefs of Police, 71
Canadian Council on Muslim Women, 91
Canadian Divorce Act of 1986, 169, 171
Canadian federal prisons, 302
Canadian Ministry of the Solicitor General, 71
Celeste, R., 277
Charlotte, North Carolina, experiment, 130
Chicago, 63
Child abuse:
    and assaultive behavior, 15, 18
Childhood violence:
    and assaultive behavior, 11, 18, 27
Children's Law Reform Act, 170, 183
Child sexual abuse accommodation syndrome, 250
Citizen Complaint Center (Washington, D.C.), 69-70
Civil/restraining orders, 67.
    See also Orders of protection (OP)
Class:
    and assaultive behavior, 11-13
Community support:
    victims' perspectives on, 84-86

Conflict Tactics Scale, 20, 76, 81, 207, 213, 214, 217, 223
Connecticut, 72
Coordinating Committee on Family Violence (London, Ontario), 73
Court process:
    victims' experience/satisfaction with, 82-83
Court Reform Task Force, 167
Coverture, doctrine of, 63
Culture of power, 96, 97
    and relational culture, 101-103, 111, 121
    definition of, 101
    imposition of, 109-119
    law and, 99-101
    police as agents of, 103-105

Decision-making power:
    and assaultive behavior, 17
Depression:
    and assaultive behavior, 16
    victimization of women and, 248
Divorce test, 66
Domestic Abuse Project of Minneapolis, 72-73
Domestic violence:
    definition of, 182
    identification of risk markers for, 30
Domestic violence counselors:
    certification of in Colorado, 198
    training of, 301-302
Domestic Violence Emergency Response System (Winnipeg, Manitoba), 90
Domestic violence treatment, 293
    anger-management approach to, 200-202
    cognitive-behavioral therapy, 199-200
    different approaches to, 195-205
    early surveys on outcomes of, 206-207
    insight-oriented therapy, 197
    in U.S. Marine Corps, 212

outcome research problems and, 220-225
outcomes of, 205-225
profeminist perspectives on, 202-203
studies on outcome of, 207-220
systems/interactional therapy, 197-199
theoretical issues and, 196-203
treatment format issues in, 203-205
ventilation therapy, 196
Duluth, Minnesota, 3, 140
Duluth Domestic Abuse Intervention Program (DAIP), 215
Dutton, D., 298

Edmonton, Alberta, 90
Education level:
    and assaultive behavior, 12

Fair Justice Acts, The, 153
Family Law:
    wife assault and, 170
Family Mediation Canada, 167, 177
    clients of, 178
Family Service London (Ontario), 84, 86
Fawcett, F., 236
FBI, 66
Forum on Concerns About Mediation in Cases of Abuse to Women and Children, 184

Garcia, I., 243
Griegg, M., 233, 234

Hamilton, A., 298
Hamilton Unified Family Court, 167, 166, 167, 178
    court-based mediation services of, 166
Hess, C., 238
Hispanic Americans:

wife assault among, 12
Hughes, F., 236
Husbands who assault, 9-30

Idaho, 240
Illinois:
   self-defense jury instructions in, 268
Indianapolis, 139, 143
   drop-permitted policy in, 153, 157
   victim-initiated complaints in, 132,
      137
Indianapolis Domestic Violence Prose-
      cution Experiment, 150-151,
      156, 157, 159
Interventions:
   behavioral, 29
   cognitive, 29
   criminal justice, 25
   for emotionally volatile wife assault-
      ers, 29
   for family-only type wife assaulters,
      28-29
   for generalized aggressor wife
      assaulters, 28
   response to different types of, 24-27

Jurisprudence, U.S.:
   androcentric, 100
   bias against women in, 101

Kansas:
   no self-defense jury instructions in,
      267

Landau, B., 184
Law, the:
   and culture of power, 99-101
Law enforcement:
   as culture of power, 96
Learned helplessness theory, 245
   adult factors, 246
   childhood factors, 245
Legal Aid (Ontario), 178

London, Ontario, 3, 63, 73, 74, 82, 83,
      87, 88, 90
   primary prevention programs in, 92
London Cultural Interpretation Ser-
      vice, 76
London Family Consultant Service, 74
London Family Court Clinic, 73, 76
London Police Force, 73, 75, 76, 77, 90
   and attitudes regarding mandate, 78-
      80
   and effectiveness of arrest policy, 74
   and response of victims of violence,
      81-86
   and victim's experience/satisfaction
      with court process, 82-83
   criminal records of, 77
   Patrol Operations Branch Survey on
      Partner Assault, 77
   response of to charging policy, 77-
      78
   Uniform Division of, 77
Los Angeles Conciliation Court, 166

Mandatory arrest policies, 4
Maricopa Task Force Against Domestic
      Violence, 119
Marion County, Indiana:
   criminal justice system of, 143
   domestic violence program in, 143,
      146
Marion County, Indiana, prosecutor's
      office:
   no-drop policy of, 144-145
Marital conflict (divorce) mediation,
      166-170, 292
   analysis of effect of wife assault on,
      181-184
   reasons for growth of, 167-170
   research on effect of on wife
      assault, 176-178
   theory of effect of on wife assault,
      172-176
Marital Conflict Index, 20
Marital Decision-making Power Scale,
      20
Marital rape, 24

Marlowe-Crowne Social Desirability
    Scale, 20, 22, 214
Masochistic Personality Disorder, 249
Michigan Alcohol Screening Test, 20
Millon Clinical Multiaxial Inventory
    (MCMI), 14, 19, 20, 22, 26, 217,
    222
Milwaukee police experiment, 130
Minneapolis Citizens' Dispute Settle-
    ment Project, 69, 86
Minneapolis Domestic Abuse Program
    (DAP), 216
Minneapolis Domestic Violence Experi-
    ment, 97, 98, 129, 138
Minneapolis Police Experiment, 25, 86
Minnesota:
    self-defense jury instructions in, 268
Minnesota Multiphasic Personality
    Inventory (MMPI), 14, 19, 222
M'Naghten Rule, 240
Morella, C., 253
Mutual combat, 117

National Clearinghouse for the Defense
    of Battered Women, 279
National Institute of Justice, 65, 86, 97,
    98
Nevada, 240
New Mexico:
    self-defense jury instructions in, 268
New York:
    homicide trial, 276
    self-defense jury instructions in, 268
New York City Police Department, 71
No-drop prosecution policies, vii, 4
Norman, J., 263-265, 266, 267, 269,
    280
Norman, J. T., 263-265
North Carolina:
    State v. Norman case in, 263-267
North Carolina appellate courts, 264
North Carolina Court of Appeals, 266
North Carolina law, 267
North Carolina self-defense law, 266
North Carolina Supreme Court, 266,
    269, 270

North Dakota:
    self-defense jury instructions in,
        268
Novaco Anger Index, 15, 20, 215, 224

Oakland Police Department training
    bulletin, 88
Omaha study of police response, 102-
    103, 130, 138
Ontario, Canada, 65
Ontario Association of Family Media-
    tors, 184
Ontario Attorney General, Committee
    on Mediation in Family Law of,
    181
Ontario Family Law Act of 1986, 183
Orders of protection (OP), 100-101,
    115, 140
Ostfoff, S., 279

Papp, A., 91
Patriarchal attitudes:
    and assaultive behavior, 17, 18
Pennsylvania:
    no self-defense jury instructions in,
        267
Personality disorders:
    and assaultive behavior, 14, 18
Phoenix, Arizona, Police Department:
    presumptive arrest policy of, 109,
        111, 114
    racist attitudes in, 113
    sexist attitudes in, 113-114
Police:
    and wife assault, 37-123
    antivictim response by, 42, 43, 66
    as agents of culture of power, 103-
        105
    as wife assaulters, 42
    attitudes of toward wife assault, 40-
        43
    battered women and, 96-121, 291
    impact of laying assault charges by,
        62-94
    mediation response by, 44, 69

Police arrest practices:
  history of, 62-63, 291
Police department policies/practices,
    63-64
  in Detroit, 64
  police training guides and, 64
Police education/training, 88-89
  community interaction and, 89-91
  in Canada, 88-89
  in Oakland, California, 88
  in Saskatchewan, 89
Police intervention, 43-45, 57-58
  and public opinion, 37-59
  training course (San Jose, Califor-
    nia), 68
Police response, 93
  criminal justice system support and,
    64-65
  external politics and, 118-119
  factors influencing, 64-68
  ideological considerations and, 112-
    116
  in Kansas, 66
  in Kansas City, 69
  internal politics and, 118
  legal considerations and, 111-112
  organizational factors and, 67-68
  police attitudes and, 66-67
  police injury and, 65-66
  practical considerations and, 116-
    118
  victim injury and, 64
  victim's wishes and, 67
  women's perceptions of, 119-120
Policing:
  as social service, 38
Post sexual abuse syndrome, 250
Post traumatic stress disorder (PTSD),
    249
  battered woman syndrome and, 247
  learned helplessness theory and, 245
  major symptom clusters of, 247
Pound, R., 166
Power imbalance:
  and assaultive behavior, 17, 18
Primary prevention programs, 92
Proarrest policy development, 70-74

Canada Evidence Act and, 71
  lawsuits and, 71-72
  legislative changes and, 70-71
  research and community models
    and, 72-74
  sexual assault laws and, 71
  warrantless arrest provisions and,
    70
Project Outreach (Hayward, Califor-
    nia), 68
Psychic numbing, 23

Rainbow Family Crisis and Counseling
    Program (Phoenix, Arizona), 69
Rape trauma syndrome, 250
Rational choice deterrence theory, 101-
    102
Recidivism, post-treatment:
  risk factors for, 26-27
Relational culture:
  battered women and, 105-109
  culture of power and, 101-103, 111,
    121
  definition of, 102
Relationship conflict, 165
  and assaultive behavior, 16, 18
Right of chastisement, 62-63, 101
Royal Canadian Mounted Police
    (R.C.M.P.), 71, 77, 89

San Francisco, 73
San Francisco Family Violence Project,
    72
San Francisco Police Department, 72
Santa Barbara LEAA Family Violence
    Program, 143, 145
Saskatchewan police training, 89
Self-esteem, low:
  and assaultive behavior, 16, 18
Sexual assault:
  and assaultive behavior, 16, 18
Solicitor General of Canada, 73, 90,
    91
South Asian Family Support Services
    (Toronto), 91

Stress:
and assaultive behavior, 15-16
Supreme Court of Canada, 294
Supreme Court of Ontario, Family Law
Division of, 170

Taylor-Johnson Temperament Analysis,
207
Texas, 243
Toronto, Ontario, 48, 91, 184
police response to black women
assault victims in, 92
South Asian community of, 91
Toronto Police Force, 78
Treatment attrition:
risk factors for, 25-26

U.S. Attorney Gerneral's Task Force on
Family Violence, 97, 98
recommendations of for wife assault
prosecutors, 148
U.S. National Institute of Justice, 4
Unemployed, the:
wife assault among, 12

Vancouver Assaultive Husbands
Project, 298
Victim-initiated complaints, 132, 139,
150, 151, 153, 157
in Indianapolis, 132, 137
Victims of violence, 81-86
cross-cultural issues and, 91-92
effect of violence on, 81
Victim-witness support programs,
vii
Victoria Family Violence Project, 298
Violent crime:
and assaultive behavior, 17
Violent relationship dynamics, 245-247
cycle theory of violence in, 245
development of learned helplessness
in, 245-246
Violent relationships:
termination of, 246-247

Warrantless police arrests, 132, 150,
151, 153, 158
Washington, D.C., 63, 131
Washington State, 117
primary aggressor policy in, 117
self-defense jury instructions in, 268
Washington State Supreme Court, 239
Wife assault:
analysis of effect of on mediation,
181-184
and family law, 170-172
and spousal/child support decisions, 171, 172
and the courts, 127-225
and training of mediators, 184
criminalization of, 97-99
cumulative research on, 298
dynamics of, 252
integrated community response to, 3
legal responses to, 289-303
Massachusetts Bay colony and, 45
perceived seriousness of, 39-40
prevention of, 299-301
public attitudes toward legal responses to, 45-47
recent research on, 295-302
religious teachings and, 45
research on effect of mediation on,
176-178
temperance movement and, 46
theory of effect of mediation on,
172-176
victims of, 233-280
women's movement and, 3
Wife assault cases:
alternative prosecution policies in,
150-151
attrition and, 140-143
evaluations of prosecution policies
in, 148-151
future prospects for interven-
tion/evaluation of, 289-303
goals of intervention in, 295-296
prosecution versus no prosecution
in, 149-150
prosecutorial tracking in cases of,
143-148

protection orders and, 140
Wife assaulters, 9-30
  arrests of, 138-139
  charging decisions in prosecuting,
    136-138
  court-mandated treatment of, vii, 3,
    145, 146, 156-157, 158, 188-
    225, 293, 295, 296
  criminal prosecution of, 127-160
  diversionary measures aimed at, 68-
    70
  incarceration of, vii, 3
  intervention and, 24-29
  issues/problems in prosecuting, 136-
    148
  pretrial concerns in prosecuting,
    138-143
  process of prosecuting, 132-136

  prosecutor's role in prosecuting,
    135-136, 292
  reasons for court-mandated treat-
    ment of, 189-190
  research on court-mandated treat-
    ment compliance of, 191-195
  research recommendations on court-
    mandated treatment of, 194-
    195
  types of, 18-19, 21-23, 27-29, 290
  types of court mandates for, 190-191
  victim complaints and, 139-140
Wife beating, 39, 40
Wife murder, 39
Wife slapping, 39, 40
Women's Community House (London,
    Ontario), 76, 84, 86
Wyoming, 243

About the Contributors

Gary W. Austin holds a Ph.D. in clinical psychology with a specialty in marital problem solving. He has been employed by the London Family Court Clinic for 10 years, is the Director of the London Custody and Access Project and of the Mediation Service, and is Adjunct Assistant Professor in the Psychology Department of the University of Western Ontario. Previously, he conducted cognitive-behavioral therapy with patients at the London Psychiatric Hospital. His research activities include: factors affecting the resolution of custody and access disputes; follow-up evaluation of custody and access cases; incidence of spouse abuse; clinical problems of young offenders; sexual abuse of children; the measurement of anger problems in young offenders; and family violence issues.

Desmond Ellis holds a B.A. from the University of Leicester, Great Britain, an M.A. from McMaster University, Ontario, and a Ph.D. from Washington University, St. Louis, Missouri. He is Project Director of the Mediation Pilot Project funded by the Attorney General of Ontario. He is currently preparing an introductory sociology text on crime and deviance.

Kathleen J. Ferraro is Associate Professor in the School of Justice Studies and core faculty in Women's Studies at Arizona State University.

She has published articles on woman battering, the shelter movement, and the legal response to battering. Currently, she is editing a book, *Child Abuse and Woman Battering,* and she is the director of a project to study homelessness in Maricopa County, Arizona.

David A. Ford is Associate Professor of Sociology at Indiana University in Indianapolis and President of University Research Associates. He is principal investigator for the Indianapolis Prosecution Experiment. He also directs the Training Project on Family Violence for Indiana Law Enforcement Officers, a program of curriculum development and implementation for required continuing education of all officers in the state. A longtime advocate for battered women, he has worked with numerous community groups dedicated to protecting and empowering battered women.

Jessica P. Greenwald is a doctoral candidate in forensic-clinical psychology at the University of Nebraska-Lincoln. She is currently an advanced fellow in the Victims of Violence Program at Cambridge Hospital, Department of Psychiatry, Harvard Medical School, having completed her clinical internship at the New York University-Bellevue Hospital Center in New York City. Her research and clinical interests are focused on psycholegal issues in domestic violence situations.

L. Kevin Hamberger, Ph.D., is Associate Professor of Clinical Family Medicine in the Department of Family and Community Medicine, Medical College of Wisconsin, Milwaukee. He conducts research on characteristics of domestically violent men and on how these characteristics relate to treatment outcome. He currently chairs the Kenosha Domestic Abuse Intervention Project community task force and the Group on Violence Education for the Society of Teachers of Family Medicine. In addition, he conducts an ongoing program of treatment for domestically violent men.

Stephen D. Hart is Assistant Professor of Psychology at the Mental Health, Law, and Policy Institute, Simon Fraser University, and a research consultant with the BC Forensic Psychiatric Services Commission. He completed his Ph.D. in clinical-forensic psychology at the University of British Columbia. His primary research interest is criminal psychopathy; he has also done research and clinical work in the areas of wife assault and mentally disordered offenders.

Elaine Hastings is a clinical/research services co-ordinator at the London Family Court Clinic. She has an Honours B.A. in Psychology and English from the University of Guelph, Ontario. She was Assistant Director of a shelter for battered women prior to joining the clinic in 1988. Her clinical experience with victims includes advocacy work and facilitating groups for battered women and for child witnesses of woman abuse. She has had extensive involvement with victims/child witnesses through young offender work, custody and access matters, child welfare cases, and preparation of child witnesses for court. As well, her work at the clinic has included several research, prevention, and training projects related to issues around woman abuse.

James E. Hastings received his Ph.D. from the University of Wisconsin in 1971. He is presently the psychologist on the Spinal Cord Injury Service at the Zablocki V.A. Medical Center, and Associate Professor of Psychiatry at the Medical College of Wisconsin in Milwaukee. He has had extensive experience in cardio-pulmonary rehabilitation, and in the treatment of chemical dependency. Prior to moving to Milwaukee, he was Assistant Professor of Psychology at Bowling Green State University in Ohio. He is the author or co-author of 35 professional publications. He is married and has three children.

N. Zoe Hilton is Research Psychologist at the Mental Health Centre, Penetanguishene, Ontario. She holds an M.Phil. from the University of Cambridge Institute of Criminology and a Ph.D. in Psychology from the University of Toronto. She has conducted group therapy for sex offenders at the Mental Health Centre and previously at the Clarke Institute of Psychiatry, Toronto. She has worked with battered women as a researcher and volunteer. Her current research interests include aggression in relationships among high school students and psychiatric patients, and the assessment of cognitive distortions among sex offenders.

Peter G. Jaffe is Director of the London Family Court Clinic and a member of the Management Committee of the London Custody and

Access Project. He is Adjunct Associate Professor in the Department of Psychology and the Department of Psychiatry at the University of Western Ontario. He received his undergraduate training from McGill University in Montreal (1970) and his Ph.D. in clinical psychology from the University of Western Ontario (1974). Most of his clinical work and research involves children and adolescents involved with police or the courts, either as delinquents or victims of family violence or custody disputes. Jaffe was founding Chairperson of the London Co-ordination Committee on Family Violence and is currently actively involved in research on the impact of family violence on children. He has also been instrumental in the foundation of the Battered Women's Advocacy Clinic and is former chairperson of its Board of Directors. He is on the Management Committee of the Family Consultant Service of the London Police Department. Most recently, he was appointed to the Canadian Panel on Violence Against Women.

Gregory R. Johnson is currently a third-year law student at the University of Nebraska-Lincoln, where he received his B.A. in journalism in 1989. His primary interests are in environmental law.

Mary K. Kenning received her M.A. and Ph.D. degrees in clinical psychology from the University of South Dakota. She is currently a senior psychologist with the Hennepin County Court System in Minneapolis, Minnesota. Her research and clinical interests include the assessment and treatment of family violence and sexual abuse.

Lucille Pope is a doctoral student in the Committee on Law and the Social Sciences at Arizona State University. She was Coordinator of the Montana Coalition Against Domestic Violence from 1986 to 1990. She has been a battered women's advocate since 1979 and a trainer of criminal justice system personnel on the topic of domestic violence.

Mary Jean Regoli is Research Coordinator of the Pediatric Psychology Laboratory at Indiana University in Bloomington. She is coinvestigator for the Indianapolis Prosecution Experiment. She also assists Bloomington's domestic violence and rape crisis center, Middle Way House, Inc., in an ongoing evaluation of the prosecution of family abuse cases in Monroe County, Indiana.

Deborah Reitzel is a graduate student in clinical psychology at the University of Western Ontario. Formerly Research Assistant at the London Family Court Clinic, she has been actively involved in several family violence projects at the clinic, including development and implementation of wife assault and violence prevention programs in the secondary school systems in London and Southwestern Ontario; a comparison of dispositions given to perpetrators of wife assault versus sentences given to men who assault women not known to them; an investigation of the satisfaction of victims of wife assault with the response of the police and the criminal court system; and a study comparing the coping strategies and problem-solving abilities of children who have experienced different forms of familial abuse (i.e., physical, sexual, child witnesses of wife assault).

Ronald Roesch is Professor and Director of Clinical Training at the Department of Psychology, Simon Fraser University. He received his Ph.D. from the University of Illinois in 1977. His interests in forensic and community psychology include competency to stand trial, the provision of mental health services to jail detainees, and the psychological effects of child sexual abuse. He is editor of *Law and Human Behavior,* the official journal of the American Psychology-Law Society (APA Division 41). He is also Executive Director of the Mental Health, Law, and Policy Institute at SFU, and Chair of the Board of Directors of the BC Institute on Family Violence.

Daniel G. Saunders, Ph.D., is Assistant Professor at the University of Michigan, School of Social Work, where he teaches courses on methods for preventing domestic violence and conducts research on the topic. His current research is on predictors of post traumatic stress in battered women and a comparison of cognitive-behavioral and psychodynamic treatments for men who batter. He has numerous publications, covering the assessment and treatment of men who batter, public and professional attitudes about domestic violence, and battered women's use of violence.

Alan J. Tomkins received his training in law (JD) and social psychology (Ph.D.) at Washington University. Since 1986 he has been a faculty member with the Law/Psychology Program at the University of

Nebraska-Lincoln, where he studies, teaches, and writes about psycholegal issues related to social and domestic violence, including topics such as acquaintance rape, battered women, child maltreatment, and perinatal exposure to harmful substances. He also has interests in the use of social science evidence in litigation, both as a general matter and with particular application to discrimination cases.

Lenore E. A. Walker, Ed.D., is a licensed psychologist in independent practice with Walker & Associates in Denver, Colorado, and Executive Director of the Domestic Violence Institute. She is a diplomate in clinical psychology qualified by the American Board of Professional Psychology and has pioneered the introduction of expert witness testimony on the "battered woman self-defense" in U.S. courts. Her research on the psychological effects of being a battered woman and the dynamics of the battering relationship began in the 1970s with research funded by the National Institute of Mental Health. She lectures internationally at the invitation of governments, private groups, and world health organizations. Her psychology interests have concentrated on women's mental health issues and stopping all forms of violence against women and children. She has written 9 books and more than 50 articles and book chapters, including *The Battered Woman* (1979), *Women and Mental Health Policy* (1984), *The Battered Woman Syndrome* (1984), *Feminist Psychotherapies* (1988 with M. A. Dutton), *Handbook on Sexually Abused Children* (1988), and *Terrifying Love: Why Battered Women Kill and How Society Responds* (1989).

Laurene J. Wilson is a graduate student in clinical psychology at the Department of Psychology, Simon Fraser University. She is currently completing her M.A., examining objective and subjective indicators of quality of life in mentally disordered offenders. Her primary interest is the impact of deinstitutionalization on the criminal justice system.